The English in the Twelfth Century

IMPERIALISM, NATIONAL IDENTITY
AND POLITICAL VALUES

Six of the greatest twelfth-century historians – William of Malmesbury, Henry of Huntingdon, Geoffrey of Monmouth, Geoffrey Gaimar, Roger of Howden, and Gerald of Wales – are analysed in this collection of essays, focusing on their attitudes to three inter-related aspects of English history. The first theme is the rise of the new and condescending perception which regarded the Irish, Scots and Welsh as barbarians; set against the background of socio-economic and cultural change in England, it is argued that this imperialist perception created a fundamental divide in the history of the British Isles, one to which Geoffrey of Monmouth responded immediately and brilliantly. The second theme treats chivalry not as a mere gloss upon the brutal realities of life, but as an important development in political morality; and it reconsiders some of the old questions associated with chivalric values and knightly obligations – home-grown products or imports from France? The third theme is the emergence of a new sense of Englishness after the traumas of the Norman Conquest, looking at the English invasion of Ireland and the making of English history.

JOHN GILLINGHAM is Emeritus Professor of History at the London School of Economics.

T0374962

The English in the Twelfth Century

IMPERIALISM, NATIONAL IDENTITY
AND POLITICAL VALUES

John Gillingham

THE BOYDELL PRESS

First published 2000
Transferred to digital printing

ISBN 978-0-85115-732-0 Hardback
ISBN 978-1-84383-425-0 Paperback

The Boydell Press is an imprint of Boydell & Brewer Ltd
PO Box 9, Woodbridge, Suffolk IP12 3DF, UK
and of Boydell & Brewer Inc.
668 Mt Hope Avenue, Rochester, NY 14620, USA
website: www.boydellandbrewer.com

A CiP catalogue record for this book is available
from the British Library

This publication is printed on acid-free paper

To Rees
for friendship and inspiration

Contents

Acknowledgements

This book would not exist had it not been for the generosity of the Leverhulme Trust. The Trust funded two years research leave in 1991–3, and virtually everything which I have written between 1992 and 1998 is the product of those two years of freedom to think about the subject.

These essays deal with English history at a time when French influence on English society was at its height, and they try to do so in British and Irish perspective. How else, we might ask, considering both the political concerns and the academic fashions of the last quarter century. After all, 1975 witnessed the publication of both Michael Hechter's *Internal Colonialism* and J. G. A. Pocock's 'British History: a Plea for a New Subject' in the *Journal of Modern History*. However it took me at least ten years to notice what was going on around me – a first stab at the now not so new subject being my 'Images of Ireland, 1170–1600', *History Today* 37 (February 1987), and I remain grateful to a colleague, David Stevenson, for the initial challenge to talk about 'Imperialism in the Middle Ages' at an LSE Study Weekend on Imperialism at Cumberland Lodge.

Since then many more individuals and institutions have helped to sustain my interest in the subject. The late Lewis Warren was kind enough to invite me in 1988 to The Queen's University of Belfast to be a member of that most privileged of groups – the guests wined and dined by the Wiles Trust in return for the arduous duty of attending the Wiles Lectures and talking about them afterwards with the sacrificial Lecturer, in this case Rees Davies. I am even grateful to the University of Newcastle for inviting me to deliver the Special Lectures in History on three consecutive days in 1990, and so give me some slight sense of what it must have been like for Rees. Writing those three lectures on 'The Beginnings of English Imperialism' forced me to clarify my thoughts – always a help, and especially so when it comes to making an application to the Leverhulme Trust.

Three of the essays first appeared as papers given at the Battle Conference on Anglo-Norman Studies. Under successive directors – Allen Brown, Marjorie Chibnall and Christopher Harper-Bill – that conference has for twenty years been a source of friendship and keen discussion, in the lecture room, dining room and garden of Pike House, as well as next door in The Chequers. Two were written as a the result of generous invitations from presidents and officers – above all Eleanor Searle and Warren Hollister, whose recent deaths have been sad blows to all working on this period – of the Conference's sister organisation, the Haskins Society.

Another source of regular stimulus has been the annual Formation of English State colloquium at St Peter's College, Oxford, organised by Gavin Williams. I am particularly grateful to him and to Philip Corrigan. One day I hope to make time to follow up at least some of the reading with which the latter has so liberally deluged me.

I am especially grateful to Lesley Johnson, for her part in organising a series of three conferences on Nationality and National Identity under the auspices of the Centre for Medieval Studies at the University of Leeds, as well as for her encouragement and for ensuring (together with Ian Short) that I kept my eyes open to the implications of vernacular sources.

Although the focus of these essays remains irredeemably English, I could not have tackled these matters without a great deal of help and advice from experts in Irish, Scottish, Welsh and French history. What I know of Irish history I owe very largely to the kindness of Sean Duffy, Marie Therese Flanagan, Robin Frame, Jim Lydon, and Katharine Simms. For Scottish history I am much indebted to Archie Duncan, Sandy Grant and Keith Stringer; for twelfth-century Welsh history to Rees Davies and Huw Pryce; for Frankish/French history to Jane Martindale and Jinty Nelson. This is not to say that I could manage the English history on my own. Here I owe debts above all to James Campbell, David Carpenter, Jim Holt, John Prestwich and Patrick Wormald.

The questions I have asked have all been essentially parasitical upon the ideas of Rob Bartlett and Rees Davies; at a more general level (and one therefore not reflected in footnotes dealing with the particular) the basic assumptions which I have brought to these questions have been deeply influenced by the work of Susan Reynolds.

In 1995 Richard Barber made the rash suggestion that I bring together my work in this area, and I thank him for that, as well as for all the help he has given to a computer near-illiterate in bringing this project to completion.

Finally I once again have very good cause to thank colleagues and friends at the University of London, and in particular members of seminars at the Institute of Historical Research. Even after knowing some of them for more than thirty years they still have the ability to spring surprises.

Source Details

'The Beginnings of English Imperialism', *Journal of Historical Sociology* 5,4 (1992), pp. 392–409. By permission of Blackwells Publishers.

'The Context and Purposes of Geoffrey of Monmouth's *History of the Kings of Britain*', *Anglo-Norman Studies* XIII, 1991 (Boydell, 1992), pp. 99–118.

'Conquering the Barbarians: War and Chivalry in Twelfth Century Britain', *The Haskins Society Journal* 4, 1992 (Boydell, 1993), pp. 67–84.

'Henry II, Richard I and the Lord Rhys, *Peritia* 10 (1996), pp. 225–236.

'The Travels of Roger of Howden and his Views of the Irish, Scots and Welsh', *Anglo-Norman Studies* XX (1998), pp. 151–169.

'The Foundations of an Disunited Kingdom', in eds. A. Grant and K. Stringer, *Uniting the Kingdom? The Making of British History* (Routledge, 1995), pp. 48–64. By permission of Routledge.

'Gaimar, the Prose *Brut* and the making of English History', in ed. Jean-Philippe Genet, *L'Histoire et les nouveaux publics dans l'Europe médiévale* (Publications de la Sorbonne, Paris, 1997), pp. 165–176. Reprinted by permission of Publications de la Sorbonne.

'Henry of Huntingdon and the Twelfth Century Revival of the English Nation', in eds. S. Forde, L. Johnson and A. Murray, *Concepts of National Identity in the Middle Ages* (Leeds Texts and Monographs, 1995), pp. 75–101. By permission of Leeds Studies in English. University of Leeds.

'The English Invasion of Ireland', in eds. B. Bradshaw, A. Hadfield and W. Maley, *Representing Ireland: Literature and the Origins of Conflict, 1534–1660* (CUP, 1993), pp. 24–42. By permission of CUP.

'Thegns and Knights in Eleventh Century England. Who was then the Gentleman?', *Transactions of the Royal Historical Society* (6th series, 5, 1995), 129–153. Reprinted by permission of the Royal Historical Society.

'The Introduction of Knight Service into England', *Anglo-Norman Studies* IV, 1981 (Boydell, 1982), pp. 53–64, 181–187.

'1066 and the Introduction of Chivalry into England', in eds. G. Garnett and J. Hudson, *Law and Government in Medieval England and Normandy. Essays in honour of Sir James Holt* (CUP, 1994), pp. 31–55. By permission of CUP.

'Kingship, Chivalry and Love. Political and Cultural Values in the Earliest History written in French: Geoffrey Gaimar's *Estoire des Engleis*', in ed. C. Warren Hollister, *Anglo-Norman Political Culture and the Twelfth Century Renaissance* (Boydell, 1997), pp. 33–58.

'Some Observations on Social Mobility in England between the Norman Conquest and the Early Thirteenth Century', in eds. A. Haverkamp and H. Vollrath, *England and Germany in the High Middle Ages* (Oxford University Press, 1996), pp. 333–355. By permission of OUP.

Abbreviations

A-N	Anglo-Norman
ANS	*Anglo-Norman Studies*
ASC	*Anglo-Saxon Chronicle*, ed. D. Whitelock *et al.*, London, 1969
ASE	*Anglo-Saxon England*
BIHR	*Bulletin of the Institute of Historical Research*
BL	British Library
Cal. Docs. France	*Calendar of Documents preserved in France*, I, 918–1206, ed. J. H. Round, Her Majesty's Stationery Office, London, 1899
CM	Matthew Paris, *Chronica Majora*, ed. H. R. Luard, RS, 1872-84.
EHD	*English Historical Documents*, 2nd edn. i, ed. D. Whitelock, London, 1979; ii, ed. D. C. Douglas, London, 1981
EHR	*English Historical Review*
FW	Florence of Worcester, *Chronicon ex Chronicis*, ed. B. Thorpe, London, 1848–9
GND	William of Jumièges, *Gesta Normannorum Ducum*. Cited by book and chapter for reference to editions by E. van Houts, Oxford, 1992–5, and by J. Marx, Rouen, 1914
GS	*Gesta Stephani*, eds. K. R. Potter and R. H. C. Davis, Oxford, 1976
HE	*Historia Ecclesiastica*
HH	Henry of Huntingdon, *Historia Anglorum*. Cited for reference to the editions by D. Greenway, Oxford, 1996, and, in square brackets, by T. Arnold, RS, 1879
HRB	*Historia Regum Britanniae*
Hyde	*Liber Monasterii de Hyda*, ed. E. Edwards, RS, 1886
JMH	*Journal of Medieval History*
JW	*The Chronicle of John of Worcester*, vol. 2, eds. R. R. Darlington and P. McGurk, Oxford, 1995
LE	*Liber Eliensis*, ed. E. O. Blake, Camden Society, London, 1962
NHI	*A New History of Ireland. II. Medieval Ireland*, ed. A. Cosgrove, Oxford, 1987
n.s.	new series
Orderic	Orderic Vitalis, *Historia Ecclesiastica*, ed. M. Chibnall, Oxford, 1969–80
OV	Orderic Vitalis, *Historia Ecclesiastica*, ed. M. Chibnall, Oxford, 1969–80
PR	Pipe Roll
RBE	*Red Book of the Exchequer*, ed. H. Hall, RS, 1896

Regesta	*Regesta Regum Anglo-Normannorum*, vol. ii, eds. C. Johnson and H. A. Cronne, Oxford, 1956
RHF	*Recueil des historiens des Gaules et de la France*
RIS	*Rerum Italicarum Scriptores*
Rot. Chart	*Rotuli Chartarum*, ed. T. D. Hardy, Record Commission, London, 1837
RS	Rolls Series
SD	*Symeonis Monachi Opera Omnia*, ed. T. Arnold, RS, 1882–5.
Thorpe	Geoffrey of Monmouth, *The History of the Kings of Britain*, trans. L. Thorpe, Harmondsworth, 1966
TRHS	*Transactions of the Royal Historical Society*
WM	William of Malmesbury, *De Gestis Regum Anglorum*. Cited by chapter number for reference to editions by W. Stubbs, RS, 1887, and by R. A. B. Mynors *et al.*, Oxford, 1998
WP	William of Poitiers, *Gesta Guillelmi*. Cited by book and chapter for reference to editions by R. Foreville, Paris, 1952, and by R. H. C. Davis and M. Chibnall, Oxford, 1998

Introduction

The English in the Twelfth Century:
Imperialism, national identity and political values

All the essays reprinted here deal with the English at a critical period in their history – the 150 or so years from the eve of the Norman Conquest to the reign of King John, a period when they were brought into new and vitally important relationships with both continental Europeans and the 'Celtic' world. The matter of national identity, always complex and often controversial, was especially so at a time when 'England was a cultural and linguistic melting pot';[1] a time when the Anglo-Normans – a useful term coined by eighteenth-century historians – were becoming 'English', and were invading the lands of their 'Celtic' – another useful as well as potentially misleading eighteenth-century term – neighbours.[2] As Raphael Samuel observed, 'British history makes "Englishness" problematical and invites us to see it as one among a number of competing ethnicities.'[3] Moreover, in the demise of slavery and in the rise of chivalry, it was also a period which saw significant changes, new ways of treating human beings, both at the base and at the top of the social hierarchy in England.

In these essays I am primarily concerned with perceptions and values, with some – but by no means all – of the perceptions and values which were taken for granted by decision-making politicians, not with the perceptions and values discussed explicitly by theologians and other theorists. That is to say I wish to discover those perceptions and values which shaped the conduct of war and politics. Since the politicians rarely wrote anything themselves, I have relied chiefly upon the words – and the silences – of contemporary historians, in the belief that the ideas and assumptions revealed by these authors as they told and re-told the histories of their own and former times can give us, however imperfectly, a better understanding of the assumptions and values of their less bookish contemporaries than any other form of surviving evidence. It is to approach the historians of the past as though they were, in Karl Leyser's phrase, 'the intelligence officers of society's aims and directions'.[4]

---

[1] I. Short, 'Patrons and Polyglots: French Literature in Twelfth-Century England', *Anglo-Norman Studies* 14 (1992), 244.

[2] Although there are strong arguments for placing inverted commas round the word 'Celtic', in these essays the sign would lose force through over-use and probably become tiresome, so I shall not do it again here.

[3] R. Samuel, 'British Dimensions: Four Nations History', *History Workshop Journal* 40 (1995), vi.

[4] K. Leyser, *Communications and Power in Medieval Europe*, ed. T. Reuter (London, 1994), vol. 1, 231.

Central to this undertaking are the historical writings of six twelfth-century intelligence officers: William of Malmesbury, Henry of Huntingdon, Geoffrey of Monmouth, Geoffrey Gaimar, Gerald de Barri (better known as Gerald of Wales) and Roger of Howden. All were either Englishmen or were writing for audiences in England. Four of them wrote histories of the English: William, Henry and Roger in Latin (though Roger's goes under the title *Chronica*), and Gaimar in French. Three of them, William of Malmesbury, Geoffrey of Monmouth, and Gerald de Barri are among the most creative authors ever to write in this country. The least known of the six, Geoffrey Gaimar, also seems to have been a pioneer – his *Estoire des Engleis* is the earliest extant history of any country written in French. All six were members of the traditional clerical elite, and one, William of Malmesbury, was a monk. But it is a mistake to imagine that all clerks were spokesmen for ecclesiastical or religious values. In these essays I shall focus on what they, and some of their fellow-authors, men such as William of Poitiers, Orderic Vitalis, William of Newburgh, Richard of Hexham and the unknown continuators of the *Anglo-Saxon Chronicle*, can be made to reveal about crucial aspects of secular political culture.

Part One. Imperialism

These six essays focus on relations between the ruling elite in England and the Celts. For many centuries the English have regarded Celtic peoples, Welsh, Irish and Highland – i.e. Gaelic-speaking – Scots, all of them fellow-Christians, as cultural inferiors, lawless and immoral savages: in short, as barbarians. That this condescending set of attitudes has been of fundamental importance in the history of the British Isles has usually been more apparent to the Irish, Scots and Welsh than to the English. None the less it has underpinned, sometimes explicitly, English policies designed to seize and then, for much longer periods, to keep control of the Celtic 'fringe'. It is my contention that this set of attitudes first emerged in the 'years of destiny' of the twelfth century. By 'imperialism' I have in mind not merely empire-building but that form of territorial expansion where the invaders possess a strong and long-lasting feeling of superiority, so that the 'centre' continues to despise the culture of newly acquired regions, which in consequence remain 'mere' provinces. It seems appropriate that 'imperialism', a word which – in its modern, as opposed to its Napoleonic, sense – emerged in political debates in 1870s and 1880s about Irish Home Rule, should be applied to a period which witnessed the English invasion of Ireland.

The first essay, 'The Beginnings of English Imperialism', sets the scene in broad-brush strokes for the more detailed studies which follow. It emphasises William of Malmesbury's precocious awareness of a new sense of Anglo-French superiority over the Celts. The imperialists' belief that they enjoy a superior culture is reflected in William's view of David I of Scotland as a ruler whose own upbringing at the English court led him to encourage the Scots 'to live in a more civilized style, dress with more elegance and eat in a more refined manner'.

I was reminded of this passage when reading an account of a Pathé newsreel describing Kemal Atatürk as a benign autocrat who imported the best British hotel housekeepers 'to teach Turkish women how to lay the table with knives and forks, and to keep their homes in a European manner' (*New Statesman*, 27 Feb. 1998). Norbert Elias, in his emphasis on the importance of 'manners' and on the transition from warrior to courtier, recognised, but did not give enough weight to, eleventh- and twelfth-century developments while at the same time, as a prisoner of the myth of the Renaissance, he over-estimated those of the fifteenth century.[5]

The second essay sees Geoffrey of Monmouth as a Welshman, perhaps of Breton descent, living and working at Oxford, in the heart of England,[6] sensing the emergence of the new attitude amongst the chattering classes there in the 1130s, and in reaction to this, re-furbishing traditional Welsh tales with the aim of securing cultural respectability for his own nation. To this end, as well no doubt as in the hope of advancement, he dedicated his work to the most powerful members of Anglo-Norman political society. If his object was to persuade not just his own people, but also the English, then he clearly failed; the English would continue to look down on the Welsh. In another sense, of course, Geoffrey succeeded triumphantly. His *History of the Kings of Britain* is one of the supreme achievements of the historical imagination, presenting almost 2,000 years of British history in one majestic sweep. It rapidly became a best-seller, throughout continental Europe as well as in the British Isles, and thanks to its central creations – the figures of Arthur and Merlin – had an immediate, immense and so far permanent impact on literature and art. With only the most fragmentary and disjointed source material at his disposal, Geoffrey had created a coherent and artistic whole. It was also almost entirely a work of fiction – the first great work of the Oxford school of history.

The third essay, 'Conquering the Barbarians', contrasts Anglo-French and Celtic practices in the conduct of war and in the treatment of prisoners of war. It focuses on how the perception of these contrasts contributed to the labelling of Celts as barbarians. Crucial here is the survival of slavery in the British Isles into the twelfth century, the contrast between its disappearance in early twelfth-century England and the continuation of the practice for some time in Celtic lands. Lawrence of Durham, writing in the early 1130s, noted the end of the slave trade and explicitly associated its passing with Norman rule. 'After England began to have Norman lords then the English no longer suffered from outsiders that which they had suffered at their own hands; in this respect

---

[5] N. Elias, *The Civilizing Process* (Oxford, 1994), 68ff, 158–60, 467–70. I, of course, propound a counter-myth, that of the 'Twelfth-Century Renaissance', see below, pp. 18, 150.

[6] Rees Davies in his Inaugural Lecture as Chichele Professor of Medieval History at Oxford drew attention to the Welsh tale, *Cyfranc Llud a Llefelys*, interpolated into Welsh translations of Geoffrey of Monmouth's *History of the Kings of Britain*, in which King Lud measured the length and breadth of the island of Britain and found Oxford at its focal point, Rees Davies, *The Matter of Britain and the Matter of England* (Oxford, 1996), 2.

they found foreigners treated them better than they had themselves' and he then went on to say that in Scotland and Ireland, where lords of their own people ruled, the old custom continued, if on a lesser scale.[7] Lawrence particularly objected to the custom of selling members of one's own family into slavery, and this is what he had in mind here. My concern, not just in this essay but in several others, is chiefly with an alternative method of recruitment of slave labour, war as slave hunt, a kind of total war which Celtic peoples continued to practice and which English commentators condemned as barbarous. It was against this background that men who liked to think of themselves as humane Christians justified the less 'civilized' ways in which they then waged war in lands beyond the pale.

The fourth and fifth essays are devoted to two important elements in the prevailing view of relations between kings of England and the Celts in the second half of the century. The first considers what Gerald de Barri and Roger of Howden have to say about relations between Henry II and Richard I and the greatest Welsh prince of the time, Lord Rhys; it challenges the traditional contrast between Henry II, allegedly a king who took the 'British' dimension of politics seriously, and the son who is supposed to have neglected it. The second is a study of Roger of Howden, a 'civil servant' historian who – I argue here – remained at the heart of government, attached as it were to the 'Foreign Office', for much longer than previously suspected. It investigates his views of the Irish, Welsh and Scots – virtually official ones – and looks at the way they began to change in the light of his own experiences, in particular his journeys to Scotland. The sixth essay, 'Foundations of a Disunited Kingdom', sets these perceptions into a wider context, the demographic, economic and political developments of the eleventh and twelfth centuries, emphasising the importance of the crisis of Stephen's reign and the relative ease with which Henry II was able to re-impose the New Order.

Part Two. National Identity

If the essays in Part I focused chiefly on what the people living in twelfth-century England thought of their Celtic neighbours, the three here focus more on what they thought of themselves, on the question of their self-identity and of

---

[7] 'Sed postquam Anglia dominos cepit habere Normannos, nuncquam hoc Anglici passi sunt ab alienis quod saepe passi sunt a suis, et hac in parte sibi meliores invenerunt extraneos quam se ipsos. Scotia autem et Hybernia, dominos habens de gente sua, nec omnino amisit nec ut olim exercet hunc morem suum'. *Life of S. Brigid* in ed. W. W. Heist, *Vitae sanctorum Hibernie* (Brussels, 1965), 1. I owe this reference to the kindness of Rob Bartlett. A case for regarding Lawrence, monk of Durham, as the most interesting writer of the hundred years after the Norman Conquest has been made by A. G. Rigg, *A History of Anglo-Latin Literature 1066–1422* (Cambridge, 1992), 54–61. A monk who compares his own frustration at not having time to write poetry to that of a eunuch with a beautiful girl could conceivably have enlivened the cloister.

their Englishness. The early shaping of the political concept of England and of English ethnic identity has been much discussed, most recently by Alfred Smyth.[8] That England was a nation-state by 1066 has been powerfully argued by James Campbell and Patrick Wormald.[9] Indeed a recent and very wide-ranging study by Adrian Hastings treats England as the prototype nation and nation-state.[10] Were there also English nationalists in 1066? There cannot possibly have been according to those for whom print and industrial society, the creation of a mass reading public, are the sine qua nons of nationalism. England in 1066 was, in Ernest Gellner's terms, an agrarian or agro-literate society. It follows that for him, to misquote a famous passage from *Nations and Nationalism*, the English-man who woke up on Boxing Day morning 1066 to hear that William the Norman had been crowned and anointed king might well have asked whether the new rulers were less corrupt and grasping than the old ones, but if his wife asked him what language the new ruler spoke, the hapless husband 'would give her a sharp look, and wonder how he would cope with all the new difficulties when, at the same time, his wife had gone quite mad'. In Gellner's view something must have happened since those agro-literate days because 'the wife's query, once so manifestly mad, [has] become the question which is now uppermost in almost everyone's mind'.[11] Yet a contemporary writer, indeed one attached to the new ruler's headquarters staff, William of Poitiers, noted in passing that after Hastings the English were still reluctant to recognise William of Normandy as king because 'it was their highest wish to have no ruler who was not a fellow countryman'.[12] It is also clear that language was crucial to their distinction between a 'fellow countryman' and a Norman, since in post-1066 English language sources such as the *Anglo-Saxon Chronicle* the Normans are almost always called not Normans but French, i.e. are principally identified by the language they spoke and the culture to which they belonged. Gellner defined nationalism as 'a theory of political legitimacy which requires that ethnic boundaries . . . should not separate the power-holders from the rest'.[13] Clearly this was a theory which William of Poitiers was perfectly well able to understand and which he believed conformed to the highest wish of the leaders of the English. Of course there were other theories of political legitimacy around, indeed the principal point of William of Poitiers' book was to urge those other

[8] 'The Emergence of English Identity, 700–1000' in ed. A. P. Smyth, *Medieval Europeans. Studies in Ethnic Identity and National Perspectives in Medieval Europe* (London, 1998).
[9] 'Let me state a certainty. Late Anglo-Saxon England was a nation state', James Campbell, 'The Late Anglo-Saxon State: A Maximum View', *Proceedings of the British Academy* 87 (1995), 47. P. Wormald, '*Engla Lond*: the Making of an Allegiance', *Journal of Historical Sociology* 7 (1994).
[10] Adrian Hastings, *The Construction of Nationhood. Ethnicity, Religion and Nationalism* (Cambridge, 1997), chapter two, and a forthright discussion of the word 'nation', pp. 14–19.
[11] Ernest Gellner, *Nations and Nationalism* (London, 1983), 127–8.
[12] *The Gesta Guillelmi of William of Poitiers*, ed. and trans. R. H. C. Davis and M. Chibnall (Oxford, 1998), 146–7, cf. 182–3.
[13] Gellner, *Nations and Nationalism*, 1.

theories with all the eloquence at his command, even at one stage addressing the land of England directly: 'and you too, English land, would love him and hold him in the highest respect; you would prostrate yourself entirely at his feet, if putting aside your folly and wickedness you could judge more soundly the kind of man into whose power you had come'.[14] It seems that here, carried away by his rhetoric, William went even further than Gellner. The wife's question was not only folly, it was wickedness. But evidently lots of people were asking it. As Susan Reynolds has emphasised, a correspondence between a kingdom and a people was assumed to be natural, and so much taken for granted that learned writers did not so much discuss it as make it an unreasoned premise of their political arguments.[15] Nationalism, as the case of Scotland in the age of Wallace and Bruce suggests, is associated more with a threat to a nation than with industrialisation. It is just that the War of English Independence was lost.

More problematic is the question of when the English nation re-emerged after the traumas of the Norman Conquest.[16] By the 1090s the English author of the *Anglo-Saxon Chronicle* felt able to refer to Rufus as 'our king'. And for the next two hundred years there is no evidence of a linguistic patriotism associated with pride in English and hostility to French. Indeed by the end of the twelfth century England could be compared to a 'fair meadow' which surpassed all other kingdoms 'in all pleasures and in nobility' – and this by a poet writing in French.[17] As the case of modern Ireland shows, a strongly held patriotism can perfectly well be expressed in the language of the former invader. Hence the appearance in the 1130s of an English history written in French and sympathetic to Hereward the Wake would seem to mark an important stage in the re-emergence of an English nation. Although it is often assumed, presumably on the basis of his name and the language in which he wrote (though neither of these are safe indicators), that Geoffrey Gaimar was French, what little is known about him associates him entirely with England and primarily with Lincolnshire. I see no reason why he, and very many of his contemporaries, should not have said 'Je suis Anglais.' In the essay on Gaimar and the making of English history I tried to recover his perception of Anglo-Saxon history, for it was this perception which the prose *Brut* ensured would be the standard one from the fourteenth to the sixteenth century, but which was then, together with the rest of Gaimar's work, lost to the view of historians – to such an extent indeed that Gaimar became a forgotten historian. Given Gaimar's perception of the centrality of a king's role in the making both of the *Anglo-Saxon Chronicle* and of a single English kingdom, it is intriguing to wonder what this early twelfth-century

[14] *Gesta Guillelmi*, 156–7.
[15] S. Reynolds, *Kingdoms and Communities in Western Europe 900–1300* (Oxford, 1984), 250.
[16] For discussion of this see E. van Houts, 'The Memory of 1066 in Written and Oral Traditions', *Anglo-Norman Studies* 19 (1996), 167–79 and 'The Trauma of 1066', *History Today* 46 (October 1996).
[17] Chardri, *Le Petit Plet*, ed. B. S. Merrilees (Anglo-Norman Texts XX, Oxford, 1970), 41–2. Though the author was prepared to concede that English knights drank too much.

author might have made of Adrian Hastings's late twentieth-century argument that nations emerge out of ethnicities partly under the pressures of the state and partly as a result of the development of a literary vernacular.[18]

Geoffrey of Monmouth, while telling William of Malmesbury and Henry of Huntingdon to steer well clear of the history of the Britons, left to them the task of writing 'the history of the Saxons'. Whether or not Geoffrey failed, there can be no doubt that William and Henry succeeded. These two gave England its history. As Rees Davies puts it, 'their accounts became the standard, one almost might say the definitive version of early English history and were subsumed into future histories down the generations . . . they wrote histories which were secular, political, progressive, one might almost say Whiggish. The future of English historiography lay with them.'[19] 'Henry of Huntingdon and the Twelfth-Century Revival of the English Nation' is a study of this influential historian's views of the English and Norman peoples in the context of his own sense of national self-identification. Why did he choose to dwell on the perjury and treachery of Normans in what he wrote in the 1140s, if – as I argue – by that date the English no longer saw themselves as a subject people oppressed by a Norman elite?

The last essay in this part, 'The English Invasion of Ireland' looks at the events of the 1160s and 1170s as described by contemporaries. In arguing that, by and large, the invaders thought of themselves as English and were referred to by the Irish of the day as *Saxain*, it sets out to expunge from the vocabulary of modern historians the habit of referring to the twelfth-century invaders of Ireland as 'Normans' or as 'Anglo-Normans' – not, as has recently been pointed out, an easy task since these terms have become 'well-rooted usage'.[20] Optimistically I hope that an improvement in Anglo-Irish relations will gradually allow us, on both sides of the Irish Sea, to face the fact – as until the mid-nineteenth century we did – that those who invaded Ireland eight hundred years ago were English. Central to this essay (and an important figure in several others) is Gerald de Barri. Although he was partly Welsh, and although in his fifties he came to identify himself strongly with Welsh causes, in his early writings, those with which I am concerned here, he was much more of a spokesman for the English point of view. There can be no doubt that the personal histories of these authors embody much of the problematic of national identity and political culture in this period. As Rees Davies has written of Geoffrey of Monmouth

[18] Hastings, *Construction of Nationhood*, 2–3, 150–1, 158–9, 165. In the light of this emphasis it is worth noting the range of subjects – legal, topographical, a Bestiary and much religious – covered by French literature written in England by 1140. See Short, 'Patrons and Polyglots', 229–49.

[19] Davies, *The Matter of Britain*, 15–16. Cf. R. R. Davies, 'The Peoples of Britain and Ireland, 1100–1400: IV. Language and Historical Mythology', *TRHS* 6th ser. 7 (1997), 18–20.

[20] Entry on 'Normans' in ed. S. J. Connolly, *The Oxford Companion to Irish History* (Oxford, 1998) signed RRF(rame). See also the entry for 'Anglo-Norman invasion' signed MTF(lanagan).

and Gerald, 'Both men were, in their different ways, victims, exponents, and beneficiaries of their own cultural ambivalence; they were men of the frontiers; therein undoubtedly lay part of the richness of their characters and the fertility of their imaginations.'[21] To a lesser extent the same can be said of William of Malmesbury and Henry of Huntingdon, both men of mixed English and Norman descent.

Part Three. Values and Structures

Four of the essays in this part deal with the themes of chivalry, knightly values and knightly obligations. Chivalry is treated not as a 'polite veneer', a mere tinsel gloss prettifying brutal realities, but as a fundamental political morality, a matter of life and death. The contrast which twelfth-century historians saw between the chivalric values of English and French knights on the one hand, and the savagery of Celtic warfare on the other, led naturally to a number of questions. How real was the contrast? If real, for how long had it existed, and how had it come about? I have considered some of these questions in Part One. Here I focus more on the matter of '1066 and All That'. Were knights and knightly obligations a post-1066 French import? Did the Norman Conquest result in a diffusion of French chivalry to England as part of that process of cultural homogenization which Robert Bartlett has labelled 'the Europeanization of Europe'.[22] Or were all these things to be found in England before 1066? These are the questions addressed in three essays: 'Thegns and Knights in Eleventh-Century England: Who was then the Gentleman?', 'The introduction of knight service into England' and '1066 and the Introduction of Chivalry into England'. The essay on knight service was written in 1981 – considerably earlier than the other essays here – but is of a piece with them in relying heavily upon narrative sources, and particularly upon their silences. In this I was following the method already adopted by John Prestwich, whose reading of contemporary narratives, including Geoffrey of Monmouth, had led him to observe that 'the feudal system is as inconspicuous in their pages' as it is prominent in the pages of historians writing many centuries later.[23]

The fourth essay in this part returns to Geoffrey Gaimar. It explores his *History of the English* as the earliest securely dated work with a claim to be considered as chivalric literature, a book offering unparalleled insights into the thought-world of the secular aristocracy of the early twelfth century, women as well as men. In presenting William Rufus in what was to become unfamiliar light as a model king, and doing so in the language of the court, Gaimar illustrates,

---

[21] Rees Davies, *The Matter of Britain*, 7.

[22] R. Bartlett, *The Making of Europe* (Harmondsworth, 1993), chapter 11.

[23] J. O. Prestwich, 'The Military Household of the Norman Kings', *English Historical Review* xcvi (1981), 31–3; reprinted in ed. M. Strickland, *Anglo-Norman Warfare* (Woodbridge, 1992).

amongst much else, the significance of the hunt as a courtly activity and the high value placed on good-humoured self-restraint – two respects in which comparison with the essay on 'Thegns and knights' indicates continuity across the divide of 1066.

The last essay is primarily concerned with the opportunities for advancement open to men born into the knightly class, with their 'life chances'. Compared with Ireland, Wales and Gaelic Scotland, England has been judged to be 'a more open and mobile society'.[24] As a new English identity became more securely established in the mid-twelfth century, so also the people of England were able to enjoy more freedoms and more opportunities: freedom from slavery and from the system of child oblates; more opportunities as emigrants and colonizers, as well as greater educational opportunities as more schoolmasters were to be found in town and village – this last a development which undoubtedly played a part in producing that remarkable crop of historians at work in twelfth-century England whose writings have formed the backbone of these essays.

The emphasis on histories rather than on records is in part a reaction to the fashion of historians earlier in this century. I prefer to avoid what Timothy Reuter has called 'the standard trope of English medievalists: narrative sources unreliable, back to the archives'.[25] I have sometimes exploited record evidence – as in the English royal charters which establish Richard I's itinerary in the autumn of 1189 or the Glasgow charters which prove Roger of Howden's presence in Scotland – but with the exception of the essay on social mobility with its rather forlorn attempt to be as quantitative as possible, this type of evidence has generally been asked to play a supporting role. Even when using records I find the stories told by forgeries or casual allusions in the narrative sections of charters more interesting than the formulae of address or witness lists – although I ought to record that the original stimulus for the idea that there was a precise political and military context for Geoffrey of Monmouth's enthusiasm for King Arthur and his great court at Caerleon came from seeing the words 'King Morgan' in the witness list of a charter. In part, of course, privileging narratives is a matter of taste. 'As an old-fashioned historian, I enjoy reading narrative sources more than I like reading administrative and judicial records.'[26] But equally obviously it is also a matter of the questions asked. In these essays I have asked questions about the thought-world of the English political elite considered in relation to their ancestors and their neighbours, in France and in Britain and Ireland, taking as axiomatic that the

[24] R. R. Davies, 'The Peoples of Britain and Ireland 1100–1400: I. Identities', *TRHS* 6th ser. 4 (1994), 9.

[25] T. Reuter, 'The Making of England and Germany, 850–1050: Points of Comparison and Difference' in ed. A. Smyth, *Medieval Europeans* (London, 1998), 62–3.

[26] J. Gillingham, *Richard Coeur de Lion. Kingship, Chivalry and War in the Twelfth Century* (London, 1994), xi.

way men and women see the world – how they think it is and how they think it ought to be – very considerably shapes how they act.

To write 'men and women' is rather more than a mere formula. Geoffrey Gaimar's *Estoire des Engleis* was commissioned by a woman, Constance FitzGilbert. So too was William of Malmesbury's hugely influential *Deeds of the Kings of the English*. The imagined community of the Britons created by Geoffrey of Monmouth was one in which women such as Cordelia and Gwendolen played a powerful part. Historians writing in the 1130s and 1140s – William of Malmesbury, Henry of Huntingdon, Geoffrey of Monmouth and Geoffrey Gaimar – could not but be aware of the central and active role of the Empress Matilda; authors writing in the 1180s and 1190s – Gerald de Barri, and Roger of Howden – similarly witnessed a number of decisive interventions by Eleanor of Aquitaine. Of course in other ways this is very circumscribed history. Its subject matter is the history written by members of the elite for the elite. This side of 'four nations' history is top-down history, 'even, after a fashion, drum-and-trumpet history'.[27] Sadly, of course, there is no direct evidence of the views of 'ordinary' people in Britain and Ireland in the twelfth century. However absence of evidence does not entitle us to generalize on the basis of Eugen Weber's *Peasants into Frenchmen* and assert that peasants everywhere had no sense of belonging to a nation – indeed even in France there was a nation, though geographically a much smaller one than late twentieth-century France.[28] None the less it is clear that in twelfth-century England, despite its small size and the density of its administrative network, there was no nation in the 'modernist' sense which would limit the word 'nation' to those societies where the masses shared a sense of collective identity with the elite – usually said to exist only after print and/or print and capitalism had created a mass reading public.[29] In Gellner's terms the medium itself, irrespective of the specific messages transmitted, is what matters: 'the core message is that the language and style of the transmissions is important, that only he who can understand them, or can acquire such comprehension, is included in a moral and economic community, and that he who does not and cannot, is excluded'.[30] In twelfth-century England too many monoglot English felt excluded by not being able to speak French – and this holds even though English itself had become a vernacular of the French-speaking minority of the population of England as early as the third or even second post-Conquest generation.[31] Even so, in the light of 'or can acquire

---

[27] Samuel, 'British Dimensions', xiv.

[28] Hastings, *Construction of Nationhood*, 26–7.

[29] As most eloquently in E. Gellner, *Nations and Nationalism* (1983) and B. Anderson, *Imagined Communities* (1983, 2nd edn, 1991). For helpful discussion of the theories see A. D. Smith, 'National Identities: Modern and Medieval?' in eds. S. Forde, L. Johnson, A. V. Murray, *Concepts of National Identity in the Middle Ages* (Leeds, 1995).

[30] Gellner, *Nations and Nationalism*, 127. In view of Gellner's masculine pronoun here, the point made by Michael Clanchy, cited in note 32, needs to be kept in mind.

[31] I. Short, '*Tam Angli quam Franci*: Self-Definition in Anglo-Norman England', *Anglo-Norman Studies* 18 (1995), 156.

such comprehension', the judgement of Frank Barlow on one aspect of mid-twelfth-century England becomes important. 'By 1154 the existence of elementary education was taken for granted: that is to say, there was a basic education available to everyone who wanted and could afford it; and the clever poor would often be educated free.'[32]

One of the ingredients of twelfth-century English consciousness was the sense that 'we' live in a much urbanised and commercialised society, in short in a more developed economy, than do the Celts. Hence those 'modernists' who are prepared to concede that 'proto-nationalist ideas existed, at least in embryonic forms, in commercial societies like early modern England and Holland'[33] might at least consider the possibility that the 'imagined community' of twelfth-century England may also have been, in their terms, 'proto-nationalist'. Modernising forces do not begin with the Reformation. Finally there is one area in which in my view – and in the absence of direct evidence for their views – it is none the less highly likely that the 'masses' shared the consciousness of the political elite and the intelligentsia. Given that the 'imperialist' disdain for Celtic peoples rationalised and justified the dispossession of Welsh and Irish to the advantage not just of the elite but also of the 'ordinary' English-born villagers and townspeople who migrated there in huge numbers and 'made good', it would be surprising if there was not considerable agreement on this point across the whole English social spectrum. Hence the Irish protest against a world in which even the Saxon who lacked breeding and wealth was regarded as more noble than a high-status Gael.[34]

In preparing these essays for this volume, I felt I had no choice but to up-date many of the notes. For this I blame the editors of the Oxford Medieval Texts series who in the last few years have published so many excellent new editions of the historians on whom I had been working – since 1995 alone new editions of William of Malmesbury's *Gesta Regum*, Henry of Huntingdon's *Historia Anglorum*, *The Chronicle* of John of Worcester, the *Gesta Guillelmi* of William of Poitiers and the *Gesta Normannorum Ducum* of William of Jumièges have appeared. Once embarked on revising the footnotes it seemed foolish not also to draw attention to some of the more recent relevant literature. This has not been carried through systematically, but I thought that something would be more useful than nothing. Similarly it seemed better to correct mistakes. To two of the essays I have added postscripts.

Since these essays are so closely inter-related my habit of repeating myself will

---

[32] F. Barlow, *The English Church 1066–1154* (1979), 229. Moreover 'instruction in reading was primarily domestic: by one individual to another, most typically by mother to child'. M. T. Clanchy, *Memory to Written Record*, 2nd edn (Oxford, 1993), 13, 198, 245.

[33] B. O'Leary, 'On the Nature of Nationalism. An Appraisal of Ernest Gellner's Writings on Nationalism' in *The Social Philosophy of Ernest Gellner*, eds. J. A. Hall and I. Jarvie, *Poznan Studies in the Philosophy of the Sciences and the Humanities* 48 (n.d.), 88–9.

[34] See below, p. 9.

be visible here. Some of the most blatant overlaps have been cut but on balance it seemed better to let many of the repetitions stand, on the assumption that readers (apart perhaps from reviewers) were much more likely to read single essays rather than plough their way through the whole book.

Part One. Imperialism

1

The Beginnings of English Imperialism

I

As is well-known, 'a large part of medieval and modern "British" history can be seen as a process of conquest and forcible anglicisation, extending of course to Ireland as well as to Wales and Scotland'.[1] Corrigan and Sayer suggest, surely rightly, that for the English to construe the brutality of conquest and/or the rapacity of commerce as a 'civilizing mission', 'took a national culture of extraordinary self-confidence and moral rectitude'.[2] From what date can an English national culture of this type be said to exist? In what social, economic and political context did the set of cultural images which 'provided the moral energy for English imperialism' first emerge? Imperialism as a subject has been very largely monopolized by modern historians and as a group they tend to think that there is a great divide, often labelled the Renaissance, between their world and that of the 'Middle Ages'.[3] Thus most modern historians have associated the emergence of this 'national culture' with what they see as profound changes in government, religion and society in the sixteenth and seventeenth centuries. This consensus is reflected in, for example, Hugh Kearney's *The British Isles. A History of Four Nations* (1989), where Chapter Seven, entitled 'The Making of an English Empire', begins: 'In the early sixteenth century, a new period began in the history of the British Isles. It was characterised by the emergence of an "English empire", or, more precisely, an empire based on the wealth, population and resources of southern England over the rest of the British Isles.' Naturally the historical sociologists who, with necessary optimism, rely on historians for the data from which they construct their theories, tend to accept this dating. Michael Hechter, for example, surveying the relation between core and periphery in the

---

[1] G. E. Aylmer, 'The Peculiarities of the English State', *Journal of Historical Sociology*, 3, 1990, 94.

[2] P. Corrigan and D. Sayer, *The Great Arch: English State Formation as Cultural Revolution*, Oxford, 1985, 193–4.

[3] Although ancient historians have attempted systematic comparisons with modern imperialism (P. A. Brunt, 'Reflections on British and Roman Imperialism', *Comparative Studies in Society and History*, 7, 1965; M. I. Finley, 'Colonies – an Attempt at a Typology', *TRHS*, 5th ser., xxvi, 1976), I know of no 'medieval' equivalents.

British Isles over a remarkably long period (from the Romans to the twentieth century), wrote that, 'From the seventeenth century on, English military and political control in the peripheral regions was buttressed by a racist ideology which held that Norman Anglo-Saxon culture was inherently superior to Celtic culture.'[4] Corrigan and Sayer trace the imperialist culture 'from the heroic myths of the "elect nation" in the sixteenth and seventeenth centuries to the more philistine, secular and complacent but no less missionary motifs of the nineteeth'.[5] Here I shall first argue that an imperialist English culture emerged in the twelfth century, then suggest reasons why it emerged some four hundred years earlier than is commonly supposed.

At first sight there is something of a paradox here since for most people the hundred years or so after the Norman Conquest was a time when Frenchmen ruled the roost, when the English were an oppressed people and their culture a necessarily subordinate one – hardly the most plausible soil for the growth of an imperialising English culture. Thus the momentous expansionist movement of soldiers, settlers and ruling elites from England into Wales, Scotland and Ireland which characterised the twelfth and thirteenth centuries, if interpreted in imperialist terms at all, is generally seen as Norman rather than English imperialism. Once again Kearney's chapter titles nicely reflect this widespread perception. Chapter five, beginning in 1066 and covering the twelfth and thirteenth centuries, is called 'The Norman Ascendancy'; chapter six, dealing with the next two centuries, is called 'The Decline of the Norman French Empire'.[6] One of the most striking symptoms of this view is the use of the nineteenth-century term 'the Norman Invasion' – now omnipresent in Ireland – to refer to the invasion of 1169–70, whence book titles such as *Ireland under the Normans* or *Ireland before the Normans*.[7]

Since this perception is both widespread and seriously misleading, it is perhaps best to begin with a few observations on the subject. No one would deny that the Norman Conquest created a deeply divided society. But these divisions passed. In this context the question is, when? In my view it took a long time, i.e. two generations, perhaps seventy years, but by the 1130s and 1140s the French connexion was no longer a source of national or ethnic tension. In his entry for 1107 the author of the *Anglo-Saxon Chronicle* wrote 'it was the forty-first year after the French had been in control of this country'. The next time (1127) the Chronicle refers to 'the French', it is not as those who are not us and rule over us, but as those who are not us because they are the subjects of the king of France. By this date French is no longer the language of foreign oppressors, it is

---

[4] M. Hechter, *Internal Colonialism. The Celtic Fringe in British National Development*, London, 1975, 342.

[5] Corrigan and Sayer, 194. But as they make explicit, p. 11, their primary concern was with 'English state formation in England', a subject on which they take their analysis much further back in time.

[6] H. Kearney, *The British Isles. A History of Four Nations*, Cambridge, 1989.

[7] On this subject see below, pp. 145–60.

already, as it was in the thirteenth century, the polite language of the English elite (whether perceived as oppressive or not).[8]

What are the implications of this for the sense of identity of the French-speaking members of the landholding elite? In this context the views of one of the greatest English historians, William of Malmesbury, are particularly revealing. His main historical work, the *Deeds of the kings of the English*, completed by 1125, survives in a lot of manuscripts and was very widely known.[9] He wrote history, as he himself said, 'out of love for my country'.[10] By his *patria* he meant not some cross-Channel Anglo-Norman realm but England. Not surprisingly he has long been thought of as a very 'English' historian. When Sir Richard Southern suggested that there was 'a distinctive character to English historical writing' based upon 'a tradition of research which had been started in the twelfth century and renewed in the sixteenth century', he identified William as 'the most talented' of all the twelfth century researchers. The tradition which Southern had in mind was essentially an antiquarian one, one which, in his words, 'had the great merit of beginning with the ordinary needs of life, and not with any intellectual programme whatsoever'.[11] I am not entirely convinced that this quite does justice to William. In his own view he was the most important English historian since Bede, i.e. for four hundred years, and he certainly saw a very clear pattern in the course of English history. As he makes explicit in his reflections on the significance of 1066, William looked upon English history as a progress from barbarism to civilisation – a smug assumption in which he was to be followed by many modern historians of England, from David Hume onwards.

In William's view the civilising process started at the sixth-century court of King Ethelberht of Kent. Since Ethelberht was the first English king to be converted it is easy to assume that William equated civilisation with Christianity.[12] In fact in William's eyes the process predated the king's conversion. The critical moment was his marriage to Bertha, the daughter of the *rex Francorum*, since it 'was by this connexion with the French that a once barbarous people began to divest themselves of their wild frame of mind and incline towards a gentler way of life'. Later William described how the ninth century King Egberht of Wessex, in exile in France, learned foreign ways 'very different from his native barbarism', for the French, William observed, 'are unrivalled

---

[8] On this subject see below, pp. 123–42.

[9] A. Gransden, *Historical Writing in England c.550 to c.1307*, London, 1974, 178–9; B. Guenée, *Histoire et Culture historique dans l'Occident médiéval*, Paris, 1980, 250–1, 270.

[10] William of Malmesbury, *Gesta Regum Anglorum*, ed. and trans. R. A. B. Mynors, R. M. Thomson and M. Winterbottom, Oxford, 1998, Book One, Prologue. Henceforth I shall cite the *Gesta Regum* as WM and by chapter, since the division into chapters is the same in both the new Oxford Medieval Text edition and in Stubbs's Rolls Series edition.

[11] R. W. Southern, 'Aspects of the European Tradition of Historical Writing: 4. The Sense of the Past', *TRHS*, 5th ser., xxiii, 1973, 253, 263.

[12] W. R. Jones, 'The Image of the Barbarian in Medieval Europe', *Comparative Studies in Society and History*, 13, 1971, 391–2.

among western nations in military skill and in polished manners'. In this passage it is the present tense which is particularly striking. In William's view then it was French culture, not Christianity alone, which made the English civilised.[13] Naturally William saw this as a process which was continuing in his own day. In political terms he perceived the battle of Hastings as 'a day of disaster for our sweet country'. He lamented that even now (c.1120), no Englishman was able to hold high office in England – though he also believed that this state of affairs was about to end.[14] For William, Norman conquest and continuing domination was one thing, but the acquisition of French culture and customs quite another. In William's eyes the more 'Frenchified' England and the English became, the better. In this cultural context for a man to use the French language need not be a denial of his English identity, of a sense of continuity with the Anglo-Saxon past – any more than the use of English by the Irish, Scots and Welsh of today necessarily separates them from a keen awareness of their own national pasts. It might be objected that a highly cultivated monk writing in Latin is no guide to the feelings of people outside monasteries, but it should be remembered that William was no recluse but a widely travelled man who had good connexions with the royal court.

Then there is the evidence of the *Estoire des Engleis* by Geoffrey Gaimar (c.1140). Gaimar's milieu was secular, aristocratic Lincolnshire society. His English history goes from the Anglo-Saxon settlements to the court of Henry I. He is capable of admiring Hereward the Wake and of criticising William the Bastard. Since Gaimar's is the earliest history known to have been written in the French language, it is worth dwelling on the fact it was precisely a history of the English and not – as might have been expected – a history of the French.[15] What it shows is that French-speakers living in England could see the Anglo-Saxon past as their past. The king and a tiny handful of the very greatest magnates, holding vast estates in Normandy as well as in England and Wales, may have thought of themselves primarily as Frenchmen, but the overwhelming majority of the landowners of England knew that they were English, French speaking, of mixed ancestry – as William of Malmesbury was – (usually French on their father's side and proud of their forefathers' achievements), but English even so.[16]

What the writings of Malmesbury and Gaimar suggest is that nineteenth- and twentieth-century scholars, when looking for evidence of a sense of English identity, have taken too Germanic a view. Here, it may well be, is a context in which seventeenth-century developments in the history of ideas have been important: the notion that the qualities which made English institutions the best

---

[13] On this subject see below, pp. 28–9.
[14] WM, cc. 227, 245, 419.
[15] I. Short, 'Gaimar et les débuts de l'historiographie en langue française', in *Chroniques nationales et Chroniques universelles*, Göppinger Arbeiten zur Germanistik 508, Göppingen, 1990.
[16] See below, pp. 99–100.

and the freest in the world were an inheritance from Germanic or Teutonic forefathers, i.e. the beginnings of the Stubbsian view that English history was 'the pure development of Germanic principles'.[17] One result of this emphasis was – and still is – the assumption that the Englishman could not recover his true identity until he had shaken off the Norman Yoke, until after 1204 when John lost Anjou and Normandy and the French connexion was very largely broken. But to apply this much later definition of English identity to the Francophile and francophone twelfth century is to be anachronistic. In the twelfth century the French language was increasingly becoming the *lingua franca* of a cosmopolitan, Europe-wide community. To speak it, or write songs in it, was one way of showing that you were the sort of Englishman who counted, who shared the civilised values of western Europe. This was clearly not an insular sense of Englishness, but it was, for all that, a kind of Englishness.[18] And though the twelfth-century Englishman 'failed' to feel a 'healthy contempt' for continentals, he undoubtedly came to feel distinctly superior to his fellow-islanders, the 'Celts'. If 'a defining characteristic of imperial expansion is that the center must disparage the indigenous culture of peripheral groups',[19] then this is of critical importance.

II

Consider the assumptions of the unknown author of the *Gesta Stephani* writing in the 1140s. England he describes as 'the seat of justice, the abode of peace, the apex of piety, the mirror of religion'. Wales, by contrast, he saw as 'a country of woodland and pasture . . . abounding in deer and fish, milk and herds, but breeding a bestial type of man'. Happily by 1135 the activities of Richard Fitz Gilbert and his fellows, imposing peace on the Welsh by castle-building and law-making, 'had made the country so to abound in peace and productivity that it might easily have been thought a second England (*secunda Anglia*)'.[20] Some years earlier William of Malmesbury had described King David I of Scotland as 'made civilised by his upbringing amongst us. In consequence the rust of his native barbarism was polished away.' Indeed William portrays David as a kind of missonary for civilisation among the Scots, promising no less than three years exemption from taxes to any of his subjects 'who would live in a more civilised style, dress with more elegance and learn to eat with more refinement'. Later in

---

[17] H. A. MacDougall, *Racial Myth in English History*, Montreal, 1982, 31–70, 102.

[18] It has been suggested (G. W. S. Barrow, *The Anglo-Norman Era in Scottish History*, Oxford, 1980, 6–7) that 'from the 1070s to the 1170s the English were less confident about their own identity than in any period of their history before this present generation'. This may be so, but however uncertain on this score the present generation may be, who would go so far as to deny their Englishness?

[19] Hechter, 64.

[20] *Gesta Stephani*, eds. K. R. Potter and R. H. C. Davis, Oxford, 1976, 15–17.

the century Ralph Diceto, dean of St Paul's, London, visualised the Irish coming to Henry II and promising to embrace English customs.[21] In these and similar passages there is a very strong sense that 'we' in England are civilised; 'they' in Wales, Scotland and Ireland are crude barbarians.

Amongst the clerical elite a prevailing perception of the otherness and inferiority of Celtic peoples is easy to document.[22] John of Salisbury, writing in the 1150s, said that the Welsh 'are rude and untamed; they live like beasts and though they nominally profess Christ, they deny him in their life and ways'.[23] 'Who would deny that the Scots are barbarians?' wrote another mid twelfth-century English author.[24] The north countryman William of Newburgh, often, in the light of his observations on Thomas Becket and King Arthur, regarded as the most judicious of twelfth-century historians, refers to a Scottish army as 'a horde of barbarians'. That this was more than a routine condemnation of an invader is made clear by his description of their behaviour. 'Everything was being consumed by the Scots, to whom no food is too filthy to be devoured, even that which is fit only for dogs. It is a delight to that inhuman nation, more savage than wild beasts, to cut the throats of old men, to slaughter little children, to rip open the bowels of women.'[25] Then, of course, there is Gerald de Barri – usually but misleadingly known as Gerald of Wales[26] – on the Irish. 'They are so barbarous that they cannot be said to have any culture . . . they are a wild people, living like beasts, who have not progressed at all from the primitive habits of pastoral farming.'[27]

Work done by historians such as Robert Bartlett and R. R. Davies since the early 1980s has shown that by the mid and late twelfth century such views were commonplace. But when did such attitudes first emerge? This question has not so far been explicitly addressed.[28] Medievalists, who as a group tend not to fall

---

[21] WM c. 400; Diceto, *Opera Historica*, ed. W. Stubbs, RS, 1876, i.350–1.

[22] W. R. Jones, 'England against the Celtic Fringe: a Study in Cultural Stereotypes', *Journal of World History*, 13, 1971; R. Bartlett, *Gerald of Wales*, Oxford, 1982; R. R. Davies, 'Buchedd a moes y Cymry. The manners and morals of the Welsh', *Welsh Historical Review*, xii, 1984–85.

[23] *The Letters of John of Salisbury*, vol. 1, ed. W. J. Millor, H. E. Butler, and C. N. L. Brooke, London, 1955, 135–6.

[24] *De Expugnatione Lyxbonensi*, ed. and trans. C. W. David, New York, 1936, 106–7. 6. When twlfth-century English authors referred to 'Scots' and 'Picts', they generally had the Irish-speaking inhabitants of the Highlands and Galloway in mind. In this period Lowland Scotland was being transformed by urbanisation and an influx of English settlers, the aristocrats among them French-speaking. This point in particular should be borne in mind whenever I over-simplify by lumping Ireland, Wales and Scotland together.

[25] William of Newburgh, *Historia Rerum Anglicarum*, ed. R. Howlett in *Chronicles of the Reigns of Stephen, Henry II and Richard I*, vols. 1 and 2, RS, 1884, i.181–3.

[26] On his name see below, p. 155.

[27] Gerald of Wales, *The History and Topography of Ireland*, trans. J. O' Meara, Harmondsworth, 1982, 101.

[28] However there are implicit answers to the question in such statements as 'The Norman Conquest accentuated differences between the Celtic and English worlds by importing

into 'the early modern trap', sometimes write as though this set of attitudes has always existed, as though it was in the nature of the Anglo-Saxon to despise the Celt. Sir Maurice Powicke, for example, referred to 'that age-long racial struggle of Celt and Teuton'.[29] But neither a traditional enmity between neighbours, nor the virtually universal feeling that 'we' are 'better' than 'them', is the same thing as the imperialist view that certain people are so inferior as to belong to a distinctly lower order of society. The imperialist view is one which leads to a striking inversion of other otherwise deeply engrained values so that, for example, a fourteenth-century Irish court historian could complain bitterly of a world turned upside down where the general rule was 'that the Gael is ignoble though a landholder and the Saxon noble though he lack both breeding and wealth'.[30]

One of William of Malmesbury's most creative and influential achievements was to introduce this imperialist perception of Celtic peoples into history. It is true, of course, that an imperial outlook had existed in earlier centuries. Some tenth-century English kings had claimed to be overlords of Britain. King Edgar, for example, has been called 'the most imperial of the late Anglo-Saxon rulers'[31] – and so in a sense he was. He was buried at Glastonbury together with – or so it was believed – the great saints of the British Isles: Patrick, David, Gildas and Aidan. But as that grand assemblage of saints shows, the culture of Celtic peoples was not disparaged in tenth-century Wessex. The West Saxon court was happy to see its great king associated in the grave with men from Ireland, Wales and Iona. In the tenth century Anglo-Saxons and Celts shared a common cultural world in which Ireland could still be regarded as a source of learning and virtue.[32] Tenth-century English kings may have been imperial rulers in that they ruled, or claimed to rule, over a number of kingdoms; but they were not imperialists.

Reading works written within the Anglo-Saxon world during the ninth, tenth and eleventh centuries what strikes me is the absence of any clearly defined attitude towards the Welsh, the Scots and the Irish. It is as though they were

---

into England the Norman feudal regime, continental urban institutions, and the reformist ideals of Roman Christianity' and 'From the time of the Norman Conquest forward these tribal, pastoral, politically decentralized, and economically marginal societies of oats-and barley-growing, meat-eating and milk-drinking cattle raiders stood in marked contrast with the agrarian, feudalized, town- and village-dwelling, politically consolidated and more affluent society of wheat-growing and wine-drinking Englishmen', Jones, 'England against the Celtic Fringe', 155–6. There are clearly important points made here, but also some highly questionable interpretations of the role of the Norman Conquest.

[29] *Walter Daniel's Life of Ailred, Abbot of Rievaulx*, ed. and trans. F. M. Powicke, London, 1950, xlvii.

[30] Cited by R. Frame, *Colonial Ireland, 1169–1369*, Dublin, 1981, 109 and by R. R. Davies, *Domination and Conquest. The experience of Ireland, Scotland and Wales*, Cambridge, 1990, 119.

[31] J. Campbell, 'Some Twelfth-Century Views of the Anglo-Saxon Past', *Peritia*, 3, 1984, 139.

[32] D. Bethell, 'English monks and Irish reform in the eleventh and twelfth centuries', *Historical Studies*, 8, 1971.

regarded as simply people like any other. In the case of the Welsh this is particularly striking since Bede had described the British king Cadwalla of Gwynedd as *barbarus* – and the Welsh were the successors of the Britons. Yet Bede's view of a fellow Christian seems to have found no echo until the twelfth century. During the previous three centuries Latin authors use the word *barbarus* as a synonym for pagan; the pagan Vikings are frequently referred to as barbarians. By contrast the various authors of the Anglo-Saxon Chronicle treat the Welsh and the Scots neutrally, occasionally even sympathetically. But William adopted a distinctly different tone.[33] For him the Celts, Irish, Scots and Welsh, are 'barbarians'. In other words he is discarding the familiar concept of barbarian as equivalent to pagan, and formulating a new one – one which allowed for the possibility of Christian barbarians. Indeed in William's eyes even people who were so Christian that they went on crusade could none the less be barbarians. Thus when recounting Pope Urban II's preaching of the crusade, he tells us that some of those who responded to Urban's call lived *in nationibus barbaris*: and he lists them, the Welsh, Scots, Danes and Norwegians. It looks as though William's extraordinary familiarity with classical literature and his admiration for the ancient world,[34] has enabled him to 'rediscover' the classical concept of the barbarian, and 'discover' that it applied to Celtic peoples in his own day. This is indeed antiquarian research, but hardly 'programme-free'.

III

Why did William's perception of Celtic peoples as barbarians become commonplace? To answer this question, it is first necessary to sketch in the perceived characteristics of the barbarous Celt. I do this under three heads: the barbarian at work, the barbarian at war and the barbarian in bed.

1. *The barbarian at work.* This is, of course, a misnomer since it was widely believed that the barbarian was thoroughly indolent – 'given only to leisure and devoted only to laziness', as Gerald described the Irish.[35] By the later twelfth century it was conventional to see the Celtic regions as fundamentally pastoral economies and to comment on the absence of towns, commerce and agriculture. The earliest author to make this explicit was William of Malmesbury, when drawing a striking contrast between England (seen as belonging to a more advanced European order) and Ireland. 'Whereas the English and the French live in market-oriented towns enjoying a more cultivated style of life, the Irish live in rustic squalor, for owing to the ignorance of the farmers their land is

---

[33] See below, pp. 27–8.
[34] R. M. Thompson, *William of Malmesbury*, Woodbridge, 1987.
[35] Gerald, *History and Topography*, 102.

inadequately cultivated.'[36] William evidently accepted the ancient notion that pastoral economies were unlikely to be able to sustain civilised life; and the comment of the author of the *Gesta Stephani* that Wales bred a bestial kind of people, suggests that he shared similar assumptions.

2. *The barbarian at war*. I turn to Richard of Hexham's description of a Scottish attack on Northumbria in 1138.

> By the sword's edge or the spear's point they slaughtered the sick on their beds, women who were pregnant or in labour, babies in their cradles or at their mothers' breasts, and sometimes they killed the mothers too. They slaughtered worn-out old men, feeble old women, anyone who was disabled. They killed husbands in front of their wives. Then they carried off their plunder and the women, both widows and maidens, stripped, bound and roped together they drove them off, goading them with spears on the way. Their fate was either to be kept as slaves or sold on to other barbarians in exchange for cattle.[37]

What struck this author was the savagery of a war targeted against non-combatants. But for combatants too the risks of engaging in Celtic warfare were observably high. Gerald de Barri, for example, contrasts French warfare with Irish and Welsh warfare: 'The French ransom soldiers; the Irish and Welsh butcher them and decapitate them.'[38]

3. *The barbarian in bed*. It was generally agreed that Celtic sexual and marital customs were animal-like. According to Richard of Hexham (c.1140), the Scots were 'those bestial men who think nothing of committing incest, adultery and other abominations'.[39] Gerald writes of the Irish in similar tones. 'They get their living from beasts and live like beasts. . . . an adulterous and incestuous people which shamefully abuses nature herself'. According to John of Salisbury, the Welsh 'live like beasts . . . despising the law of marriage, they keep concubines as well as wives; whenever it suits them they get rid of them – for a price – to other men. They do not blush to indulge in incest. Their king Owain, for example, the prince of these barbarians, abuses the daughter of his uncle.'[40]

IV

Such are the perceptions. The question is: are they based on reality? Essentially the answer is yes. Clearly in some respects these authors exaggerated – for

[36] WM, c. 409.

[37] Richard of Hexham, *Chronicles of the Reigns*, iii.156–7. For similar descriptions written by other English contemporaries see below, pp. 44–6.

[38] Gerald, *The Journey through Wales*, trans. L. Thorpe, Harmondsworth, 1978, 269.

[39] Richard of Hexham, 157.

[40] Gerald, *History and Topography*, 101, 118; *Letters of John of Salisbury*, i.135–6.

example, the extent to which Celtic peoples relied upon pastoral farming. None the less there is plenty of evidence that in all of these spheres, economic, military and marital there were highly significant differences between twelfth-century England and contemporary Celtic realms.

1. *Economy*

A comparative chronology of economic development within the British Isles suggests that the fundamental differences between highland and lowland zone were being sharply accentuated during the course of the tenth and eleventh centuries. By the end of that period many English people no longer lived in isolated farmsteads or in hamlets but in villages and market towns.[41] In England there is clear evidence of the growth of a money economy. By the end of the tenth century moneyers were at work in some 70 English towns; 'a very considerable intensification of minting' was taking place. Although a graph of the volume of coinage in circulation in England would certainly not show a constant upward trend from the tenth to the thirteenth century, the fact remains that by the 1220s – the date of the earliest extant figures for mint production – huge amounts of silver were being coined and pumped into the economic system, by the mid-thirteenth century in quantities which were not to be surpassed until the nineteenth century.[42] By contrast, the highland zone and Ireland lagged some centuries behind. Put very roughly, the Celtic regions in the twelfth century looked rather like eighth-century England: a dispersed settlement pattern of farms and hamlets, not many coins, very few towns – and these situated on the coasts where they serviced international trade, not the needs of villagers going to their local market.[43] One symptom of this fundamental transformation of England – urban growth and commercialisation of the countryside – was the appearance in England of settlements of Jews, seemingly moving across the Channel in the wake of the Norman Conquest – said William of Malmesbury. Jewish communities were established first in London and the south, then gradually spread west and north as far as Newcastle.[44] Up to the time of their expulsion (1290) there were no Jewish settlements in Scotland, Wales or Ireland. In economic terms England can be put into the context of European development described as 'the most profound and most permanent change that overtook Western Europe between

[41] C. Taylor, *Village and Farmstead*, London, 1983; D. A. Hinton, *Archaeology, Economy and Society. England from the fifth to the fifteenth century*, London, 1990.

[42] P. Spufford, *Money and its Use in Medieval Europe*, Cambridge, 1988, 87–94, 202–5. See R. H. Britnell, *The Commercialisation of English Society, 1000–1500*, Cambridge, 1993.

[43] A. A. M. Duncan, *Scotland. The Making of the Kingdom*, Edinburgh, 1975, 463; T. B. Barry, *The Archaeology of Medieval Ireland*, London, 1987; W. Davies, *Wales in the Early Middle Ages*, Leicester, 1982.

[44] R. B. Dobson, *The Jews of Medieval York and the Massacre of March 1190*, Borthwick Papers No. 45, York, 1974, 1–11; H. G. Richardson, *The English Jewry under the Angevin Kings*, London, 1960, 1–22.

the invention of agriculture and the industrial revolution', the growth of towns, markets and manufactures which together with government institutions of a new force, networks of officials, 'transformed Europe from a society of gift exchange into a money economy, with profound results for its entire structure of values and social custom'.[45] These are the changes described by James Campbell as 'the preliminary to the European conquest of the world'.[46]

We may if we like, from the vantage point of the twentieth century, look back at medieval England and see it as an overwhelmingly rural society, a primitive economy. But this is precisely the attitude adopted by twelfth-century Englishmen when they looked towards their Celtic neighbours. 'The Irish', in Gerald's words, 'have not progressed at all from the primitive habits of pastoral farming. For while mankind usually progresses from the woods to the fields, and then from fields to settlements and communities of citizens, this Irish people scorns work on the land, has little use for the money making of towns and despises the rights and privileges of the civil life.' Ireland, Wales and the highlands and islands of Scotland were perceived as poor and primitive societies – primitive in that they had failed to climb the ladder of evolution of human societies which twelfth-century intellectuals like Gerald took for granted.[47] By contrast the English saw themselves as prosperous, peaceful, law-abiding, urbanised and enterprising. As Richard of Devizes was to put it (in 1190s), 'no one keen on making money need die poor here'. For Richard FitzNigel (in the 1180s), England was a land characterised by its 'untold riches' and by 'the natural drunkeness of its inhabitants'.[48] A land of yuppies and lager louts.

A further aspect of English economic development and social change was also important in helping to establish the set of imperialist images: the demise of slavery. Slavery, a significant feature of Anglo-Saxon society, was dead and gone by the early decades of the twelfth century. But not from contemporary Ireland, Wales and Scotland – though this is a history which still remains to be written. To William of Malmesbury slavery was a degrading and inhumane instition, and he condemned as 'barbarians' those like the Irish who practised it. For John of Salisbury one of the indicators of Welsh barbarism was the fact that they engaged in the slave trade; and very obviously one of the things Richard of Hexham detested about the Scots was their involvement in slaving.[49]

---

[45] R. I. Moore, *The Formation of a Persecuting Society*, Oxford, 1987, 102.

[46] J. Campbell, 'Was it Infancy in England? Some Questions of Comparison' in *England and her Neighbours 1066–1453. Essays in Honour of Pierre Chaplais*, eds. M. Jones and M. Vale, London, 1989, 17.

[47] Gerald, *History and Topography*, 101–2; Bartlett, *Gerald*, 176.

[48] *The Chronicle of Richard of Devizes*, ed. J. T. Appleby, London, 1963, 64; Richard FitzNigel, *Dialogus de Scaccario*, ed. and trans. C. Johnson, F. E. L. Carter and D. Greenway, Oxford, 1983, 87.

[49] See below, pp. 45–7.

2. *War and Chivalry*

The socio-economic fact of slavery carried with it military implications.[50] From the mid-twelfth century onwards English observers found war as slave hunt utterly repellent, for it involved a form of total war, an attack not just on the property of non-combatants – as, in the form of ravaging, was the norm of warfare everywhere in Europe – but on their persons too. In order to capture potential slaves and drag them off into slavery it was in practice necessary to kill not only anyone who put up a fight, but also anyone who got in the way, elderly parents and young children for example – those categories of persons whom it was uneconomic to put to work but whose lamenting, clinging presence impeded the operation.[51] Thus the shocked language with which so many contemporary authors – Henry of Huntingdon, Orderic, Richard and John of Hexham – described the Scottish invasions of the North in 1137 and 1138, whereas in earlier centuries Scottish raids had been referred to in much more neutral terms by authors who, as members of slave-owning, slave-raiding societies themselves, presumably took for granted the basic characteristics of this form of war.

The new non slave-owning English culture explains why contemporaries of the Battle of the Standard (1138) portrayed it not just as a battle between Scots and English, but as a titanic and ferocious struggle between two different cultures. Moreover accounts of the English victory at the Standard throw further light on the varying rates of economic development within Britain. The Scots lost because although they had an 'innumerable army', they had only 200 mailed soldiers.[52] Although they possessed archers they were very short of arrows. In terms of the manufacture of arms and ammunition the English economy, above all its iron industry, easily outperformed the Scottish economy, and the Welsh economy, and the Irish. It was not heavy cavalry as such – the so-called 'feudal knights' – which dominated campaigns in Wales and Ireland in the twelfth century. It was armour and firepower – the armour worn by soldiers fighting on foot as well as on horseback, the firepower of mounted archers as well as of foot archers. In addition, of course, the English had the capacity to build castles and to stock them on a scale far beyond anything their Celtic neighbours could manage.[53] Hence it was the English who were the expansionist power within the British Isles.[54]

[50] O. Patterson, *Slavery and Social Death*, Cambridge, Mass., 1982, 113–21.

[51] J. F. Ade Ajayi, 'Samuel Ajayi Crowther of Oyo' in *Africa Remembered*, ed. P. D. Curtin, Madison, 1967, 303.

[52] M. Strickland, 'Securing the Border: Invasion and the strategy of defence in twelfth-century Anglo-Scottish Warfare', *ANS*, xii, 1989–90, 191–4.

[53] See, for example, M. T. Flanagan, 'Irish and Anglo-Norman warfare in twelfth-century Ireland' in eds. T. Bartlett and K. Jeffery, *A Military History of Ireland*, Cambridge, 1996, 52–75.

[54] R. Bartlett, 'Technique militaire et pouvoir politique, 900–1300', *Annales, Économies, Sociétés, Civilisations*, 41, 1986. For further development of these points see below, pp. 49, 103.

Throughout the British Isles succession disputes were one of the commonest causes of armed conflict. In the Celtic realms they were often fought out with great ferocity, losers being either killed or mutilated. Madog ap Meredith, for example, emerged as ruler of Powys in 1132 after two of his uncles and four cousins had met one or other of these fates.[55] Welsh politics, like Irish and Scottish politics, was unquestionably a bloody business for the leading participants.[56] To an observer like Gerald de Barri, who at this stage of his career saw himself as a representative of English civilisation, all this was thoroughly reprehensible. When a prince died, he noted, 'the most frightful disturbances occur . . . people being murdered, brothers killing each other and even putting each other's eyes out, for as everyone knows from experience, it is very difficult to settle disputes of this sort'.[57] And indeed this is not how succession disputes were handled in twelfth-century England. In earlier centuries power struggles within and between Anglo-Saxon royal dynasties seem to have provoked similar levels of violence, but by the twelfth century disputes about succession to high political office or succession to great estates, were handled, not without violence of course, but with violence which was controlled so as to spare the lives of the royals and aristocrats who engaged in it. Compared with Celtic politics the so-called 'anarchy of Stephen's reign' was a very 'gentlemanly' affair. This was a chivalrous society.[58] In this sort of society, as Gerald observed, captured soldiers were ransomed, whereas in Wales and Ireland they were butchered and decapitated. Here too is another measure of English economic development, since the chivalrous custom of sparing the lives of high-ranking captives, either ransoming them for money or using them as bargaining counters in order to obtain possession of castles or towns were humane options which were not so readily available in societies which lacked castles and towns, and where coin was in relatively short supply.[59]

3. Sex and marriage

The outraged language used by English authors when referring to the 'scandalous' sexual mores and marriage laws of the Celts reflects the way that in twelfth-century England, as in the most of 'civilised' Europe, men and women had come to accept that marriage was a matter of church law, not of secular law.[60] This increasingly meant that Christian ideas of marriage – that it

[55] R. R. Davies, *Conquest, Co-existence and Change. Wales 1063–1415*, Oxford, 1987, 71–4.
[56] On this see my essay 'Killing and Mutilating Political Enemies in the British Isles from the Late Twelfth to the Early Fourteenth Century: A Comparative Study' in ed. B. Smith, *Britain and Ireland 900–1300: Insular Responses to Medieval European Change*, Cambridge, 1999.
[57] Gerald, *The Journey through Wales*, 26.
[58] See below, pp. 209–29.
[59] This helps to explain why when in Ireland the English tended to treat the Irish 'in Irish fashion', see below, pp. 41–58.
[60] C. N. L. Brooke, *The Medieval Idea of Marriage*, Oxford, 1989, 124–42.

should be monogamous, permanent and involve prohibitions against marrying cousins – came to be accepted as social norms, often breached, no doubt, but norms none the less. Celtic societies, however, continued to regulate these matters according to their ancient laws. In earlier centuries there had been a fundamental similarity between English and Celtic marriage customs – Edward the Elder (899–924), for example, married several women, one of them his second cousin, with different degrees of formality. An eleventh-century English law code still found it necessary to assert that no man should have more than one wife. But developments from the late Saxon period onwards[61] meant that by the twelfth century customs had perceptibly diverged. Celtic marriage law was now regarded as thoroughly disreputable – especially, of course, by the most enthusiastic 'reformers'. Thus it is not surprising that it should be in the matter of sex and marriage and within the circle of ecclesiastical reformers that we can detect the earliest signs of the approach of a new and hostile attitude to Celtic peoples. In Lanfranc's eyes, Irish marriage law – a traditional law which made provision for divorce and re-marriage – was not a law of marriage but a law of fornication. A little later, Anselm of Canterbury was to accuse the Irish of wife-swapping 'in the way that other men exchange horses'.[62] For as long as Celtic societies remained true to their traditional family law – in Wales into the late middle ages, in Ireland into the seventeenth century – there were to be real differences here, and ones which did much to shape English hostility.

But Celtic family law did more than just upset a few puritanical ecclesiastics. At the level of high politics it also had significant consequences. By allowing Welsh or Irish kings to have a number of wives it made it more likely that they would have a number of sons and this increased the number of males with a claim to succeed, all the more so since Celtic custom posited no great gulf between 'legitimate' and 'illegitimate' sons. This had the effect of making succession disputes both more frequent and more complicated as different segments of the royal kindreds put in their bids for power.[63] Given the ferocity of these conflicts, the term used by anthropologically-minded historians – 'segmentary strife' – is a faintly anodyne one.[64]

In much of Europe by the twelfth century changes in the laws of marriage and in the customs of inheritance had led away from political conventions which simply took it for granted that successions would be fought over to conventions which were slightly more peaceful. This is a development which

[61] P. Stafford, *Unification and Conquest. A Political and Social History of England in the Tenth and Eleventh Centuries*, London, 1989, 41–2, 163–8.
[62] Cited in Bartlett, *Gerald*, 43–4.
[63] J. B. Smith, 'Dynastic Succession in Medieval Wales', *Bulletin of the Board of Celtic Studies*, 33, 1986.
[64] A term which, as pointed out in B. Bradshaw, 'Nationalism and Historical Scholarship in Modern Ireland', *Irish Historical Studies*, 26, 1988–89, reflects, in part at least, the tendency of historians to retreat into anthropological or sociological euphemism when discomfited by the violence of the past in their own society.

seems to go together with the recognition of the rights of daughters as heiresses – in England, but again not in the Celtic world. Thus 'Welsh medieval history has none of those heiresses whose fortunes and fate are such a prominent feature of the territorial politics of medieval England.'[65] Similarly in Ireland, both property and political office could be inherited only by males – at any rate in the centuries before the English invasion of Ireland, when it clearly suited the invading Strongbow, husband of Aoife, daughter of Dermot, king of Leinster, that his wife should be recognised as her father's heiress.[66]

V

The perception of Celtic societies as barbarous obviously functioned in part as an ideology of conquest. This is evident from the language of the *Gesta Stephani* on the benefits which the new rulers brought to Wales as also from the kinds of justification – like the papal bull *Laudabiliter* (forged or not) – which Gerald de Barri and others put forward in order to legitimise Henry II's conquest of an island to which he had no claim of the conventional type (i.e. based on some alleged hereditary right). But if I am right about the attitudes of authors in the ninth, tenth and eleventh centuries, then it is equally clear that the English had been invading Welsh – and Cornish – lands for centuries without needing an imperialist ideology. The greater significance of the imperialist outlook was the barrier it set up between conqueror and conquered – a barrier which inhibited assimilation. In Hechter's terms, 'if the state conquers a peripheral territory without making the assertion of cultural superiority, assimilation is much easier to achieve'.[67] There are, it is true, a few signs that some late eleventh-century French observers did regard the English as barbarians, but this perception soon passed, presumably because it had little basis in real differences between northern French and English society.[68] By 1166 an 'English' revolt against Norman rule is unimaginable. The descendants of William's followers had become English, speaking French, but living by English law, within a framework of English institutions, aware that they were the heirs of an English past. This is not how the newcomers lived in Wales and Ireland – though once again lowland Scotland was different.

For many centuries England and the Celtic world had been very similar societies.[69] But in the course of the tenth, eleventh and early twelfth centuries profound European economic, social, military and cultural developments

[65] R. R. Davies, 'The status of women and the practice of marriage in late-medieval Wales' in *The Welsh Law of Women*, eds. D. Jenkins and M. Owen, Cardiff, 1988, 101.
[66] M. T. Flanagan, *Irish Society, Anglo-Norman Settlers, Angevin Kingship*, Oxford, 1989, 95.
[67] Hechter, *Internal Colonialism*, 64.
[68] See below, p. 57.
[69] P. Wormald, 'Celtic and Anglo-Saxon Kingship: Some further thoughts' in *Sources of Anglo-Saxon Culture*, ed. P. E. Szarmach, Kalamazoo, 1986.

affected the south-east of Britain, a wealthy region close to centres of learning, much more rapidly and intensively than they did a remote upland fringe.[70] By the twelfth century this development meant that they had grown sufficiently far apart for the differences between them to be visible to contemporaries. The author who first gave clear expression to this perception of 'otherness' and who did so in terms of the classical contrast between civilisation and barbarism was William of Malmesbury. Some writers, Orderic Vitalis and Henry of Huntingdon, for example, were not immediately converted to seeing Britain and British history through William's eyes, but incidents in the late 1130s, when Scottish and Welsh troops 'barbarously' invaded England, seem to have persuaded even them that William's terms of reference made good sense.[71] As William's ideas were taken up, repeated and elaborated many times over in the next few decades, so a new, negative and condescending attitude to Celtic peoples was established, one which was to endure over many centuries. In the field of British history William was the most creative and influential of all English historians. That his ideas, themselves owing much to the depth and intensity of his own immersion in the literature of the ancient world, struck so many chords is doubtless due in part to the intellectual and cultural movement labelled the Twelfth Century Renaissance – here, as generally, a much more important movement than the later Renaissance of the fifteenth and sixteenth centuries. For all that he was a monk living in a formally – and in many respects self-consciously and radically reforming – Christian society, William's revival of Greco-Roman modes of perception resulted in the Christian view of the world, one which divided men and women into two basic groups – Christian and non-Christian – being decisively supplemented by a non-religious system of classification, one which divided men and women into the civilised and the barbarians. In the course of British history this was to be the great divide, the creation of an imperialist culture.

[70] R. Frame, *The Political Development of the British Isles 1100–1400*, Oxford, 1990, 72–3.
[71] See below, pp. 101–5.

2

The Context and Purposes of Geoffrey of Monmouth's *History of the Kings of Britain*

It is unlikely, to say the least, that there could ever be a single satisfying explanation of a book as extraordinary and influential as Geoffrey of Monmouth's *History of the Kings of Britain*.[1] Covering almost two thousand years and the reigns of ninety-nine kings it is so full of material of different kinds that almost anyone who reads it with a particular interest in mind will be able to pick out passages which support their own interpretation. This, of course, is what I shall be doing. The History (HRB) is particularly susceptible of myriad interpretations since it is shot through and through with ambiguity. In one of its most famous passages, for example, we are told that at the battle of Camblann 'Arthur was mortally wounded and was thence taken to the Isle of Avalon to have his wounds healed.' Moreover central to the book's structure – as also to Geoffrey's later work, the *Vita Merlini* – is prophecy.[2] HRB contains not only the Prophecies of Merlin; there are also prophecies at the book's beginning – notably Diana's prophecy foretelling the destiny of Brutus and his descendants – and at its end, when the 'angelic voice' speaks of the return of Britons.[3] It is of the nature of prophecy, even when its main thrust is plain, that it should contain all

---

* This paper, indeed this whole collection, owes a great deal – much more than its footnotes imply – to the kindness and critical acumen of Rees Davies.

[1] *The Historia Regum Britanniae of Geoffrey of Monmouth. I. Bern, Burgerbibliothek, MS 568*, ed. Neil Wright, Cambridge 1984, c. 178; Geoffrey of Monmouth, *The History of the Kings of Britain*, trans. Lewis Thorpe, Harmondsworth 1966, xi, 2. All passages from Geoffey of Monmouth will be cited in this double fashion in order to facilitate use of other editions. For the differences, textually minor but historically interesting, between the Bern MS and Geoffrey's original text see Wright, liv–lix, and below, pp. 38–9.

[2] H. Pähler, *Strukturuntersuchungen zur Historia Regum Britanniae des Geoffrey of Monmouth*, Bonn 1958, 140–41.

[3] HRB, cc. 16, 112–17, 205; Thorpe, i.11, vii.3–4, xii.17. A version of the Prophecies of Merlin seems to have been in Orderic's hands by 1135–36 (Orderic Vitalis, *Historia Ecclesiastica*, ed. M. Chibnall, Oxford Medieval Texts, 1969–80, vi, 380–88), and this is often taken to mean that Geoffrey had started writing before then. Probably he had, but it is also possible that Orderic used a text which was in circulation before Geoffrey composed the HRB version. See below, n. 110. Julia Crick, *The Historia Regum Britanniae of Geoffrey of Monmouth. III. A Summary Catalogue of the Manuscripts*, Cambridge 1989, 330–32, has counted more than seventy manuscripts of the Prophecies as a separate work.

manner of unknown quantities and ambiguities. In HRB Geoffrey himself tells us that after Merlin had delivered himself of his prophecies 'ambiguitate verborum suorum astantes in admirationem commovit'. Here, of course, lies endless scope for misinterpretation – just as, at Arthur's great court at Caerleon, it was misinterpretation of prophecy which contributed to the launching of the fateful campaign against Rome.[4] Even so there are I think a few things of which we can be tolerably sure. We can be confident that Geoffrey had completed HRB very shortly before January 1139, when Henry of Huntingdon saw it at Bec and was bowled over by what he read.[5] I think that we are also entitled to accept Neil Wright's view that the work was originally and primarily dedicated to Robert of Gloucester.[6] Indeed both date and dedication are vital to my understanding of Geoffrey's purposes. I also believe that the main thrust of HRB can be discerned. In trying to sum it up in a few words I do not think I can do better than paraphrase another Geoffrey, Geoffrey Barrow: Geoffrey was a Welshman whose object was to secure cultural respectability for his own nation.[7]

In saying this I am implying some measure of disagreement with three interpretations which have been influential, even dominant, for much of this century. In my view there is something to be said for all three interpretations, but all give undue weight to subsidiary themes. I shall consider them briefly before moving on to offer my own interpretation. The first is the notion that Geoffrey had no serious political purpose but that, as Sir John Lloyd put it, 'his first and last thought was for literary effect'.[8] In recent years, and particularly since the publication of Christopher Brooke's brilliant study of 'Geoffrey of Monmouth as a Historian' in 1976, it has been generally thought that the effect for which he was striving was a humourous one, that he was writing parody. Although, as Brooke acknowledged, parody can be written with serious intent, in his view the political motivation was clearly subordinate to the 'mockery and mischief'.[9] For Valerie Flint, though there was an over-riding purpose behind

---

[4] HRB, cc. 118, 160; Thorpe, viii.1, ix.17.

[5] Although many scholars have preferred 1136, I entirely agree with Wright, xi–xvi, in accepting what is essentially Tatlock's argument, J. S. P. Tatlock, *The Legendary History of Britain*, Berkeley 1950, 433–34. Given the close connections in the diocese of Lincoln between Henry and Geoffrey, and the fact that until January 1139 Henry had been hunting in vain for information on events before Caesar, it is very unlikely that HRB can have been completed for long before it came to the assiduous Henry's attention.

[6] Wright, xii–xv, especially since it is clear from the terms of the joint dedication to Stephen and Robert that Robert can be referred to as *consul* as well as *dux*.

[7] G. W. S. Barrow, 'Wales and Scotland in the Middle Ages', *Welsh Historical Review*, x, 1980–81, 305.

[8] J. E. Lloyd, *A History of Wales*, London 1939, vol. 2, 528.

[9] Christopher Brooke, 'Geoffrey of Monmouth as a historian' in ed. C. Brooke et al., *Church and Government in the Middle Ages*, Cambridge 1976, 77–91. Though granting that there were passages likely to 'appeal to a Welsh audience' he felt that 'if the Celtic hope was uppermost in his mind, or the Norman empire, he could easily have made his interest much clearer'. Thus John Clark, 'Trinovantum – the evolution of a legend', *Journal of Medieval History*, 7, 1981, 143, has Geoffrey writing 'tongue in cheek'.

the parody, in her opinion it had nothing to do with national politics but was intended to exalt non-monastic virtues and styles of life.[10] I agree with her that there was a serious purpose behind this entertainment, but given the overwhelmingly political and military content of Geoffrey's history I think it more likely that it had to do with matters of politics, the politics of cultural nationalism.

This brings me to the second of the three interpretations, the belief that Geoffrey was much more concerned with the Anglo-Norman elite than with the Welsh. Clearly since all his work was dedicated to prominent members of that elite, he must in a sense have been writing for them. But the questions remain: in what sense and in whose interest? Was Geoffrey basically an ambitious man seeking preferment, telling the elite what he thought they wanted to hear?[11] Or were his concerns more complicated, ambiguous even?[12] Undoubtedly HRB contains strains which would have struck a chord with the ruling elite. As Normandy and England slid into civil war after Henry I's death, Geoffrey's frequent references to the damaging effects of discord have an obvious point.[13] Indeed as Neil Wright has suggested the two double dedications 'to men who newly found themselves enemies', first to Robert and Waleran of Meulan, then to Robert and King Stephen, could well be construed as 'a powerful, if covert, plea for unity'.[14] But warnings against discord could have applied to the Welsh just as much as to the Anglo-Normans, even more so, many would have said.[15] It has also been powerfully argued, and widely accepted, that Arthur's empire was in some way a pre-figuration of the Norman Empire, that the figure of Arthur was formed in the image of Charlemagne, or Alexander, and that in the line of British kings descended from Brutus, Geoffrey was providing the contemporary kings

[10] Valerie I. J. Flint, 'The *Historia Regum Britanniae* of Geoffrey of Monmouth: parody and its purpose. A suggestion', *Speculum*, liv, 1979, 447–68. That some readers were indeed disturbed by HRB's relatively secular and non-monastic tone is suggested by some early alterations to the text, *The Historia Regum Britanniae of Geoffrey of Monmouth. II. The First Variant Version*, ed. Neil Wright, Woodbridge 1988, l, lxxv.

[11] On this assumption there was little point in writing for the Welsh for, as G. H. Gerould put it, 'The Welsh of that day did not furnish prime ministers to England, with deaneries and bishoprics in their gift', 'King Arthur and Politics', *Speculum*, ii, 1927, 38. Cf. T. D. Kendrick, *British Antiquity*, London 1950, 9.

[12] 'Did Geoffrey, like others after him, find his mixed loyalties, emotions and hopes rather a problem?' is the question asked by Brynley F. Roberts, 'Geoffrey of Monmouth and the Welsh Historical Tradition', *Nottingham Medieval Studies*, xx, 1976, 40. Cf. Stephen Knight, *Arthurian Literature and Society*, London 1983, 64–66 (a reference I owe to the kindness of Ruth Harvey).

[13] Especially HRB c. 185; Thorpe xi.9, where Geoffrey employs a direct approach using the second person singular, 'you foolish people . . . never happy but when you are fighting one another'. See W. F. Schirmer, *Die frühen Darstellungen des Arthurstoffes*, Köln 1958, 25.

[14] Wright, xv.

[15] When in the *Life of Merlin* Geoffrey again adopts a direct approach he has Wales in mind. 'Kambria gaudebit suffuso sanguine semper/ Gens inimica deo, quid gaudes sanguine fuso?', *The Vita Merlini*, ed. J. J. Parry, Urbana (Illinois) 1925, lines 601–2.

of England with 'a genealogy older and more distinguished than that of the Frankish rulers descended from Charlemagne'. This, in Wright's words, 'was a history in which the new Norman masters of Britain could take pride'.[16]

One difficulty with this line of argument is that it is not easy to show that this is how contemporaries read it. Perhaps this is why some commentators have suggested that Geoffrey was serving the political interests not of the Norman kings, but of the Angevin monarchy.[17] Clearly the figure of Arthur was well-known at the Angevin court, but that is very different from the idea that Henry II was thought of as Arthur's heir.[18] As William Leckie has shown, many people were well aware of the problems which Geoffrey's history posed, especially his history of the sixth and seventh centuries, and not until the end of of the twelfth century did any English historian treat Geoffrey in a reverential way – indeed Leckie very plausibly suggests that William of Newburgh's famous and fierce attack on Geoffrey's veracity may have been a reaction against a recent trend.[19] In that case, so far as the kings of England were concerned, HRB would have remained a highly dubious source of propaganda until very late in the twelfth century.[20] If what was wanted was a predecessor with claims to all Britain then

[16] Marjorie Chibnall, *Anglo-Norman England 1066–1166*, London 1986, 211; Wright, xix; Gerould, 45, 49; Tatlock, 305–20; Schirmer, 28–30. A study which appeared after the first publication of this essay, Francis Ingledew, 'The Book of Troy and the Genealogical Construction of History: the Case of Geoffrey of Monmouth's *Historia regum Britanniae*', *Speculum*, 69, 1994, 665–704, while setting Geoffrey within a stimulating and truly Galfridian literary perspective which reaches from Vergil and St Augustine to Sir Thomas Gray's *Scalacronica*, also denies Geoffrey's Welshness and makes him an unambiguous spokesman for 'the Norman world view'. This neither makes any allowance for mixed loyalties, see above, n. 12, nor does it take account of the prediction of a return to insular domination by the Welsh, to which Ingledew himself refers, 701 n. 188. Nor does emphasis on Geoffrey's Norman credentials throw much light on the way he 'torpedoed the smug Anglocentricity' of William of Malmesbury and Henry of Huntingdon, Rees Davies, *The Matter of Britain and the Matter of England*, Oxford 1996, 10.

[17] R. Howard Bloch, *Etymologies and Genealogies. A Literary Anthropology of the French Middle Ages*, Chicago 1983, 82. Cf. 'the prophecies might be read as referring to the Angevin empire rather than to a Celtic revival', Brooke, 'Geoffrey', 88.

[18] Ulrich Broich, 'Heinrich II als Patron der Literatur seiner Zeit', *Wissenschaftliche Abhandlungen der Arbeitsgemeinschaft für Forschung des Landes Nordrhein-Westfalen*, xxiii, 1962, 90–92. Thus neither the fairly long passage about Arthur in *Draco Normannicus* nor the passing allusions in Benoit (ed. C. Fahlin, *Chronique des ducs de Normandie par Benoit*, Uppsala 1951–67, lines 33, 592–96, 41, 284–88) assign him any such role. I am not persuaded by the ingenious but overcomplicated interpretation of the Arthur passage in *Draco Normannicus* offered by Peter Johanek, 'König Arthur und die Plantagenets', *Frühmittelalterliche Studien*, xxi, 1987, 384–89.

[19] R. William Leckie, *The Passage of Dominion*, Toronto 1981, 73–101. Thus the two earliest chroniclers to take Geoffrey more or less on trust are Diceto and Gervase of Canterbury, both writing c.1188 to c.1200. This ties in with the date at which Gerald of Wales first mentions Arthur and points more to Richard's reign than to Henry's. See below, nn. 20, 23.

[20] It was suitable only for the most far-fetched claims, e.g. the assertion that Rufus planned to go to Rome 'pur chalenger, Lancient dreit de cel pais, Ke i out Brens e Belins', Gaimar,

Edgar could perform that function much more securely. Indeed, as both Ailred of Rievaulx and Roger of Howden noted, Edgar was to the English what Charlemagne was to the French, or indeed, as Howden added, as Arthur to the Britons.[21]. As this remark of Howden reminds us, in the twelfth century the British history belonged to the Britons, not to the kings of England, for whom the possibility of Arthur's return fighting-fit from the Isle of Avalon would have been an uncomfortable prospect. By the end of the century, however, not only were the problems of Geoffrey's reliability gradually being forgotten, but also the discovery at Glastonbury of Arthur's body, still bearing terrible wounds, meant that he could now be regarded as truly dead and buried.[22] Only now could the British history be expropriated and made politically useful to the kings of England. My impression is that the first king of England to associate himself with Arthur was Richard the Lionheart.[23] But to suppose that it was for this that Geoffrey wrote HRB is indeed to endow him with prophetic powers. At the end of the century William of Newburgh had no doubt that HRB was 'written to please the Britons'.[24] What is much more to the point, this is what the author himself implied when he said that it was the Britons who should garland him for what he had done for them in what he called his *Gesta Britonum*.[25]

L'Estoire des Engleis, ed. A. Bell, Anglo-Norman Texts, Oxford 1960, lines 5966–8. The status of Brennius and Belinus was less insecure than that of Arthur, which might explain Gerald de Barri's treatment of early Irish 'history' in his *Topographia Hibernica* (*Giraldi Cambrensis Opera*, v, ed. J. F. Dimock, RS 1867, 148), where what seems to be the earliest manuscript mentions them but not Arthur. By 1189, however, Gerald is willing to give more countenance to Arthur, both in the *Topographia* and in the *Expugnatio Hibernica*, ed. A. B. Scott and F. X. Martin, Dublin 1978, 148. Not surprisingly William of Newburgh was very dismissive of claims to Ireland based on Arthur, *Historia Rerum Anglicarum*, ed. R. Howlett in *Chronicles of the Reigns of Stephen, Henry II and Richard I*, RS 1884, i, 166. Walter Ullmann's suggestion ('On the influence of Geoffrey of Monmouth in English history', in ed. C. Bauer, L. Boehm and M. Muller, *Speculum Historiale*, Freiburg 1965, 272–73) that John of Salisbury may have used HRB in the 1150s in order to persuade Pope Adrian IV to grant Ireland to Henry depends upon a rather forced translation of a passage from the *Metalogicon* and receives no support from the text of *Laudabiliter* itself. Elsewhere, moreover, John was very scathing indeed about claims based on HRB. See *The Letters of John of Salisbury*, ed. W. J. Millor and C. N. L. Brooke, Oxford 1979, ii, 666–69.

[21] Roger of Howden, *Chronica*, ed. W. Stubbs, RS 1868, i, 64 (using the *Historia post obitum Bedae*); Aelred, *Genealogia Regum Anglorum*, Pat. Lat. 195, col. 726.

[22] The various accounts of this episode are conveniently brought together in Gerald of Wales, *The Journey through Wales and The Description of Wales*, trans. L. Thorpe, Harmondsworth 1978, Appendix 3; also E. K. Chambers, *Arthur of Britain*, London 1927, Records 25–26.

[23] Roger of Howden, *Gesta Regis Ricardi*, ed. W. Stubbs, RS 1867, ii, 159, where Richard possessed Caliburn, the sword of Arthur, *rex Britonum*. By the time Howden edited this passage for his *Chronica* (iii, 97), Arthur had become *rex Anglie*.

[24] Newburgh i, 14.

[25] 'Vos ergo Britanni, Laurea serta date Gaufrido de Monumeta. Est etenim vester, nam quondam prelia vestra, Vestrorumque ducum cecinit scripsitque libellum, Quem nunc Gesta vocant Britonum celebrata per orbem.' *Vita Merlini*, lines 1525–29.

For the Britons. But for which Britons? For the Bretons, for the Cornish, for the Welsh or for some combination of all or any two of them? Here I come to the third interpretation, the idea that Geoffrey was more Breton than Welsh, or at any rate that he sympathised with the Bretons much more than with the Welsh. According to the great Geoffrey scholar Tatlock, Geoffrey showed 'strong and steady favouritism for the Bretons and contempt for the Welsh'. 'Nothing', he wrote, 'is more certain than this.'[26] Undoubtedly nothing is more certain than that this view is widely held, especially, interestingly enough, among the leading Welsh scholars of Welsh medieval history – who should, I suppose, see these things more clearly than a Saxon can.[27] But essentially the theory that Geoffrey was anti-Welsh is based on his criticisms of the Welsh of his own day, and on grounds such as these we might as well argue that the sympathies of Wulfstan, the author of the *Sermo Lupi ad Anglos* were not with English, or that Gildas's sympathies weren't British. The belief that the present generation is sinful, and being punished by God for its sins, was surely too commonplace for it to lend support to any such theory.

Whether or not Geoffrey was of Breton descent, the fact is that he identified himself as 'from Monmouth' and, to judge from HRB, he knew that region better than any other.[28] Moreover linguistic evidence has been adduced to show that he was familiar with Welsh, but not with Breton.[29] In any case the key to Geoffrey's outlook is not the belief that recent generations of Welshmen have been corrupt but rather the direct line of continuity which he traces between Britons and Welsh. 'Britain', Geoffrey explains at the outset, 'is inhabited by five peoples, Normans, Britons, Saxons, Picts and Scots. In former times, before the other peoples came, the Britons occupied the land from sea to sea. Then the vengeance of God overtook them because of their pride . . .' The book ends with God's vengeance, famine and disease striking down the Britons and allowing the Saxons to occupy the island, 'opposed only by those pitiful

[26] Tatlock, 414, 443 and indeed virtually passim, so strongly does he take this view. So also Schirmer, 20. However see G. H. Gerould's review of Tatlock in *Speculum*, xxvi, 1951, 223–24. Other scholars are inclined to emphasise the pro-Cornish strain in Geoffrey's writing, notably O. J. Padel, 'Geoffrey of Monmouth and Cornwall', *Cambridge Medieval Celtic Studies*, 8, 1984, 1–27. Pähler argued that Arthur's description of a square pond in which four different kinds of fish lived, each keeping to its own corner (HRB c. 150; Thorpe, ix.7), was a plea on behalf of the oppressed peoples of Britain by an author who himself belonged to one of these communities, Pähler, 78–81.

[27] J. E. Lloyd, 'Geoffrey of Monmouth', *EHR*, lvii, 1942, 466–67. It was presumably this train of thought which led to the description of Geoffrey as 'a Norman-Breton ecclesiastic' by Rachel Bromwich, *The Welsh Triads*, 2nd edn Cardiff 1978, lxxxv. Cf. 'Geoffrey's *History* shows scant sympathy for the Welsh', R. R. Davies, *Conquest, Coexistence and Change. Wales 1063–1415*, Oxford 1987, 106. But see now Davies, *The Matter of Britain*, 5–11.

[28] Tatlock, 68–77.

[29] T. D. Crawford, 'On the Linguistic Competence of Geoffrey of Monmouth', *Medium Aevum*, li, 1982, 152–62. I am grateful to Vanessa Barker for drawing this to my attention. Cf. Tatlock, 82. Like William of Malmesbury and Henry of Huntingdon no doubt Geoffrey spoke French.

remnants of the Britons who dwelt in the forests of Wales'. And these remnants *iam non vocabantur Britones sed Gualenses.* Clearly here it is the Welsh, not the Bretons, who are the heirs of the Britons.[30] Moreover, as above all Brynley Roberts has emphasised, HRB is of a piece with traditional Welsh historiography, with its themes of British unity, rivalry with Rome, loss of sovereignty to the Saxons and the hope of future recovery.[31] Indeed in one respect Geoffrey seems to be more Welsh even than the Welsh; he locates Arthur's court in Wales at Caerleon, whereas earlier Welsh tradition seems to have placed it in Cornwall.[32] The focus of all this is clearly Welsh or, at the very least, British seen from a Welsh angle. Moreover although scholars still argue whether Geoffrey's – doubtless fictitious – 'very ancient book in the British tongue' was in Breton or Welsh, at least Gaimar, writing c.1140, i.e. very soon afterwards, seems to have believed that it was a Welsh book, a *geste* of the British kings.[33] However the notion that Geoffrey was hostile or indifferent to the Welsh has been a widespread one and, as will be plain, it has had important consequences.

I intend to focus on two points that have long been recognised as among the most remarkable features of the History. First its epilogue, the extraordinary words addressed to William of Malmesbury and Henry of Huntingdon, telling them to steer clear of the History of the Britons.[34] Second, King Arthur's crown-wearing at Caerleon, widely regarded as the structural and dramatic climax of his History. I begin with Henry of Huntingdon, whose *Historia Anglorum* was first published in the early 1130s. According to Henry it is history 'which chiefly distinguishes rational beings from brutes. For brutes, whether they are men or animals, neither know nor wish to know anything about their origins or their history.'[35] To be without a history was the mark of

---

[30] HRB cc. 5, 204, 205, 207; Thorpe, i.2, xii.16, 17, 19. That 'the Britons are now called the Welsh' was common parlance among early twelfth-century chroniclers, e.g. *De gestis regum*, i, 135, 148 (see n. 36); Orderic ii, 276, iv, 138.

[31] Roberts, 29–40. Possibly, as Bromwich points out, this was also Breton tradition, but it seems unnecessarily complicated to try to associate Geoffrey, given his known connections in south-east Wales, with a Breton tradition of which we cannot be sure, when with the 'pseudo-learned Welsh tradition' we can stay on firmer ground (Bromwich, xcvi, cxxvi).

[32] Bromwich, 275; Padel, 19–20.

[33] Robert of Gloucester had had a *geste* translated from 'books about the British kings belonging to the Welsh'. Gaimar used this (as well as other books) in the composition of his own history, adding details, he tells us, 'Ke li Waleis ourent leisse'. Gaimar, *Estoire*, lines 6432–63. I am grateful to Ian Short for discussion of this convoluted passage. Cf. Brooke, 'Geoffrey', 83. In HRB c. 23, Thorpe ii.1, *lingua Britannica* clearly means Welsh, as noted by Thorpe, 39. For close discussion of the relationship between HRB and Gaimar see now Ian Short, 'Gaimar's Epilogue and Geoffrey of Monmouth's *Liber vetustissimus*', *Speculum*, 69, 1994, 223–43.

[34] HRB c. 208; Thorpe, 284.

[35] *Henry, Archdeacon of Huntingdon: Historia Anglorum*, ed. and trans. D. Greenway, Oxford Medieval Texts, 1996, 4–5 [Henry of Huntingdon, *Historia Anglorum*, ed. T. Arnold, RS 1879, 2–3].

the beast. Yet the Britons had virtually no history. At any rate the learned world knew virtually nothing about it. As William of Malmesbury had written, 'what notice the Britons had attracted from other peoples they owed to Gildas'.[36] Indeed precisely this is Geoffrey's starting point. 'It has seemed a remarkable thing to me that apart from mention of them by Gildas and Bede, I have not been able to discover anything at all on the kings who lived here before the Incarnation of Christ, or indeed about Arthur and all those who followed on after the Incarnation.'[37] Geoffrey, of course, filled the gap in magnificent style. But he did much more. If what the contemporary world of learning knew about the Britons was derived from the pages of Bede and Gildas, then they knew little good of them. In Bede's eyes the Britons were barbarians, and so it is naturally as barbarians that they re-appear in Henry of Huntingdon.[38] Geoffrey's Britons, however, are very far from being barbarians.

This may seem obvious, but it is important to see it in context. Although Bede had emphatically portrayed the seventh century British king Cadwalla as a barbarian,[39] this view of a fellow Christian seems to have found no echo until the twelfth century. Reading works written in England during the ninth, tenth and eleventh centuries, what strikes me is the absence of any sharply defined attitude towards the Welsh. Aethelweard, for example, consistently treats Danes as barbarians, but his occasional references to Britons are neutral in tone. For him the word 'barbarian' is a synonym for 'pagan'. The author of the Life of Edward the Confessor sees the Welsh as 'an untamed people' (*gens indomita*) and once again it is the Danes and Norwegians who are called barbarous.[40] The many different contributors to the *Anglo-Saxon Chronicle* all treat the Welsh either neutrally, or occasionally, after the Norman Conquest, even sympathetically, as under the year 1094 when we are told of the Welsh fight against 'the French who had deprived them of their land'.[41] In the Latin version of the chronicle composed at Worcester this has become 'the Welsh seeking their

---

[36] Since both the old standard edition, *De Gestis Regum Anglorum*, ed. W. Stubbs, RS 1887, and the new standard, *Gesta Regum Anglorum*, volume 1, ed. and trans. R. A. B. Mynors, R. M. Thomson and M. Winterbottom, Oxford 1998, share the same division of the work into chapters, for simplicity's sake I shall cite this as WM followed by chapter number, in this case c. 20.

[37] HRB c. 1; Thorpe, i.1. Thus Sigebert of Gembloux writing his universal chronicle in 1111 could say nothing of the origins of the Britons. On the absence of British history see Tatlock, 428–31.

[38] *Bede's Ecclesiastical History of the English People*, ed. B. Colgrave and R. A. B. Mynors, Oxford 1969, I, 2 (p. 22); *Huntingdon*, ed. Greenway, 34–35 [ed. Arnold, 18].

[39] Bede, II, c. 20 (p. 202).

[40] *The Chronicle of Aethelweard*, ed. A. Campbell, London 1962, 22–23, 31, 36–49, 52; *The Life of King Edward*, ed. and trans. F. Barlow, 2nd edn 1992, 15, 86–89. The latter author seems slightly more critical of the Scots than of the Welsh.

[41] *ASC*, 171. This was probably written soon after the event, C. Clark, *The Peterborough Chronicle 1070–1154*, 2nd edn Oxford 1970, xxi.

liberty'.[42] Indeed even as late as the 1130s the Worcester chronicler remains remarkably sympathetic to the Welsh cause.[43]

But by the 1130s John of Worcester is beginning to look a little old-fashioned. A different view of the Welsh has taken root. By 1125 William of Malmesbury is writing of the Welsh as barbarians. His comment on Harold's campaign against the Welsh in 1064 was that it subordinated *omnem illam barbariem*.[44] This language was not in his sources. It reflects William's own view of the world. William's underlying assumption is that 'we' – the Anglo-French – are civilised and 'they', the Welsh, Scots and Irish, are not.[45] This view of the Welsh was clearly fully developed by the late 1140s, when the author of the *Gesta Stephani* was writing. He sees Wales as 'a land abounding in deer, fish, milk and herds', and one which breeds 'men of an animal type'; the Welsh we learn are a *barbara gens*, characterised by 'untamed savagery'.[46] By the second half of the twelfth century this view of the Welsh had become the standard one. As Chrétien of Troyes put it, 'Gallois sont tuit par nature, Plus fol que bestes en pasture'.[47] Twentieth century historians, above all Robert Bartlett and Rees Davies, have produced extremely illuminating analyses of the contemptuous attitude of self-consciously civilised peoples towards the more pastoral peoples on the fringes of twelfth century Europe, but they have not really traced the emergence of this attitude – though it seems to me one of the most important ideological developments in medieval Britain, one which was to shape much subsequent history.[48] In this context the writings of Orderic Vitalis are peculiarly interesting, since he wrote so much and over so long a period, from c.1115 to

[42] Florence of Worcester, *Chronicon ex Chronicis*, ed. B. Thorpe, London 1848–49, ii, 35, 41 where William II is said to have intended to kill all Welshmen.

[43] 'Walenses in defensione suae nativae terrae', *The Chronicle of John of Worcester*, ed. J. R. H. Weaver, Oxford 1908, 43. For connections between the churches of Worcester and South Wales see David Crouch, 'Urban: First Bishop of Llandaff, 1107–34', *Journal of Welsh Ecclesiastical History*, vii, 1989, 3; Wendy Davies, 'St Mary's Worcester and the *Liber Landaviensis*', *Journal of the Society of Archivists*, iv, 1972, 459–85.

[44] WM c. 196; cf. cc. 327, 396, 401.

[45] This is made explicit in William's comment on David of Scotland being made *curialior* through contact and upbringing 'amongst us' so that the rust of Scottish barbarism was polished away, WM, c. 400. Amongst the earliest exponents of this attitude to Celtic society were two reform-minded Italians, Lanfranc and Anselm. It is reflected in the comment that St Asaph in 1125 was vacant *pro vastitate et barbarie*, Hugh the Chantor, *The History of the Church of York*, ed. C. Johnson, 2nd edn, Oxford Medieval Texts, 1990, 52–53, 206–7.

[46] *Gesta Stephani*, ed. K. R. Potter and R. H. C. Davis, Oxford 1976, 14, 172, 194.

[47] Chrétien de Troyes, *Le Conte du Graal*, ed. W. Roach, 2nd edn, Geneva 1959, lines 243–44.

[48] Robert Bartlett, *Gerald of Wales*, Oxford 1982, above all chapter 6, 'The Face of the Barbarian'; R. R. Davies, 'Buchedd a moes y Cymry. The Manners and Morals of the Welsh', *Welsh History Review*, 12, 1984–85, 155–79; R. R. Davies, *Domination and Conquest*, Cambridge 1990, 20ff, 113ff; W. R. Jones, 'England against the Celtic Fringe', *Journal of World History*, 13, 1971, 155–71. There are some intriguing thoughts on the change in attitude in Denis Bethell, 'English Monks and Irish Reform in the Eleventh and Twelfth Centuries', *Historical Studies*, 8, 1971, 111–35.

c.1141. Whereas references to the Welsh in passages written before the mid-1130s are either neutral or even sympathetic in tone, by the mid-1130s he is using strong but strikingly ambiguous language – they are barbarians, yet a Christian and badly oppressed people for all that. By 1140 the sympathy seems to have gone; his vocabulary is more uniformly hostile and condescending.[49]

In other words in 1125 William of Malmesbury is giving expression to a relatively new point of view, one that is becoming fashionable and powerful. For this reason it is, I think, worth looking closely at William's concept of the barbarian – a term which he uses noticeably more frequently than other contemporary historians. Paradoxically the best approach to this is through William's treatment of the civilised, the English.[50] Their history was, in his eyes, a progress from barbarism to civilisation; he makes this explicit in his reflections on 1066.[51] The civilising process started at the court of King Ethelberht of Kent. Since Ethelberht was the first English king to be converted it is easy to assume that William equated civilisation with Christianity.[52] In fact in William's eyes the process predated the king's conversion. The critical moment was his marriage to Bertha, the daughter of the *rex Francorum*, since it 'was by this connexion with the French that a once barbarous people began to divest themselves of their wild frame of mind and incline towards a gentler way of life'.[53] The ninth century case of King Egberht of Wessex makes explicit that it was not conversion which did it, since Egberht was already a Christian before he went into exile in France. But it was in France that he learned foreign ways which in William's words were 'very different from his native barbarism'. For, as William put it, the French 'are unrivalled among western nations in military skill and in polished manners'. In this passage it is the present tense which is particularly striking.[54] Of Sigeberht King of East Anglia we are told that 'all his barbarism was polished away by his

---

49 Orderic, ii, 138, 216, 228, 234, 260–62, 276; iv, 138; vi, 536, 542. It is not merely that Orderic becomes more critical as the Welsh give more trouble. Although he doesn't mince his words about the Angevin attacks on Normandy in 1136–38 (vi, 470, 526), he compares them with infidels not with barbarians.

50 That the English were civilised is not a view Paschal II shared, as is clear from the language of his letters as copied in Eadmer, *Historia novorum in Anglia*, ed. M. Rule, RS 1884, 135, 185–86. However William of Malmesbury, though he used Eadmer, did not allow papal opinion to colour his view of his own people. In Eadmer's own case it is clear that once he had direct experience of the Scots he became more critical of Scottish customs. Cf. Bethell, 127.

51 Whereas formerly the English *vultu et gestu barbarico, usu bellico, ritu fanatico vivebant*, gradually they had become civilised thanks to their conversion, to peace and the passage of time: WM c. 245. As for an early Anglo-Saxon like Hengest, he had been *barbarus*, preferring *omnia cruentius quam civilius*, WM cc. 7–8.

52 As does W. R. Jones, 'The Image of the Barbarian in Medieval Europe', *Comparative Studies in Society and History*, 13, 1971, 391–92.

53 'Tum vero Francorum contubernio gens eatenus barbara ad unas consuetudines confoederata, silvestres animos indies exuere, et ad leviores mores declinare.' WM c. 9.

54 'Est enim gens illa et exercitatione virium, et comitate morum cunctarum occidentalium facile princeps. (Egbert) mores longe a gentilitia barbarie alienos indueret.' WM c. 106.

upbringing among the French'; when he returned home he founded schools so that rustics could learn the delights of letters.[55] In William's view then it was French culture, not Christianity alone, which made the English civilised. In his own day William felt that it was French scholars and poets, men like John of Tours, Hildebert of Le Mans and Godfrey of Winchester who represented a revival of correct Latinity after the 'barbarism' of authors like Aethelweard and of antique literary and ethical values.[56] Indeed in William's eyes even people who were so Christian that they went on crusade could none the less be barbarians. Thus when recounting Urban's preaching of the crusade, he tells us that some of those who responded to Urban's call lived *in nationibus barbaris:* and he lists them, the Welsh, Scots, Danes and Norwegians.[57] If Christians like the Welsh were to be looked upon as barbarians then the familiar concept of the barbarian, one which equated pagan and barbarian, – as Aethelweard had done – had to be discarded and a new, classicizing one formulated. William's achievement was to introduce this concept into English history. Presumably this is related to the depth and intensity of his immersion in classical literature.[58]

William also saw civilisation in socio-economic as well as in cultural terms. This comes across very clearly in his view of Irish society, a society he describes in terms of an explicit contrast with English and French society. 'Whereas the English and the French live in market-oriented towns enjoying a more cultivated style of life, the Irish live in rustic squalor, for owing to the ignorance of the farmers their land is inadequately cultivated.'[59] For William of Malmesbury then towns and an appropriate knowledge of agriculture (*scientia cultorum*) were bases of civilisation. One implication of this was that more pastoral economies, like the Welsh, were unlikely to sustain civilised life – connexions of this sort were certainly in the mind of the author of the *Gesta Stephani*. A second implication, of course, was that it had to have been the Romans who brought civilisation to Britain, for as everyone who had read Bede knew, it was as a result of Roman rule that cities, lighthouses, bridges and roads were built in Britain.[60] Naturally historians like William of Malmesbury and Orderic Vitalis believed that towns like Bath and Carlisle were founded by Julius Caesar.[61]

---

[55] WM c. 97.

[56] As pointed out by R. M. Thomson, *William of Malmesbury*, Woodbridge 1987, 13, 17, 71–72. See William of Malmesbury, *De gestis pontificum Anglorum*, ed. N. E. S. A. Hamilton, RS 1870, 172, 195 (where John of Tours looks upon the English monks as barbarians); also WM c. 340.

[57] WM c. 348.

[58] Among English scholars only John of Salisbury matches the breadth of his reading, Thomson, 6–10.

[59] WM c. 409. Gerald de Barri was still making similar points about the Welsh economy many decades later. 'The Welsh do not live in towns, villages or castles . . . they pay no heed to trade, shipping or industry', *Opera*, vi, 180, 200 (*Descriptio Cambriae*, i.8, 17).

[60] Bede I, 11 (p. 40), where we also learn that the Romans had possessed a *ius dominandi* over the islands beyond Britain.

[61] *De gestis pontificum*, 194, 291; Orderic, vi, 518.

It is against the background of a revival of the classical concept of barbarian, and in consequence the growing fashion for dismissing the Celtic peoples as barbarians, that we must read Geoffrey's History. According to Geoffrey, Bath was founded by the British king Bladud and Carlisle by King Leil. Doubtless, as Valerie Flint has emphasised, all this was meant to tease William, but it also has a much more serious purpose.[62] In Geoffrey's eyes town foundation is one of the proper activities of the good king. It often goes together with building roads, encouraging agriculture and issuing laws, – also, of course, an activity associated with the Romans. Thus when Brutus's followers first arrived in this island, 'they began to cultivate the fields'; Brutus himself built a city, New Troy, and issued laws.[63] Like Leil and Bladud, subsequent competent rulers do the same things. Belinus builds cities and roads. Dunvallo built temples, issued laws which are said to be well-known to the English even to this day; among other things Dunvallo's laws protected the roads and the ploughs of the farmers. Another outstanding law-giver was Marcia, whose laws Alfred translated and called the Mercian law. Gorbonianus encouraged the farmers to till the soil (*colonos ad agriculturam animabat*). Lud was such a *gloriosus edificator urbium* that New Troy came to be re-named London.[64] Geoffrey, in other words, asserts not only that the Britons had a long and heroic history of migration and successful war, but that they had long been civilised.

Being civilised themselves it was not at all surprising that they had looked upon the Saxons as barbarians – as readers of Gildas and 'Nennius' would have known they had.[65] Nor surprising that they had shared the contempt of the twelfth century Anglo-Norman world for the Scots, Picts and Irish.[66] In a sense all this is obvious. What, I think, is not so obvious is the cultural and intellectual juncture at which Geoffrey settled down to write in these terms. He was writing

---

[62] HRB cc. 29–30, Thorpe, ii.9–10; Flint, 453–57.

[63] HRB cc. 21–22; Thorpe, i.16–18. In Bede's eyes when an English king issued laws it was *iuxta exempla Romanorum*, II, 5 (p. 150).

[64] HRB cc. 34, 47, 49, 53, 69, 127; Thorpe, ii.17, iii.13, 16, 20, iv.16, viii.9. See A. Gransden, *Historical Writing in England c.550 to c.1307*, London 1974, 206–7, on Geoffrey's 'hall-marks of good kingship'. The model did not go unnoticed. According to his later twelfth-century life, under the rule of Gruffydd ap Cynan (d.1137), 'he increased all manner of goods in Gwynedd, and the inhabitants began to build churches in every direction therein, and to plant . . . and to make orchards and gardens, and surround them with walls and ditches, and to construct walled buildings, and to support themselves from the fruit of the earth after the fashion of the Romans'. *The History of Gruffydd ap Cynan*, ed. A. Jones, Manchester 1910, 155.

[65] E.g. HRB cc. 191, 194, 206; Thorpe, xii.2, 5, 18. Some readers found the 'Nennian' view that the Saxons were barbarians a bit disquieting, cf. *Historia Brittonum. The 'Vatican' Recension*, ed. D. Dumville, Cambridge 1985, 5.

[66] Tatlock 18, 80. In HRB cc. 148–49; Thorpe, ix.5–6, the Scots and Picts, peoples with a Christian clergy, are treated as barbarians. So too are the Irish whom Geoffrey, like other twelfth-century observers, describes as *gens nuda et inermis*, HRB cc. 149, 153; Thorpe, ix.6, 10. Undoubtedly one of the significant omissions from HRB is any allusion to Patrick in Ireland.

just at the time when the learned Anglo-French world with which he was familiar was beginning to despise Welshmen, to write off the Britons as barbarians, as brutish creatures without a history. It is in this fundamental sense that his history was inspired by Henry of Huntingdon and William of Malmesbury. It is not just that he was taking the mickey out of them; nor just that his figure of Arthur was inspired by William's remark that Arthur was worthy of a genuine history, not just of being dreamed of in bogus legends.[67] More importantly the whole conception and structure of the History was a refutation of attitudes which had been gaining currency in advanced intellectual circles, and which were now well on the way to becoming part of the established view of insular history. Right at the end of his history he alludes to, and even concedes the possibility, that the modern Welsh are indeed barbarians. 'From now on the Britons were called Welsh, the word deriving either from the name of their leader Gualo, or of queen Galeas, or from their barbarism.'[68] But by setting this concession to modern taste in a framework of his own making, a fictional history of highly civilised pre-Roman British kings, the effect Geoffrey achieves is anything but dismissive. After all the whole history began with Brutus and that party of Trojans who, after their defeat by the Greeks, chose to retreat into the forest depths, preferring to live like wild animals (*ferino ritu*), eating meat and grass – i.e. putting up with a pastoral economy – rather than remain under the yoke of Greek slavery.[69] There is a parallel here with the situation of the twelfth century Welsh; and what their ancestors had done once the Welsh could do surely do again. Thus no medieval Welshman made the mistake of thinking Geoffrey anti-Welsh.[70]

But there is rather more to Geoffrey's timing than this. Geoffrey finished writing shortly before January 1139. Presumably he was hard at work in the years immediately after the death of Henry I. During Henry's reign the Anglo-French advance into Wales had been so overwhelming that, in the words of the *Gesta Stephani*, Wales was becoming a second England, law-abiding, prosperous and civilised.[71]

---

[67] WM c. 8.

[68] HRB c. 207, Thorpe, xii.19.

[69] HRB c. 8, Thorpe, i.4.

[70] As is clear from the number of Welsh *Bruts*, the Welsh recognised the line of continuity which Geoffrey drew between them and the Britons. Here, after all, Geoffrey had been doing no more than draw on Welsh tradition, one which remained strong. 'The Welsh being sprung by unbroken succession from the original stock of Britons, boast of all Britain as theirs by right' – such, at any rate, are the words which Gerald attributes to Hubert Walter, W. S. Davies, 'Giraldus Cambrensis: De Invectionibus', *Y Cymmrodor*, xxx, 1920, 84–85.

[71] *Gesta Stephani*, 14–17, where what the Normans did to Wales is described as *constanter excoluere*, 'they perseveringly civilised it'; 'they imposed law and made the land productive'. From a Welsh point of view this meant that Henry's reign ended 'with four years in succession without there being any history', *Brut Y Tywysogyon, Red Book of Hergest Version*, ed. T. Jones, Cardiff 1955, 113. See R. R. Davies, 'Henry I and Wales', *Studies in Medieval History presented to R. H. C. Davis*, ed. H. Mayr-Harting and R. I. Moore, London 1985, 132–47. The marcher lords in South Wales were well in at Henry's court, very different, as

One sign of this was the gradual undermining of the position of native Welsh kings, as was noted by the well-informed Worcester chronicler under the year 1093.[72] As David Crouch has recently put it, 'he was a little precipitate but generally correct. The intrusion of the power of the Anglo-Norman monarchy into the heart of Wales undermined the use of the word *rex* by Welsh rulers and their scribes. Welsh magnates of greater influence and pretensions resorted increasingly to the titles *princeps* or *dominus*.'[73] Not surprisingly the Welsh resented what the Normans were doing to them. According to the Welsh chronicle (under the year 1114), it seemed that the French were aiming 'to exterminate all the Britons completely, so that the Britannic name should never more be remembered'. In 1116 'many young hotheads', followers of Gruffudd ap Rhys, a Welsh prince in revolt against Henry I, were moved by 'an urge to restore and renew the Britannic kingdom'.[74]

Their opportunity came when Henry died in December 1135. The news was greeted by outbreaks of revolt in several different parts of Wales at once, 'the great revolt' as Sir John Lloyd called it.[75] With hindsight the rebellion of 1136–8 looks nothing more than a brief reverse eddy in the tide of history, flowing inexorably towards the ever-increasing Anglicisation of Wales. But is this how it was seen in 1136 and 1137? In 1136 and 1137 the Anglo-Normans in Wales were overtaken by a series of dramatic disasters. Twice they were defeated in pitched battle. Two leading magnates, Richard fitz Gilbert of Clare and Payn Fitz John, were killed. The whole of Cardigan was overwhelmed; Carmarthen and the neighbouring districts of Cantref Mawr and Cantref Bychan were captured. The Welsh made further advances in the north-east, in the area between the Clwd and the Dee, in Maelienydd and on the Shropshire border. After a few attempts to retrieve the situation, attempts which cost a great deal of money but only led to further setbacks, King Stephen – or so we are told by his biographer – took the strategic decision to leave the Welsh to their own devices, hoping that they would start to quarrel amongst themselves and bring about their own ruin.[76] Doubtless in the long run he was right, but one of the

Judith Green makes clear, from the men who were given estates on the northern frontier, 'Aristocratic Loyalties on the Northern Frontier of England, c.1100–1174', *England in the Twelfth Century*, Cambridge 1990, 83–100.

[72] When Rhys ap Tewdwr was killed in 1093 'ab illo die regnare in Walonia reges desiere', Worcester, ii, 31.

[73] David Crouch, 'The Slow Death of Kingship in Glamorgan, 1067–1158', *Morgannwg*, xxix, 1985, 30. On the subject of the titles adopted by twelfth-century Welsh rulers see now D. Crouch, *The Image of Aristocracy in Britain 1000–1300*, London 1992, 85–94; H. Pryce, 'Owain Gwynedd and Louis VII: the Franco-Welsh Diplomacy of the First Prince of Wales', *The Welsh History Review*, 19, 1998, 1–28, esp. 21–24.

[74] *Brut*, 78–81, 86–87.

[75] This is Lloyd's title for Section II of Chapter XIII ('The National Revival') of his *History of Wales*. In the words of a contemporary, the rebels 'collaetantes per omnes se Waloniae fines audacter effuderunt', *Gesta Stephani*, 16.

[76] *Gesta Stephani*, 20.

remarkable features of the revolt of 1136–7 is the way in which the rulers of three separate Welsh principalities, ancient kingdoms, Maelienydd, Gwynedd and Deheubarth, inspired it seems by Gruffudd ap Rhys of Deheubarth – the leader of the 'young hotheads' of 1116 – were able to put aside their traditional rivalries and join together against the foreign invader.[77]

It may be possible to obtain further insight into the atmosphere in the aftermath of the great revolt if we can date a little-known text, the Anglo-Norman *Description of England*, to the 1140s. Once thought to have been written by Gaimar, this attribution was denied, on stylistic grounds, by Alexander Bell, who accordingly omitted it from his edition of Gaimar's *Estoire des Engleis*. Moreover though Bell dated the *Estoire* to c.1140, he was reluctant to date the *Description* at all closely.[78] In consequence it fell into a kind of limbo, from which fortunately it has recently been rescued.[79] In three out of the four extant manuscripts of the *Description* it is incorporated into the *Estoire* in one way or another and a date in the 1140s is tempting, partly because it suits my argument, but partly also because the *Description* contains a reference to Carlisle as 'a new bishopric'. Not only was Carlisle founded in 1133 but it went into abeyance early in the 1150s.[80] Now in the *Description* we find the following passage. 'Well have the Welsh revenged themselves, Many of our French they have slain, Some of our castles they have taken, Fiercely they threaten us, Openly they go about saying, That in the end they will have all, By means of Arthur, they will have it back . . . They will call it Britain again.'[81] Here too there can be no doubt that the figure of Arthur was perceived as a threat to the Anglo-Norman rulers.

Let us suppose that in 1136 Geoffrey was hard at work writing his History. What, I wonder, was the effect of the extra-ordinary news from Wales likely to be? There are one or two intriguing parallels between incidents in the Welsh revolt and Geoffrey's history. The prominent role played by Geoffrey's queens – Cordelia, Gwendolen and Marcia – has long been noted and often linked, plausibly enough, with the contemporary role played by the Empress Matilda.[82]

---

[77] Davies, *Conquest*, 47–48; Lloyd, 470–72. Not until 1139 does the *Brut Y Tywysogyon* take up its routine theme of Welsh internal strife.

[78] *Estoire*, ed. Bell, xii–xiii.

[79] Lesley Johnson and Alexander Bell, 'The Anglo-Norman *Description of England*', *Anglo-Norman Anniversary Studies*, ed. Ian Short, 1993, 11–47.

[80] Gaimar, *Estoire des Engleis*, ed. T. D. Hardy and C. T. Martin, RS 1888–89, II, 212. In suggesting a date as early as the 1140s I am merely pushing a little further points made by Bell himself, *Estoire*, xii–xiii.

[81] *Estoire*, ed. Hardy, 213–14. The possibility that this is an allusion to thirteenth-century Welsh revolts is further diminished if we date MS D to the late twelfth rather than to the early thirteenth century. See Johnson, 'The Anglo-Norman *Description*', n. 5 and *Jordan Fantosme's Chronicle*, ed. R. C. Johnston, Oxford 1981, xliv. Once we are in the twelfth century then Stephen's reign seems the most likely time since it witnessed by far the most dramatic Welsh revolt of that century, one which created a 'sense of triumph in the Welsh principalities and of disaster in the marcher lordships', David Walker, *Medieval Wales*, Cambridge 1990, 47.

[82] Tatlock, 286–88. See also J. Gillingham, 'Love, Marriage and Politics in the Twelfth

But perhaps even more dramatic was the part played by Gwenllian, wife of Gruffudd ap Rhys. According to Gerald, while her husband went north to seek allies in Gwynedd, she herself went to war, riding at the head of an army 'like a second Penthesilea, Queen of the Amazons'. In Gerald's Latin her name was Guendoloena, the name of the most warlike of Geoffrey's queens.[83] Historians have not found it so easy to find contemporary resonances for a much more central episode, Guinevere's betrayal of Arthur, but it is at least worth noting that when Gruffudd ap Rhys was killed in 1137 it was, according to John of Worcester, because he was deceived by the treachery of his wife.[84]

I turn now to my second focus, to Arthur and his court, to what Christopher Brooke called 'the most revealing passage', the famous account of the Pentecostal crown-wearing at Caerleon, the town 'that principally captivated Geoffrey's imagination'.[85] Scholars have often asked, why Caerleon? Christopher Brooke discussed the question in terms of the location of the seat of the primate of Britain, Geoffrey's archbishop of Caerleon. In ecclesiastical terms, as Brooke suggests, this was just a piece of mockery, a tease, all that mattered was that it was not Canterbury, nor York, nor London, nor Winchester, nor Llandaff, nor St David's. 'Thus he declared a pox on all their houses, and can have intended nothing but mockery and mischief.'[86] In terms of Welsh churches, Geoffrey's joke was a particularly pointed one since in the 1120s and 1130s both Llandaff and St David's were making ambitious claims. 'If Wales must have an archbishopric (and why not?) we will place it where our fancy takes us – at Caerleon, "situated in a passing pleasant position on the river Usk".'[87] But why does our fancy take us precisely there? Perhaps some local pride, since it's not far from Monmouth – though it is certainly not the sort of local pride which Bishop Urban of Llandaff would have appreciated.[88] Most scholars also follow Tatlock in pointing to 'the ancient remains at the obscure Caerleon' which 'appealed to Geoffrey's historical imagination'.[89] I do not doubt

Century', *Forum for Modern Language Studies*, xxv, 1989, 202–303, esp. 295–96, for Geoffrey's recognition of the greater political importance of heiresses in this period.

[83] Gerald, *Opera*, vi, 79 (*Itinerarium* i.9); HRB cc. 24–25; Thorpe, ii.4–5.

[84] 'Dolo coniugis suae circumventus', John of Worcester, 43. Since Gwenllian had been killed at Kidwelly, this was presumably a subsequent wife – as indeed Guinevere was later thought to be, Gerald of Wales, *The Journey*, 282, 287.

[85] Brooke, 'Geoffrey', 80; Davies, *Conquest*, 106.

[86] Brooke, 'Geoffrey', 82.

[87] Christopher Brooke, 'The Archbishops of St David's, Llandaff and Caerleon-on-Usk' in N. K. Chadwick, K. Hughes, C. Brooke, K. Jackson, *Studies in the Early British Church*, Cambridge 1958, 201–11, esp. 210.

[88] He had died in 1134. His successor Uthred was not consecrated until 1140, but had been involved in Urban's campaign for the greater glory of Llandaff: *Llandaff Episcopal Acta, 1140–1287*, ed. D. Crouch, Cardiff 1988, xii–xiii. Doubtless the more Geoffrey knew of the making of the Book of Llandaff (on which see Wendy Davies, '*Liber Landaviensis*. Its Construction and Credibility', *EHR*, 88, 1973, 335–51) the greater his amusement in preferring Caerleon, Brooke, 'The Archbishops', 205–6, 232–33.

[89] Tatlock, 70–71. The ruins did make an impression, HRB c. 72; Thorpe, iv.19.

that these are among the motives which led Geoffrey to site the metropolitan church at Caerleon, but what is at issue in this particular episode – the climax of HRB – is not a church's foundation, but a king's crown-wearing. According to Geoffrey, Arthur's father, King Uther, had worn his crown at London.[90] So why Caerleon for Arthur's? As Tatlock rightly observed, Geoffrey's 'chief interests are war and politics' and it is therefore I suggest within a military and political context that we should seek an answer.[91]

In Tatlock's view, Caerleon's 'prominence is assuredly not due to any importance in his day'.[92] But here I think Tatlock's insistence that Geoffrey's sympathies were all Breton has misled him. In 1136 two Welsh princes, the brothers Morgan and Iorwerth ap Owain ambushed and killed one of the greatest magnates, Richard of Clare. They then descended from the hills and seized the castles of Usk and Caerleon. By the end of the year the elder brother Morgan controlled virtually all the lands which had once belonged to his grandfather, that King Caradog who had destroyed Harold's hunting-lodge at Portskewett in 1065.[93] A few years later, in a charter issued at some date between 1143 and 1154, we find Morgan being accorded the title king in one of the earldom of Hereford charters.[94] As David Crouch has observed, 'it can only be that Morgan had taken up the kingship that is supposed to have died with his grandfather, Caradog, and even got his neighbour Earl Roger of Hereford to acknowledge it'.[95] Caerleon was to remain the centre of Morgan's lands until he was killed in 1158.[96] For some one

---

[90] HRB c. 137; Thorpe, viii.19. On the Crown of London as symbol of British sovereignty, see Roberts, 32, 37.

[91] Tatlock, 345. On the underlying strategic importance of the Caerleon region see J. Campbell, 'The United Kingdom of England. The Anglo-Saxon Achievement' in ed. A. Grant and K. J. Stringer, *Uniting the Kingdom? The Making of British History*, London 1995, 46–47.

[92] Ironically this comes not only from a very great Geoffrey scholar but one who believed that if his work had shown anything, it was that when studying Geoffrey it always pays to look at contemporary history, Tatlock, 70, 190, 425. Perhaps it was Sir John Lloyd's determination to free Geoffrey's life from any association with the notorious forger Iolo Morganwg that led that great historian of medieval Wales in the same direction and to conclude that 'the real Geoffrey had no interest in Glamorgan', Lloyd, 'Geoffrey', 462–64. For Caerleon and Glamorgan see below, n. 99.

[93] *Gesta Stephani*, 16; Gerald, *Opera*, vi, 47–48 (*Itin.*, i.4); Crouch, 'The Slow Death', 33.

[94] 'Charters of the Earldom of Hereford, 1095–1201', ed. D. Walker, *Camden Miscellany*, xxii, 1964, no. 36.

[95] Crouch, 'The Slow Death', 35–36, was the first to recognise the significance of this witness list. The next witness to this charter, William de Chesny, takes us into circles within which Geoffrey moved. He was castellan of Oxford from 1142 (see *Gesta Stephani*, 130 n.) and brother of that Bishop of Lincoln, formerly canon of St George's, Oxford, to whom Geoffrey dedicated his *Vita Merlini*.

[96] 'And along with him was killed the best poet, and he was called Gwrgant ap Rhys. And then Iorwerth ap Owain, Morgan's brother, ruled the land of Caerleon', *Brut*, 137. Morgan's association with 'the best poet' must have helped to ensure the fame of his exploits. Intriguingly Iorwerth married – though at an unknown date – Angharad, daughter of Bishop Uthred of Llandaff.

with Geoffrey of Monmouth's background and interests there can have been no place of greater, or more dramatic, possibly portentous political interest in 1136 or 1137 than Caerleon. And if, as seems most likely, Morgan resumed the ancestral title in the euphoria of 1136–7, then when Geoffrey was writing the later sections of his History, there was once again a king in South Wales, a British king at Caerleon.

If Geoffrey of Monmouth must have been aware of the events of 1136 at Caerleon, so also must have been the man to whom he dedicated his History, Robert of Gloucester. Twice Geoffrey explains that Caerleon is in Glamorgan.[97] In the 1130s the lord of Glamorgan was none other than Robert of Gloucester. If Robert was thinking of taking up the fight on his sister's behalf then he either had to inflict a rapid and comprehensive defeat upon the Welsh or come to terms with them. Caught up as he would be with the struggle in England the one thing he could not afford was a long war of attrition against the rampant Welsh. In effect he probably had no choice. As R. R. Davies says 'The Welsh were now potential allies in the struggle in England rather than an enemy to be defeated.'[98] Among those who did in fact join Robert against Stephen was a man whom Orderic called 'Morgan the Welshman who held Usk'.[99] He is the only Welshman mentioned by Orderic in a list of Robert's allies and he is of course our Morgan.

But how would contemporaries feel about an alliance between Earl Robert and the Welsh? This, after all, was not a minor or peripheral matter. Given the history of the previous hundred years Welsh military and political support was likely to be an important element in a struggle for power in England. Indeed, as it turned out, it looks as though King Morgan and Welsh troops were to play a major part in the battle of Lincoln and in the capture of King Stephen.[100] As early as 1139 Orderic noted that Robert has called the Welsh to his aid and that these barbarians – as they are called, he observes – having been let loose over England are causing untold havoc: 'daily the sons of God are slaughtered like

[97] HRB cc. 72, 156; Thorpe, iv.19, ix.12. See Tatlock, 69.
[98] Davies, *Conquest*, 47.
[99] Orderic, vi, 518. Morgan's conquests included patronage over Goldcliff priory, a dependency of Bec – where Henry of Huntingdon saw a copy of HRB in January 1139. David Crouch has pointed to the evidence for a deal between Earl Robert and Morgan, probably clinched before the end of 1136, as well as indications that Robert came to terms with other neighbouring Welsh princes, Crouch, 'The Slow Death', 33–35. Given the fact that Morgan and Iorwerth were to refer to Robert of Gloucester as their lord, and that the Anglo-Norman lords of Caerleon whom they ousted were adherents of Stephen (first Walter de Clare, then, after his death in 1138, Gilbert fitz Gilbert, Stephen's earl of Pembroke), there may well be local political significance in Geoffrey's statement that Caerleon lay in Glamorgan. Not until the 1170s did the Clares, at least temporarily, manage to recover control here. See M. T. Flanagan, *Irish Society, Anglo-Norman Settlers, Angevin Kingship*, Oxford 1989, 139–41, and esp. 157 n. 88; Davies, *Conquest*, 275.
[100] According to Orderic the front rank of Robert's army was composed of 'a fierce mob of Welshman' and it was the greater number of footsoldiers and Welshmen that won the day, Orderic, vi, 542. For Morgan ap Owain's presence at the battle see below, p. 98.

cattle by the swords of the Britons'.[101] A few years later the author of the *Gesta Stephani* is complaining of Robert's employment of the 'unbridled barbarousness of the Welsh'.[102] How comfortable would a highly civilised, intellectually aware Anglo-Norman like Robert of Gloucester feel about having barbarians as allies? It is I think worth noting the contrast between the two great writers who sought Robert's patronage: Geoffrey of Monmouth and William of Malmesbury. William never once mentions the fact that Robert has Welsh allies or employs Welsh troops.[103] Given his views on the barbarous nature of the Welsh is it far-fetched to guess that William's silence on this subject is an embarrassed silence? Geoffrey, of course, was in a totally different situation. He had probably already set out on his task of giving the Welsh an honourable and civilised past. With the rapidly moving events of 1136 and 1137 that task became an even more urgent one. It was no longer just a question of rescuing the reputation of a people from the disdain of a few historically minded scholars, a people who seemed, after all, to be on the way out, in a country being turned into a 'second England'. It was now also a question of giving a distinguished pedigree to a people that had suddenly begun to play once more – as their prophecies said they would – a major part in the politics of Britain. And if the Welsh were now allies of Robert of Gloucester, then might not Geoffrey's counter-history now have the extra advantage of being politically convenient to his patron?[104]

Finally, it seems to me, as indeed to many commentators, that the mood of the History changes considerably once Merlin and Arthur enter upon the scene.[105] King Arthur presides over a magnificent and fashionable court, but otherwise the world in which he lives is entirely dominated by war. He founds no towns, issues no laws, shows no concern for the well-being of farmers. He is a warrior-king, a figure from an heroic age, endowed with some overtones of chivalry to bring him up-to-date, but in no sense a paradigm of good civilian kingship. In this he is perceptibly different from Geoffrey's earlier British kings. Arthur is also different because Geoffrey explicitly associates him with the British hope of recovery of sovereignty. The day when the Britons come into their own again is 'the day which Merlin had prophesied to Arthur'.[106] Arthur,

---

[101] Orderic uses similar language (*beluino more barbariem suam . . . exercuerunt*, including the disembowelling of pregnant women) to describe the Scottish invasion of 1138. Cf. n. 49.

[102] 'effrenemque Walensium barbariem', *Gesta Stephani*, 172.

[103] This is an aspect of William's discretion which has not, I think, been observed hitherto, cf. R. B. Patterson, 'William of Malmesbury's Robert of Gloucester: a Re-evaluation of the *Historia Novella*', *American Historical Review*, lxx, 1965, 983–97.

[104] In passing G. H. Gerould suggested that one of Geoffrey's purposes was 'to flatter the followers of Earl Robert who had Celtic blood', 'King Arthur', 47. I owe the term 'counter-history' to Rees Davies.

[105] Thorpe, 20–22.

[106] HRB c. 205; Thorpe, xii.17. Unless, perhaps, the Arthur referred to here was none other than Geoffrey himself, an ambiguous, half-joking allusion to the nickname given to a man known to be obsessed with the figure of legend, Padel, 1–4. Cf. the self-identification of Gerald as 'Silvester', *Opera*, v, 20 n. 20.

though mortally wounded at Camblann, was conveyed to the Isle of Avalon to recover and, by implication, to return. Presumably this aspect of Geoffrey's treatment may simply be because Arthur was already associated with the British hope.[107] But it is possible that the theme of recovery may not have been in Geoffrey's mind from the beginning; at any rate he makes no allusion to it in the early parts of the book, not even when he mentions Arthur.[108] It is not until he reaches the Prophecies of Merlin that Geoffrey first refers to the British hope, and then he does so in very powerful and unmistakable terms, so powerful indeed that Tatlock believed they could not have been written by Geoffrey.[109] 'The people that is oppressed shall prevail in the end, for it will resist the savagery of the invaders. The Boar of Cornwall shall bring assistance and will trample their necks beneath its feet . . . Cadwallader shall summon Conan and shall make an alliance with Albany. Then the foreigners shall be slaughtered and the rivers run with blood.'[110] Up until this point Geoffrey had dealt with only two of the main themes of Welsh tradition: the theme of rivalry between Britain and Rome, and the theme of loss of dominion to the Saxons. But from this moment on his history is brought within the framework of another theme, one which had been an integral part of Welsh historiography since at least the tenth century, the theme of deliverance and renewal.[111]

Now Geoffrey himself tells us that he paused during his writing of the History, at a time when, as he put it, 'Merlin began to be talked about very much'; that he then composed a version of the Prophecies of Merlin and dedicated it to Bishop Alexander of Lincoln, before returning to the task of completing his History.[112] What all this makes possible, it seems to me, is that the theme of the British recovery entered Geoffrey's History just at that moment when it seemed to be becoming historical reality, when, in the words of the *Description*, 'Openly they go about saying, That in the end they will have it all, By means of Arthur, They will get it back.' We know at any rate that one very early reader of HRB revised the text both in order to play down the theme of the treachery of the Saxons and also in order, as Neil Wright puts it, 'to record unequivocally that the national hero was dead', to put an end, in

---

[107] WM c. 287. Though see Roberts, 40 n. 37.

[108] HRB c. 1; Thorpe, i.1.

[109] Tatlock, 405, 414–15.

[110] HRB cc. 112, 115; Thorpe, vii.3. See M. J. Curley, 'A New Edition of John of Cornwall's *Prophetia Merlini*', *Speculum*, lvii, 1982, 245–46, for the identification of Conan and Cadwallader. It is not entirely certain that Orderic's copy of the Prophecies of Merlin included explicit references to the British hope. His initial summary of the Prophecy ends with the Britons 'driven beyond the shores of the Ocean', and then his extract *de Merlini libello*, though it ends with the words 'Deinde revertentur cives in insulam' – which might be taken as an allusion to the British hope – neither includes the phrase which follows immediately in Geoffrey's version, *nam discidium alienigenarum orietur*, nor any of the subsequent passages.

[111] For discussion of these themes, Roberts, 32–40; Davies, *Conquest*, 77–80.

[112] HRB c. 109; Thorpe, vii.1.

other words, to the ambiguity which had surrounded Arthur's fate after the Battle of Camblann.[113] As these alterations to the text make plain, Geoffrey's history in its original form was felt to be playing with political fire and to be disturbingly anti-English.

To sum up. Geoffrey was a complex and ambiguous writer and I don't mean to imply that I have explained him. But I do want to suggest that among the complexities and ambiguities within which he operated were, at one level, the 'twelfth century Renaissance' perception of the Celtic peoples in general, and the Welsh in particular, as barbarians. To this perception he provided a powerful rejoinder.[114] In the event it was not one powerful enough to offset the contemporary realities of a Welsh pastoral economy and an 'unreformed' Welsh social structure. English writers continued to regard the Welsh as a barbarous and primitive people. At another level, and perhaps at a later stage of composition, he responded to a much more immediate political and military situation, the electrifying excitement of the great revolt of 1136–7, the capture of Caerleon by Morgan, King Morgan, and the dilemma which that posed for his patron Robert of Gloucester. And it is surely appropriate to end with a question. Did he fail here as well? Or was this the highly-charged atmosphere in which his relatively prosaic history took flight? In which he was inspired to bring off his greatest coups, Merlin the magician-prophet and Arthur the all-conquering British king, the 'two personages who were to give Geoffrey of Monmouth his place in the development of European literature?'[115]

---

[113] Wright, lvi–lix. On the other hand in his *Vita Merlini* Geoffrey makes explicit the promise of Arthur's recovery, lines 929–40.

[114] In this sense he may be said to have 'sought to stimulate and satisfy the curiosity of the Normans about the peoples they had come to dominate'. Robin Frame, *The Political Development of the British Isles, 1100–1400*, Oxford 1990, 8.

[115] Thorpe, 21.

3

Conquering the Barbarians: War and Chivalry in Twelfth-Century Britain and Ireland

I begin with an incident which occurred on the south coast of Ireland in the summer of 1170. A small invading force of men-at-arms and archers won a fiercely contested engagement at the creek of Baginbun against the men of Waterford and their Irish allies. According to the rhyme first written down by Richard Stanihurst in the sixteenth century:

> At the creeke of Baginbun
> Ireland was lost and won.

As a result of their victory the English found themselves in possession of some 70 prisoners. What was to be done with them? According to Gerald de Barri, his cousin Raymond le Gros took the view that their lives should be spared; and the arguments put into Raymond's mouth are, to my mind, of exceptional interest. If we had killed them in battle, he says, that would have enhanced our reputation. But now that they have been taken prisoner they are no longer our enemies, they are human beings. They are not rebels, nor traitors, nor thieves, just men defeated by us while they were defending their country. Let us be merciful, for clemency is most deserving of praise. Without mercy, victory is wicked and bestial. Moreover their ransom would be much more advantageous to us than their deaths because it will add to our soldiers' pay and give an example of noble conduct.

But Raymond was opposed by Hervey de Montmorency and Hervey's arguments are equally noteworthy. In essence his case was that foreign countries cannot be conquered by clemency. Only when we have completed our conquest, he says, can we afford to show mercy. In the meantime while the whole population of Ireland is plotting our destruction, we must be ruthless. Moreover let Raymond answer this. If they had been victorious, would they have ransomed us? In the end it was Hervey's arguments which found favour with his fellow soldiers. According to the *Song of Dermot and the Earl*, they handed an axe to a lady called Alice of Abervenny who had lost her lover in the fight, and

* This article was made possible by the generosity of the Leverhulme Trust in providing me with that most precious of commodities, time for research and writing.

she decapitated all the prisoners. Then their bodies were thrown over the cliff's edge. But Gerald himself did not share the majority view. In his judgment the victors misused their good fortune by displaying deplorable and inhuman brutality. In return for the lives of their prisoners they could have received a huge sum or they might have obtained the town of Waterford itself.[1] In his reflections on the massacre after Baginbun Gerald de Barri throws into dramatic relief many different aspects of the subject that I propose to consider here: the conduct and perception of war in Britain and Ireland in the twelfth century.

From the time that the kingdom of England emerged in the course of the tenth century it is clear that it was generally this kingdom which was the dominant and expansionist power within the British Isles. By one means or other English men and women, whether English speaking or French speaking, pushed and shoved their way north and west, into Scotland, Wales and Ireland. Sometimes they could claim to have been invited in by one or other local ruler, but more often than not they met with resistance; they had to fight, especially in Wales and Ireland. The history of this expansion is therefore in large part a military history, a history of wars of conquest and attempted conquest. Military men, in R. R. Davies's phrase, 'set the tone and called the tune'.[2] Here I wish to focus on the place of the twelfth century in that military history. I do so for two reasons. First, because it was in the twelfth century that these wars became genuinely imperialist wars. It was in this century that the English learned to despise their Celtic neighbours and to think of themselves as belonging to a higher level of civilisation. In the history of the British Isles this was to be a decisive turning-point. Second, because the conquerors thought of themselves as 'chevaler nobles & curteis'.[3] At times, as the Waterford debate indicates, some of them were aware that they were falling short of their own standards, but felt they could justify this: they were in a conquest situation and, as Hervey de Montmorency's rhetorical question showed, they felt they were only doing what their barbarous enemies would have done to them. The warfare of Celtic peoples throws notions of chivalric conduct into sharp perspective, and by doing so offers us some important clues as to the nature and origins of chivalry.[4]

---

[1] Giraldus Cambrensis, *Expugnatio Hibernica*, ed. and trans. A. B. Scott and F. X. Martin (Dublin, 1978), 58–65, 300 (hereafter cited as *Expug.*); *The Song of Dermot and the Earl*, ed. G. H. Orpen (Oxford, 1892), 110–11. Interestingly, in view of the arguments which Gerald puts into his mouth, Hervey de Montmorency later dropped out of the conquest of Ireland and became a monk at Canterbury, where voices criticising the whole enterprise could be heard. On why the invaders should be called 'English' see pp. 145–60. Indeed, except for the Anglo-Norman Orderic Vitalis, almost all the authors whose words I shall be quoting thought of themselves as English rather than Norman or Anglo-Norman, so English is the term I shall almost invariably use.

[2] R. R. Davies, *Domination and Conquest. The experience of Ireland, Scotland and Wales 1100–1300* (Cambridge, 1990), 64.

[3] *Song of Dermot*, line 1812; Davies, *Domination*, 29–30.

[4] Matthew Strickland, *War and Chivalry. The Conduct and Perception of War in England and Normandy, 1075–1217* (Cambridge, 1996), 291–329, 337–40. I am enormously indebted to

I must make a distinction. By 'imperialism' I do not mean what medieval historians sometimes call 'imperial overlordship' – the claims made by some tenth-century English rulers such as King Edgar to be overlords of Britain.[5] But the culture of Celtic peoples was not disparaged at the tenth-century West Saxon court. Anglo-Saxons and Celts continued to share what Dennis Bethell called 'a common cultural world in which Ireland was still regarded as a source of learning and virtue'.[6] Tenth-century English kings may have been imperial rulers in that they ruled, or claimed to rule, over a number of kingdoms; but they were not imperialists. By the late twelfth century, however, this is exactly what they were.

I have argued elsewhere that William of Malmesbury was the first English historian to adopt a new and contemptuous attitude to Celtic peoples.[7] Whereas writers for at least the previous three centuries had been content to take an essentially Christian view of the world, dividing men and women into two basic groups, Christian and non-Christian, William also used a non-religious system of classification, dividing them into the 'civilised' and the 'barbarians'. In the earlier period the word *barbarus* had been synonymous with *paganus*, but in William's eyes the Christian Celts of his own day were 'barbarians'. His negative view of Celtic peoples rapidly became the dominant one. Why was this? Why did William's attitude prove to be so catching? His perception and its formulation owed much to his profound classical scholarship, to his love and admiration for the values of the Ancient World; and the Twelfth Century Renaissance meant that other members of the clerical elite came to share his learned admiration for antiquity. But what was it about Celtic peoples that made them seem so barbarous to William and his readers? The ideals of the religious reform movement undoubtedly supply part of the answer. As the Anglo-Norman clergy gradually became a 'reformed' clergy, so they also became aware of resistance to 'reform' in the Celtic churches. Eadmer's view of the Scots, for example, became much more hostile after his own brief experience of the Scottish church as a failed bishop of St Andrews.[8] But few Anglo-Norman churchmen visited the Celtic realms and, on the whole, until Gerald de Barri told them about Ireland and Wales in works written in the 1180s and 1190s, English and Norman writers knew very little about any Celtic society. Yet already by the middle of the twelfth century most members of the clerical elite

---

Matthew Strickland's kindness in giving me a copy of his Cambridge thesis before the book was published.

[5] James Campbell, 'Some Twelfth Century Views of the Anglo-Saxon Past', *Peritia* 3 (1984): 139; Davies, *Domination*, 4–5. See also above, p. 9.

[6] Denis Bethell, 'English monks and Irish reform in the eleventh and twelfth centuries', *Historical Studies* 8 (1971): 117–18, 125–26.

[7] See above, pp. 27–9. The author of *Quadripartitus*, perhaps writing a little later than William of Malmesbury, also referred to the barbarity of Ireland, F. Liebermann, *Die Gesetze der Angelsachsen*, 3 vols. (Halle, 1903–16), 1: 534.

[8] Eadmer, *Historia Novorum in Anglia*, ed. Martin Rule, RS (London, 1884), 279–86..

seem to be convinced that Celts were barbarians. 'Who', for example, 'would deny that the Scots are barbarians?' was the question confidently put by the author of *The Conquest of Lisbon*.[9]

To see why this was so we should, I think, turn to those parts of the twelfth-century image of the barbarian on which modern scholars have had little to say. Thanks to work done particularly by R. R. Davies and Robert Bartlett it is now very well-known that the Celtic barbarian was believed to live in unenterprising fashion in a primitive, pastoral economy, wallowing in bestial sexual and marital customs.[10] Modern scholars, on the other hand, have had very litttle to say about the barbarian at war.[11] But twelfth-century writers did, and they did so in a deluge of vituperation which began quite suddenly in about 1140.

This is because after Henry I's death the Welsh and the Scots seized the military initiative and in the late 1130s began to intervene within England with devastating effect. Describing King David's invasion in 1138, Orderic writes: 'a ferocious army of Scots invaded England with the utmost brutality and gave full rein to their barbarity (*barbariem suam*), treating the people of the borders with bestial cruelty. They spared no one, killing young and old alike, and even butchered pregnant women by savagely disembowelling them with their swords.' Henry of Huntingdon uses similar language. 'They ripped open pregnant women, tossed children on the points of their spears, butchered priests at the altars; they cut off the heads of images of Christ on the cross and exchanged them for the decapitated heads of their own victims.' On several occasions during his account of the same Scottish invasion, Richard of Hexham applies words like 'barbarian' or 'barbarism' to King David's army. In Ailred's account of the Battle of the Standard Archbishop Thurstan exhorted his men to defend themselves *contra barbaros*. Espec told the troops they were fighting not against men but beasts. At the same time Orderic and others were beginning to use similar language about the Welsh at war.[12] This is not how we make war is

---

[9] *De Expugnatione Lyxbonensi*, ed. and trans. C. W. David (New York, 1936), 106–7. He presumably has the Irish speaking Scots in mind since to twelfth-century authors the English speaking subjects of the Scottish kings were English.

[10] Robert Bartlett, *Gerald of Wales* (Oxford, 1982), esp. chapter 6, 'The Face of the Barbarian'. R. R. Davies, 'Buchedd a moes y Cymry. The manners and morals of the Welsh', *Welsh History Review* 12 (1984–85): 155–79. See now R. R. Davies, 'The Peoples of Britain and Ireland, 1100–1400: II. Names, Boundaries and Regnal Solidarities', *TRHS* 6th ser. 5 (1995): 1–20.

[11] There are brief comments and interesting suggestions in Robert Bartlett, 'Technique Militaire et Pouvoir Politique, 900–1300', *Annales* 41 (1986): 1135–59, esp. 1147–52. The Scottish barbarians have been systematically treated in Strickland, *War and Chivalry*, see above, n. 3. See also his article, 'Securing the North: Invasion and the Strategy of Defence in Twelfth-Century Anglo-Scottish Warfare', *ANS* 12 (1989): 177–98.

[12] Orderic Vitalis, *Historia Ecclesiastica*, ed. M. Chibnall, 6 vols. (Oxford, 1969–80), vi. 518; Richard of Hexham, *De Gestis Regis Stephani* and Ailred of Rievaulx, *Relatio de Standardo* both in *Chronicles of the Reigns of Stephen, Henry II and Richard I*, ed. R. Howlett, 4 vols., RS (London, 1884–90), 3: 160, 163, 165, 182, 188 (hereafter cited as *Chronicles*); Henry, *Archdeacon of Huntingdon, Historia Anglorum*, ed. and trans. D. Greenway (Oxford, 1996),

the unspoken but crystal clear message. Not even Flemish mercenaries made war like this – a point made explicit a generation later by Jordan Fantosme when referring to the activity of Flemings during William the Lion's invasion of the North: 'They burned the countryside; but God showed his love for these goodly peasants (*gentilz paisanz*) who had no protection, in that their mortal enemies, the Scots, were not there, for they would have beaten, killed and ill-treated them.'[13] Ravaging and burning the countryside were essential ingredients of chivalrous warfare – indeed I have argued that they were the main ingredients – but killing unresisting non-combatants was not.[14]

What are we to make of the language of writers like Orderic, Henry of Huntingdon, and Richard and Ailred of Hexham? Do we have here essentially baseless atrocity stories, or do they reflect the reality of Celtic warfare? Some of the charges may indeed be fictions,[15] but there is, I think, an important underlying reality. Consider another atrocity story, the description of Malcolm Canmore's invasion of the north in 1070 which comes from the *History of the Kings* attributed to Symeon of Durham. (I shall return later to the question of author and date.)

Gazing upon the church of St Peter, blazing with the flames kindled by his men . . . he commanded them no longer to spare any of the English nation, but either to slay them all or drive them away under the yoke of perpetual slavery. When his men received their King's licence it was pitiable to see what they did to the English: old men and women were either beheaded by swords or stuck with spears like pigs destined for the table. Torn from their mothers' breasts, babes were tossed high in the air, and caught on the spikes of spears fixed close together in the ground. The Scots, crueller than beasts, delighted in this cruelty as in the sight of games . . . Young men and girls, all who seemed fit for work, were bound together and driven away into slavery. When some of the girls dropped to the ground exhausted by the pace of the slave-drivers, they were left to die where they fell. Malcom watched all these things without pity; merely ordering his slave-drivers to make haste.[16]

710–11; 261 in Thomas Arnold's Rolls Series edition (London, 1879). Both editions will be hereafter cited as HH, with Arnold's pagination in square brackets. On views of the Welsh see above, pp. 27–8.

[13] *Jordan Fantosme's Chronicle*, ed. and trans. R. C. Johnston (Oxford, 1981), lines 1175–78.

[14] John Gillingham, 'War and Chivalry in the *History of William the Marshal*' in ed. P. R. Coss and S. Lloyd, *Thirteenth Century England II* (Woodbridge, 1988), 1–13; reprinted in Gillingham, *Richard Coeur de Lion. Kingship, Chivalry and War in the Twelfth Century* (London, 1994) and in ed. M. Strickland, *Anglo-Norman Warfare* (Woodbridge, 1992). Even the dreaded routiers only tortured to get money, Strickland, *War and Chivalry*, 311–13. Thus in Normandy in 1118 villagers assumed that they could safely follow a raiding party 'planning to buy back their stock or recover it somehow', Orderic, vi. 250. Eleanor Searle kindly drew my attention to the implications of this passage.

[15] Notably Ailred's accusation that they ate their victims' flesh, *Chronicles*, 3: 187, 189.

[16] Symeon of Durham, *Opera Omnia*, ed. Thomas Arnold, 2 vols., RS (London, 1882–85), 2: 191–92. 'Go they must or be killed on the spot' was how one victim of a slave raid in early

This, in other words, is war as slave hunt. So it was again when David invaded the north in 1138. Of the Galwegians on that expedition, Richard of Hexham wrote, 'these bestial men, once they were weary of abusing their prisoners in the manner of brutish animals – for they regarded adultery, incest and other abominations as being of no account, – either made them slave women or sold them for cattle to other barbarians'. Similarly the sale of prisoners into foreign parts had been a feature of the Welsh revolt of 1136–7.[17] The systematic slave hunt involved a form of total war, an attack not just on the property of non-combatants but on their persons too. In order to capture potential slaves, generally women but sometimes young men as well, and drag them off into slavery it was in practice necessary not only to kill anyone who put up a fight but also anyone who got in the way. Not only husbands but also elderly parents and young children, all those categories of persons who would move too slowly or whom it was uneconomic to put to work, but whose lamenting, living, clinging presence would have impeded the whole operation.[18]

There was, of course, nothing new about war as slave hunt. So why were the writers of the mid-twelfth century making so much fuss about it? Once the question has been posed the answer is an obvious one – and a fundamental one, significant because part and parcel of a far-reaching transformation of society. In England economic development and social change resulted in the demise of slavery in the early twelfth century.[19] By contrast in the less developed

nineteenth-century Nigeria summed up the fate of 'women who were bowed with age' and 'children who were younger than myself' – he was then about fourteen, J. F. Ade Ajayi, 'Samuel Ajayi Crowther of Oyo' in ed. P. D. Curtin, *Africa Remembered* (Madison, 1967), 303.

[17] *Chronicles*, 3: 157; *The Chronicle of John of Worcester*, ed. J. R. H. Weaver (Oxford, 1908), 43, where the author also deplores the killing of the innocent.

[18] That men, especially husbands, were more commonly killed than made captive is suggested by Richard of Hexham, *Chronicles*, 3: 156, 170; also by John of Hexham, *The Chronicle of John, Prior of Hexham*, ed. J. Raine, *The Priory of Hexham*, Surtees Society 44 (1863), 2 vols., 1: 116 (hereafter cited as John of Hexham). Here maidens and widows, their men having been killed, were roped together and dragged naked into captivity. Similarly the Welsh revolt of 1136 involved the killing of husbands and children and the enslavement of women, according to the Gloucester continuator printed in *Florentii Wigorniensis Monachi Chronicon ex Chronicis*, 2 vols., ed. B. Thorpe (London, 1848–49), 2: 96. In a twelfth-century Irish version of events at Limerick in 967, all those fit for war were killed while girls and young women 'soft, silk-clad and blooming' were enslaved, *Cogadh Gaedhel re Gallaibh*, ed. J. H. Todd, RS (London, 1867), 78–81. On this see P. Holm, 'The Slave Trade of Dublin, ninth to twelfth centuries', *Peritia* 5 (1986): 338–39, a reference I owe to the kindness of James Lydon. On the gender distinction, Orlando Patterson, *Slavery and Social Death* (Cambridge, Mass., 1982), 120–21.

[19] John S. Moore, 'Domesday Slavery', *ANS* 11 (1988): 191–220, refers in passing to the effects of landlord policy and the cash-nexus on the progress of slaves into free labouring groups in southern England, and the disappearance of slavery in England is considered by David A. E. Pelteret, *Slavery in Early Medieval England* (Woodbridge, 1995), 251–59, but I know of no analysis of the demise of slavery in the British Isles to match 'The survival and extinction of the slave system in the early medieval West' in Pierre Bonnassie, *From Slavery to Feudalism in South Western Europe* (Cambridge, 1991).

economies of the Celtic lands slavery continued to flourish. In William of Malmesbury's opinion slavery was a degrading and inhumane institution and those who practised it, like the Irish, he called 'barbarous'. The fact that the Welsh continued to engage in the slave trade was, in John of Salisbury's eyes, one of the principal indicators of their barbarism. According to Gerald de Barri, the English invasion of Ireland was God's punishment on the Irish for their involvement in the monstrous crime of slavery.[20]

One implication here is that in earlier periods English observers, themselves members of a slave owning, slave raiding, slave trading society, would not have noticed anything peculiarly repellent in Celtic warfare. This does seem to have been the case. Even when the English were on the receiving end, the *Anglo-Saxon Chronicle* adopts a laconic and neutral tone when dealing with campaigns which involved enslaving prisoners. In 1079, for example, 'King Malcolm came from Scotland with a great army which harried the land of the Northumbrians as far as the Tyne, and slew many hundreds, taking home much money and treasure, and carrying off people into captivity.'[21] This is very different from the way the writers of the 1140s and 1150s described the invasion of 1138. But it also, of course, contrasts sharply with Symeon of Durham's description of Malcolm's 1070 raid. This is in fact an extremely revealing case. The text of the *Historia Regum*, as we have it, dates not from the first third but from the second half of the twelfth century. It contains, as H. S. Offler showed, mid-twelfth-century interpolations made at Hexham.[22] And the tone of these interpolated passages is markedly different from the rest of the chronicle, more emotional, more violently anti-Scottish. The description of Malcolm's raid, being one of these interpolations, was written by an author who lived in a society which no longer practised slavery and who had himself lived through the invasion of 1138; this was 1070 seen through mid-twelfth-century eyes.

Thus one of the vital moments in the European history of freedom, the demise of slavery, has led to old-fashioned warfare being regarded as unnaturally cruel and barbarous. This is clear from Orderic's condemnation of Robert of Rhuddlan, despite the fact that he was one of St Evroul's benefactors. 'For fifteen years he harried the Welsh mercilessly . . . some he slaughtered on the spot like cattle, others he kept for years in fetters, or forced into a harsh and unlawful slavery. It is not right that Christians should so oppress their

[20] *The Vita Wulfstani of William of Malmesbury*, ed. R. R. Darlington, Camden Society, n.s. 11 (1928): 42; *The Letters of John of Salisbury*, 2 vols., ed. W. J. Millor and H. E. Butler, 1: 135; *Expug.*, 70.

[21] *The Anglo-Saxon Chronicle*, ed. and trans. Dorothy Whitelock et al. (London, 1961), 159. See also the cases cited by David Pelteret, 'Slave Raiding and Slave Trading in Early England', *Anglo-Saxon England* 9 (1981): 107–8, 111.

[22] H. S. Offler, 'Hexham and the *Historia Regum*', *Transactions of the Architectural and Archaeological Society of Durham and Northumberland*, n.s. 2 (1970): 51–62, esp. 53, 55.

[23] Orderic, iv. 138–39.

brothers.'[23] Orderic wrote these words shortly before the death of Henry I and it was in the light of this view of slavery and the slave hunt that he and his fellow authors were shocked by the old style warfare which the revival of Welsh and Scottish military fortunes brought so forcibly to their attention in the early years of Stephen's reign. Earlier, writing in the 1120s, Orderic had taken a sympathetic view of the Scots, even in one passage describing them as people who loved peace and quiet.[24] Not any more. From now on anyone who read William of Malmesbury's *Gesta Regum* could not but agree with the hostile perception of Celts offered by that most creative and influential of historians. This is why the Battle of the Standard is portrayed by contemporaries not just as a battle between Scots and English but as a titanic and ferocious struggle between two opposing cultures, the civilised and the savage.[25] It is this perception which makes the Standard one of the most important battles in British history.

King David I of Scotland, of course, as leader of an army of barbarians was in a difficult and ambiguous position. After all he had been brought up in the English court and he was, at least according to William of Malmesbury, keen to civilise the Scots. 'To all of his subjects who would learn to live in a more civilised style, dress with more elegance and eat with more refinement, David promised no less than three years exemption from taxes.'[26] The papal legate Alberic, whom David welcomed at his court, is said to have made the Scots, in particular the Galwegians, promise to release slaves captured in 1137–8 and in future wars to spare children, women, the old and infirm, killing only those who fought against them.[27] But to judge from accounts of the Scottish invasion of the north in 1173–4 not much had changed by then. William of Newburgh, by reputation the most thoughtful and judicious of twelfth-century English historians, is particularly fierce in his condemnation of the conduct of what he explicitly called 'a huge horde of barbarians' during their 1174 raid. 'Everything was being consumed by the Scots, to whom no kind of food is too filthy to be devoured, even that which is fit only for dogs. It is a delight to

[24] Orderic, ii. 218; iv. 70, 278. On Orderic's changing view of the Welsh, see above, pp. 27–8.

[25] William E. Kapelle, *The Norman Conquest of the North* (London, 1979), 227, describes these hysterical accounts as 'the usual result of contact between agriculturists and a semipastoral folk given to plundering and slaving from an inaccessible homeland' – when the agriculturists are no longer slavers, I would add.

[26] William of Malmesbury, *De Gestis Regum Anglorum*, ed. William Stubbs, 2 vols., RS (London, 1887–89), c. 400. I shall cite this work as WM and by chapter number since both this edition and the new one, *Gesta Regum Anglorum*, vol. 1, ed. and trans. R. A. B. Mynors, R. M. Thomson and M. Winterbottom (Oxford, 1998) share the same division into chapters. Curiously C. Stephen Jaeger, *The Origins of Courtliness* (Philadelphia, 1985), 181, completely mistranslates this passage and in consequence mistakenly sees David as 'alone among contemporary monarchs to be lauded for having resisted courtly luxury'. For Henry II's attempt to make political capital out of a 'civilised' cuisine, see Roger of Howden, *Chronica*, ed. William Stubbs, 4 vols., RS (London, 1868–71), 2: 32, cited below, p. 104.

[27] *Chronicles*, 3: 171; John of Hexham, 121.

that inhuman nation, more savage than wild beasts, to cut the throats of old men, to slaughter little children, to rip open the bowels of women.'[28]

Of course Celtic warfare was old-fashioned in another sense as well, technologically. Here too accounts of the Battle of the Standard are very revealing. The Scots lost because although they had an 'innumerable army', they had only 200 mailed soldiers. Thus they suffered terribly from the fire of the English archers, to which they could make little response, for although they had archers themselves they were very short of arrows.[29] Time and again the sources comment on the lack of body armour of Celtic soldiers.[30] It is these details which make plain why it was the English who were the expansionist power within the British Isles. We are already witnessing an unequal struggle between an industrially advanced power and a pastoral economy. A fully equipped man in mail armour would be carrying some 40 pounds of expensive iron.[31] The English economy was able to cope with the mass-production of armour and ammunition (i.e. arrowheads) and thus the English were able to mow down the inadequately armoured Irish, Welsh and native Scots. In general there is a lot of nonsense written about the dominance of heavy cavalry – 'feudal' or otherwise – in the 'medieval' centuries. Certainly it wasn't cavalry which dominated so many campaigns in Wales and Ireland in the twelfth century, it was armour and firepower.[32] Also, of course, the capacity to build castles and to stock them. This too is a measure of the economic transformation which England had undergone – but which Wales and Ireland had not, and Scotland only to a very limited extent.

[28] *Chronicles*, 1: 182–83.
[29] HH, 714–17, [263]; *The Chronicle of John of Worcester*, 51; *Chronicles*, 3: 196–97; John of Hexham, 120.
[30] On the Scots, for example, 'Nudi ipsi et paene inermes progressi adversus cuneos loricatos et iccirco invulnerabiles', John of Hexham, 120; 'seminudis natibus', 'gladiis et telis nostris nudum obiciunt corium', 'inermis Scottus', *Chronicles*, 3:186. For Gerald on the Welsh, see *Descriptio Kambriae* in *Giraldi Cambrensis Opera*, ed. J. S. Brewer et al., 8 vols., RS (London, 1861–91), 6: 180, 210 (hereafter cited as *Descriptio*) and on the Irish, *Topographia Hibernica*, ibid., 5: 150. Cf. 'Unequal they engaged in battle/ The foreigners and the Gael of Tara/ Fine linen shirts on the race of Conn/ And foreigners in one mass of iron', cited by J. F. Lydon, *The Lordship of Ireland* (Dublin, 1972), 158. On the use of armour to mark the contrast between Greek and barbarian see W. R. Connor, 'Early Greek Land Warfare', *Past and Present* 119 (1988): 25.
[31] Bartlett, 'Technique militaire', 1136–37; Lydon, *Lordship*, 40–41 on the scale of Henry II's preparations for the invasion of Ireland.
[32] *Expug.*, 248. Throughout his narrative of the invasion of Ireland Gerald consistently provides numbers of archers and men-at-arms. In William of Newburgh's judgment, Irish boldness was easily defeated *a loricatis et sagitariis*, *Chronicles*, 1: 238. According to Wace, King Arthur conquered Ireland because the Irish 'furent trop nu: n'orent hauberc, n'orent escu, ne saietes ne conuisseient, ne od arc traire ne saveient. E li Bretun, qui arcs teneient, espessement a els traheient', *Le Roman de Brut de Wace*, ed. I. Arnold, 2 vols. (Paris, 1938–40), lines 9681–86. It was in terms of firepower, not horsepower, that Henry of Huntingdon, HH, 392–93, [202–3], explained the victory at Hastings over 'gentem nec etiam sagittas habentem'.

In a famous passage on the battle of Brémule (1119) Orderic observed that the knights on both sides were all clad in mail and, in his view, it was partly as a result of this that out of the 900 knights engaged only three were killed.[33] It was possible to batter down a heavily armoured soldier, to beat him into submission without either killing or seriously wounding him. In hand to hand combat in Celtic countries this was an option – a humane option – which hardly existed. Moreover when large numbers of cavalry were engaged, soldiers had the option of deliberately aiming at the horses, a tactic which enabled them to bring down their enemies while aiming to miss their bodies. Inevitably this tactic was less often practised when war was waged in terrain unsuited to cavalry, i.e. in Celtic countries.[34] By and large, however, I think that historians of war and chivalry are inclined to exaggerate the importance of cavalry tactics. It was, after all, effective body armour which made realistic games of combat possible. It was the widespread availability of quality armour, therefore, not the new cavalry tactic of the couched lance, which led to the rise of tournaments. Couched lances led to jousting whether in real fighting or in pretended fighting, but tournaments have to be distinguished from jousts and in tournaments the great bulk of the fighting was done with mace and sword.[35] And I observe that the earliest clear references to tournaments date from the 1120s, not long after the battle of Brémule.[36]

I can no longer avoid the troublesome concept of chivalry, so elusive of definition. Irrespective of what twelfth-century vernacular authors meant by the

[33] Orderic, vi. 240–41. On Orderic's views see Christopher J. Holdsworth, 'Ideas and Reality: Some Attempts to Control and Defuse War in the Twelfth Century' in *The Church and War*, ed. W. J. Sheils, Studies in Church History 20 (Oxford, 1983), 59–78; Marjorie Chibnall, *The World of Orderic Vitalis* (Oxford, 1984), 132–45.

[34] Orderic, v. 218–19; vi. 348–51. On the relative usefulness of infantry and cavalry in Ireland and Wales see Gerald de Barri's comments, *Expug.*, 246–48 and *Descriptio*, 220–21.

[35] As William of Malmesbury's account of the battle of Lincoln shows, lances were the main weapon in the joust, the prelude to battle (*proludium pugne . . . quod iustam vocant*), but not in the main action itself; those armed with lances fled when the enemy cavalry, armed with swords, and clearly intending to break through the royalist lines, launched a charge, Malmesbury, ed. Stubbs, 2: 571. The role of the joust was clarified by M. H. Jones, 'die tjostiure uz vunf scharn (Willehalm 362, 3)' in ed. K. Gärtner and J. Heinzle, *Studien zu Wolfram von Eschenbach. Festschrift für Werner Schröder* (Tubingen, 1989), 429–441. To judge from the earliest extended descriptions of tournaments in *L'Histoire de Guillaume le Maréchal*, ed. P. Meyer, 3 vols. (Paris, 1891–1901), although lances were used, especially in the preliminaries when the jousters were engaged – e.g. lines 3499–3505, 4801–2, 4989–91 – the overwhelming bulk of the fighting was done with mace and sword. Thus it was the Marshal's ability to take literally resounding blows, particularly on his helmet – e.g. lines 5000, 6073 – and return them with interest – like a woodcutter chopping down oaks (line 2959) – that made him a tournament champion. Without effective protection for the participant's head, neck and shoulders the tournament is unthinkable.

[36] But Geoffrey Malaterra, *De Rebus Gestis Rogerii Comitis*, Muratori, RIS 5, Book I, cap. 23, writing c.1100, may have envisaged young men clashing *ad militiam exercendam* as participants in a kind of impromptu tournament. Cf. Richard Barber and Juliet Vale, *Tournaments* (Woodbridge, 1989).

word 'chevalerie', modern historians writing in English generally use the word 'chivalry' to refer to a set of attitudes and conventions shared between the great aristocrats and their *milites*. It is with chivalry in this sense that I am concerned; not with chivalry as an order of knighthood, a social class, but with the code of values associated with that class.[37] Most elements of the code – admiration for courage, loyalty, largesse and prowess on foot and on horseback – unquestionably pre-date the twelfth century. In all societies dominated by military aristocracies and in which army commanders were expected to lead from the front, there was bound to be a certain camaraderie and some shared values between the nobles and their armed followers. Chivalry defined in these terms can be found, for example, in ninth-century Francia. But these are not the values upon which I wish to focus here; nor am I here concerned with the legitimisation of warfare in Christian terms.[38] Rather, and in part reflecting current English usage – the language in which I am trying to write – what I am looking for is evidence of the attempt to limit the brutality of war by treating the defeated in a more humane fashion. Seen in this perspective the crucial questions are ones which historians of chivalry have hardly asked: when did warfare become less harsh? And for whom? At what date, and where, can we find the earliest indications that these matters were governed by a system of shared values, a code of honour?[39] Sidney Painter called this code 'courtesy' – a choice of words which clearly reveals the terminological problems which this subject involves.[40] He suggested that 'the earliest instances of knightly courtesy

---

[37] See the discussion of the various meanings of chivalry in Maurice Keen, *Chivalry* (New Haven and London, 1984), 1–6.

[38] Karl Leyser, 'Early Medieval Canon Law and the Beginnings of Knighthood' in *Institutionen, Kultur und Gesellschaft im Mittelalter. Festschrift für Josef Fleckenstein*, ed. L. Fenske, W. Rösener and T. Zotz (Sigmaringen, 1984), 549–66; reprinted in K. Leyser, *Communications and Power in Medieval Europe. The Carolingian and Ottonian Centuries*, ed. T. Reuter (London, 1994). Janet Nelson, 'Ninth-century Knighthood: the Evidence of Nithard' in *Studies in Medieval History presented to R. Allen Brown*, ed. Christopher Harper-Bill, Christopher Holdsworth and Janet L. Nelson (Woodbridge, 1989), 255–66 (hereafter cited as *Studies*); reprinted in J. L. Nelson, *The Frankish World* (London, 1996); cf. 'The ninth century was already an age of chivalry' in the sense of engaging in violence consecrated in the service of God (even when it involved Christian Frank against Christian Frank), Janet Nelson, 'Violence in the Carolingian world and the ritualization of ninth-century warfare' in ed. Guy Halsall, *Violence and Society in the Early Medieval West* (Woodbridge, 1998), 90–107. Nor indeed am I concerned with chivalry in Jean Flori's sense, i.e. as the royal ethic transferred to knights when, for one reason or another, kingship is perceived as failing, *L'essor de la chevalerie, XI–XII siècles* (Geneva, 1986).

[39] Although the conduct of war was not his subject, Stephen Jaeger emphasised the significance of the Middle Ages as the period 'when knights first took it upon themselves to mitigate the violence typical in any warrior class with ideals of restraint and mercy'. His comments on Jean of Marmoutier, Hartmann and Wolfram suggest that he may have seen the late twelfth century as the crucial period, *Origins of Courtliness*, 204–5, 246–9, 261.

[40] Sidney Painter, *French Chivalry* (Baltimore, 1940), 33–34. As a word for a pattern of conduct intended to ameliorate the brutality of war, 'courtesy' has the advantage of being closer to twelfth-century French usage; 'chivalry' the advantage of being closer to modern

in the realm of war appeared in the late eleventh and twelfth centuries'; however he dealt with the subject in a very cursory fashion.[41] There may well be instances earlier than those to which Painter referred. Philippe Contamine suggested that 'with the Carolingians war between Christians may have lost a little of the harshness and bestial savagery which it possessed during the Merovingian period'.[42] Pierre Bonnassie has pointed to the ninth century as a period when war became a less significant factor in the recruitment of slaves.[43] But while acknowledging the potential force of these observations as indicating fruitful fields for further research, for the moment I am inclined, exactly as Painter was, to give a good deal of weight to some of the stories which Orderic, writing in the early 1130s, told about William Rufus.

In July 1098 William Rufus took Ballon in Maine and allowed some prisoners to be released on parole until after dinner. When some of his followers objected that the prisoners might escape, Rufus replied that he did not believe a true knight would break his word, for if he did he would be despised for ever as an outlaw (*exlex*).[44] Elsewhere Orderic comments that Rufus 'was not cruel in his treatment of knights but gracious and courteous'. A little later in his account of the battle of Brémule Orderic used the famous phrase *notitia contubernii* – the soldiers' awareness of 'fellowship in arms' – as part of his explanation of why those fleeing were captured not killed.[45] When, at the council of Rheims in October 1118, Henry I had been accused before Pope Calixtus II of acting *contra omne ius et fas detestabiliter*, it was on account of his treatment of his captured brother Robert. A little later Orderic recorded the count of Flanders' protest against Henry I's treatment of the prisoners taken at Bourgtheroulde (1121); 'you are doing', said the count, 'something contrary to our customs'. Henry had his reply ready but Orderic's formulation is a significant one: *rem nostris ritibus inusitatem*.[46] As will be obvious by now there are two threads that link all these

English usage. Because in modern French 'chevalerie' is closer to 'knighthood' than is the English 'chivalry', Philippe Contamine referred to 'un code de la guerre courtoise', *La Guerre au Moyen Age* (Paris, 1980), 413, and Michael Jones translated it as 'a code of chivalric warfare', Contamine, *War in the Middle Ages*, trans. M. Jones (Oxford, 1984), 255.

[41] Painter, *French Chivalry*, 44–45. He confuses matters by treating 'courtesy' together with 'love of glory', so it is hardly surprising that those authors who have followed Painter have found difficulties with the subject, e.g. J. T. Johnson, *Just War Tradition and the Restraint of War* (Princeton, 1981), 126–48.

[42] Contamine, *War*, 265. He went on to observe that there has been 'insufficient historical research in this area', but see now Paul Fouracre, 'Attitudes towards violence in seventh-and eighth-century Francia' in Halsall, *Violence and Society*, 60–75.

[43] Bonnassie, *From Slavery to Feudalism*, 32–34, without however making clear that this applies to West rather than East Francia. Cf. Contamine, *War*, 266. Presumably the Peace and Truce of God also helped to protect non-combatants.

[44] Orderic, v. 244, written c.1134. Cf. *Jordan Fantosme's Chronicle*, lines 1863–64 where Bernard of Balliol brings down William de Mortemer (though the translation here is misleading), then 'puts him on parole as is customary with a knight'.

[45] Orderic, v. 238; vi. 240–41.

[46] Orderic, vi. 256, 352. Cf. WM c. 406.

episodes: one is the taking and keeping of prisoners, the other is the notion that there is some body of law or custom that regulates these matters. The assumption that this custom would be observed enabled enemies to trust each other's word and made war a more humane business than it might otherwise have been. I am reminded of the young Parzifal in Wolfram's poem receiving his first lesson in chivalry. 'Temper daring with mercy. When you have won a man's submission in battle, accept it and let him live unless he has done you some mortal wrong.' I think also of the story in John of Marmoutier's *Historia Galfridi* where Geoffrey of Anjou releases some captured knights and does so with the words: 'Are we not knights, should we not therefore owe a special compassion to knights?'[47]

Compassion. This brings me back to the dilemma facing the victors of Baginbun in 1170. Although the English or French knight no longer went on slaving expeditions he still, of course, faced the problem of what to do with captured combatants. Here too Gerald de Barri saw a sharp contrast between Celtic practice and what he called *Gallica militia* – words which, in honour of Sidney Painter, I would translate as 'French Chivalry'. 'There, in France, knights are held in captivity, here they are decapitated; there they are ransomed, here killed.'[48] Indeed the English invaders' treatment of Askulv, the Norse ruler of Dublin, in 1171 makes a striking contrast with the famous story of how Rufus released Helias of Maine despite the latter's vow to do all he could, once he was free, to undermine William's power.[49] Originally held for ransom, Askulv was publicly beheaded as soon as he told his captors that if they let him go he would return in force.[50]

Ransom. Although Orderic makes no explicit mention of ransom in his account of Brémule, elsewhere he makes plain that he realised the importance of ransoms in contemporary warfare.[51] Again there's obviously nothing new about ransoms, but a widespread convention of ransoming is much easier to operate in a relatively highly monetised society – not a description applicable to the Celtic economy. Moreover it is clear that in return for the life of very high status prisoners a very high price could be demanded: a city for example. Because Geofrey Martel captured the count of Blois he was able to acquire Tours. Rufus obtained Le Mans thanks to the capture of Count Helias. Other prisoners could

[47] Wolfram von Eschenbach, *Parzival*, trans. A. T. Hatto (Harmondsworth, 1980), 96; *Chroniques des Comtes d'Anjou*, eds. Louis Halphen and René Poupardin (Paris, 1913), 194–96.

[48] *Expug.*, 246; repeated in *Descriptio*, 220.

[49] Orderic, v. 248. The various versions of this story show how deep an impression it made. For William of Malmesbury, c. 320, it was an illustration of Rufus's *praeclara magnanimitas* which put him on a par with Julius Caesar. Gaimar makes it one of the highlights of a great and courtly reign, *L'Estoire des Engleis*, ed. A. Bell, Anglo-Norman Texts (Oxford, 1960), lines 5925ff. Rufus, Frank Barlow observed, 'undoubtedly played a part in developing the knightly code of behaviour which became known as chivalry', *William Rufus* (London, 1983), 118. On Gaimar's treatment of Rufus see below, pp. 241–5.

[50] *Expug.*, 76–78; *Song of Dermot*, lines 2468ff.

[51] E.g. Orderic, iv. 48, v. 216.

be used as bargaining counters to acquire castles.[52] Obviously it seemed to Gerald de Barri that in 1170 it might have been possible to obtain possession of Waterford in return for the lives of those taken at Baginbun. But how frequently could this have been a realistic option in societies which lacked towns and castles? i.e. societies like Wales, Ireland and Scotland up to the reign of King David. It is a mark of the transformation of Lowland Scotland presided over by David that Henry II was able to release William the Lion in 1174 in return for possession of five key castles including Edinburgh and Stirling.[53]

If in Celtic countries there were still relatively few strongpoints from which territory could be controlled, then how were enemies to be defeated not just for a day but for the longer term? Only, I suggest, by putting them out of action – by killing them or mutilating them. This goes some way towards explaining the extra-ordinary savagery of Celtic political conflict – and conflict struck outside observers as being part and parcel of Celtic society. Not only were there a large number of rival political units, but succession customs meant that these units were themselves often subject to internal power struggles, to what anthropologically minded historians have called 'segmentary strife'.[54] In these 'vicious conflicts' the losers were often murdered or mutilated. Madog ap Meredith, for example, emerged as ruler of Powys in 1132 after two of his uncles and four cousins had met one or other of these fates.[55] Welsh politics was unquestionably a bloody business for the leading participants. Thus the entry for 1130 in the *Brut y Tywysogyon*: 'Iorwerth ap Llywarch was slain by Llywelyn ap Owain in Powys. Soon after that, Llywelyn ap Owain was deprived of his eyes and his testicles by Maredudd ap Bleddyn. In that year Ieuf ap Owain was slain by the sons of Llywarch ab Owain, his first cousins. At the close of the year Madog ap llywarch was slain by Meurig, his first cousin, son of Rhiddid.'[56] Similarly in Ireland and Scotland. In 1141 Diarmait Mac Murchada killed or blinded 17 members of the royal families of Leinster. It was by killing and mutilating rivals that the line of David secured its hold on the throne of Scotland in the twelfth

[52] *Chroniques des comtes*, 57–58, 235; Orderic, v. 246; *Gesta Stephani*, ed. K. R. Potter and R. H. C. Davies (Oxford, 1976), 116, 148, 176–78. On all these points see Strickland, *War and Chivalry*, 183–96.

[53] Davies, *Domination*, 8–10. This feature of Celtic lands was not lost on contemporary English observers, e.g. according to the Anglo-Norman *Description of England*, after Arthur's days there were no cities left in Wales, *Estoire des Engleis*, ed. T. D. Hardy and C. T. Martin, 2 vols., RS (London, 1888–89), 1: 286. On this text and the views of William of Malmesbury and Gerald de Barri on Ireland and Wales, see pp. 27–9, 33. For the development of burghs and sheriffdoms in Scotland, *An Historical Atlas of Scotland c.400– c.1600*, eds. Peter McNeill and Ranald Nicholson (St Andrews, 1975), 30–31. For Ailred's praise of David as a promoter of castles, towns and trade, see *Pinkerton's Lives of the Scottish Saints*, 2 vols., ed. W. M. Metcalfe (Paisley, 1889), 2: 279.

[54] J. B. Smith, 'Dynastic Succession in Medieval Wales', *Bulletin of the Board of Celtic Studies* 33 (1986): 199–232. The prevalence of segmentary strife limited the effectiveness of taking hostages.

[55] R. R. Davies, *Conquest, Coexistence and Change. Wales 1063–1415* (Oxford, 1987), 59–61, 91.

[56] *Brut Y Tywysogyon, Red Book of Hergest Version*, ed. T. Jones (Cardiff, 1955), 112–13.

and thirteenth centuries.[57] To an observer like Gerald de Barri who saw himself as a representative of English civilisation, this was all very reprehensible. When a prince died, he noted, 'the most frightful disturbances occur . . . people being murdered, brothers killing each other or putting each other's eyes out. As everyone knows from experience, it is very difficult to settle disputes of this sort.'[58] And indeed this is not how succession disputes were handled in twelfth-century England. In England disputes over succession to high office, or succession to great estates, certainly involved violence, but it was violence which was controlled so as to spare the lives of the royals and aristocrats who engaged in it. Compared with Celtic politics the so-called 'anarchy of Stephen's reign' was a very 'gentlemanly' affair. What all this suggests is that the conventions of chivalry were appropriate to a certain stage of socio-economic development, one which England had reached by the twelfth century, but which Celtic countries had not.[59]

Once again, as with the history of slavery, we are witnessing fundamental developments – pointed to by William of Newburgh when he observed that modern Ireland was like Anglo-Saxon England.[60] The frequent power struggles within and between the Anglo-Saxon royal dynasties also often ended bloodily, both for the royals themselves and for their aristocratic companions. Consider Bede's account of how Cadwalla conquered the Isle of Wight and 'endeavoured to wipe out all the natives by merciless slaughter'; two young brothers of the island's king were hunted down and put to death. Or his story of Imma, the Northumbrian noble who, captured on the morrow of a battle, was sold into slavery because his captors believed him to be a peasant. As Bede makes explicit, had they known he was a noble they would have killed him.[61] Such a story would be perfectly plausible in the twelfth-century Celtic world, but was inconceivable in chivalrous England – for, to repeat, chivalry involves violence controlled so as to spare the lives of the leading combatants. In chivalrous society low-born combatants might, if captured, be summarily put to death – especially if they were archers or crossbowmen – but not nobles.[62] Indeed even the vast majority of commoners, the non-combatants, no longer in danger of being either massacred or enslaved, were now significantly better off than before.

---

[57] *A New History of Ireland. II, 1169–1534*, ed. Art Cosgrove (Oxford, 1987), 26–27. A. A. M. Duncan, *Scotland. The Making of the Kingdom* (Edinburgh, 1975), 166, 196–97, 529, 546.

[58] *Descriptio*, 211–12; and on Ireland, *Topographia*, 167–68.

[59] Contrast Jaeger's view that 'in terms of *Realpolitik* it was then and always will be practical for a warrior to put his vanquished enemies to death', *Origins of Courtliness*, 235 – a view which does not explain why the receptiveness of warriors to 'the courtly ideals of the learned clergy' varies from one period to another. Although Patterson, *Slavery*, 106–7, argues that 'there is no relation between the level of development of a victorious group and its treatment of prisoners', he also notes that 'among all the advanced states of Africa, Asia and Europe upper-class captives were usually ransomed'.

[60] *Chronicles*, 1: 167.

[61] Bede, 3.14; 4.16, 22.

[62] Strickland, *War and Chivalry*, 180–81, 223.

This prompts the question: how and when did the English elite become chivalrous? Was it after Hastings and as a result of the Norman Conquest? 1066 and All That strikes again. For if chivalry was, as I have argued, a set of values appropriate to certain socio-economic conditions then its emergence must be related to what R. I. Moore calls 'the most profound and most permanent change that overtook Western Europe between the invention of agriculture and the industrial revolution', the growth of towns, markets and manufactures which together with the extension of 'government institutions of a new force, networks of officials', 'transformed Europe from a society of gift exchange into a money economy, with profound results for its entire structure of values and social custom'.[63] These are changes far too fundamental to be attributed to the influence of any one ethnic or cultural community. Moreover in England the processes of industrialization and monetization certainly long pre-dated the Norman Conquest.[64] Yet within this over-arching socio-economic and cultural framework it is worth considering the view that the Normans did make a difference. Not because they were more chivalrous in the horsy sense than the Anglo-Saxons; they probably weren't.[65] But because political *mores* in Normandy may have been becoming more humane after the minority of William the Bastard. By contrast conflict in England in the reign of Edward the Confessor was still relatively savage, as it had been in the reigns of Aethelred II and Cnut.[66] Thus it is at least possible that Norman indignation at the fate of Alfred the Atheling and his companions in 1036, killed, mutilated or enslaved, may have been more than just politically motivated synthetic outrage.[67] When William of Normandy is compared with Anglo-Danish rulers, there does seem to be something in William of Poitiers' insistence that he was a paragon of clemency.[68]

[63] R. I. Moore, *The Formation of a Persecuting Society* (Oxford, 1987), 102.

[64] Richard Hodges, *The Anglo-Saxon Achievement* (London, 1989), chapter 6 entitled 'The First English Industrial Revolution'; David A. Hinton, *Archaeology, Economy and Society. England from the fifth to the fifteenth century* (London, 1990).

[65] R. H. C. Davies, *The Medieval Warhorse* (London, 1989), 70–77.

[66] To judge from events in 1064 court politics in England were still a dangerous game. In the eleventh century 'a barbarian, iron-age strain was never far distant from the monarchies of the British Isles', G. W. S. Barrow, *Kingship and Unity. Scotland 1000–1306* (London, 1981), 24. But if in contemporary Normandy it was no longer thought decent to kill or mutilate aristocratic enemies openly, then perhaps there were ways round this. David Douglas, *William the Conqueror* (London, 1964), 408–15, pointed to the number of allegations of secret poisoning in eleventh-century Normandy and the contrast in this respect with England. The points made in this paragraph are further developed below, pp. 209–31.

[67] See *Encomium Emmae Reginae*, ed. A. Campbell, Camden Society, 3rd ser. 72 (1949): lxiv–lxvii.

[68] *The Gesta Guillelmi of William of Poitiers*, ed. and trans. R. H. C. Davis and M. Chibnall (Oxford, 1998), 38–39, Book 1, c. 25; *pace* Jaeger, *Origins of Courtliness*, 200. But ravaging when taken to extremes, as in William's harrying of the north, could result in the massacre of non-combatants by famine and in the enslavement of refugees. Unlike the duke's atrocity at Alençon, this was presumably too prominent an event for William to omit it, see John Gillingham, 'William the Bastard at War', in *Studies*, 141–42, 150, re-printed in ed. M. Strickland, *Anglo-Norman Warfare* and in S. Morillo, *The Battle of Hastings* (Woodbridge, 1996).

And it is surely significant that the only high status political opponent William ever put publicly to death was the Englishman, Waltheof, and by English law, whereas the lives of the French rebels of 1075 were spared because, in Orderic's words, they were dealt with *secundum leges Normannorum*.[69] The shift visible here was to be a most important one. In twelfth- and thirteenth-century England nobles were neither killed at court nor executed for treason as they had been in earlier centuries – and as they were to be again in the fourteenth century and after, 'the ages of blood', as Maitland called them.[70]

At the least it remains thought-provoking that those twelfth-century historians who had the widest range of intellectual interests, I mean William of Malmesbury and Gerald de Barri, were convinced that the best standards of their age both in war and in peace were quintessentially French. For Gerald it was *gallica*, not *anglica*, *militia*. 'The French', wrote William 'are unrivalled among western nations in military skill and polished manners.'[71] Although William as a patriotic Englishman certainly regarded the Norman Conquest as a political catastrophe he also believed that it was French schools and French culture which had made England a civilised country.[72]

In the eleventh and early twelfth centuries there were Frenchmen like William of Poitiers, Ivo of Chartres and John of Tours, as well as Italian-born popes and prelates like Paschal II and Lanfranc, who looked upon the English as a barbarous people.[73] But my impression is that by the mid-twelfth century no one any longer thought like this. Not only had the English learned to speak French, but English society had shared to the full in that fundamental socio-economic and cultural transformation of Europe. By contrast Celtic society hadn't – or hardly at all. As Robin Frame points out, wealthy regions close to centres of learning and ruled by a strong, unitary kingship were likely to be more receptive to economic and cultural trends than upland areas ruled by a collection of competing minor dynasties.[74] It is surely significant that there were no Jewish settlements anywhere in Scotland, Wales or Ireland. For many centuries the English and Celtic worlds had been very similar.[75] But by the mid-twelfth century

---

[69] Orderic, ii. 314, 318. Orderic also disapproved of the killing of Tostig and Hardrada, ii. 176.

[70] 'For two centuries after the Conquest, the frank, open rebellions of the great folk were treated with a clemency which, when we look back to it through the intervening ages of blood, seems wonderful', F. Pollock and F. W. Maitland, *The History of English Law before the time of Edward I*, 2 vols. (Cambridge, 1968), 2: 506. However he omitted the case of William of Aldrie, hanged by Rufus – unjustly said Malmesbury, c. 319. See also C. Warren Hollister, 'Royal Acts of Mutilation: the Case against Henry I', *Albion* 10 (1978).

[71] WM c. 106.

[72] See above, pp. 5–6. Cf. Orderic, ii. 256.

[73] Poitiers, *Gesta*, 128, 132, 166, Book 2, cc. 17, 20, 37; *The Letters of Ivo of Chartres*, J. P. Migne, *Patrologia Latina*, 162: 219–20 (no. 215) – a reference I owe to the kindness of Lynn K. Barker; *The Letters of Lanfranc*, ed. and trans. Helen Glover and Margaret Gibson (Oxford, 1979), 30; Paschal II's words were cited by Eadmer, *Historia Novorum*, 135, 185–86; for the views of John of Tours see WM c. 340.

[74] Robin Frame, *The Political Development of the British Isles 1100–1400* (Oxford, 1990), 72–73.

[75] This point has been powerfully argued by Patrick Wormald, 'Celtic and Anglo-Saxon

they had grown sufficiently far apart for the differences between them to be visible to contemporaries. The English 'belonged to a new world. And they knew it.'[76] From William of Malmesbury onwards they chose to articulate their sense of superiority by exploiting the vocabulary of barbarism and civilisation.

So it was that in the twelfth century civilised warriors entering barbarian territory intending to conquer and to settle found themselves facing an awkward series of choices. They could abide by the chivalrous conventions which they now took for granted elsewhere; or they could choose to set them aside. This was the dilemma with which I began, the issue at stake in the debate between Raymond le Gros and Hervey de Montmorency. Given the small number of the invaders it made sense to adopt the ruthless option and because Celtic peoples were perceived as barbarians it did not seem difficult to justify waging a barbarous war against them. The victors of Baginbun were not the first to take this road. Gerald often praises Henry II for his clemency, especially for the way he released prisoners taken during the 1173–4 rebellion. But those fortunate captives were French and English. By contrast Henry mutilated Welsh hostages in 1165, blinding and castrating the sons of princes and, according to one report, cutting off the noses and ears of female hostages.[77]

As a result of twelfth-century developments in the conduct and perception of war, the Irish, the Irish-speaking Scots and the Welsh all came came to be seen as barbarous savages who fought war in an uncivilised fashion. In this same period, as R. R. Davies has observed, the Scottish court was gradually allowed to enter the 'exhilarating international world of aristocratic fellowship and customs', but for the Welsh and the Irish the door to the charmed circle of international chivalry remained firmly closed.[78] Moreover whereas the English attempt to conquer Scotland was to be a comparatively short-lived one, the conquests of Wales and Ireland were both prolonged and fought with scant regard for chivalry. Wales and Ireland had come, in the twelfth century, to be seen as lands beyond the realms of chivalry; there the story of conquest was 'refuelled in each generation by grisly new massacres'.[79] In these twelfth-century developments some fundamentals of the shape of British history over many centuries can already be discerned.

Kingship: Some Further Thoughts' in ed. P. E. Szarmach, *Sources of Anglo-Saxon Culture* (Kalamazoo, 1986).
[76] Davies, *Domination*, 10.
[77] *Expug.*, 122–24, 128, 220. Taking female hostages is itself extraordinary; their fate is reported by Howden, *Chronica*, 1: 240, following the Melrose Chronicle, see below pp. 78, 83 n.
[78] Davies, *Domination*, 51.
[79] Davies, *Domination*, 26. Some examples cited in Lydon, *Lordship*, 169, 176, 195, 290. For an example of the way the uncomfortable protestations of the victors of Baginbun resurfaced centuries later see Thomas Churchyard, *A Generall Rehearsall of Warres* (London, 1579), Q, iii, where Sir Humphrey Gilbert's practice of building avenues of Irish heads was described, 'which course of government might be thought cruel, in excuse whereof it is to be answered. That he did but then begin that order with them, which they had in effect ever tofore used toward the English.'

4

Henry II, Richard I and the Lord Rhys

In 1171 Henry II decided to invade Ireland. As a consequence of this, as the author of the *Brut y Tywysogyon* was well aware, he decided to make peace with the ruler of Deheubarth, the Lord Rhys.[1] Lewis Warren was unorthodox in doubting whether this meant a real change in Henry's policy – for, he wrote, 'It is difficult to believe that Henry II at any time intended the conquest of Wales and its assimilation into the English state.'[2] But he was entirely orthodox in thinking that a settlement was made in 1171–2 which lasted until it came to an abrupt end with the accession of Richard I in 1189. This view had all the weight of Sir John Lloyd's authority behind it, and it still remains the general consensus.[3] In Lloyd's words, 'The death of Henry II marks an epoch in the relations between England and Wales as surely as that of Henry I.'[4] In October 1189 Count John escorted the Lord Rhys to Oxford to meet Richard I. But the newly crowned king of England, wrote Roger of Howden, refused to see the Welsh ruler 'as the king his father had been accustomed to do' and so Rhys returned angrily to his own lands.[5] Naturally Warren understood Howden's comment as validating his own view of Henry II as a peace-loving king. 'Peace with England rested upon personalities, and the ties could be easily broken: within a few months of Henry's death, Richard I's stupid mishandling of Rhys put the whole position in South Wales in jeopardy.'[6] This view too continues to

---

* This essay first appeared in a volume in memory of Lewis Warren.
[1] Thomas Jones (ed.), *Brut y Tywysogyon, Red Book of Hergest Version* (Cardiff 1955), s.a. 1171. Since there are, for my purposes, no substantial differences between the different versions of the *Brut y Tywysogyon* I shall, as here, cite only this one.
[2] W. L. Warren, *Henry II* (London 1973), 161. The only hint Gerald de Barri gave of a change of policy on Henry's part was when he was tricked into believing that Wales was an unproductive and primitive land fit only for beasts, J. S. Brewer, J. F. Dimock and G. F. Warner (ed.), *Giraldi Cambrensis Opera* (8 vols, RS, London 1861–91), vi 81–82. But that was in 1163.
[3] R. R. Davies, *Conquest, Coexistence and Change. Wales 1063–1415* (Oxford 1987), 53–54, 218–23, 271, 275, 290–92. H. Pryce, 'Gerald's Journey through Wales', *Journal of Welsh Ecclesiastical History* 6 (1989), 17–34: 26; D. Walker, *Medieval Wales* (Cambridge 1990), 50.
[4] J. E. Lloyd, *A History of Wales*, 3rd edn (London 1939), 573.
[5] Roger of Howden, *Gesta Regis Henrici Secundi et Ricardi Primi*, ed. W. Stubbs (2 vols, RS, London 1867), ii 97; Roger of Howden, *Chronica*, ed. W. Stubbs (4 vols, RS, London 1868–71), iii 23. The phrase alluding to Henry's custom appears only in Howden's later work, the *Chronica*.
[6] Warren, *Henry II*, 169.

be widely shared.[7] No one would expect me to agree with this view of Richard I. Lewis Warren would probably have been disappointed if I did. In 1985 he sent me a characteristically generous letter about something I had written on Magna Carta,[8] but observing that I had 'given a very Warren-ish interpretation. Come, come, this won't do. How can students be expected to find arguments for tutorials if we both say the same?'

In this article I shall do my best to avoid a Warren-ish interpretation. I shall argue that the notion of a détente lasting until 1189 is a modern construct which exaggerates the extent to which Rhys and Henry II were committed to peace; that in 1189 it was Rhys not Richard who unleashed war; that there is no evidence that Richard, before his departure on crusade, 'neglected' Wales any more than that he 'neglected' England – indeed there is hitherto unnoticed evidence for a meeting between Richard and the Welsh in 1189; and finally that the Welsh policy of his early years, when he and his ministers were using the services of none other than Gerald de Barri must have worked reasonably well since not a single Welsh prince can be shown to have joined the alliance of John and Philip Augustus in 1193–94.

It is, of course, obvious that after 1171–72 Henry's relations with the Welsh became much more peaceful than they had been in the first dozen years of his reign. 'The settlement of 1171–2 marks the end of an era.'[9] Henry launched no more invasions. But there was nothing specific to Wales about this, the result, as Lloyd put it, of Henry learning from the experience of his earlier invasions and perhaps taking to heart the words of the wise old Welshman that 'come what may, no other people than this and no other language than that of Wales, will answer on the great Day of Judgement for this little corner of the earth'.[10] The fact is that after his 1173 invasion of Brittany, Henry II launched no more invasions anywhere. The relentless belligerence of his early years was everywhere at an end. After the great revolt of 1173–74, he remained on the defensive, trying to retain control in the face of the threat, actual or potential, posed by alliances between members of his own family and neighbouring rulers, above all – but not only – the kings of France.

It was this revolt of 1173–4 which, according to Warren, 'gave the Welsh princes an opportunity which they readily seized to respond to Henry II's liberality with loyalty'.[11] It is certainly clear that Rhys went out of his way to help Henry. But not all the princes of south Wales did so, indeed very probably

---

[7] Davies, *Conquest*, 223, 292; A. D. Carr, *Medieval Wales* (London 1995), 46; A. D. Carr, 'Anglo-Welsh Relations, 1066–1282' in ed. M. Jones and M. Vale, *England and her Neighbours 1066–1453* (London 1989), 121–138: 126.

[8] John Gillingham, 'Magna Carta and Royal Government' in L. M. Smith (ed.), *The Making of Britain: The Middle Ages* (London 1985), 41–54.

[9] Davies, *Conquest*, 54. On the king's last invasion of Wales see P. Latimer, 'Henry II's Campaign against the Welsh in 1165', *Welsh Historical Review* 14 (1989), 523–52.

[10] Lloyd, *History of Wales*, 554. These were the words with which Gerald ended his *Description of Wales*, *Giraldi Opera*, vi 227.

[11] Warren, *Henry II*, 167.

many did not. The account in the *Brut* is unusually full for the years from 1171 to 1176 and its author was well aware of Henry's wider concerns and the opportunities which this created. In 1173, as he noted, 'While the kings were contending beyond the sea' Iorwerth ap Owain of Gwynllwg captured Caerleon and his son Hywel entered and subdued the whole land of Gwent Is-Coed 'except the castles', taking hostages from the chief men of the whole land.[12] Gerald too makes clear that Iorwerth and Hywel were taking advantage of Henry's troubles in 1173–74.[13] Iorwerth ap Owain had very good reason to take up arms when the chance came. His son Owain had been killed in 1172 while under safe-conduct on his way to peace-talks with Henry II at Usk. For that reason, wrote the *Brut*, Iorwerth and Hywel 'and many others in no way trusting the king, ravaged the king's territory as far as Hereford and Gloucester, slaying and burning and plundering without mercy'.[14] We lack similar information about the activities of other south Welsh princes in 1173–74, but when the Lord Rhys took a whole company of them with him to the 1175 conference at Gloucester with Henry II, the *Brut* explicitly refers to them as those 'who had been in opposition to the king': they were Cadwallon ap Madog of Maelienydd, Einion Clud of Elfael, Einion ap Rhys of Gwerthrynion, Morgan son of Caradog ap Iestyn of Glamorgan, Gruffudd ap Ifor ap Meurig of Senghenydd, Iorwerth ab Owain of Caerleon and Seisyll ap Dyfnwal of Gwent Uwch-Coed.[15] Mapping the territories of these princes would suggest plenty of opposition.[16]

Clearly the Gloucester conference of 1175 saw Henry and Rhys publicly co-operating to preserve the peace, and there is an intriguing parallel between that and the 1175 treaty of Windsor with the king of Connacht.[17] There were further conferences between Henry II and the Welsh, headed by Rhys ap Gruffydd, in 1177 and, on the whole, a sort of peace survived until 1183. At any rate there was no major royal invasion of Wales until John took a large army to the relief of Carmarthen in the autumn of 1189. The fact that the *Brut* becomes laconic in the extreme for the years from 1177 to 1186 – it does not even mention the 'serious revolt in western Glamorgan in 1183–4' – helps to create an impression of relative peace. Of course, given the structure of Welsh politics, even a 'relative peace', it has been powerfully argued, was a considerable achievement. The more fragile the concordat of 1171–72, the more it was threatened by the 'ambitions of Marcher lords and the impetuosity of Welsh princelings', the more

---

[12] *Brut*, s.a. 1173.

[13] In his *Journey through Wales* i 5, *Giraldi Opera*, vi 60.

[14] *Brut*, s.a. 1172.

[15] *Brut*, s.a. 1175. Seisyll ap Dyfnwal had been one of the princes whom the *Brut* reports as 'seized through treachery by the king's men' in 1172.

[16] However the opposition may have been confined to the south. Howden, *Gesta Regis*, i 51 names David and Evayn as two Welsh kings on Henry's side in 1173, probably Dafydd of Gwynedd and Owain Cyfeiliog of Powys. See Lloyd, *History of Wales*, 551–53 for these identifications.

[17] Davies, *Conquest*, 291.

admirable the 'personal trust' between Henry II and the Lord Rhys on which the peace is said to be based.[18]

But was Henry II any more to be trusted in 1175 than in 1172? Immediately after the Gloucester conference the massacre at Abergavenny – the treacherous killing of Seisyll ap Dyfnwal, his wife and seven year-old son as well as 'many of the chieftains of Gwent' – led the author of the *Brut* to comment that 'none of the Welsh dared place their trust in the French'.[19] The allusiveness of the post-1176 *Brut* means for details of the revenge taken by the men of Gwent in 1182 we are dependent on the accounts given by Gerald and Roger of Howden.[20] There is no evidence that Rhys was involved in 1182.[21] Of course it is possible to interpret the killings of 1175 and 1182 as occurring despite the best efforts of Henry II and Rhys. Certainly, in another incident, Henry punished those who killed Cadwallon ap Madog of Maelienydd in 1179, regarding it, according to Diceto, as an offence against his honour, since Cadwallon had been ambushed while under the king's safe-conduct.[22] Similarly, according to Gerald in the first recension (c.1191) of his *Journey through Wales*, William de Briouze, lord of Abergavenny, was punished for his involvement in the 1175 masacre by being deprived of an office he had been expecting. Some punishment! Indeed if that was all the punishment he received, it would not be surprising if there had been rumours that the political will behind the massacre was the king himself. By the time of the later recensions of his *Journey*, Gerald makes no bones about it. In his view Briouze was merely *executionis non impeditor*. He pins the blame firstly on Ranulf Poer, sheriff of Hereford, *machinator* (and hence killed by the men of Gwent in 1182) and secondly on Henry II, *auctor*. In the first recension he was less emphatic, but none the less clear that Henry II was involved.[23] Gerald's judgements are often, of course, highly prejudiced, and may well have been in this case too.[24] Even so we should at least bear in mind that he was in a remarkably good position to have heard many different accounts of what happened at Abergavenny. Not only because of his own Welsh and English family connections and his later (c.1184) recruitment to the royal court, but also because he was appointed archdeacon of Brecon in about 1175, i.e. just at the time of the massacre – and William de Briouze was lord of Brecon as well as of Abergavenny.

If there is a question mark against Henry II, there is also one against Rhys's commitment to peace after 1175. Much turns on the extent of his involvement

[18] Davies, *Conquest*, 222, 292.
[19] *Brut*, s.a. 175.
[20] *Giraldi Opera*, vi 51–52 (*Journey through Wales*, i 4); Howden, *Gesta Regis*, i 288–89.
[21] Though J. H. Round thought there was, *Pipe Roll 30 Henry II* (London 1912), xxvii.
[22] W. Stubbs (ed.), *Radulfi de Diceto Opera Historica* (2 vols, RS, London 1876), i 437–38. Diceto took a very English and hostile view of Cadwallon's career and understood the motives of those who killed him.
[23] *Giraldi Opera*, vi 49–53.
[24] For an analysis of Gerald on Henry II see above all Robert Bartlett, *Gerald of Wales 1146–1223* (Oxford 1982), 58–93.

in the hostilities of 1183–84, which are reported by the Margam Annals, though wrongly dated there, as Round showed, to 1185. Evidence from the Pipe Roll for 1183–84 and the Margam Annals shows that five castles, Kenfig, Cardiff, Newcastle, Newport and Neath, were attacked and a sixth, Carmarthen, was put into a state of readiness.[25] This was a serious revolt, but who was behind it? Morgan ap Caradog of Glamorgan or his uncle, the Lord Rhys? Round took it for granted that it was that 'restless prince, Rhys ap Griffin'. For J. B. Smith it was Morgan ap Caradog. For him, Rhys though also at war, was a background figure.[26] However Round was surely right to associate these events with Howden's report on Henry II's return to England after a two year absence. According to Howden, 'Henry gathered the army of England to advance into Wales to attack Rhys and his accomplices who in the last two years had ravaged the king's land and killed his men. In fear and under safe-conduct Rhys came to Henry at Worcester and swore . . . to return the lands and castles which he had taken by force of arms while the king was away.'[27] Evidently Roger of Howden, and hence presumably the English court, thought Rhys was the real leader of this Welsh offensive.

If Rhys had been a force for restraint for the last twelve years, why did he now change tack? Perhaps because he felt that the English crown was getting uncomfortably close to Deheubarth and realised that he had an opportunity to do something about it at once. As J. B. Smith observed, the signal for this revolt was probably given by the death of the lord of Glamorgan, Earl William of Gloucester, on 23 November 1183. Traditionally war broke out on the death of a powerful ruler – as had happened in 1135 and was to happen again in 1189. A hundred years later a Neath author was to complain that the value of his house's estates in Gower was diminished by the Welsh habit of ravaging whenever a lord of Gower died.[28] But in 1183 there may have been rather more to it than this. The heiress to the earldom of Gloucester was betrothed to the king's son John, still young enough to be a pliant tool of his father's will. From 1183 Glamorgan was retained in king's hands.[29] In addition it may already have been known that the crown was about to acquire the lordship of Gower. Although this may not

[25] H. R. Luard (ed.), *Annales Monastici* (5 vols, RS, London 1864–69), i 17–18; *Pipe Roll 30 Henry II*, 110–11. Perhaps it was during the assault on one of these castles that Cadwallon ap Caradog was killed 'in the presence of so many of his own and his brothers' troops', *Giraldi Opera*, vi 69.

[26] *Pipe Roll 30 Henry II*, xxvii; J. Beverley Smith, 'The kingdom of Morgannwg and the Norman Conquest of Glamorgan' in *Glamorgan County History* vol. 3, ed. T. B. Pugh (Cardiff 1971), 37–38.

[27] *Gesta Regis*, i 314. Lloyd read Howden differently. For him at Worcester Rhys 'promised the fullest amends for all the misdeeds of his underlings', *History of Wales*, 569.

[28] 'in permutatione dominorum multototiens vastata fuit a Walensibus' in F. R. Lewis, 'A History of the Lordship of Gower from the Missing Cartulary of Neath Abbey', *Bulletin of the Board of Celtic Studies* 9 (1938), 149–54: 153. I owe this reference to the kindness of Rees Davies.

[29] Smith, 'Glamorgan', 39.

have happened until after the death of the earl of Warwick (November 1184), the extravagant and impecunious earl had apparently already sold Gower to the king in order to meeet his debts.[30] In other words by late 1183 it may have been clear that royal power in south Wales was increasing. Henry's overlordship was one thing, but direct crown rule in Gower and in Glamorgan, above all western Glamorgan, was another. It may be worth noting that the most impressive feature of the Welsh revolt, in the eyes of the Margam Annalist, was their employment of a siege engine at Neath, the westernmost of the Glamorgan castles, and the one which would have been of most concern to a ruler of Deheubarth who longed to recover control of the commotes of Cydweli and Gower.[31] But if the events of 1183 caused concern, they also created an opportunity. Once again Henry II's troubles with his sons had come to a head and in consequence he was detained on the continent by the affairs of Aquitaine and conflicts between Richard, John and Geoffrey. However in the event the king's return and muster of an army of invasion was enough to bring Rhys to heel at Worcester in July 1184. The events of 1183–84 suggest that any trust there may have been between Henry II and the Lord Rhys was now dead.[32] Hence the increased expenditure on royal castles in South Wales.[33] Hence too, it may be, Henry's recruitment of Gerald de Barri as an advisor on Welsh affairs from c.1184 and Gerald's claim that he 'single-handedly, by his own labour and diligence . . . turned aside not a few of Rhys' great armies from the king's land, which the prince was preparing to invade'.[34] Perhaps the sack of Tenby by Maelgwyn ap Rhys in 1187 was carried out against his father's will – though there is no evidence either way – but it evidently won the admiration of the author of the *Brut* and can have done nothing to allay suspicion.

The tone in which the *Brut* reports Richard's accession does not immediately suggest that the character of the new king aroused hostility. 'Henry died. And after him Richard his son was crowned king – the best and doughtiest knight.' Perhaps admiration for a crusader king is not surprising in the light of the concern for Jerusalem indicated by the *Brut* author's entries for 1185 and 1188.[35] But Henry's death was patently regarded as an opportunity. As Huw Pryce put it, 'On hearing of Henry II's death, the Lord Rhys launched a series of devastating and widespread attacks on Anglo-Norman strongholds in south Wales.'[36] Gerald describes the devastation of Pembroke and Rhos, the siege of Carmarthen and the capture of Laugharne and Llanstephan.[37] Even more than

[30] Lewis, 'A History of the Lordship', 150–51.
[31] Davies, *Conquest*, 218.
[32] Especially in the light of Rhys's failure to produce the hostages required in 1184, *Gesta Regis*, i 317; *Chronica*, ii 290.
[33] M. T. Flanagan, *Irish Society, Anglo-Norman Settlers, Angevin Kingship* (Oxford 1989), 129 n. 69.
[34] *Giraldi Opera*, i 60. As Gerald, in his autobiography (1208 or later), remembers it, the king whose lands he saved was Henry II.
[35] *Brut*, s.a. 1185, 1187, 1188, 1189.
[36] Pryce, 'Gerald's Journey', 31.
[37] *Giraldi Opera*, vi 80; and see i 24 for the attack on the Flemings of Rhos. J. Williams ab

Neath, these castles were strategically vital to an ambitious ruler of Deheubarth, enabling him to cut the land route between south-west Wales and the Marcher lordships further east. This was an area which, in Rees Davies's words, 'the princes of Deheubarth longed to recover'.[38] Unlike Rhys, however, Richard I seems to have been keen to preserve peace. According to Gerald, no sooner was Henry dead than Richard, aware of what the Welsh reaction to the news of his father's death might be, on the advice of Baldwin of Canterbury, sent Gerald de Barri to preserve the peace: 'missus est ab eo, consilio Cantuariensis archiepiscopi, ad servandum pacem in Walliae finibus propter regum mutationem Giraldus archidiaconus cum literis multis'. After various mishaps in Normandy and Ponthieu, Gerald reached London, saw the justiciar and then immediately hurried on to Wales where he gave Count Richard's letters to those to whom they were sent, and so helped to restore peace to a land whch had been greatly disturbed as a consequence of the king's death (*patriam prae morte regis valde turbatam*).[39]

Whether Gerald was as successful as he claims is doubtful. According to Gervase of Canterbury, who had strong Canterbury reasons for watching the new king's movements and policies very closely, when Richard reached Winchester (14 August 1189), he was informed that the Welsh had launched raids into England. His first thought was to deal with this at once, but he was persuaded by his mother to proceed with his coronation, which took place on 3 September.[40] From 11 to 18 September he then held a great council at Geddington and nearby Pipewell Abbey. It was there that he gave an important military command to John, whom he had recently created lord of Glamorgan by marrying him to Hawise of Gloucester on 29 August.[41] John was to take a large army against Rhys ap Gruffydd for, in Howden's words, 'the king of Southwales had broken the peace and refused to obey his commands'.[42] Howden's next sentence is worth quoting in full. 'Caeteri vero reges Wallorum ad eum venerunt apud Wirecestre, et foedus pacis cum eo inierunt.' Stubbs understood 'him' to be John, and it has been understood in that sense ever since.[43] But it is,

---

Ithel (ed.), *Annales Cambriae* (RS, London 1860), 57 gives further details, including the ravaging of Gower and the destruction of the castle of Carnwyllion.

[38] Davies, *Conquest*, 218 and the map on 220.

[39] *Giraldi Opera*, i 80–81, 84.

[40] W. Stubbs (ed.), *The Historical Works of Gervase of Canterbury* (2 vols, RS, London 1879–80), i 457.

[41] Moreover one of Richard's very first acts had had important implications for Welsh politics: the grant of the marriage of Strongbow's daughter (and hence the lordship of Striguil and a claim to Pembroke) to William Marshal. On the lordship of Pembroke in this period, Flanagan, *Irish Society*, 135.

[42] *Gesta Regis*, ii 87–88. According to the *Annales Cambriae*, 57, John took with him *exercitus totius Angliae*. The scutage for the army of Wales left a very considerable imprint on Exchequer records, see in particular D. M. Stenton (ed.), *The Great Roll of the Pipe for the second year of the reign of King Richard I* (London 1925), as well as those for subsequent years.

[43] E.g. Lloyd, *History of Wales*, 575; K. Norgate, *John Lackland* (London 1902), 25; J. T. Appleby, *England without Richard* (London 1965), 24.

I suggest, much more likely that the 'him' was Richard. From Geddington the court moved to Warwick (19–20 September), then to Feckenham on 22 and 23 September and was back at Warwick on 28 September.[44] The royal manor of Feckenham was the headquarters of the Forest of Feckenham, the western boundary of which came 'to the very walls of Worcester'.[45] It cannot be proved that Richard visited Worcester, but given that Feckenham is only some 10 miles away, and given the existence of gaps in his known itinerary, e.g. 24–26 September, it is hard to believe that on one (or more) of those days he did not travel the extra few miles. Although conceivably John might also have passed through Worcester, he was probably travelling fast to join up with an army mustered to march to the relief of Carmarthen.[46] In any case John's absence from the royal court between 19 September and 11 November means that it is not possible to show that he was even anywhere near Worcester in the critical weeks.[47] All in all it seems most likely that while Richard sent one brother to Rhys and would soon send another, Geoffrey, to bring the king of Scotland to his court (where by the Quitclaim of Canterbury he would free the Scots from the terms of the Treaty of Falaise, thus winning their friendship and admiration), he himself went to Worcester where he met the other kings of Wales in late September.[48] It was presumably here that he received their promise not to attack England while he was on crusade.[49]

Nothing about Richard's conduct of policy in 1189 suggests that this was a king who would needlessly insult a man such as the Lord Rhys. Doubtless Rhys was insulted by Richard's refusal to meet him, but it is plain that he had not waited to be insulted before going on to the attack. More likely Richard refused to meet Rhys when John brought him to Oxford in October, because he already knew the terms of the peace which John had made with Rhys and had no

[44] L. Landon, *The Itinerary of King Richard I* (Pipe Roll Society, London 1935), nos. 57–64. On 27 September Richard was at 'Browd'.

[45] R. H. Hilton, *A Medieval Society. The West Midlands at the End of the Thirteenth Century* (London 1966), 15, 242.

[46] Troops and military supplies were being assembled at Gloucester, Stenton, *Great Roll of the Pipe*, 4, 53. See also J. Hunter (ed.), *The Great Roll of the Pipe for the first year of the reign of Richard I* (London 1844), 130, 163. On William Marshal as sheriff of Gloucester and lord of Striguil see D. Crouch, *William Marshal* (London 1990), 62–64.

[47] Landon, *Itinerary*, nos. 55, 120. Similarly missing from the witness lists to Richard's charters during these weeks is William fitz Audelin – one of those quit of paying scutage on the grounds that they served with the army in Wales. On his earlier career see Flanagan, *Irish Society*, 135, 285–304.

[48] Who these other Welsh kings were is not known. Dafydd of Gwynedd was very likely one of them since he was, after a fashion, Richard's uncle. The presence of the bishops of Bangor and St Asaph at the coronation indicates men going to and fro between the royal court and Wales, especially since there is no evidence that they, unlike the bishop of St David's and the Irish bishops who attended Richard's coronation, also stayed on for the council of Pipewell, *Gesta Regis*, ii 85; Landon, *Itinerary*, nos. 41, 54.

[49] J. T. Appleby (ed.), *The Chronicle of Richard of Devizes* (London 1963), 7.

intention of ratifying them.[50] It is certainly possible that Howden meant his reference to Henry's custom of meeting Rhys as an implicit criticism of Richard, as modern historians assume; but it is at least worth considering the possibility that he intended the opposite – a criticism of Henry II. In the light of what had happened in 1184, Howden may have come to feel that meetings with Rhys were a waste of time.[51] Contemporary allusions to Henry II's customary conduct are often critical in tone.[52] In any case whatever Richard's Welsh policy was in the autumn of 1189, it seems likely that one of the experts whose views he consulted before refusing to see Rhys was none other than Rhys' own kinsman, Gerald de Barri. Before he left England (December 1189), Richard attached Gerald to the staff of William Longchamp and presumably approved the release from his crusading vows which he obtained from the papal legate. Soon Longchamp was to offer him the bishopric of Bangor.[53] As Huw Pryce notes, 'Gerald's efforts appear to have been appreciated.'[54]

The Welsh princes kept the promises they had made in 1189.[55] In 1193, when John tried to take the throne while Richard was a prisoner in Germany, he obtained support neither from the king of Scotland nor from any Welsh prince.[56] Perhaps this was because Richard was a crusader – though so far as John, Philip Augustus and Leopold of Austria were concerned, that seems to have made no difference. Nor, of course, did the fact that John took the cross in 1215 help him much, if at all. It may well be that family feuding inhibited the rulers of Deheubarth and Gwynedd from intervening effectively in England in 1193–94, but it seems unlikely that all the princes of Wales were so incapacitated. Here again Gerald may have performed a useful service, for he informs us that at this time he was sent into Wales by the queen and by Walter of Coutances.[57] At any

[50] *Annales Cambriae*, 57 for the *pax privata* between Rhys and John. See Norgate, *Lackland*, 25–26.

[51] Above n. 34. In any case Howden was not much interested in the Welsh whom he looked upon as poor and savage, *Gesta Regis*, i 90–91, ii 46. He gave noticeably more attention to Irish as well as to Scottish affairs. See below pp. 81–6.

[52] See for example *Gesta Regis*, i 346; Gervase, *Historical Works*, i 382; and for general commentary J. Gillingham, 'Conquering Kings: contemporary perceptions of Henry II and Richard I' in T. Reuter (ed.), *Warriors and Churchmen in the High Middle Ages. Essays presented to Karl Leyser* (London 1992), 163–78.

[53] *Giraldi Opera*, i 84–85.

[54] Pryce, 'Gerald's Journey', 31.

[55] Not Rhys, of course, because he had made no promise. Obviously the result of this was that Rhys continued his war, capturing St Clear's at Christmas 1189, building Kidwelly castle, capturing Nevern in 1191, Lawhaden in 1192, and besieging Swansea. The capture of Wiston in 1193 by his son Hywel Sais looks to be the continuation of a campaign concentrating on Dyfed, as far from England as it is possible to get.

[56] In 1141 Welsh kings had even gone as far east as Lincoln to lend crucial military support to an earl of Gloucester; not in 1193 when it was John who held the earldom. On the Welsh at the battle of Lincoln see pp. 36, 98.

[57] *Giraldi Opera*, i 295–96. This marked the end of Gerald's career as a royal clerk. The rapidity and apparent enthusiasm with which he switched sides – his Welsh *levitas*? – in the

rate the loyalty and restraint shown by England's 'Celtic' neighbours in 1193 stands in marked contrast to those other moments – 1135–54, 1173–74, 1215–16 – when the king of England was in trouble and when the Welsh, Scots and, in 1173–74 the Irish too, took full advantage of it.[58]

'These two nations, the Welsh and Irish, constantly feed on the hope of recovering all the lands which the English have taken from them.' So wrote Gerald de Barri, recounting a teasing conversation between him and Rhys ap Gruffudd in a Hereford garden in the 1180s – indeed he attributed the thought, by implication at least, to Rhys himself.[59] But modern opinion is that whatever other Welsh or Irish leaders may have fed on, Rhys ap Gruffudd came to trust Henry II and so to renounce that hope during Henry's lifetime. Here I have argued that in fact Rhys continued to hope and to take whatever chances came along, in 1183–84 as well as in the summer of 1189. Moreover the evidence that he launched his attacks in 1189 as soon as he heard that Henry was dead is so overwhelming that it would be hard to see why historians came to associate the end of peace with Richard's refusal to see him in October, were it not for the fact that it fitted the entrenched belief that Richard was indifferent to the politics of England, let alone to the politics of England's 'Celtic' frontiers.[60] Only this assumption can explain Stubbs' failure to consider the possibility that it was Richard, not John, who met Welsh kings at Worcester in 1189. Only this same assumption can explain why we have all unthinkingly followed Stubbs in this. This, of course, merely confirms me in my view that the great weakness of my biography of Richard I is that there are many instances of that king's remarkable competence as a ruler to which I failed to draw attention.[61]

faction fighting at the English court from 1191 to 1193 must have raised doubts about his reliability, and it may have been this (about which he is noticeably silent) as much as the Welsh family connexions (about which he protests so much) which ended his career – none the less he continued to be paid a substantial retainer until early in John's reign, Bartlett, *Gerald*, 19, 65.

[58] Gillingham, 'Foundations', below, pp. 107–8.

[59] *Giraldi Opera*, i 60.

[60] 'Richard's devotion to the crusade and to other interests remote from his duties as an English king had the same practical effect as the nerveless and vacillating rule of Stephen', Lloyd, *History of Wales*, 573.

[61] J. Gillingham, *Richard the Lionheart* (2nd edn, London 1989). Lewis Warren was the first to point out to me that my concentration on the Plantagenet lands in France had led me to neglect Richard's dealings with the Irish, Scots and Welsh. He was right. Regrettably the book contains not a single reference to Irish or Welsh rulers, and too few to William of Scotland. I have now tried to remedy this, see *Richard I* (New Haven and London, 1999).

5

The Travels of Roger of Howden
and his Views of the Irish, Scots and Welsh

Writing in what Antonia Gransden called 'a golden age of historiography in England', Roger of Howden was, in Sir Richard Southern's judgement, 'the best historian of the English crown in the twelfth century'.[1] When I began work on this paper my intention was to consider what Roger of Howden, an English historian writing from near the centre of English government, had to say about the Irish, Scots and Welsh, and to think about what he did not say as much as about what he did say. He did not, for example, call them 'barbarians' as contemporaries such as Ralph of Diceto, Gerald de Barri and William of Newburgh did.[2] Why not? Was it because the word 'barbarian' was too highly-charged for a dull and matter of fact historian? After all, in the view of his editor, William Stubbs, what Howden gives us is 'a passionless, colourless narrative'.[3] As David Corner observed, 'It has often been asserted that Roger of Howden's historical writings lack a personal touch. It is generally held that the works lack interest because they rarely display anything more than the slightest prejudice.'[4] Or was it because he saw the British Isles in a much wider context than other English historians did? After all, he was the most widely travelled of all medieval English historians. He used the word 'barbarian' very rarely, once when following the terminology of Emperor Manuel's letter explaining the defeat at Myriocephalon in 1176, and a second time, probably again following the language of a source, when he noted that Robert Guiscard received a papal license to subdue 'barbarous nations'.[5] In the first case it refers to Turks; in the second, it appears to refer to Greeks as much as to Muslims. His own preferred

---

[1] A. Gransden, *Historical Writing in England c.550 to c.1307*, London 1974, 219; R. W. Southern, 'England's First Entry into Europe' in his *Medieval Humanism and other Studies*, Oxford 1970, 150.

[2] See R. Bartlett, *Gerald of Wales 1146–1223*, Oxford 1982, 158–210; also below, pp. 82, 93.

[3] *Chronica Rogeri de Hovedene*, ed. W. Stubbs, 4 vols., RS 1868–71, i.lxix; from now on cited as *Howden.*

[4] D. Corner, 'The *Gesta Regis Henrici Secundi* and *Chronica* of Roger, Parson of Howden', *BIHR* lvi, 1983, 137.

[5] *Gesta Regis Henrici Secundi Benedicti Abbatis. The Chronicle of the Reigns of Henry II and Richard I*, ed. W. Stubbs, 2 vols., RS 1867 (from now on cited as *Gesta Regis Henrici*), i.129, ii.200, and see *Howden*, ii.102–4 for the full text of Manuel's letter.

words for Muslims were 'pagans' or 'Saracens'. When he wrote 'Barbariem' he meant specifically the Barbary Coast rather than, as William of Malmesbury had when writing about Wales, a barbarous region.[6]

In trying to answer such questions it soon became clear that while for students of later twelfth-century Ireland and Scotland, there is no English historian more important than Roger of Howden, this certainly does not apply to Wales, about which he had very little to say. While it might seem natural that a northerner, as Howden certainly was, would write more about Scotland than Wales, it was not immediately evident why he would write more about Ireland than Wales. What follows is, in all essentials, a continuation of the approach to Howden pioneered by David Corner. As he pointed out, 'variations in structure, content and tone can only be understood through an appreciation of the particular ways in which specific pieces of information were obtained'.[7] As I tried to work out how Roger obtained his information on Ireland, Scotland and Wales, I found I was increasingly drawn into a reconstruction of his career, his journeys and his contacts. In the limited space available this means that his views of the Irish, Scots and Welsh, though not disregarded, have taken second place. Yet another Englishman has ended up by relegating the Celtic lands to the fringe of his analysis.

It may be useful to start by sketching what I take to be the present view of Howden's historical work and career. It is now accepted that he wrote the *Gesta Regis Henrici et Ricardi*[8] as well as the *Chronica* which has always gone under his name. He originally wrote in annals, from Christmas to Christmas, entering information as it came to him, and the bulk of the *Gesta* takes this form, though when the work was put into its present form (MS BL Cotton Vitellius E. xvii) in 1192–3, he took the opportunity to include short histories of some other countries, Byzantium, the kingdom of Jerusalem and Norway, in a manner which broke though the annalistic format. The *Gesta* begins at Christmas 1169 (the beginning of the year 1170) and he probably made notes from then on, though his account of Becket's murder suggests that the narrative was not composed until after September 1172.[9] It looks as though there was a pause in the composition in 1177. One manuscript (MS BL Cotton Julius A.xi) only goes as far as that, and there is evidence in the Barnwell Chronicle that this version circulated separately.[10]

In 1192–3 he began the work of extending, revising and continuing the *Gesta*, turning it into a new work, the *Chronica*.[11] He provided a long prelude, beginning

---

[6] *Gesta Regis Henrici*, ii.199; for William of Malmesbury's usage see above, p. 27.

[7] Corner, 'The *Gesta Regis*', 144.

[8] The title by which it is generally known is based on a title in MS BL Cotton Julius A.xi. Howden himself referred to his work, or at any rate to its main thread, as *historia*, *Gesta regis Henrici*, i.45, 331.

[9] *Gesta Regis Henrici*, i.xlv.

[10] *Gesta Regis Henrici*, i.xxiv–xxv.

[11] The first folio of the earliest manuscript (BL Royal MS 14.C.2 – Stubbs's A) of the first

at 732. For the years up to 1148 this was taken almost – but not quite – verbatim from a north country compilation known as the *Historia post obitum Bedae*. Then, for the gap between 1148 and 1170, he used the Melrose Chronicle – though seemingly much more sporadically and freely than he had used the northern *Historia*.[12] Finally he continued his contemporary history until his own death, late in 1201 or in 1202. In Howden's *Chronica*, wrote Stubbs, 'we have the full harvest of the labours of the Northumbrian historians'.[13] Stubbs saw him as the historian who provided 'the great store of facts' for the reigns of Henry II and Richard; hence his prefaces to six Rolls Series volumes are mostly about those 'facts' and very little about Howden's outlook or method of working. Until recently historians mostly followed in Stubbs' footsteps. Indeed the more twentieth-century historians valued record evidence above chronicle evidence, the more they have appreciated Howden's habit of including the texts of many documents, a high proportion of which survive only thanks to Howden. Sir James Holt emphasised how much our knowledge of the assizes of Henry II owes to this practice.[14] Were it not for Howden, we would not possess the text of the 1175 Treaty of Windsor between Henry II and Rory O'Connor, the earliest extant treaty between English and Irish kings. Were it not for Howden, we would not have the texts of a dozen papal letters relating to the Scottish church between 1180 and 1192.[15] But the positivist approach to Howden, regarding him as a reliable repository of facts and documents, left him looking worthy but dull; in consequence his works were for long 'neglected as sources for the study of the processes involved in writing medieval chronicles'.[16]

Roger was a royal clerk, first clearly visible as such when, as he himself reported, he went on a diplomatic mission to the ruler of Galloway in late 1174.[17] By that time, probably earlier in the year and in succession to his father, he had acquired Howden and the 'princely' revenues which made this parsonage 'an especially rich prize'.[18] In 1175 he was entrusted with the task of inviting vacant monasteries to send deputations of monks to court so that new abbots could be elected.[19] Although this was the last occasion on which Roger

---

part of the *Chronica* is missing so the conventional title *Chronica magistri Rogeri de Hovedene* comes, more or less, from MS BL Arundel 69 (Stubbs's B). If it was an exact copy of A (*Howden*, i.lxxvii–lxxx), then the title may be Howden's own.

[12] I am not persuaded by the suggestion that he used a non-Melrose 'Scottish source' as argued in A. O. and M. O. Anderson, *The Melrose Chronicle*, London 1936, xii–xiv.

[13] *Howden*, i.xiii.

[14] J. C. Holt, 'The Assizes of Henry II: the Texts' in eds. D. A. Bullough and R. L. Storey, *The Study of Medieval Records*, Oxford 1971, 86.

[15] R. Somerville, *Scotia Pontificia*, Oxford 1982, nos. 92, 100, 101, 110, 141, 142, 150, 151, 152, 153 and perhaps 156 (*Cum universi Christi*). Also Clement III's letter to Henry II about St Andrews, *Gesta Regis Henrici*, ii.57.

[16] Corner, 'The *Gesta Regis*', 144.

[17] *Gesta Regis Henrici*, i.80. However it is likely that, as Stubbs suggested, his royal service began when the *Gesta* began, i.e. Christmas 1169, *Howden*, i.lxvi.

[18] F. Barlow, 'Roger of Howden', *EHR* 65, 1950, 352–60.

[19] *Gesta Regis Henrici*, i.91–2.

mentioned himself by name in his historical writing, it was certainly not the last time he acted as a royal servant. In the *Gesta* he gave the text of the 1184 Assize of Woodstock and and said that in each circuit the king appointed two clerks and two knights as justices but he named none of them.[20] It is only from pipe roll evidence that we know that he became a justice of the forest.[21] In other words he was capable of referring to his own activites without mentioning himself by name – a matter of critical importance for this paper.

He went on the Third Crusade – the key discovery which first showed that Howden and the author of the *Gesta* were one and the same.[22] He joined Richard I at Marseilles in August 1190, leaving him at Acre on 25 August 1191 in order to return to France in the company of Philip Augustus. He saw Philip celebrate Christmas 1191 at Fontainebleau, 'impudently boasting that he was going to lay waste the lands of the king of England'.[23] Roger then entered – or perhaps re-entered – the *familia* of Hugh du Puiset and remained in the bishop of Durham's service until the bishop died at Howden on 3 March 1195. David Corner demonstrated that after 1191 Roger occasionally attended the king's court for brief periods, for example 25 March to 3 May 1194 and 13 to 17 June 1194, but that for most of the time he was elsewhere. He contrasted the annals for 1173 and 1174 with those for 1195 and 1196, pointing out that whereas in the former 'there is no document specifically concerning Yorkshire affairs', in the latter 'every document included would have been available in the parson's home county'. He also showed that at the end of his life Howden was getting information from the new bishop of Durham, Philip of Poitou, and from a Yorkshire landowner, Robert of Thornham. Hence the now prevailing view that after Roger returned from crusade 'his parish rather than the court was his base'.[24]

In this paper I shall suggest that the contrast between the 'court diary' – as it is sometimes termed – of Howden Part I and the diary of a country parson of Howden Part II is not as great as is sometimes thought, and that to say that 'he retired to Howden', as one historian has done, is much too simple.[25] Why if he had retired to his Yorkshire parsonage in 1192, does his chronicle for 1197 contain virtually nothing on English matters, and only one sentence about the north of England?[26] The answer, I suspect, is because in 1197 he was on his travels yet again, that the year saw one or more of his visits to the papal curia. His history, I shall argue, was never so much a court diary as a journal of his

[20] *Gesta Regis Henrici*, i.323–4.
[21] *PR 31 Henry II*, 3, 186. He last served as a justice of the forest in 1189–90.
[22] D. M. Stenton, 'Roger of Howden and Benedict', *EHR* 68, 1953, 574–82.
[23] *Gesta Regis Henrici*, ii.235.
[24] Corner, 'The *Gesta Regis*', 131, 143–4; D. Corner, 'The earliest surviving manuscripts of Roger of Howden's *Chronica*', *EHR* 98, 1983, 309–10.
[25] J. Gillingham, 'The unromantic death of Richard I', *Speculum* 54, 1979, 24; reprinted in J. Gillingham, *Richard Coeur de Lion*, London 1994, 161.
[26] *Chronica*, iv.17–34. The one sentence, on p. 17, could be regarded as news from court.

own travels. It followed the court when he followed the court, but when he was away from court – albeit often in the king's service – then it reflected his own journeys. This explains not only what he wrote but also what he didn't write. Consider his account of the great war of 1173–4. While Henry II stayed on the continent during the first half of 1174, Howden provided a detailed narrative of the Scottish invasion and of rebel activity in the north of England, but was very brief and vague about what the king was doing. By contrast his account of military activity in 1173 had focussed on events such as the sieges of Verneuil and Dol in which Henry himself had been involved; indeed from Roger we would not even know that William the Lion invaded the north in 1173 as well as in 1174.[27] During the months of war in 1173 Howden was at court; during the first half of 1174 he wasn't, he was in England. His language reflects this. In 1173 he writes of people 'coming' to Normandy and 'crossing' to England. In 1174 he writes of them 'coming' to England.[28]

Two articles published in the early 1980s took issue with Stubbs's view that Howden rarely allowed the reader to catch a glimpse of his personal character or sympathies.[29] I suggested that he was a committed crusader and that this contributed to his increasingly critical view of Henry II.[30] David Corner showed that in the early 1190s he sympathised with Hugh du Puiset against both William Longchamp and Geoffey of York.[31] Certainly he was far from passionless. He was often heated on subject of Archbishop Geoffrey of York's quarrels with his dean and chapter. He was vitriolic about the MacWilliams and their bids for the Scottish throne.[32] He consistently took a hostile view of Philip Augustus, seeing him as a tyrannical ruler.[33] He described a papal legate, Hugo Pierleone, as a limb of Satan, a shepherd who on seeing the wolf coming deserted his flock.[34]

So how did the notion that he was generally dull and neutral come about? Partly because he included the full texts of so many official documents – even to an extent that he himself thought a bit much. But perhaps primarily because he was undeniably neutral between Becket and Henry II and since the *Gesta*'s first year ran from Christmas 1169 to Christmas 1170, anyone who reads Howden begins with the Becket dispute and hence obtains a powerful first impression of his even-handedness. For him, as Barlow wrote, 'although Thomas Becket had been a martyr, Henry II was king'.[35] True, but there was probably more to it than

---

[27] *Gesta Regis Henrici*, i.45–71.
[28] *Gesta Regis Henrici*, i.49, 60, 66, 68.
[29] Though at least twice he used the first person singular, once to condemn, once to express scepticism, *Gesta Regis Henrici*, i.124, ii.196.
[30] J. Gillingham, 'Roger of Howden on Crusade' in ed. D. O. Morgan, *Medieval Historical Writing in the Christian and Islamic Worlds*, School of Oriental and African Studies 1982; reprinted in *Richard Coeur de Lion*, 141–53, esp. 151–2.
[31] Corner, 'The *Gesta Regis*', 137–8.
[32] *Gesta Regis Henrici*, ii.7–9.
[33] *Gesta Regis Henrici*, i.244, ii.229.
[34] *Gesta Regis Henrici*, i.105.
[35] Barlow, 'Roger of Howden', 360.

this. In the early 1170s Howden was, I suggest, a protégé not of Hugh du Puiset but of none other than the archbishop of York, Roger of Pont l'Evêque, the chief enemy of the Becket group. His history was much more concerned with the church of York than with the church of Durham. In the fighting of 1174 he noted the deeds of the army of Yorkshire, one of whose commanders was the archbishop's constable, Ralph de Tilly.[36] In the quarrels of 1174–5 between York and Canterbury he consistently presented events from York's point of view, and criticised Archbishop Richard of Canterbury for oppressing monasteries and bribing the papal legate.[37] According to Roger, Archbishop Richard died of a stress-related disease, the stress brought on by a vision in which God appeared to him, saying 'You have wasted the goods of my church, now I shall waste you.'[38] In the 1170s he highlighted York's claims over the Scottish church.[39] If Howden was a member, as Stubbs suggested, of the *familia* of Hugh du Puiset, York's suffragan, might this be enough to explain his pro-York stance? But was he? It has been suggested that it was with Hugh's support that Roger got his parsonage; after all, the manor of Howden belonged to the bishop of Durham and the church to the prior and convent.[40] Moreover Corner has shown that from 1189 to 1195 there was a close relationship between Bishop Hugh and Roger's history.[41] However Corner was not concerned with the 1170s and 1180s, and had no need to address the question of how Roger got his parsonage.

The certificate by which Archbishop Roger instituted Roger as parson of Howden, after the resignation of Robert, was dated by Clay to 1167–74 on the basis of the group of York clerics in the witness list.[42] Now in a letter written from Anagni on 19 July (and hence datable to 1173 or 1174 or 1176), Alexander III prohibited the prior and convent of Durham from granting the church of Howden 'to anyone at the behest of any lay power and in particular not to Roger son of the Robert who now holds it'.[43] Combining these two documents it seems that Roger was instituted as parson in 1173–4 and that – as was natural given the church's importance and wealth – lay power was at work. But this effectively rules out Bishop Hugh having any influence. As Scammell noted, this was 'the lowest ebb of Puiset's political fortunes', when he was deeply

---

[36]   *Gesta Regis Henrici*, i.65, 68–9.
[37]   *Gesta Regis Henrici*, i.80–1, 89–90, 104–5, 112–14.
[38]   *Gesta Regis Henrici*, i.311.
[39]   *Gesta Regis Henrici*, i.111, 117, 166–7.
[40]   *Gesta Regis Henrici*, i.liv; Barlow, 'Roger of Howden', 353, 359.
[41]   Corner, 'The *Gesta Regis*', 134–44, esp. 139.
[42]   W. Farrer, *Early Yorkshire Charters*, ii.307 no. 978 dated by Farrer c.1172. Cf. C. T. Clay, *Yorkshire Archaeological Journal* 36, 1944–7, 417–18 who widens the dates to 1167–1173–4. Marie Lovatt, who kindly sent me a copy of the text prepared for her forthcoming edition of Roger's *acta*, inclines towards 1173–4.
[43]   Cited and dated in Barlow, 'Roger of Howden', 354–6. For a parson of Howden with a mistress see *Giraldi Cambrensis Opera*, vi.24–5.

implicated in the rebellion of 1173–4 – when Henry II, in Howden's words, believed that Hugh had served him *molle et ficte*.[44]

Moreover there are intriguing connections between the certificate of institution and Roger's history. Among the witnesses to the certificate are Geoffrey, provost of Beverley, and Master Robert Magnus. In Roger's account of 1177 he wrote with sorrow of a great storm in which Geoffrey provost of Beverley, nephew of Archbishop Roger, and Robert Magnus master of the schools of York were drowned. He wrote that Robert Magnus was a man 'endowed with every fine quality' – indeed these were the very last words he wrote before putting down his history for a while. When he took up his pen again the first words he added were further words in praise of Robert.[45] Of Howden's schooling we know nothing for certain.[46] But I suggest we consider the schools of York; it might explain why, in a certificate witnessed by the master of those schools, we find a reference to Roger's 'integrity and learning (*scientia*)'.[47] Roger was surely close to the clerks of York. In his account of the dispute of the archbishops in 1174–5, it was the indignation and the actions of York's clerks that he emphasised.[48] When he reacted angrily to what he regarded as Henry II's unjust enforcement of forest law, it was the plight of the clerks of Yorkshire that most concerned him and, in particular, the clerks of St Peter's, York. Indeed it was precisely the papal legate's failure to protest to Henry II that led to Roger calling him a limb of Satan.[49]

Consider too the contrast between the way Howden reported the deaths of Hugh of Durham and Roger of York. When Hugh died, he gave date and place (3 March 1195, at Howden), and added nothing more. But when Archbishop Roger died in 1181, he noted that he bequeathed all his goods to the poor – calling this admirable conduct which would redound to his praise in perpetuity – and that he had ruled his province happily and well (*feliciter*) for more than twenty-seven years.[50] In the light of the strong York connection running through Howden's early career and writing, I suggest that it was Roger of Pont l' Evêque who drew the learned man to the king's attention.[51] If this was so, then everything that Howden wrote about the Becket dispute should have been conditioned on the one hand by his recognition that Becket was a martyr

---

[44] G. V. Scammell, *Hugh du Puiset*, Cambridge 1956, 147; Archbishop Roger by contrast served Henry well in the crisis of 1174, *Gesta Regis Henrici*, i.68–9, 160–1.

[45] *Gesta Regis Henrici*, i.195. Robert was also master of the hospital at York, as was Paulinus to whom Roger also gave high praise, *ibid.*, i.349.

[46] 'We may imagine him the son of a well-to-do tenant of the monastery [Durham] and sent for his education to the monastic school at Durham', *Howden*, i.xiv.

[47] I am grateful to Christopher Holdsworth and Marie Lovatt for pointing out that this was not a standard formula.

[48] *Gesta Regis Henrici*, i.80–1, 89–90.

[49] *Gesta Regis Henrici*, i.94, 99, 105.

[50] *Gesta Regis Henrici*, i.282–3.

[51] *Gesta Regis Henrici*, i.122 for one certain and one probable case of Archbishop Roger securing promotion for his clerks.

for God's law and for the privilege of the church, and on the other by his own loyalty and respect for his patron, the victim of character assassination at the hands of Becket's followers.[52]

After Archbishop Roger's death and in the absence of any successor at York until 1189, Howden probably became more closely attached to Hugh of Durham, especially since both of them carried a responsibility for relations with the Scots. When Howden went on the diplomatic mission to Gilbert and Uhtred of Galloway in November 1174, it was his report back to Henry II in Normandy in December which shaped the king's refusal to accept Gilbert's offer of submission.[53] Had Henry accepted Gilbert's offer, then the so-called treaty of Falaise between the kings of England and Scotland could not have taken the form it did. Among the witnesses to that treaty was 'Roger the chaplain'. I am inclined to accept E. L. G. Stones's identification of this Roger as the historian.[54] But irrespective of whether or not Howden was 'Roger the chaplain', there is no doubt that early in his career in royal service we see him playing an important diplomatic role in Anglo-Scottish affairs. The 1174 mission is well-known. But I suspect that he was just as important in the same diplomatic role in the last ten years of his life – when he is said to have left royal service.

Take, for example, the entry in which he tells us that Gregory bishop of Ross died in February 1195 and was succeeded by Reginald called Macer, a monk of Melrose, and then adds the remarkable information that in the cathedral of Ross (which is called Rosemarkie) there lies the body of Pope Boniface IV who (as can be read in church histories) received the Pantheon in Rome from Phocas and dedicated it to Mary. For Stubbs this was merely one of Roger's rare mistakes, confusing Boniface IV with a perhaps non-existent first bishop of Ross.[55] But how did Roger come to make it? A Roger of Hoveden witnessed

[52] *Howden*, ii.7–9 for the text of the harsh letter sent to Archbishop Roger by Alexander III, and which Howden omitted from the work he composed during Roger's lifetime.

[53] *Gesta Regis Henrici*, i.80.

[54] *Anglo-Scottish Relations 1174–1328. Some Selected Documents*, ed. E. L. G. Stones, London 1965, 5. Stubbs (*Howden*, ii.82) had considered this possibility but he rejected it on the grounds that Roger could not have returned from a conference in Galloway on 23 November in time to witness a treaty dated 8 December 1174 (*Diceto*, i.396–7). However although Roger's own copy of the treaty placed it at Falaise, both Diceto's copy and the extant Exchequer copies put it at Valognes. It seems that the two kings came to an agreement while William was still in prison at Falaise, but that a more formal document was drawn up at Valognes, before being finally ratified at York in August 1175. Quite apart from the possibility that Roger might have met Gilbert south of Galloway, I would in any case have thought there was time for him to get from there to Valognes, close to the port of Barfleur, by 8 December. He would have had to travel fast (approx. 350 miles from Carlisle to Portsmouth in 10 days) but the short time allowed for his mission to the vacant abbeys in 1175 suggests that he could, and it is clear that in view of the offer made by Gilbert to hold Galloway of the king of England, haste was needed.

[55] *Howden*, iii.284. For a view of a saintly first bishop of Ross which is rather less sceptical than Stubbs's see A. MacDonald, *Curadán, Boniface and the Early Church of Rosemarkie*, Groam House Museum 1992.

two Melrose charters, both lacking place-dates, the first, Bishop Jocelin of Glasgow's grant of the church of Hassendean to Melrose, the second, the confirmation by the Glasgow dean and chapter. In 1971 Geoffrey Barrow identified this Roger of Hoveden with the historian – a second instance of a historian of Scotland making an identification which seems to have escaped historians of historical writing in England.[56] This one must be right. The charter of confirmation was also witnessed by Bishop Reginald of Ross. Although the bishop's charter was once thought to date from 1193, recent close analysis by Professor A. A. M. Duncan has shown that both charters relate to the same transaction and were issued at Melrose between mid-September and early December 1195. Presumably Roger used a meeting with the new bishop of Ross at Melrose to brush up his knowledge of both ancient and modern Scottish church history.[57]

What was Howden doing in Scotland at this time? In his *Chronica* we are told that at Christmas 1195 Hubert Walter was at York, sent there by Richard to speak with William about a marriage between Richard's nephew Otto and William's eldest daughter Margaret. 'For it had been agreed', Howden continues, 'that William would give Margaret the whole of Lothian, and Richard would give Otto and Margaret and their heirs the whole of Northumbria and the county of Carlisle, and that Richard would hold the whole of Lothian with its castles while William would hold Northumbria and Carlisle with their churches. However the queen of Scotland was now pregnant so William, hoping that God would give him a son, no longer wished to stand by that agreement.'[58] When had this provisional agreement been negotiated and by whom? If by Howden, then this would explain why he was well-informed about both William's scheme to make Otto his heir and the earlier opposition to it, on the grounds that it was not the custom of the kingdom. 'Although the king had many who went along with his wishes, yet Earl Patrick and many others opposed the scheme. They said they would not recognise his daughter as a queen because it was not the custom of that kingdom (*consuetudo regni illius*) that a woman should have the kingdom so long as there was a brother or a nephew who could have it by right (*de jure*).'[59] Clearly the provisional agreement of late 1195 could have been immensely important for Anglo-Scottish history, but then so the business of the status of Galloway in 1174 could have been, and in that Howden's role at the preliminary stages is beyond doubt.

A visit or visits to Melrose would also throw much light on the writing of

---

[56] *Liber S. Mariae de Melros*, Bannatyne Club 1837, nos. 121, 122. *Regesta Regum Scottorum, II. The Acts of William I*, ed. G. W. S. Barrow, Edinburgh 1971, 361; cf. K. J. Stringer, *Earl David of Huntingdon*, Edinburgh 1985, 284 n. 89.

[57] For discussion and dating of these charters (and some others relating to the same transaction) I am indebted to a forthcoming paper by A. A. M. Duncan, 'Roger of Howden and Scotland'.

[58] *Howden*, iii.308.

[59] *Howden*, iii.298–9.

history. As Barrow pointed out, Howden made 'considerable use of the Melrose Chronicle in his own historical work'.[60] This is true so far as the *Chronica* is concerned, but does not apply to the *Gesta*. If he began to work on the *Chronica* in 1192–3 a visit to Melrose in 1193 would fit remarkably well; however Professor Duncan's re-dating of Bishop Jocelin's charter means that there is no longer clear evidence for Howden's presence at Melrose as early as this. Indeed he suggests that Howden's decision to convert his account of contemporary events into a history reaching back to the eighth century may have been taken as late as 1195 and have been inspired by the opportunity to take notes from the Melrose Chronicle enabling him to fill what was otherwise an awkward gap in his knowledge of history. This is possible, though so too is the possibility that Howden had contacts with Melrose – and hence at least indirect access to the Melrose Chronicle – before 1195.[61] Also possible is that Howden ventured at least to embark on his grander scheme before he came across the Melrose material which helped him to bridge the period between 1148 and 1170.[62]

Did Howden visit Scotland between 1174 and the 1190s? I am inclined to think that he did, and more than once. A curious detail in the *Gesta* suggests that he was probably in Galloway in late 1176. He reports that the papal legate Vivian sailed to Ireland from Whithorn on 24 December 1176.[63] This precision about an apparently minor point is most readily explicable if Howden himself was there. It is not hard to see a political context in which he might have been sent to Galloway. Gilbert of Galloway and King William attended a council at Feckenham (near Worcester) in October 1176 and Roger may have been deputed to conduct Gilbert, the legate and perhaps also King William north after the council.[64] The structure of the *Gesta* suggests that Howden was not at

---

[60] *Regesta*, ed. Barrow, 361.

[61] On this see A. A. M. Duncan, 'Roger of Howden and Scotland'. In this paper Archie Duncan demonstrates that Howden was actually a canon of Glasgow and raises the interesting possibility that his contacts with the later bishop of Ross dated back to the period when Reginald was still just a monk at Melrose. Such earlier contacts could have enabled Howden to obtain copies of Urban III's letters of 31 July 1186, one to Jocelin of Glasgow and the abbots of Melrose, Newbattle and Dunfermline, and one to King William, since these texts are given only in the *Chronica* (ii.312–14), not in the *Gesta*. Cf. also *Scotia Pontificia*, no. 100.

[62] What I think is not plausible, however, is the suggestion I made in the original version of this article, based upon the identification of the *Gesta* as one of Fordun's sources (*Scotichronicon by Walter Bower*, ed. D. E. R. Watt, vol. 4, Aberdeen 1994, xxii), that Howden took a copy of his own *Gesta* to Melrose and left it there to be fed into Scottish historical writing. Archie Duncan's arguments have persuaded me that this is very unlikely indeed.

[63] *Gesta Regis Henrici*, i.136–7. His interest in the detail of Vivian's escort can be seen in the small detail added in *Howden*, ii.99.

[64] *Gesta Regis Henrici*, i.126. Roger the Chaplain witnessed a charter given at Feckenham, *Calendar of Patent Rolls, 1247–58*, 259–60. I am very grateful to Michael Staunton for sending me copies of charters witnessed by Roger the Chaplain, several (including this one which I would provisionally date 1174 × 12.10.76) not noted by Eyton.

court between 17 October 1176 and mid-January 1177.[65] Subsequently in reporting provisions made by Henry II in May 1177 he reports that Vivian, on his way to see Henry II at Winchester, had disembarked at Chester – another minor detail about which he is curiously precise, but precison which might make sense if it had been Howden himself who brought Vivian from Chester to Winchester.[66] At Winchester on 3 June 1177 Vivian obtained 'letters of protection and safe-conduct' from Henry to return to Scotland where he held a council at Edinburgh shortly before 1 August. At Edinburgh he suspended the bishop of Whithorn for refusing (on the grounds that he was a suffragan of York) to attend a council of the Scottish church. This was news which was likely to reach Roger wherever he was, and the knowledge he has of events at Henry's court suggests he remained there for some weeks after 3 June.[67] Amongst much else he reports that the king of Scotland came, at Henry II's summons, to a council meeting at Winchester which lasted from 1 to 8 July 1177.[68] Howden then followed Henry II's movements in great detail for the next few days (9–12 July), but after that had nothing more to say on the subject until 15 August, except for the vague statement that the king spent a week at Stanstead (near Portsmouth) before returning to Winchester.[69] Why the gap between 12 July and 15 August? Was this because Roger himself was no longer at court? He noted that on 12 July Henry sent a messenger to the archbishop of York.[70] If Howden himself was the messenger this would explain neatly both how he came to know about the difficulties which a suffragan of York had with Legate Vivian and why he had virtually nothing to report on Henry II's actions between 12 July and 15 August. When he went north did he also act as escort for the king of Scotland on his way back from the meeting at Winchester? We know that Roger was later to be very interested in matters of escort between England and Scotland since he provides a detailed account of the arrangements for conducting a Scottish king to the English court.[71] We know too that in 1191 he was given the sensitive task of accompanying Philip Augustus back from crusade, presumably with a watching brief. Was this because he already had a proven track-record in this kind of work?

If this had become his role in royal service by the later 1170s, it would help to explain how he became such an authority on the long dispute which followed King William's attempt to intrude his chaplain Hugh into the see of St Andrews after the electors had already chosen a candidate of their own, Master John the

---

[65] *Gesta Regis Henrici*, i.127–132.
[66] *Gesta Regis Henrici*, i.161.
[67] *Gesta Regis Henrici*, i.166–7.
[68] *Gesta Regis Henrici*, i.177–8, 180.
[69] *Gesta Regis Henrici*, i.182, 190.
[70] *Gesta Regis Henrici*, i.181.
[71] *Howden*, iii.244–5. It is clear from this that the clergy of Durham and York would share in the responsibility for conducting the Scottish king. The incumbent of the parsonage of Howden would be well placed to take his share. Cf. *Gesta Regis Henrici*, ii.97 for another instance of Roger's interest in the matter.

Scot. It has been suggested that his narrative of this dispute was derived from the many papal letters he quoted.[72] But he provides some information not in the letters, for example on the involvement of John's uncle, Bishop Matthew of Aberdeen, and on the king burning down Matthew's house in revenge.[73] In any case there would still be the question of how he got those letters. Take, for example, the letters written by Alexander III in 1180 or 1181 and relating to the involvement of the papal legate Alexius in the disputed election.[74] According to Howden, Alexius and John the Scot travelled to Scotland *cum conductu domini regis Anglie*. After Alexius rejected and excommunicated King William's candidate, and consecrated John the Scot at Edinburgh in June 1180, he, John and Matthew of Aberdeen then took refuge from the king's wrath with Henry II in Normandy. Suppose Howden travelled with them. Suppose too that when Henry summoned William to his court, it was Howden who carried the king's writ of summons and then escorted him to Normandy.[75] This would explain in the most economical fashion how Roger got the pope's letters and how he came to be so well-informed about events in Scotland in 1180 and then in Normandy in early 1181, including details of Henry II's conferences with Philip of France and Archbishop Laurence of Dublin's death at Eu in February.[76] An alternative possibility would be that the letters (together with the additional information) were passed on to him by Roger of York or by Hugh of Durham, both of whom were involved in the St Andrews dispute. But given that their involvement would necessarily also have meant the involvement of clerks associated with them, this might only bring us back again to Howden himself. It is certainly likely that Howden travelled back to England in July 1181 with the two kings and attended the council of Nottingham, where he learned how Donald MacWilliam had been taking advantage of King William's absence.[77] This scenario would put Roger on the road and away from court for much of 1180, but in rather closer contact in 1181, especially from July onwards. Of course there is not a scrap of direct evidence for any of this, but it would have the advantage of explaining both the extraordinary muddle that the annal for 1180 presents and the lack of information about Henry II's itinerary in that year.[78]

The entry in the *Gesta* for 1182 includes a report on the Scottish embassy to Rome headed by Jocelin of Glasgow and the abbot of Melrose that obtained

---

[72] A. A. M. Duncan, *Scotland. The Making of the Kingdom*, Edinburgh 1975, 270 n. 19.

[73] *Gesta Regis Henrici*, i.265.

[74] *Scotia Pontificia*, nos. 92, 100, 101; *Gesta Regis Henrici*, i.263, 265, *Howden*, ii.209–10.

[75] *Gesta Regis Henrici*, i.264–6.

[76] *Gesta Regis Henrici*, i.270–2. In none of these instances is certainty about Howden's movements possible, but cumulatively they build up to a general pattern.

[77] *Gesta Regis Henrici*, i.277, 280–2. Whether or not Howden was at the meeting between Hugh du Puiset and King William at Redden he would clearly be well-informed about Archbishop Roger's excommunication of the king and about the interdict which Hugh imposed on Scotland.

[78] Stubbs reckoned with a break in composition in 1180, *Gesta Regis Henrici*, i.xlvi.

King William's absolution (11 March) and asked Lucius III to send legates to sort out the St Andrews dispute; it then reports their journey and what they did in Scotland.[79] Since one of the legates was a churchman from Yorkshire, the abbot of Rievaulx, and since Hugh du Puiset, acting as protector to John the Scot, was also involved in the protracted negotiations of this year, we might well anticipate that Roger would be well-informed about all this.[80] What we might not anticipate is that the annal for 1182 should be the shortest in the entire work. Whether he went to the papal curia himself, or went on the embassy to Frederick Barbarossa,[81] or escorted the legates, or stayed in the north of England moving into the *familia* of the bishop of Durham now that Roger of Pont L'Evêque was dead, he was certainly not much at court.

Throughout the 1180s Howden continued to be keenly interested in Anglo-Scottish politics. He reported the marriage negotiations between William and Henry in detail, noting the presence of Jocelin of Glasgow and the abbot of Melrose at the English court in 1186. When Henry II then took a big army to Carlisle to browbeat the recalcitrant Roland of Galloway, it seems likely that Roger himself was there, and was, amongst other things, delighted to see Paulinus of Leeds, master of St Leonard's Hospital at York, elected bishop of Carlisle.[82] Eyton dated Henry II's charter for Holm Cultram Abbey near Carlisle to July 1186; one of the witnesses to this charter was Roger the Chaplain.[83] Roger may well have been on the Scottish border again in 1188 as one of the *familiares* whom Henry II sent to Birgham with Hugh du Puiset to confer with the king, barons and prelates of Scotland about the collection of the Saladin Tithe.[84] As he grew older he became increasingly well informed about Scotland and its people, some of whom he must have got to know very well.[85]

How did this affect his view of Scotland and the Scots? He first mentioned the Scots in the context of their invasion of the north in 1174, and he accused them of atrocities. Slitting open pregnant women, tearing out unborn babies, tossing children upon spear points, they pitilessly massacred young and old of both sexes,

---

[79] *Gesta Regis Henrici*, i.286–7, 289–90.

[80] Hugh's role emerges from the report written by the legates, *Howden*, ii.271–2, which Roger did not include in the *Gesta*, possibly out of discretion or possibly because it was not written until he and the legates had gone their separate ways. A puzzle.

[81] He noted the consecration of John Cumin at Velletri on 21 March, and then details of Henry II's efforts on Henry the Lion's behalf, *Gesta Regis Henrici*, i.287–8.

[82] *Gesta Regis Henrici*, i.347–9.

[83] R. W. Eyton, *Court, Household and Itinerary of Henry II*, London 1878, 269. Witnessed by the chaplains Nicolas and Roger.

[84] *Gesta Regis Henrici*, ii.44–5. It could have been on this occasion that he obtained copies of some of the letters on the continuing St Andrews saga written by Clement III, *Gesta Regis Henrici*, ii.42–5, 57–8, 64–5. For discussion of the date of these letters see A. D. M. Barrell, 'The background to *Cum universi*: Scoto-papal relations 1159–1192', *Innes Review* xlvi, 1995, 116–38. For my knowledge of this article I am indebted to Archie Duncan's kindness.

[85] In addition to Jocelin of Glasgow and Abbot Arnold of Melrose, these probably included the new bishop of St Andrews, Roger Beaumont, and Reginald bishop of Ross – his likely source for events in the far north of Scotland in 1196–7, *Howden*, iv.10–12.

and beheaded priests upon their altars.[86] The importance of this passage in the *Gesta* is three-fold. First, it is largely borrowed from the account of the invasion of 1138 in the *Historia post obitum Bedae* – the history which Howden was to use for the first volume of his *Chronica*, indeed he was to use near identical words when covering the 1138 invasion in this later work. Apart from the Chronicle of Melrose, the *Historia post obitum Bedae* is the only historical work Roger is known to have used, and clearly he knew it already when writing the *Gesta*. Second, although modern Scottish historians are inclined to note 'the stereotyped nature of these accounts',[87] Roger did make changes. He added the phrase about the pitiless massacre, which he may have been moved to do because of a particular incident which he described in some detail, the massacre of the people of Warkworth by earl Duncan's troops.[88] All this suggests that, although he did not call them 'barbarians', he nonetheless shared the values of William of Newburgh for whom the Scots of 1173–4 were 'bloodthirsty barbarians'.[89] Thirdly, he described the invaders of 1174 not just as Scots (as, following the *Historia post obitum Bedae*, he was to call the invaders of 1138), but as Scots and Galwegians. Elsewhere he showed himself to be acutely aware of the differences between Scotland and Galloway, of the high level of killing and mutilating that characterised Galwegian politics, and of the tensions that existed between Scots and Galwegians.[90]

When re-writing his narrative for the *Chronica* he omitted the massacre at Warkworth – an omission which is of a piece with the generally more positive tone which Howden adopts with regard to the Scots in the 1190s. His account of the conduct of the Scottish clergy at and after the Council of Northampton in the *Chronica* gives significantly more space to the case for the independence of Scotish churches, especially as put by Jocelin of Glasgow, than he had in the contemporaneous *Gesta*.[91] Similarly in the *Chronica* he merely reports the arrival of Cardinal Vivian in 1177, whereas in the *Gesta* he twice explained that after the break-up of the Council of Northampton the Scottish bishops had 'secretly' sent envoys to Alexander III asking for his protection against the demands of the English church.[92] It is an intriguing thought that were it not for Roger we might not have the text of Celestine III's *Cum universi Christi*, the famous papal guarantee of the freedom of the Scottish church.[93] His growing sympathy for the independence of the Scottish church from the English may be paralleled by

[86] *Gesta Regis Henrici*, i.64; retained in *Howden*, ii.57.
[87] A. O. Anderson, *Scottish Annals from English Chronicles*, London 1908, 249 n. 7.
[88] *Gesta Regis Henrici*, i.66; omitted from *Howden*, ii.60.
[89] *Historia Rerum Anglicarum of William of Newburgh*, in *Chronicles of the reigns of Stephen, Henry II and Richard I*, ed. R. Howlett, 4 vols., RS 1885–90, i.177.
[90] *Gesta Regis Henrici*, i.67–8, 79–80, 95, 126, 210, 313, 339–40.
[91] *Gesta Regis Henrici*, i.111–12; *Howden*, ii.91–2.
[92] *Howden*, ii.98; *Gesta Regis Henrici*, i.112, 117. The emphasis on the underhandedness of the Scots is much stronger in the Julius MS (reflecting his view in 1177) than in the Vitellius MS (reflecting a revision of c.1192).
[93] According to Robert Somerville, the one other manuscript could have been copied from Howden, *Scotia Pontificia*, 143.

a sympathy for the independence of the Scottish kingdom. Thus he commented that those who attended the Canterbury Council of December 1189 went home 'praising King Richard's great deeds' – deeds which included the Quitclaim of Canterbury.[94] He re-wrote his account of the 1188 meeting at Birgham to give the impression of a tougher and more independent-minded King William.[95] Roger's growing familiarity with the Scottish court and church is itself a symptom of the way Scotland was being increasingly drawn within the ambit of a European and English culture. He regarded King William's peace measures, based on English practice, as 'following a good example'.[96] Only the Scottish court's western and northern enemies continued to evoke the hostile tone with which he had once written about Scots in general.[97]

There could hardly be a greater contrast between Roger's knowledge of Scotland and his knowledge of Wales. Not until his entry for 1199 when Gerald de Barri raised the issue of the metropolitan status of St David's did he include a copy of a document relating to Welsh history, and that was Pope Eugenius III's letter of 1147 which Gerald had found in his search through the papal registers.[98] If he visited Wales at all, it was while travelling to and from Ireland in 1171–2, and it made no impression on him. He first mentioned the Welsh in his entry for 1174 and then it was in their role as fierce forest fighters who frightened the French.[99] His next was in reporting, under 1175, that such was the poverty of the see and the hostility of the Welsh that the bishop of St Asaph preferred to give up his bishopric rather than reside there.[100] His information on Welsh politics was limited, based on what he learned at those occasions when Welsh kings attended meetings of the English council when he was also present: Gloucester 1175, Oxford 1177, Worcester and Gloucester 1184.[101] With one or two possible exceptions, there is little sign of a developing attitude towards the Welsh.[102] From first to last they impinge on Roger's mind chiefly as

[94] *Gesta Regis Henrici*, ii.98–9, and 102–4 for the text of the Quitclaim.
[95] *Howden*, ii.338–9. The effect of the revision was noted by Duncan, *Scotland*, 235.
[96] *Howden*, iv.33.
[97] *Gesta Regis Henrici*, ii.8–9. Even a fierce Galwegian such as Roland was to end his days at Northampton, *Howden*, iv.145.
[98] *Howden*, iv.103–6. For the argument that Roger was in Rome from late 1199 to early 1200 see J. Gillingham, 'Historians without hindsight: Coggeshall, Diceto and Howden on the early years of John's reign' in S. Church, ed., *Essays on the Reign of King John*, Woodbridge 1999.
[99] This was August 1174 by which time Howden was back in France with the king, *Gesta Regis Henrici*, i.74. See also ii.46–7, 50, 68 for further indications that he saw Welsh troops in operation there. In his book, however, when up against English troops they were much less impressive, even when heavily armed, *Howden*, iv.53.
[100] *Gesta Regis Henrici*, i.90–1.
[101] *Gesta Regis Henrici*, i.92, 162, 314, 317, ii.87–8. If David Corner is right, he was on his way to Rome, not at Worcester, when Richard – not John – met some Welsh kings there in late September 1189, Corner, 'The *Gesta Regis*', 136. On the Worcester meeting see above, pp. 65–6.
[102] One possible exception is his reference, based on the Chronicle of Melrose, to Henry II's

trouble-makers.[103] When he compiled his list of the rulers of the world in 1201, though he found room for Guthred in the Isle of Man and John de Courcy in Ulster, there was no room in Roger's mind for any Welsh ruler.[104] He had, of course, been aware of the Lord Rhys of Deheubarth, but there is no sign that he was aware of the growing reputation of Llywelyn ap Iorwerth.

In terms of what Roger knew about it, Ireland falls somewhere between Scotland and Wales. From September 1171 to April 1172 his narrative deals with Henry II's expedition to Ireland *and* has nothing to say about events anywhere else. Analysis of the structure of Howden's text suggests that Roger accompanied the king to Ireland and stayed with him until March 1172 when he would have been one of the chaplains sent to Waterford with the bulk of the army while the king and his private houshold remained at Wexford.[105] If so this would explain why he was able to locate Henry II's palace at Dublin with such topographical precision.[106] This would also mean that Roger, despite being in Ireland, was not himself present at the Synod of Cashel and that for his account of it he relied upon a list of Irish episcopal sees and information supplied by his close associate Nicolas the Chaplain.[107] Further analysis of Howden's Irish information re-inforces the idea that 1177 was an important turning point in his life. Until 1177 most of his information on Irish matters clearly 'derived from royal oficials or their records'.[108] The most famous record, of course, being the treaty of Windsor, witnessed by none other than Roger the Chaplain.[109] But Roger's account of Henry II's grant of the kingdom of Limerick to Philip de

mutilation of daughters as well as sons of Rhys; the second is the tone of his account of relations between St David's and Canterbury, *Howden*, i.240, iv.103–6. In these passages he may be doing no more than reflecting the language of his source. But if that is so, he is at least not changing it. The first may have more to do with his changing perception of Henry II than with a new view of the Welsh. On the other hand the violence of English kings is common to both passages.

[103] E.g. *Gesta Regis Henrici*, i.288–9, *Howden*, iv.21, 163.
[104] *Howden*, iv.161–2. This despite the fact that he generally gave Welsh rulers the title 'king'.
[105] *Gesta Regis Henrici*, i.25–30.
[106] *Gesta Regis Henrici*, i.28–9; S. Duffy, 'Ireland's Hastings: the Anglo-Norman Conquest of Dublin', *Anglo-Norman Studies* 20, 1997, 82–5.
[107] M. T. Flanagan, 'Henry II, the Council of Cashel and the Irish Bishops', *Peritia* 10, 1996, 184–211, esp. 204–5.
[108] M. T. Flanagan, *Irish Society, Anglo-Norman Settlers, Angevin Kingship*, Oxford 1989, 224.
[109] As well as by Nicolas the chaplain. In addition to the charter for the bishops of Hereford given at Feckenham (see above n. 64), Roger and Nicolas were joint witnesses to at least five more of Henry II's charters. These were for: (1) Holm Cultram and (2) Stanley, Eyton, *Itinerary*, 269, 273; (3) two Le Mans chaplains, at Le Mans, *Cal. Docs. France*, no. 1022, there dated c.1173. L. Delisle and E. Berger, *Recueil des Actes de Henri II Roi d'Angleterre et Duc de Normandie concernant les Provinces françaises et les Affaires de France*, 3 vols., Paris 1909–20, no. 354 were more open-ended, 1156–72 × 3; (4) the bishops of Winchester, at Westminster (March 1176 since witnessed by Huguccio and the archbishop of Rouen), *Cal. Charter Rolls*, July 1317; (5) Cormeri, at Angers, from Delisle, *Recueil*, ii.307, no. 683, there dated 'after 1173'.

Briouze in June 1177 is the last occasion on which he seems to have had official documentation before him.[110] He had further information about Irish affairs in 1179, 1180, 1181, 1185 and 1186 but all of it could derive from oral sources. After 1186 he had nothing to report until 1197 – an astonishingly long gap for a writer previously so well informed. Indeed given the fact that he mentioned only briefly the two major political events in Ireland in 1185 and 1186 – John's expedition and the killing of Hugh de Lacy[111] – it looks as though he almost completely lost touch with Ireland between 1181 and 1197. From 1197 to the end of his work there are five items of Irish interest, or six, if we count his list of the rulers of the world of 1201 with the name of John de Courcy 'reigning in Ulster' at the end of it.[112] Three (or four) of these items relate to John de Courcy.[113] It seems that circles around de Courcy were now providing information and a recent re-examination of de Courcy's background has convincingly demonstrated not only his ties with Galloway but also the connections with Yorkshire and indeed with York itself.[114] Of the other two Irish items, one relates to John Cumin, archbishop of Dublin, a man long known to Howden.[115] The other deals with King John's grant of the Irish estates of Philip of Worcester and Theobald Walter to William de Briouze for 5,000 marks in 1200. Since Roger noted that Philip of Worcester escaped John's clutches by travelling through the land of the king of the Scots, it may be that he came to hear the story through his Scottish connections.[116]

What did he think of Ireland and the Irish? His account of Henry II's expedition to Ireland in 1171–2 shows that, like any right-thinking English cleric

[110] *Gesta Regis Henrici*, i.172.

[111] *Gesta Regis Henrici*, i.339, 350.

[112] *Howden*, iv.161–2. I think it unlikely that, as suggested by Orpen, this was 'a court sarcasm current at the time', G. H. Orpen, *Ireland under the Normans 1169–1216*, Oxford 1911, 137 n. 2.

[113] *Howden*, iv.25, 157, 176.

[114] S. Duffy, 'The First Ulster Plantation: John de Courcy and the Men of Cumbria' in eds. T. Barry, R. Frame and K. Simms, *Colony and Frontier in Medieval Ireland. Essays presented to J. F. Lydon*, London 1995, 1–27, esp. 6, 19–22, 24. Note especially Roger of Dunsforth, a follower of de Courcy who retired to St Mary's York in 1194. But it was probably from the papal legate Vivian (see above, pp. 78–9) that Roger learned of John de Courcy's attack on Ulster early in 1177, *Gesta Regis Henrici*, i.137–8. The fact that he mentions there the three saints of Downpatrick makes a de Courcy source tempting, but in that case the twenty year gap before the next de Courcy item would be very puzzling.

[115] *Howden*, iv.29–30. Roger the Chaplain witnessed a charter of John count of Mortain, lord of Ireland, for John of Dublin, G. Mac Niocaill, 'The Charters of John, Lord of Ireland to the See of Dublin', *Repertorium Novum* iii, 1961–4, no. 4 there dated August 1189 x early 1190. Cumin attended the royal court in 1198 at a time when Philip of Durham was there, so Philip could have been Roger's source for the quarrel between John and Cumin that erupted in 1197.

[116] *Howden*, iv.152–3. An alternative source might be the exchequer since ironically the report of the grant to William de Briouze follows immediately after the text of the newly issued *lex scaccarii* which John was later to use to justify the political destruction of the Briouze family.

of the time, he regarded Irish marriage customs as polygamous and incestuous, and that he thought of Ireland as a rainy land of mountains and bogs, a place that we – the English – could easily subjugate if only we put our minds to it – which we never do because there are more important things than Ireland.[117] Probably by 1177, and certainly by the time he re-wrote his account of events in the kingdoms of Limerick and Cork for the *Chronica*, it is clear that he shared the English view of Irish politics as kin-slaying.[118] On the other hand he was also aware of the Irish feeling that they were being cruelly treated by the incomers. He knew this by 1177, perhaps as a result of talking to Vivian when he escorted the papal legate from Chester on his return from Ireland.[119] He repeated it in his entry for 1179, adding that in consequence of Irish complaints, William fitzAudelin and Hugh de Lacy were long kept out of Henry's favour (a week being a long time in court politics). As noted by Marie Therese Flanagan, his source on this occasion may well have beeen Irish clergy, notably the archbishops of Dublin and Tuam and some of their suffragans, who came to Windsor early in 1179 on their way to the Lateran Council.[120]

According to Howden, the Irish prelates swore that in Rome they would attempt nothing to the detriment of the king or kingdom of England – and I suspect that he went with them to keep an eye on them. He certainly went to the curia on other occasions. He was there in autumn 1191 when Pope Celestine showed Philip Augustus the Veronica.[121] David Corner has made a case for him visiting Rome in 1189.[122] Turning to his entry for 1179 (some twenty-three pages in all in Stubbs's edition) we find that the first seventeen pages are devoted exclusively to the Lateran Council and to its preliminaries. The remaining pages for 1179 deal with events from Easter onwards. Bishop Hugh of Durham attended the Lateran, so he could have been Roger's source, but in that case we have to ask why, if Roger was with the king or in England, he had nothing germane to report on the first three months of the year. As before, Roger's history makes most sense as, in large part, a journal of his travels.

The same line of argument, notably the absence of any information on Henry II's movements between Christmas 1170 and August 1171, suggests that Roger was one of the royal clerks attached to the mission which Henry sent to Alexander III in 1171.[123] He was probably at the curia again early in 1183. This would explain how he came by information about the quarrel between Lucius and the Romans and how he knew what happened in the business of St Andrews at Velletri early in 1183.[124] He may well have been one of the envoys

[117] *Gesta Regis Henrici*, i.25–30, 270.
[118] *Gesta Regis Henrici*, i.173; *Howden*, ii.135–6.
[119] *Gesta Regis Henrici*, i.161, 166, 173.
[120] *Gesta Regis Henrici*, i.221; Flanagan, *Irish Society*, 260 n. 88.
[121] *Gesta Regis Henrici*, ii.228–9.
[122] Corner, 'The *Gesta Regis*', 136.
[123] *Gesta Regis Henrici*, i.19–22.
[124] *Gesta Regis Henrici*, i.293–4, 308–9. Distance from events might explain why he gave a

who put Bishop Hugh's case there in 1192 in the dispute with Geoffrey of York.[125] He was probably there again early in 1197 in the company of Philip of Poitou who put the king's case in the dispute over Les Andelys with Rouen, and who was consecrated bishop of Durham at Rome on 20 April 1197.[126]

He probably went again later that year and stayed at Rome until early 1198. From the point of view of papal history this was the most important of Roger's visits. He provides a remarkable amount of information on events from the death of Henry VI (28 September 1197) to the beginnings of Innocent III's pontificate, including his reform of the curia and his quarrel with Romans.[127] Particularly significant, because unique to him, is his account of how just before Christmas 1197 the dying Celestine III attempted to designate a successor: 'the pope offered to depose himself if the cardinals would consent to election of John of St Paul. But they replied with one voice that they would not elect him *conditionaliter* and that it was unheard of that the supreme pontiff should resign, and so there was a schism between them.'[128] Most recent historians of the papacy have tended to discount this tale on the grounds that it was 'largely based on rumour' and 'the embellishments of his own imagination'.[129] There is certainly no shortage of potential sources to explain Roger's knowledge of events in and around Rome at the turn of the year 1197–8. Archbishop Geoffrey of York seems to have been there.[130] In 1201 Cardinal John of Salerno as legate to Scotland, Ireland and the Isles, came to York, and he, Howden believed, might have become pope himself in January 1198. According to Roger's version of the papal election which followed Celestine's death, ten cardinals voted for John, but he at once chose to withdraw and throw his support behind Lothar.[131] Despite these alternative sources of information, what makes it likely that Roger himself was there, as Jane Sayers has supposed,[132] is – once again – the fact that he says very little about English affairs during the relevant months. He mentions Richard I's demand for a 300 knight army – a demand opposed by Hugh of Lincoln, one

confused account of what happened in the early stages of the Young King's war against Richard and his father.

[125] *Gesta Regis Henrici*, ii.240–45; *Howden*, iii.170, 172.

[126] *Howden*, iv.16–18. Or was this information supplied by Philip himself? But in that case why did Roger have so little to report from England? If he returned, with Philip, to the king's court in Normandy before setting off again to Rome, he could have met John Cumin there, which would explain how he came to have news from Ireland in this year, *Howden*, iv.29–30.

[127] *Howden*, iv.30–32, 44–5.

[128] *Howden*, iv.32–3.

[129] M. Taylor, 'The election of Innocent III', *Studies in Church History* 9, 1991, ed. D. Wood, 97–112, esp. 106–7.

[130] *Howden*, iv.7–8, 44–5.

[131] *Howden*, iv.174–5. Hardly 'a wild scramble of the whole college to secure election', I. S. Robinson, *The Papacy 1073–1198*, Cambridge 1990, 89. But it could well be that Howden only learned this 'inside story' of what happened on 8 January in 1201, and Cardinal John may well have liked to present himself in a good light.

[132] J. Sayers, *Innocent III*, London 1994, 8, 25.

of Roger's heroes – but he placed the meeting at which the demand was made in 1198, when in fact it occurred early in December 1197.[133] This slight chronological error is readily comprehensible if Howden was out of England at the time.

Roger of Howden's historical writings contain so much 'hard' political and constitutional material that he has been seen almost exclusively as man interested in politics and administration. But Stubbs drew attention to his miracle stories, notably the miracles associated with Sabbath Observance and the preaching tour of Eustace of Flay in 1200 and 1201. At Nafferton a cake baked on Saturday poured blood on Sunday and, according to Roger, 'he who saw bore witness and his witness is true'. As Stubbs saw, this phrase suggests that the witness was Howden himself, but he rejected the idea since a virtually identical phrase was used in the description of flying fish in the Mediterranean which 'almost to a certainty' Stubbs felt Howden could not have seen.[134] However now that it is accepted that Howden did sail the Mediterranean, it is surely likely that Stubbs's first instinct was right and that Howden did indeed insist that he saw the cake pouring blood. The tendency to marginalise Howden's piety underestimates the degree of his commitment to the crusading cause; it also underestimates the depth of his worry about heresy. Under 1182 in the *Chronica* there is a story not told in Henry II's lifetime of how Walter, servant of Eustace of Flay, heard a voice from heaven sending instructions to the king, but when Walter told Henry, he was ignored. Soon afterwards King Henry's sons Henry and Geoffrey died. What should Henry have done to avert God's punishment? At a time when heretics were being burned in many places in the kingdom of France, he should not have stopped them being dealt with in this way in his own lands where there were so many.[135] Howden's worry about heretics in Henry's lands may have been grounded in his own experience since analysis of his entry for 1178, of what he wrote and of what he did not cover, makes it possible that he was sent by the king to keep a watching brief on the anti-heresy preaching tour that went to Toulouse in that year.[136] His involvement

---

[133] *Howden*, iv.40.

[134] *Howden*, iv.xxiv, 170–1.

[135] *Howden*, ii.272–3. Characteristically for Stubbs the story was important 'as bearing on the character of Henry II', not for its bearing on the character of Roger of Howden.

[136] He has nothing on the king's movements between 6 August 1178 when he was at Woodstock and Christmas 1178, *Gesta Regis Henrici*, i.207, 220; *Diceto*, i.426. Although the bulk of his account of the anti-heresy campaign is based on the letters, the texts of which he gives, one written by Cardinal Peter and one written by Abbot Henry of Clairvaux, he adds some details which cannot be inferred from them, e.g. that the protector of heretics had two castles, one in and one outside Toulouse, *Gesta Regis Henrici*, i.199–200. On the property, including two fortresses, held by Petrus Maurandus, see J. H. Mundy, *Liberty and Political Power in Toulouse*, New York 1954, 60–61. For the date of the mission, in the autumn of 1178, see B. M. Kienzle, 'Henry of Clairvaux and the 1178 and 1181 missions', *Heresis* 28, 1997 – a reference I owe to the kindness of Elaine Graham-Leigh. In this context it may be relevant that Howden seems to have been more interested in Henry of Clairvaux, the future cardinal-bishop of Albano than he was in most cardinals.

with the 1178 anti-heresy campaign in the Toulousain would explain how he came to have a copy of the acts of the earlier Council of Lombers against heretics there, a long abridgement of which he subsequently inserted into his *Chronica* under the year 1176.[137]

To sum up. Roger of Howden was closely attached to the schools and clergy of York, and the turmoil there which followed Geoffrey Plantagenet's election as archbishop at times reduced him to despair. He may well have been introduced to royal service by Roger of Pont L'Evêque and until the archbishop died in 1181, he was more closely attached to him than to the bishop of Durham. The long vacancy at York then allowed Hugh du Puiset's influence to increase.[138] From the beginning of his career to its end, Roger always served two masters, the king and a powerful prelate. In this he was presumably no different from other royal clerks. Doubtless it was not always easy, for example when Richard I and Hugh du Puiset were at odds in 1194.[139]

Roger's royal service probably began at Christmas 1169, and he followed the court to Ireland in 1171–2. But he did not stay at court all the time until 1189 and then, after his return from crusade, leave royal service to retire to his parsonage. From very early on in his career he was employed on missions which took him away from court, and this continued to be the pattern in the 1190s. The mission to Gilbert of Galloway in November 1174 began a close involvement with Scottish business which was to last the rest of his life, and involve him in many journeys to Scotland. On some of these journeys he acted as an escort, in his master's interest keeping an eye on papal legates as well as on Scots from the king downwards. Although he became a particular expert on the Scottish church, it seems likely that he was sometimes given a responsibility for the safe-conduct of papal legates in other circumstances too.[140] When Richard I sent him back from Acre to accompany Philip Augustus, he chose an experienced diplomat well-accustomed to keeping a watching brief on the men he escorted. Although he probably made the first of many visits to the curia as early as 1171, the missions to Toulouse in 1178 and to the Lateran Council in 1179 usher in a period when his absences from court were more frequent and more prolonged than they had been up to 1177.

Until 1177 he was frequently at court, whether the court was on the continent or in England or Ireland. From 1178 until June 1184 he was only rarely at court. Between June 1184 and early 1187 he attended court for longer

---

[137] *Howden*, ii.105–17.

[138] *Gesta Regis Henrici*, ii.247–8.

[139] *Howden*, iii.245–6. Life was probably simpler once Philip of Poitou was bishop of Durham.

[140] See for example *Gesta Regis Henrici*, i.106, 117 for a possible association with Hugo Pierleone in England and Normandy, coinciding with gaps in his coverage of Henry II's movements during November–December 1175 and June–July 1176.

periods again but, continuing a pattern already set, only when it was in England.[141] From then until the end of the reign he was once again only occasionally at court, though he did go to France in the late summer of 1188, presumably reporting the failure of the negotiations at Birgham,[142] and probably again in the summer of 1189. Seen in the light of this career pattern and of the fact that Richard I was seldom in England, it should hardly come as a surprise that Roger can rarely be shown to have been at Richard I's court, except when that court was in England – and especially when relations with Scotland were high on the agenda as in April 1194. Indeed Roger of Howden's life in the 1190s looks very like a continuation of his career after 1177. After 1177, a year which marked a pause in his writing of history and may also have been darkened by personal loss, he was less often at the hub of affairs and so became increasingly cut off from former sources of information. When in the *Gesta* for 1177 Roger recorded the accession of a new Irish king of Limerick whose name he did not know, he left a blank – evidently he expected to be able to ascertain the name and fill in the blank. By the early 1190s he was so out of touch with Irish business that he neither knew the name nor left a blank, even though that king was the great Domnall Mor Ua Briain who dominated Munster politics until his death in 1194.[143]

Although it must be as certain as anything can be, that I am mistaken in my reconstruction of one or more of the individual episodes discussed here, and it is even possible that Roger of Howden was not also Roger the Chaplain, none the less I find it hard to see how the general pattern of information and of gaps in information in Howden's historical writing for the years after 1169, can be better explained than by interpreting his history as in large part a reflection of his own travels, both when he was with the court and when on service away from court. In other words he was *primarily* useful to kings not as a clerk in domestic court service or as a justice of the forest – though doubtless he was useful in these roles too – but as a clerk with special expertise in Scottish and papal business, attached, as it were, to the Foreign Office, rather than to the Home Office or Treasury. If he was, even more than previously suspected, the best travelled of all medieval English historians, and particularly if I am right in arguing that he generally travelled in government service, it would help to explain why he was politically so remarkably well-informed over so wide a geographical range – about, for example, the extent of imperial authority over the kingdom of Arles, or the system of succession to the Norwegian throne.[144] His observations have been cited with approval by modern historians of, for

---

[141] The pattern can be readily ascertained from the details relating to 'Benedict of Peterborough' which Stubbs supplied in his Outline Itinerary of Henry II, *Gesta Regis Henrici*, ii.cxxxvii–cxlviii.

[142] *Gesta Regis Henrici*, ii.44–7, including the marvel at Dunstable, 9 August 1188.

[143] *Gesta Regis Henrici*, i.173; *Howden*, ii.135–6; Flanagan, *Irish Society*, 257–8.

[144] *Howden*, iii.225–6, 271–2.

example, Barbarossa's crusade preparations,[145] of papal and Roman politics,[146] of the operation of Mediterranean galleys.[147] As Stubbs wrote, 'much must have been gained from intercourse with travellers and foreigners who made their way to court'.[148] Indeed, but much may also have been gained when he made his way to their courts. It is clear that his journeys to Scotland led not only to more information but also to growing understanding and sympathy for Scottish aspirations. His links with Ireland and especially Wales were much more tenuous. He had no ascertainable contacts with the Irish themselves after 1180, and few contacts with any Welshmen at any time. Even here, however, though in the Welsh case not until near the end of his life, there are a few hints that he was capable of seeing their side of things.

---

[145] 'der Autor der Gesta Heinrici II hat das sehr genau gesehen', R. Hiestand, 'Barbarossa und der Kreuzzug' in ed. A. Haverkamp, *Friedrich Barbarossa. Handlungsspielräume und Wirkungswesen des Staufischen Kaisers*, Sigmaringen 1992, 56.

[146] Robinson, *The Papacy*, 5, 141.

[147] Observations 'based on experience and accurate', J. H. Pryor, *Geography, Technology and War*, Cambridge 1988, 37–8, 80.

[148] *Gesta Regis Henrici*, i.xvi.

6

The Foundations of a Disunited Kingdom

I begin with the view from London. The late twelfth-century historian, Ralph, dean of St Paul's, regarded the kingdom of England as a model state – literally the model on which he believed that a new king of France, Philip Augustus, intended to pattern his own kingdom. This model state was, in Ralph's words, 'wide in extent, peacefully governed, and contained within it some very barbarous inhabitants, the Scots and the Welsh.'[1] Dean Ralph's view encapsulates two perceptions of fundamental importance for the history of the United Kingdom: the first, that the king of England is the ruler of Britain; the second, that some of his subjects are barbarians. Since in this passage Ralph was limiting his remarks to Britain, he made no mention of the latest of Henry II's acquisitions, Ireland. Had he done so, he would certainly have added the Irish to the list of Henry's barbarous subjects. By the 1180s, when Dean Ralph was writing, the foundations of an English empire had been well and truly laid – 'an empire based on the wealth, population and resources of southern England over the rest of the British Isles'.[2] That there was an English empire of Britain had been claimed two hundred years earlier still, in the 980s – and not surprisingly, given the military and political achievements of the tenth-century West Saxons. What was new about the twelfth-century empire was the assumption that some of the ruler's subjects were barbarians. Given that for all its power then and in subsequent centuries, the English state failed to introduce measures for the effective integration of the 'Celtic' parts of the British Isles which it controlled into its own, distinctively English, political community, this new assumption was to be of critical significance. It meant that those whose lands were taken, tended to remain undervalued and alienated.[3] If

---

[1] 'a tam barbaris nationibus Scotis videlicet et Walensibus inhabitatum' in *The Historical Works of Master Ralph de Diceto*, ed. W. Stubbs, 2 vols. (RS, 1876), ii.8. Ralph, it should be noted, was thinking of a time when Henry II's garrisons were installed in Scotland's largest town, Berwick, as well as in Edinburgh and Roxburgh.

[2] Hugh Kearney, *The British Isles. A History of Four Nations* (Cambridge, 1989), 106, where the phrase is applied to sixteenth-century developments.

[3] R. R. Davies, 'The English State and the "Celtic" Peoples 1100–1400', *Journal of Historical Sociology* 6 (1993), 12–13. For some of the many reasons why 'Celtic' is a very misleading, if convenient, word, see M. Chapman, *The Celts. The Construction of a Myth* (London, 1992).

English power tended to unite Britain and Ireland, English attitudes tended to divide; hence the long history of a disunited kingdom.

By the 1180s the movement that Rees Davies has characterised as 'the second tidal wave of Anglo-Saxon or English colonization', was in full flood, i.e. that migration of primarily English settlers into lowland Wales, Scotland and Ireland which began in the late eleventh century and which flowed more or less strongly for roughly two hundred years.[4] Those settlers lived dangerously. In Wales and Ireland they had muscled their way in by force of arms and, as stealers of other men's lands, they sometimes had to pay a high price. In 1171 the natives, wrote Gerald, 'cruelly put to death any English they found on the streets of Waterford or in the houses, without respect for sex or age'.[5] Even in Scotland where they were not following in the wake of military conquest, the incomers were often resented. A few years later, in 1174, after the defeat of King William of Scotland's invasion of the north of England, the Scots took their revenge. 'The towns and boroughs of the kingdom of Scotland are inhabited by English, and the Scots hate them, so they killed as many of the English as they could.'[6] Many centuries earlier, at the time of the first great tidal wave of Anglo-Saxon colonization, the lives of the settlers had been just as precarious, but at that time there had also been a strong tide flowing in the opposite direction. Irish colonization of northern and western Britain had – arguably – been just as important as Anglo-Saxon colonization of the south and east. It lay at the foundations of the kingdom of Scotland much as the Anglo-Saxon settlements led ultimately to the kingdom of England. By contrast, in the twelfth century, and with the important exception of Stephen's reign – significant for this and for other reasons (to which I shall return) – the tide appeared to be flowing in one direction only. It was not just those whose lands were being invaded who were alarmed. In 1171 the king of the Isle of Man and other lords of the Isles came to the aid of the Irish fighting to retain control of Dublin. According to Gerald, one of the reasons they did so was because 'English successes meant that they too now feared English dominion.'[7]

What lay behind those English successes? First and most obvious was the creation of the kingdom of England itself, those economic, political and military developments which changed for ever the political configuration of the British Isles. Compared with contemporary 'Celtic' societies, tenth-century England was both relatively peaceful and economically advanced. Beyond England there were

---

[4] R. R. Davies, *Domination and Conquest. The experience of Ireland, Scotland and Wales 1100–1300* (Cambridge, 1990), 12.

[5] Giraldus Cambrensis, *Expugnatio Hibernica*, ed. and trans. A. B. Scott and F. X. Martin (Dublin, 1978), 140. On contemporary use of the word 'English' to refer to the invaders see 'The English Invasion of Ireland', below, pp. 145–60.

[6] William of Newburgh, *Historia Rerum Anglicarum* in ed. R. Howlett, *Chronicles of the Reigns of Stephen, Henry II and Richard I*, 4 vols. (RS, 1884–90), i.186.

[7] Giraldus, *Expugnatio*, 78.

hardly any coins and hardly any towns – just a few coastal emporia. Economically and politically England had been transformed; 'Celtic' societies had not.[8] Not surprisingly tenth-century English kings, notably Edgar, were described by contemporaries – English ones of course – in terms which accorded them some sort of imperial overlordship over the whole of Britain. There may have been earlier Anglo-Saxon overlordships from the seventh century onwards – Bede certainly claims as much – but it was tenth-century overlordship which had staying power. In place of a British Isles composed of a large number of political communities with fluid frontiers and more or less ephemeral overlordships, from now on there was a single state in the richer lands of lowland Britain and a large number of smaller and poorer kingships to the north and west. By the time Dean Ralph wrote, England had been, with rare and transitory exceptions, a united kingdom for more than two hundred years. Wales and Ireland had continued to be politically fragmented, Ireland especially so. As William of Newburgh, writing in the 1190s, put it when explaining the background to the conquest of the Irish by the English (his words), Ireland in 1170 was like the England of long ago, a land of many kingdoms and a seemingly endless round of war and slaughter.[9] So long as England remained united, it was bound to be the dominant power. Its only rival lay in the north, but in 1100 'as a kingdom Scotland was still very much in the making. The authority of the kings of Scots was barely nominal in Galloway or Moray; in Argyll or Caithness, as of course in the Isles, it faded out in the face of a world of virtually autonomous chiefs under the loose overlordship of Norway.'[10] True, the kingdom of Scotland had not suffered the eleventh-century English fate of being twice conquered. On these grounds it can be argued that it was the Scots, not the English, who 'established the most stable and successful kingdom in Britain prior to the Norman invasion'.[11] But it was more limited in

[8] Though the process was beginning in Scotland; see e.g. B. T. Hudson, 'Kings and Church in early Scotland', *Scottish Historical Review* lxxiii (1994) and A. Grant, 'Thanes and Thanages from the eleventh to the fourteenth centuries' in A. Grant and K. J. Stringer (eds.), *Medieval Scotland: Crown, Lordship and Community. Essays presented to G. W. S. Barrow* (Edinburgh, 1993), pp. 40–7.

[9] William of Newburgh, *Historia*, 167.

[10] R. Frame, *The Political Development of the British Isles 1100–1400* (Oxford, 1990), 10–11; though see also Grant, 'Thanes and Thanages', pp. 46–7; and E. J. Cowan, 'The historical Macbeth' in W. D. H. Sellar (ed.), *Moray: Province and People* (Edinburgh, 1993).

[11] A. Smyth, *Warlords and Holy Men. Scotland AD 80–1000* (London, 1984), 238. However, as Smyth acknowledged, the king of Scots 'did not command resources comparable with those of his English counterpart'. Moreover the twelfth-century kingdom of Scotland seems to have been ethnically more divided even than Anglo-Norman England. See above, n. 6, and below, n. 58, as well as Richard of Hexham's account of ferocious splits within King David I's army in 1138. 'After the battle his men scattered, and in flight they dealt with each other not as friends but as foes. For the English and the Scots and the Galwegians and the rest of the barbarians, whenever they chanced upon each other . . . took the opportunity to kill, wound or rob the other. Thus by a just judgment of God they were oppressed as much by their own kind as by outsiders.' Richard of Hexham, *De Gestis Regis Stephani* in Howlett, *Chronicles*, iii.165–6.

extent, much poorer than England and from the late eleventh century onwards its culture was increasingly influenced by incomers from the south. Thus it was the English empire established in the tenth century – a thousand year *Reich* in the making – which really impressed itself upon subsequent historical consciousness. By the twelfth century it was commonplace for English authors to see their history in imperial terms. In this version of their past, King Edgar was the ideal ruler. According to John of Worcester, Symeon of Durham, Ailred of Rievaulx and Roger of Howden, Edgar was to the English what Charlemagne was to the French and Alexander to the Greeks.[12] This is how another twelfth-century author, Geoffrey Gaimar, described Edgar's reign.

> He held the land as emperor
> In his time he improved the land.
> Everywhere there was peace, nowhere war.
> He alone ruled over all the kings
> And over the Scots and the Welsh
> Never since Arthur departed
> Has any king held such power.[13]

Gaimar's words were taken over by the late medieval chronicle known as the prose *Brut*, the chronicle which survives in more manuscripts than any other English historical work, which was the earliest English history to be printed (by Caxton in 1480), and which had been re-printed no less than eleven times by 1528. Thus this most popular view of English history came to include the notion of an empire founded in the tenth century.[14]

After 1066, and riding on the back of Anglo-Saxon achievement, the new Norman rulers were soon to assert greater dominance both in Scotland and in Wales than their predecessors had done. From this time onwards the native Welsh histories began to acknowledge the pre-eminent position of the king of England. The *Chronicle of the Princes* referred to 'William the Bastard, prince of the Normans and king of the Saxons and Britons and Scots'. In the Red Book of Hergest version Henry I was called 'king of England and Wales and all the island besides'.[15] According to the author of the *Gesta Stephani*, after the Norman conquest of England, they added Wales to their dominion, civilized it, and 'made the land so productive as to be in no way inferior to the most fertile part

---

[12] When, at the end of the century, Roger of Howden borrowed from his predecessors this estimate of Edgar's place in English history, he added a comparison of his own, 'as Arthur to the Britons', *Chronica Magistri Rogeri de Hovedene*, ed. W. Stubbs, 4 vols. (RS, 1868–71), i.64.

[13] Alexander Bell, *L'Estoire des Engleis by Geffrei Gaimar* (Anglo-Norman Text Society, 1960), vv. 3562–8.

[14] See below, pp. 113–22.

[15] *Brut y Tywysogyon or The Chronicle of the Princes. Peniarth Ms. 20 version*, ed. and trans. T. Jones (Cardiff, 1952), 18; *Brut y Tywysogyon. Red Book of Hergest version*, ed. and trans. T. Jones (Cardiff, 1955), 113.

of Britain'.[16] In Scotland, English influence was strong at the court of Malcolm Canmore and Margaret; their anglicized son Edgar appears to have accepted that he owed his throne in part 'to the gift of King William his lord'. In 1124 the earl of Huntingdon became King David I of Scotland, accelerating the process of Anglo-Norman penetration into Scotland.[17] When, writing at the end of the tenth century, Aelfric of Eynsham referred to Roman Britain as England, it may have been just – just! – an early example of what Patrick Wormald has called 'the Englishman's tendency to confuse the identities of England and Britain'.[18] By the 1120s Henry of Huntingdon was turning it into an explicit point. 'This, the most noble of islands, 800 miles long and 200 broad, was first called Albion, then Britain and is now known as England.' And, Henry continued, its abundant wealth, including flourishing vineyards, meant that an extensive foreign trade brought in so much silver that there appeared to be more silver here than in Germany itself. Thus the inhabitants of this England were, in Henry's opinion, superior in life-style and in dress to all other peoples.[19] By the 1120s a combination of politics, war, economics and fashion was creating an apparently inexorable drive towards a culturally homogeneous island in which the over-lordship of the king of England was becoming an ever greater reality.[20]

As it happened, however, this process was to be halted, in some senses reversed, and in others profoundly transformed, during the crisis of Stephen's reign.

The Crisis of Stephen's Reign

Since English dominion depended on the unity of the English state, the prolonged civil war of Stephen's reign was the period when the empire of the kings of England was most at risk, most in danger of being overthrown by the military successes of Scottish and Welsh kings. For Stephen the decisive moment came when he was captured at the battle of Lincoln (1141). In addition to its other consequences this allowed King David of Scotland, who

---

[16] *Gesta Stephani*, ed. and trans. K. R. Potter and R. H. C. Davis (Oxford, 1976), 15.

[17] A. A. M. Duncan, *Scotland. The Making of the Kingdom* (Edinburgh, 1975), 122–7, 134–5. An army from England put Edgar on the throne, and William Rufus undoubtedly regarded him as a vassal. It is harder to be sure about what Edgar thought. The quotation comes from a charter (or diploma) which (if genuine) was issued at Durham, two years before he became king; the text is quite possibly a thirteenth-century forgery; in his later charters Edgar is simply styled 'king of Scots'. See J. Donnelly, 'The earliest Scottish charters?', *Scottish Historical Review*, lxviii (1989).

[18] P. Wormald, 'The Venerable Bede and the "Church of the English"' in ed. G. Rowell, *The English Religious Tradition and the Genius of Anglicanism* (Wantage, 1992), n. 27.

[19] *Henry, Archdeacon of Huntingdon, Historia Anglorum*, ed. and trans. D. Greenway (Oxford, 1996), 12–13, 20–21; 6, 10 in Thomas Arnold's Rolls Series edition (1879). Both editions will hereafter be cited as HH, with Arnold's pagination in square brackets.

[20] The European dimensions of these trends are best set out in R. Bartlett, *The Making of Europe. Conquest, Colonization and Cultural Change 950–1350* (London, 1993).

had already led invasions in 1137–8, to extend and consolidate his take-over of all of England north of the River Tees, including North Lancashire and parts of Yorkshire as well as all Cumberland and Northumberland. From then on until his death in 1153 King David regularly held court at Carlisle and Newcastle, and issued coin from mints at Carlisle, Corbridge and Bamburgh. After Lincoln, as Keith Stringer has pointed out, the north was bound more tightly to Scotland than ever it had been to England.[21] Arguably it was the Welsh contingents fighting for the Angevin cause at Lincoln who gave the Scots this golden opportunity. According to Orderic Vitalis, the first of Stephen's men to take to flight were those who had found themselves facing 'the fierce mob of Welshmen'.[22] The Welsh mob at Lincoln was led by three remarkable kings: Cadwaladr ap Gruffydd of Gwynedd, Madog ap Maredudd of Powys, and Morgan ap Owain from south-east Wales. All three of them had played – and would continue to play – leading roles in what Sir John Lloyd labelled the National Revival, the great Welsh revolt which had broken out following the death of Henry I. In 1136 Cadwaladr and his brother Owain led the biggest and most dramatically successful Welsh armies. In the words of the *Brut Y Tywysogyon* they were 'two exalted kings and two generous ones, two brave lions, two wise ones, defenders of the poor, slayers of their enemies, predominant in soul and body, together they upheld the whole kingdom of the Britons'.[23] Madog ap Maredudd of Powys (1132–60) was to capture Oswestry and see Welsh settlement pushed eastwards towards Cheshire and Shropshire. As a great patron of poets, Madog also was praised in extravagant language, 'a firm anchor in a deep sea'.[24] The third king, Morgan ap Owain, is less well-known, – indeed the evidence for his presence at Lincoln has until recently been overlooked[25] – but it was he who gave the signal for the great revolt by killing Richard FitzGilbert before going on to capture the castle of Caerleon. The revolt and Morgan's capture of Caerleon were, I have suggested, events of major significance in the literary history of Britain, helping to inspire Geoffrey of Monmouth's figure of King Arthur, the all-conquering British king whose reign, in Geoffrey's version, came to a grand climax with a crown-wearing at Caerleon. It is, I think, to the period of the

[21] K. J. Stringer, *The Reign of Stephen* (London, 1993), 28–36.
[22] *The Ecclesiastical History of Orderic Vitalis*, ed. M. Chibnall, 6 vols. (Oxford, 1968–80), vi.542.
[23] *Brut Peniarth*, 51; *Hergest*, 113–15.
[24] R. R. Davies, *Conquest, Co-existence and Change. Wales 1063–1415* (Oxford, 1987), 46, 49–50, 57, 233.
[25] As noted by D. Crouch, 'The March and the Welsh Kings' in ed. E. King, *The Anarchy of King Stephen's Reign* (Oxford, 1994), 273 n. 41. Morgan's presence at Lincoln is vouched for by the author of the *Liber Eliensis*, ed. E. O. Blake, Camden Soc., vol. 92 (1962), 321. Although on the authority of Sir John Lloyd, *A History of Wales* (1939), ii.478, 489, 507, this has long been thought to be a mistake, the fact that between 1140 and 1142 Bishop Nigel of Ely took refuge at Gloucester suggests that at the critical period he was well-placed to learn about Robert of Gloucester's Welsh allies and hence to pass that information on to the author of the Book of Ely.

Welsh revolt that we can date the Anglo-Norman vernacular *Description of England*, with the lines:

> Well have the Welsh revenged themselves . . . Some of our castles they have taken, Fiercely they threaten us, Openly they go about saying, That in the end they will have all, By means of Arthur they will have it back . . . They will call it Britain again.[26]

The New English

In this crisis of empire when the crown of England was in dispute and when ground was being lost to both Scots and Welsh, two perceptions took root.[27] The first was the emergence of a new sense of national identity after the traumas of the Norman Conquest. In answer to the question of the date at which the descendants of those newcomers who settled in England in the wake of the Norman Conquest began to think of themselves as English, historians have often said, 'by the end of the twelfth century'. However I am convinced that it was by 1140, at the latest.[28] If we frame the question of national identity in terms of self-identification, it is apparent that William of Malmesbury and Henry of Huntingdon, authors who left behind a sufficient body of relevant evidence for their own sense of national identity to be ascertained with reasonable confidence, both thought of themselves as English. In what they wrote in the 1120s it is possible to discern a lingering reminiscence of a perception of themselves as English in the sense of being members of a subject population – the downtrodden English oppressed by French (or Norman) lords. But by the time of their later writings this sense of oppression is absent. Now the clear sense in which they felt themselves to be English was in terms of 'we are English and we are members of a ruling elite'.

Equally striking is the work of Geoffrey Gaimar. His *Estoire des Engleis*, written in the late 1130s for the wife of a Lincolnshire landowner, is the earliest extant history written in French, yet not a history of the French, but of the English.[29] What Geoffrey's *Estoire* suggests is, as Sir Richard Southern pointed out, that by the 1130s the Francophone secular elite, the gentry of the time, could see the Anglo-Saxon past as their past, and could, for example, regard a Hereward the Wake as one of their own heroes.[30] Doubtless the king and a tiny

---

[26] See above, pp. 33–9.

[27] 'The ambitions of England's rulers . . . were given literary shape during Stephen's reign, when the kingdom was torn by civil war', M. T. Clanchy, *England and its Rulers* (Glasgow, 1983), 29–30.

[28] In what follows I am summarizing the argument in 'Henry of Huntingdon and the Twelfth-Century Revival of the English Nation', below, pp. 123–42.

[29] Manuscript evidence supports the use of the familiar title, *Estoire des Engleis*, Bell, xi. On the circumstances in which Gaimar wrote see I. Short, 'Gaimar's Epilogue and Geoffrey of Monmouth's *Liber vetustissimus*', *Speculum* 69 (1994), 323–43.

[30] R. W. Southern, *Medieval Humanism* (Oxford, 1970), 154–5.

handful of the greatest magnates, holding vast estates in Normandy as well as in England – though this too was not to be so easy in Stephen's reign after 1141 – may have thought of themselves primarily as Norman French, but the overwhelming majority of the landowners of England knew that they were English, of mixed ancestry and proud of their French forefathers' achievements, bilingual if not tri-lingual, but English none the less, believing that Old English law was their law.[31]

Now the context in which Henry of Huntingdon, that learned and poetic canon of Lincoln, most explicitly gave voice to his 'Wirgefühl' was in his account of the great battle fought in 1138 between the northern barons and the Scots, the Battle of the Standard. 'We were victorious', he wrote.[32] A contemporary of his, John of Worcester, responded in the same way. The first occasions in his chronicle that he used the word 'we' were when writing of 'our' wars against the Welsh and the Scots in 1138.[33] It looks as though one of the consequences of the wars against the Welsh and the Scots in Stephen's reign was to crystallise a newly re-emerging sense of English solidarity and identity – a solidarity which linked men from Lincoln and Worcester with northerners.

I should stress that I am concerned here with nationality in terms of self-identification. This is not necessarily how others would have identified them, almost certainly not the Scots, and certainly not the Welsh. Welsh narrative sources continue to use the term 'the French' when writing of the people whom I am calling the English. This is not surprising. The Welsh had a centuries old experience of facing invaders from the east. Before 1066 they had called them the Saxons. After 1066 when the most prominent invaders were now speaking another language, they gave them another name. The Welsh had made their identification of the invaders on the basis of language, and just because the Francophone settlers of England began to think of themselves as English, that was no reason for the Welsh to stop using a term which still made perfectly good linguistic sense to them. Not until the end of the twelfth century do Welsh sources get round to using the word 'Saxon' of French-speaking English. Native Scottish narrative sources, had any such existed, might well have seen a similar development.[34]

---

[31] On English law in the early twelfth century see P. Wormald, 'Quadripartitus' in eds. G. Garnett and J. Hudson, *Law and Government in Medieval England and Normandy* (Cambridge, 1994), 111–47.

[32] HH, 716–19, [264]. This is the one and only time he brings English and Normans together in a single *gens*, the *gens Normannorum et Anglorum in una acie*. This is the nearest any contemporary writing in England came to using a term approximating to the eighteenth-century concept 'Anglo-Norman'. A little later in the same passage Henry referred to the northern army as *populus Anglorum*.

[33] *The Chronicle of John of Worcester*, ed. J. R. H. Weaver (Oxford, 1908), 46, 49, 51.

[34] The French figure prominently in the address clauses of twelfth-century charters drawn up in Scotland as well as in England and Ireland, but I would argue that the legalistic formulae of address are, in the context of perceptions of national identity, less significant

The New Barbarians

The second perception to take root during Stephen's reign was the perception of Celtic peoples as barbarians. Thus the emerging sense of Englishness came to be partly based on the perception of Celts as significantly different and inferior. The period of the first tidal wave of Anglo-Saxon colonization had also seen great antipathies. In the early eighth century Bede was prepared to call a British king – a fellow-Christian – a barbarian and early West Saxon law codes treated the Welsh as 'second-class citizens.[35] But in the lull between the two great tidal waves, we seem to have a period – and it is an enormously long period – characterised by the absence of any sharply defined attitude towards the Welsh and Scots. Works written in England during the ninth, tenth and eleventh centuries contain none of the language of alienation and superiority which later bulks so large. Moreover it seemed to Liebermann, comparing the late Anglo-Saxon law code of the Dunsaete with the early – c.700 – laws of Wessex, that the former's even-handed treatment of Welsh and English marked 'an advance towards the reconcilation of the races'.[36] It might be argued that the absence of condemnatory language is just an apparent absence, a reflection of the paucity of sources and of the silence of those few that do exist. In this case all that would have happened is that the greater volume of sources in the twelfth century would have enabled historians belatedly to detect views which had been held for centuries. But the writings of early twelfth-century authors such as Orderic Vitalis and John of Worcester suggest that attitudes were changing during their lifetimes. Orderic was at work on his great History from c.1115 to 1141. In what he wrote about the Welsh and Scots up to the mid 1130s he is neutral or even sympathetic. But by the end of that decade his tone was very different. In 1138 the Scots 'invaded England with the utmost brutality and giving full rein to their barbarity treated the peoples of the borders with bestial cruelty'. Of the Welsh he now noted that they are called barbarians and are going around slaughtering people like cattle.[37] John of Worcester too was originally sympathetic towards the Welsh but in the late 1130s adopted a more hostile tone.[38] The Welsh rising and the Scottish invasion of the north unleashed an unprecedented deluge of

than the usage of contemporary narratives, see 'The English Invasion of Ireland', below, pp. 153–4. There are occasional references to the newcomers in Scotland and Ireland as 'French' rather than 'English' in thirteenth-century narratives – but these are exceptional and explicable in terms of the exceptional circumstances in which they were written.

[35] Bede, *Ecclesistical History of the English People*, ed. B. Colgrave and R. A. B. Mynors (Oxford, 1969), 202; *The Laws of the Earliest English Kings*, ed. and trans. F. L. Attenborough (Cambridge, 1922), 36–61. In these early centuries learned Britons from Gildas to 'Nennius' referred to the Saxons as barbarians.

[36] F. Liebermann, *Die Gesetze der Angelsachsen*, 3 vols. (Halle, 1903–16), iii.217.

[37] Orderic, vi.518, 536.

[38] Compare the sympathetic treatment of Welsh revolts during the 1090s in Florence of Worcester, *Chronicon ex Chronicis*, ed. B. Thorpe (London, 1848–9), ii.35, 41–2 with the more critical notes heard after 1135 (ibid., ii.97 and John of Worcester, 43).

vituperation over the heads of the Welsh and Scots. The language of peoples at war, doubtless, but these were peoples who had been at war with each other for many centuries without all this verbal ferocity. So why now?

I have suggested that the new vocabulary should be linked to a socio-economic development of fundamental importance: the demise of slavery.[39] Slavery went out of fashion in England in the early twelfth century. But it survived for longer in Wales, Ireland and Scotland – perhaps for not much longer, but for long enough to have had a dramatic impact upon the English-man's perception of his neighbours. Obviously those who no longer practised slavery or engaged in the slave-trade found it easy to condemn those who did. Particularly important in the context of forming opinion was the fact that the Scots, Welsh and Irish continued to practise war as slave-hunt – a kind of total war. This is how one contemporary, Richard of Hexham, described the Scots in the North in 1138. They 'slaughtered husbands in the sight of their wives, then they carried off the women together with their spoil. The women, both widows and maidens, were stripped, bound and then roped together by cords and thongs, and were driven off at arrow point, goaded by spears . . . Those bestial men who think nothing of adultery, incest and other crimes, when they were tired of abusing their victims, either kept them as slaves or sold them to other barbarians in exchange for cattle.' As this passage, like many others written in the mid-twelfth century, makes clear, war as slave-hunt was war targeted against non-combatants, whereas by this date 'civilised' war elsewhere in England or on the continent meant war against combatants and their property. But slave-raiders found it in practice necessary to kill not only anyone who put up a fight but also anyone whose lamenting or clinging presence got in the way of the business of seizing potential slaves and dragging them off into captivity. Thus the Scots, in Richard of Hexham's words, 'by the sword's edge or the spear's point slaughtered the sick on their beds, women pregnant and in labour, babes in their cradles or at their mothers' breasts or in their arms, they slaughtered worn-out old men, feeble old women, and anyone who was disabled'.[40] As Richard of Hexham's language makes plain, authors like him now regarded as utterly bestial a form of war once taken for granted as the way everyone made war and always had done. Hence the newly hysterical language applied to the conduct of the Scottish and Welsh war-parties in the later 1130s.

Once English authors had in this way been made forcibly aware of the Scots and Welsh, then they noticed other things about them. For example they began to talk about their 'nakedness'. This did not, of course, mean that they invaded England in the nude but that their lack of adequate armour made their bodies look very vulnerable – as indeed they were. Even the royal army of David of

[39] 'The Beginnings of English Imperialism', above, pp. 13–14; also 'Conquering the Barbarians: War and Chivalry in twelfth-century Britain', above, pp. 45–8.

[40] Richard of Hexham, *De Gestis Regis Stephani* in Howlett, *Chronicles*, iii.152, 156–7. Henry of Huntingdon, Ailred of Rievaulx, John of Hexham and John of Worcester all wrote of the Scots in similar terms.

Scotland at the Standard included only 200 mailed soldiers; the rest of his troops lacked body armour and in consequence, as was observed by all commentators on the battle, they suffered terribly from the fire of the English archers.[41] Similarly during the invasion of Ireland it was, in Gerald de Barri's judgment, the arrows of the English which spread terror among the Irish. Superior armour and firepower gave the invaders a decisive advantage, enabling them to win the control which gave them time to build the castles which further re-inforced and stabilised that control.[42] In terms of armour and ammunition – i.e. arrowheads – the English economy was clearly capable of out-producing that of any Celtic power. In a vivid image of Henry II's knights riding out to war, Jordan Fantosme, author of a vernacular account of the Anglo-Scottish war of 1173–4, used the contrast to make a point. 'See now the knights coming down from the castle, seizing their arms, putting on hauberks and coats of mail, lacing on their new helmets . . . in battle array they come forth from the town, some 60,000 of them . . . and not one of them but thinks himself the equal of a Welsh king.'[43] The 60,000 is, no doubt, an exaggeration, but the point remains that in Jordan's mind there were very large numbers of men who could afford to be 'royally', by Welsh standards, armed and armoured. And indeed that the numbers able to obtain high-quality armour had reached new – if still unquantifiable – levels is suggested by that other twelfth-century phenomenon: the tournament. To engage in tournaments was to proclaim your membership of a heavily armoured elite, the exclusive club of international chivalry. In the 1160s we can see a king of Scotland, William the Lion, working hard to join the club but, kings apart, there were few living north or west of England who could afford the entrance fee.

War between the English, with their towns, castles, hauberks and helmets, and any of their Celtic neighbours (including, at this stage of their development, the Scots) was an unequal struggle between an industrially advanced power and a comparatively primitive economy. Thus when twelfth-century English writers looked at the Welsh and Scots they saw savage and poorly equipped people. In consequence they looked at them with hostile and condescending eyes. As Jordan Fantosme's language implies, this attitude is unlikely to have been restricted to the Latin writing clerical elite. Chrétien of Troyes probably became familiar with the Matter of Britain at Henry II's court and, in Chrétien's *Perceval*, one of King Arthur's knights is made to observe that 'all Welshmen are more stupid than beasts of the field'. In Guillaume le Clerc's *Fergus* this characterisa-tion was transferred to the Galwegians.[44] Learned men such as Dean Ralph,

---

[41] M. Strickland, 'Securing the North: Invasion and the Strategy of Defence in Twelfth-Century Anglo-Scottish Warfare', *Anglo-Norman Studies* 12 (1989), 177–98.

[42] *Expugnatio*, 230, 248; *incastellata* was Gerald's term for a properly subjected land, *ibid.*, 232, cf. 104. Bartlett, *The Making of Europe*, 63–84.

[43] *Jordan Fantosme's Chronicle*, ed. and trans. R. C. Johnston (Oxford, 1981), vv. 153–161.

[44] Chrétien de Troyes, *Arthurian Romances*, trans. W. W. Kibler (Harmondsworth, 1991), 384; Guillaume le Clerc, *Fergus of Galloway*, trans. D. D. R. Owen (London, 1991), 4. The Galwegians seem to have been regarded as peculiarly savage by many of their neighbours.

Richard of Hexham and William of Newburgh began to refer routinely to these crude, stupid and feckless people as 'barbarians'.

But why did those who came to look down on their Celtic neigbours choose to describe them precisely as *barbari*? In earlier centuries the word 'barbarian' had been used by Latin Christian authors as a synonym for 'pagan' so *prima facie* it is odd to see it applied to the Christian Irish, Welsh and Scots.[45] I am inclined to think that at least part of the responsibility for this – one of the most devastating ideological shifts in the course of British history – should be borne by a historian: William of Malmesbury, one of the most creative of all English historians and in his influential *History of the Kings of England* (completed by 1125), an early exponent of the splendid English habit of regarding the course of English history as the triumph of civilisation over barbarism. William's crucial intellectual step was to take the religious component out of the concept of barbarian and re-define it in terms of secular and material culture. His comments on King David of Scotland show that he regarded polished manners and a sophisticated life-style as among the hallmarks of civilised society. According to William, David's promised tax exemptions to any of his subjects who would 'live in a more civilised style, dress with more elegance and learn to eat with more refinement'. And where had David acquired his notions of civilised behaviour? William was in no doubt. 'From the time he had spent with us – *familiaritas nostrorum* – he had been made more courtly and the rust of his native barbarism had been polished away.'[46] Later in the century we can see Henry II holding court at Dublin and trying to impress the Irish by a demonstration of a kind of *nouvelle cuisine*. According to Gerald, he made the Irish kings and chiefs eat crane – a bird they had never before thought of as a delicacy. Moreover Exchequer records show that Henry's logistical preparations for his 1171–2 expedition to Ireland included 569 pounds of almonds.[47]

More fundamentally, William explicitly associated high culture with economic development. Of the Irish – whom he refers to as barbarians – he says that 'ignorant of agriculture they live in rustic squalor unlike the English and French who live in towns, who are familiar with commerce and enjoy a more cultivated style of life'.[48] He clearly accepted the ancient notion that pastoral economies

---

[45] W. R. Jones, 'The Image of the Barbarian in Medieval Europe', *Comparative Studies in Society and History* 13 (1971); W. R. Jones, 'England against the Celtic Fringe: a Study in Cultural Stereotypes', *Journal of World History* 13 (1971).

[46] William of Malmesbury, *Gesta Regum Anglorum*, ed. W. Stubbs, 2 vols. (RS, 1887–9), c. 400. Since the division into chapters is the same both in this edition and in the new one, *Gesta Regum Anglorum*, vol. 1, ed. and trans. R. A. B. Mynors, R. M. Thomson and M. Winterbottom, I cite this work as WM and by chapter number.

[47] Gerald, *Expugnatio*, 96. In addition to almonds and massive quantities of ironware, Henry II's fleet to Ireland also carried 1,000 pounds of wax, presumably to seal documents and to shed light in the dark corners of the land. See J. F. Lydon, *The Lordship of Ireland* (Dublin, 1972), 40–41.

[48] WM c. 409.

were unable to sustain civilised life. Here we have one of the consequences of the unequal rate of economic development in different parts of the British Isles. Whereas for centuries the Anglo-Saxon and Celtic worlds had been, as Patrick Wormald has argued, very similar, by the early twelfth century they were different enough for the differences to be visible to contemporaries. The author who first gave expression to this perception of significant otherness was William of Malmesbury. After centuries in which the term 'barbarian' was understood in religious terms, William's remarkable familiarity with classical literature and his admiration for the values of the ancient world enabled him to re-discover the classical concept of the barbarian and to discover that it applied to Celtic peoples in his own day. In British history at any rate this is the truly significant Renaissance. William's revival of Greco-Roman modes of perception resulted in the Christian view of the world, one which divided men and women into two basic groups – Christian and non-Christian – being decisively supplemented by a non-religious system of classification, one which divided men and women into the 'civilised' and the 'barbarous'. In the course of British history this was to be the great divide, the creation of an imperialist English culture.

A New Order

It may be that William's way of seeing the societies of the British Isles would have caught on anyway. But, as it happened, ten years or so after he completed his *History of the Kings of England*, the events of Stephen's reign brought two of William's barbarians, the Welsh and the Scots, to people's attention, and did so with shocking violence. Thus the author of the *Deeds of King Stephen* began his narrative of Stephen's reign with an account of the Welsh revolt and this led him to offer an analysis of Welsh society. This he did in Malmesbury's terms. The Welsh, it appears, are a barbarous people, of untamed savagery, and they live in a 'country of woodland and pasture . . . abounding in deer and fish, milk and herds . . . a country breeding men of a bestial type'.[49] By the later twelfth century it had become commonplace to note the relative lack of towns, commerce and agriculture in Ireland and Wales.[50] The author who, above all others, took up and elaborated this point of view was Gerald de Barri. According to him, the Welsh lived almost entirely on oats and milk, cheese and butter, the produce of their herds. They ate plenty of meat but very little bread and paid no attention to

---

[49] *Gesta Stephani*, 14.
[50] However it is important for the way anglicized lowland Scotland was developing to note that in the 1150s one well-informed observer, Ailred of Rievaulx, praised King David for having made an uncultivated and barren land bring forth fruit, for building castles and towns, and for filling its markets with goods from abroad, *Eulogium Davidis Regis Scottorum* in *Pinkerton's Lives of the Scottish Saints*, ed. W. M. Metcalfe, 2 vols. (Paisley, 1889), ii.279. Perhaps the tax exemptions attributed to David by William of Malmesbury had had the desired pump-priming effect.

commerce, shipping or industry.[51] He painted a picture of Ireland as a country rich in natural resources but undeveloped owing to lack of industry on the part of the natives, a land of gold and rain-forests, where the savages whiled away their lives in brutality, sexual licence and laziness, an Eldorado waiting for the arrival of the enterprising and clean-living Englishman.[52]

Of course twelfth-century writers exaggerated the extent to which Celtic societies were pastoral; here the point is that this is how those societies were perceived and presented to English audiences. So far as Ireland and Wales were concerned, one consequence was that they were perceived as economically dependent on England and hence as vulnerable to the power of the rulers of England. According to William of Malmesbury, Irish kings were careful to remain in Henry I's good books. One who stepped out of line for a moment was quickly brought to heel by a trade embargo. 'For what would Ireland be worth if goods were not brought to it from England?'[53] According to William of Newburgh, Wales 'is incapable of supplying its inhabitants with food except by imports from neighbouring English counties – and thus it is inevitably subject to the power of the king of England'. When Gerald advised the English on how to conquer the Welsh he advocated an embargo. 'Every effort must be made to stop them from buying the cloth, salt and corn which they usually import from England. Ships manned with picked troops must patrol the coast to ensure that these goods are not brought by water across the Irish or the Severn Sea.'[54]

A second consequence of seeing Ireland and Wales as economically undeveloped was the conviction that under proper (i.e. English) management and with strong government to curb native lawlessness, they could be brought to peace and prosperity. According to the author of the *Gesta Stephani*, conquerors and settlers in Wales 'had made the country so abound in peace and productivity that it might easily have been thought a second England'. In the same vein Gerald argued that if the Irish could be compelled to obey the king of England, then they would enjoy the benefits of peace and be introduced to 'a better way of life'.[55] 'Let them eat crane', as Henry II might have said. The better way was the English way. In stark contrast to their image of their Celtic neighbours, the English perceived themselves as prosperous, urbanised, enterprising, peaceful, law-abiding and with higher moral standards. At the synod of Cashel (1172) it was announced that in future the Irish church was in all matters to be conducted in line with the observance of the English church – above all, the dean of St Paul's noted, in matters of marriage, one of many indications that church 'reformers', from the time of Pope Gregory VII and

[51] Gerald of Wales, *The Journey through Wales and The Description of Wales*, trans. L. Thorpe (Harmondsworth, 1978), 233.

[52] *Expugnatio*, 170; *The Topography of Ireland*, trans. J. J. O' Meara (Harmondsworth, 1982).

[53] WM c. 409. Gerald made a similar point. 'Ireland cannot survive without the goods and trade which come to it from Britain', *Expugnatio*, 252.

[54] William of Newburgh, i.107; Gerald, *The Journey*, 267.

[55] *Gesta Stephani*, 16; *Expugnatio*, 100, 250.

Lanfranc onwards, had regarded Celtic family law as immoral. In 1174 a captive King William was forced to agree that the church of Scotland would be subject to the English church. England's neighbours were being offered a co-prosperity sphere and a New Order. But is it not misleading to apply, as here, the vocabulary of twentieth-century imperialism to twelfth-century conditions? After all 'everyone knows' that things were different then. Looking back from the twentieth century we can see that medieval England was an overwhelmingly rural economy, a primitive society. But this was precisely what twelfth-century Englishmen saw when they looked towards their Celtic neighbours. When they called them barbarians they did not merely mean 'we are better than you'. They meant 'we are so much better as to have reached a higher stage of human development than you'.[56]

One measure of the economic and political strength of the structures underpinning the English position within the British Isles is the speed with which, after the crisis of Stephen's reign, Henry II was able to re-impose the old patterns. In Gerald's words, 'He remarkably extended the kingdom's borders and limits until they reached from the sea to the south to the Orkney Islands in the north. Within his powerful grasp he included the whole island of Britain in one monarchy.'[57] In doing this he was materially helped by the fact that divisions within Scotland and Wales were much fiercer and more fundamental than those which had recently disturbed the English kingdom. King David 'modernised' Scotland with the help of émigrés from south of the border but this may have exacerbated ethnic tensions and added to the difficulties faced by his successor, Malcolm IV. In 1157 the young king of Scots had to submit to Henry II's bullying and restore the territorial gains which David had made at English expense.[58] In 1158 Morgan of Caerleon was 'slain through treachery' by a fellow Welshman; in 1171 on his way to Ireland Henry confiscated the castle of Caerleon.[59] Part of the pattern was that those who, in Gerald's words, 'feed constantly on the hope of recovering the lands which the English have taken from them' would naturally take advantage of any serious dissension within the English establishment. For example, the rebellion of his family against Henry II in 1173–4 triggered Irish, Scottish and – by Morgan's successor, Iorwerth of

---

[56] R. Bartlett, *Gerald of Wales* (Oxford, 1982), 176, for the parallels between some of these twelfth-century concepts – the ladder of evolution of human societies and the persistence of primitive survivals – and nineteenth- (and twentieth-) century anthropological thought.

[57] Giraldi Cambrensis, *Opera*, vol. viii, ed. G. F. Warner (RS, 1891), 156.

[58] For Malcolm's problems with the Gaelic world, notably from 'the barbarous hands' of Somerled of Argyll and his kin, see the passages from the Chronicles of Holyrood, Melrose and Man and above all from the *Carmen de morte Sumerledi*, translated in A. O. Anderson, *Early Sources of Scottish History*, 2 vols. (Stamford, 1990), ii.223–4, 254–8. The point is argued vigorously in R. A. McDonald and S. A. McLean, 'Somerled of Argyll: a new look at old problems', *Scottish Historical Review* lxxi (1992). For a different view, see Duncan, *Making of the Kingdom*, 166–7.

[59] *Brut. Hergest*, 137; *Peniarth*, 66.

Caerleon – Welsh recovery attempts.[60] Similarly the war at the end of John's reign, the Magna Carta revolt as it appears from an English perspective, was also a war of the allies, the French, the Welsh and the Scots against the English – and was so perceived at the time.[61] In this war no one fought on more obstinately than did Morgan of Caerleon.[62]

There is one striking exception to this pattern. This is when Richard I was in prison in Germany and his brother John in revolt against him – a moment of acute weakness for the English crown, and an ideal opportunity for any of England's Celtic neighbours to exploit. Yet, unlike the king of France, not one of them made any attempt to do so. Not the Irish.[63] Nor the Welsh princes – perhaps thanks in part to Gerald de Barri's diplomatic activity, though at the cost of his own ecclesiastical career.[64] Nor the Scots. William the Lion not only refused to exploit the situation, he even made a substantial contribution to Richard's ransom. Peace, not war, characterised the relations between Scots and English in Richard's reign. In the words of the first historian of Scotland, John of Fordun, there was 'so hearty a union between the two countries and so great a friendship of real affection knit the two kings . . . that the two peoples were reckoned as one and the same.'[65] This, of course, was in the reign of an exceptional king.

Henry II's reign had witnessed the re-impositon of old patterns. This, indeed, is what he had set out to achieve – the recovery of what he called the rights of his grandfather. In this context Walter Map's styling of Henry I as 'king of England, duke of Normandy, count of Brittany and Maine, lord of Scotland,

---

[60] *Expugnatio*, 134. For the interdependence of these events see Gerald, *The Journey through Wales*, 119–20.

[61] Thomas Wright, *The Political Songs of England from the Reign of John to that of Edward II* (Camden Soc., 1839), 19–20. For the continuing concern of the English government with alliances of this kind see S. Duffy, 'The Bruce Brothers and the Irish Sea World, 1306–29', *Cambridge Medieval Celtic Studies* 21 (1991).

[62] See D. A. Carpenter, *The Minority of Henry III* (London, 1990), 70, 77, 192, 294, 308.

[63] To judge from the Irish annals, in Ireland it was business as usual – perhaps the only corner of Christian Europe to display no interest in the crusades. Modern books on medieval Irish history have tended to ignore Richard I's reign – a mistake as M. T. Flanagan has shown, *Irish Society, Anglo-Norman Settlers, Angevin Kingship* (Oxford, 1989), esp. 266–7, on the appointment and activities of John de Courcy as justiciar of Ireland in 1194–5.

[64] Giraldi Cambrensis, *Opera*, vol. i, ed. J. S. Brewer (RS, 1861), 295–300.

[65] John of Fordun called Richard 'that noble king of England so friendly to the Scots', *The Historians of Scotland*, vol. 4, *John of Fordun's Chronicle of the Scottish Nation*, ed. W. F. Skene (Edinburgh, 1872), 269–71. See now Walter Bower, *Scotichronicon*, ed. D. E. R. Watt et al., 9 vols. (1987–98), vol. 4, 406. Not surprisingly since Richard's 1189 Quitclaim of Canterbury released Scotland, in the words of the Melrose Chronicle, 'from that grievous state of subordination and servitude to which it had been subjected', Anderson, *Early Sources*, ii.322. As the aftermath indicated, this was a well calculated act of political generosity, of enormous advantage to Richard as well as to the independence of Scotland. However many modern English historians have preferred to echo the view expressed by Gerald (*Opera*, viii.156) that the Quitclaim represented a shameful loss to the English crown.

Galloway and of the whole English island' gives a good indication of the way men thought at Henry II's court, as does also Map's reference to 'our island England'.[66] But in some vital respects Henry's reign marked the New Order. First and most fateful was the fact that the English invaded Ireland. In the words of William of Newburgh, this meant that a people who had been free since time immemorial, unconquered even by the Romans, a people for whom liberty seemed, as he put it, an inborn right, were now fallen into the power of the king of England.[67] The second was that as a consequence of government in late twelfth-century England becoming significantly more bureaucratic, so English domination was increasingly to be expressed in institutional and administrative forms. The third was that a regime which claimed to be bringing the delights of modern government and prosperity to its neighbours was doing so at a time when the perception of the king's Celtic subjects as barbarians was no longer just the clever idea of a clever historian but had become deeply entrenched in English thought. This way of seeing and describing differences between peoples set up ideological barriers between invader and invaded, between coloniser and colonised. From the twelfth century onwards there was to be a crucial fragility at the heart of the English empire.[68]

---

[66] Walter Map, *De Nugis Curialium*, ed. M. R. James, C. N. L. Brooke and R. A. B. Mynors (Oxford, 1983), 166, 472.
[67] William of Newburgh, i.165–8.
[68] Davies, 'The English State and the "Celtic" Peoples', 10–13.

Part Two. National Identity

7

Gaimar, the Prose *Brut* and the
Making of English History

Medieval England has been described by Bernard Guenée, and with good
reason, as a country where the passion for history was 'fort vive'.[1] But it had not
always been so. As James Campbell observes, 'The learned men of Anglo-Saxon
England had left their country very ill-provided with histories . . . It is virtually
certain that for large areas of Anglo-Saxon history the inquirer of c.1100 had no
sources apart from Bede or the wretched annals of one or more versions of the
Anglo-Saxon Chronicle.' The English passion for history was, in effect, a creation
of the twelfth century. In Campbell's words, 'The greatest advances in the study
and understanding of Anglo-Saxon history made before the nineteenth century
were those of the twelfth. They were in large measure accomplished by
historians working during the reigns of Henry I and Stephen: William of
Malmesbury, Henry of Huntingdon and the author traditionally called Florence
of Worcester, but whose name was probably John.'[2] Guenée called this same
trio 'une brillante cohorte d'érudits'; in 1300 their work was still 'au fondement
même de la culture et de la conscience nationale des Anglais'.[3] In my view there
was another early twelfth-century English historian who, in his own way, was at
least as influential as those three. This was Geoffrey Gaimar.

Gaimar's *Estoire des Engleis* has long been recognised as one of the most
remarkable and pioneering of all extant medieval historical works. Composed in
the late 1130s it is the earliest extant history written in French; it was composed
in octosyllabic couplets, the classic verse form of the romance.[4] As conceived
and originally executed it was clearly a vast historical enterprise, beginning with

---

[1] Bernard Guenée, *Histoire et Culture Historique dans l'occident médiéval* (Paris, 1980), p. 318.
[2] James Campbell, 'Some Twelfth-Century Views of the Anglo-Saxon Past', *Peritia* 3 (1984),
pp. 131, 138.
[3] Guenée, *Histoire et Culture*, pp. 309, 313.
[4] Ian Short, 'Gaimar et les débuts de l'historiographie en langue française' in ed. Danielle
Buschinger, *Chroniques nationales et chroniques universelles* (Göppingen, 1990), pp. 155–63;
Alexander Bell, 'Gaimar as pioneer', *Romania* 97 (1976), pp. 462–80; M. Dominica Legge,
Anglo-Norman Literature and its Background (Oxford, 1963), pp. 27–36, 277; R. R. Bezzola, *Les
Origines et la formation de la littérature courtoise*, vol. 2 (Paris, 1960), p. 454. On the date of
writing (and much else) see Ian Short, 'Gaimar's Epilogue and Geoffrey of Monmouth's
liber vetustissimus', *Speculum* 69 (1994), 323–43.

the story of Jason and the Golden Fleece and continuing up to the accession of Henry I in AD 1100. For the period up to the mid-tenth century it comprises in large part a translation of the *Anglo-Saxon Chronicle*. Gaimar performs the *tour de force* of turning the archaic prose of the Old English annals into a national history written in fashionable French verse.[5] From Edgar's reign (957–75) until the end of his history, Gaimar's source, or more probably sources (including, very likely, oral tradition), are unknown. But whatever his sources, what he produced was what A. R. Press has called 'the earliest known and quite explicit formulation of an entirely new historiographical concept . . . a wholly secular and superbly self-possessed celebration of the world's delights, values and activities'.[6] These delights, values and activities had already, of course, been evoked in early troubadour lyrics, but in Gaimar they are fitted into an immense and entirely secular historical framework, beginning with the Golden Fleece and ending with an evocation of the pleasures of life at the court of King Henry I. There, in Gaimar's words, was 'love and gallantry, and woodland sports and jokes, and feasts and splendour'.[7] Not all of Gaimar's *Estoire* still survives; only some 6500 lines of verse, covering the period after the arrival of the Saxons under Hengist. The now lost first part seems to have been largely based on Geoffrey of Monmouth and so it is traditionally known as *L'estoire des Bretuns*.[8] At some stage this part was superseded by Wace's *Roman de Brut*, the work which precedes the *Estoire des Engleis* in all four surviving manuscripts.[9] Given this relatively small number of manuscripts, it is not surprising that Gaimar has been regarded as having been less influential than his contemporaries who wrote in Latin: William of Malmesbury, Henry of Huntingdon and John of Worcester.[10]

---

[5] I shall quote from the edition by Alexander Bell, *L'Estoire des Engleis by Geffrei Gaimar* (Anglo-Norman Text Society, 1960). The older edition by T. D. Hardy and C. T. Martin, *L'Estoire des Engles*, 2 vols. (RS, 1888–89) numbers the lines slightly differently and provides an English translation. On Gaimar's linguistic range see Short, 'Gaimar', p. 160, and Ian Short, 'Patrons and Polyglots: French Literature in Twelfth Century England', *Anglo-Norman Studies* 14 (1991), p. 244.

[6] A. R. Press, 'The Precocious Courtesy of Geoffrey Gaimar' in ed. G. S. Burgess, *Court and Poet* (Liverpool, 1981), 268–69. For further analysis of Gaimar's outlook see below, pp. 233–58.

[7] Gaimar, vv. 6505–7, 6523–24. Gaimar himself mentions an earlier work by David, but to judge from his reference to it, it dealt only with Henry I's reign and so presumably was on a much smaller scale.

[8] Bell, *L'Estoire*, pp. xii–xiii, li, lxxv–lxxvi.

[9] The manuscripts are described in Bell, *L'Estoire*, pp. xv–xviii. In three of them Gaimar is associated with two other vernacular histories, Wace and Jordan Fantosme; in the fourth with Wace, the Lay of Haveloc (A-N), Chretien of Troyes' *Perceval*, and Walter of Henley's *Hosebonderie*.

[10] Antonia Gransden, *Historical Writing in England c.550 to c.1307* (London, 1974), p. 209: 'Its popular success was small.' See the fascinating table giving the approximate manuscript numbers of some eighty histories (but not the *Brut* – the table is explicitly acknowledged to be incomplete) in Guenée, *Histoire et culture*, pp. 250–52. This gives 35 for Malmesbury's *Gesta Regum* plus 20 for his *Gesta Pontificum*, and 25 for Henry of Huntingdon's *Historia*.

However in this paper I shall argue that Gaimar was much more influential than has generally been realised. I shall do so primarily on the basis of his direct impact on the Anglo-Saxon sections of the history of England that survives in far more manuscripts than any other, and indeed which was the first English history to be printed: the prose *Brut*.

The prose *Brut* was originally composed c.1300 in French by an anonymous author, perhaps a Londoner, probably a man. (For convenience, though there is no direct evidence of gender, I shall refer to the author as 'he'.) It covered the centuries between the foundation of Britain by Brutus and the accession of Edward I in 1272. Many different continuations were then added and versions of it were translated into both English and then Latin. Its extra-ordinary success is shown by the fact that the count of extant manuscripts of all three versions stands at present at more than 230: 15 Latin, more than 50 in French and 168 in English.[11] An English version was printed by Caxton in 1480 and then again no less than twelve times before its last printing in 1528. The *Brut* became 'the nearest equivalent in medieval England to the *Grandes Chroniques* in France . . . and judging by the surviving number of copies it appears to have enjoyed a wider circulation in England than the *Grandes Chroniques* were to do in their own country'.[12] No other single work can give us a better idea of how English men and women in the fourteenth, fifteenth and early sixteenth centuries viewed their past.

Yet although the remarkable popularity of the *Brut* has long been perfectly familiar to historians of England, hardly any work has been done on the original text of c.1300. Even historians of historical literature like John Taylor and Antonia Gransden have been more interested in the more or less contemporary accounts offered by the fourteenth and fifteenth century continuations than in the original *Brut*'s narrative of earlier history. In that sense, like historians of politics, they have tended to study the *Brut* primarily as evidence for events, rather than as a work of historical literature in its own right. Unquestionably for historians looking for reliable information about the distant past the *Brut* had little or nothing to offer. In the damning verdict of Friedrich Brie, the German scholar who edited an English version of the *Brut* at the start of this century, 'als Ganzes genommen hat der Brute of England so viele Fehler als es für ein geschichtliches Werk zu besitzen möglich ist'.[13] So the original French prose *Brut* has been neglected. There is still no edition of it, despite – or perhaps

---

[11] The best introduction to the *Brut* is John Taylor, *English Historical Literature in the Fourteenth Century* (Oxford, 1987), pp. 110–32. For the manuscripts see Lister M. Matheson, 'Historical Prose' in ed. A. S. G. Edwards, *Middle English Prose* (New Brunswick, 1984), pp. 232–33, a reference I owe to the kindness of Lesley Johnson.

[12] Taylor, *English Historical Literature*, p. 113. For evidence that the *Brut* was also known in France, see Paul Meyer, 'De quelques chroniques anglo-normandes qui ont porté le nom de *Brut*', *Bulletin de la Société des anciens textes français* 4 (1878), pp. 104–45.

[13] Friedrich W. D. Brie, *Geschichte und Quellen der mittelenglischen Prosachronik, 'The Brute of England' oder 'The Chronicles of England'* (Marburg, 1905), p. 9.

because of – its 50 manuscripts.[14] Virtually nothing has been done on its sources since Brie's 1905 sketch.[15]

Here I shall concentrate on the *Brut*'s Anglo-Saxon history, chapters 102–127 in the English version, the most neglected chapters in a neglected work.[16] Whereas the first hundred chapters have at least attracted some slight attention from the many scholars who have succumbed to the spell of Geoffrey of Monmouth and King Arthur, the *Brut*'s account of Anglo-Saxon history has been forgotten.[17] What is crystal clear, however, is that the author of the *Brut* knew Gaimar's *Estoire* (either as a whole or in part) and sometimes followed it very closely indeed.[18] If we assume, perhaps rashly, that the whole of the *Estoire* was available to him, then the *Brut* author was extremely selective, for his narrative of Anglo-Saxon history is much shorter than Gaimar's. From the first 2000 lines of Gaimar, he took virtually nothing except the story of Haveloc the Dane. This means that he omitted nearly all of the driest part of Gaimar, the translation of the *Anglo-Saxon Chronicle* annals for the seventh, eighth and early ninth centuries. On the other hand he also took nothing at all of the last 1500 lines. This means that he omitted some of Gaimar's liveliest passages, so his selection cannot have been made only on literary grounds.

He first became really interested in the *Estoire* at that point where Gaimar explained the production of the *Anglo-Saxon Chronicle*. According to Gaimar, so violent and lawless were the politics of the time (eighth and ninth centuries) that people were confused and hardly knew where they stood. In an attempt to get things straight monks and canons of abbeys kept written records which were then collected together in the form of a big book kept chained at Winchester and for which King Alfred was responsible. Here the *Brut* simply takes Gaimar's verse and renders it into French prose.[19] For the next 25 chapters Gaimar remained the dominant influence. In chapter 103 the *Brut* follows him in telling

[14] In preparing this paper I looked at just three copies of the French *Brut*, BL Cotton Cleopatra D VII, BL Add. 18462 (a) and (b).

[15] Brie, *Geschichte und Quellen*, pp. 32–43. Despite variations between the various copies of the French *Brut*, it is obvious that the author had Gaimar in front of him. Sometimes he turned verse into prose by the simple method of letting one line run into another.

[16] *The Brut or Chronicles of England*, ed. F. W. D. Brie, Early English Text Society cxxxi (1906).

[17] Thus the summary description of the French prose *Brut* as 'a chronicle which added to Geoffrey (of Monmouth)'s romance a more factual account of British history from the time of the Norman Conquest to the reign of Edward I', Taylor, *English Historical Literature*, p. 111, effectively eliminates Anglo-Saxon history.

[18] Brie, *Geschichte und Quellen*, pp. 40–41; thus H. Matter, *Englische Gründungssagen von Geoffrey of Monmouth bis zur Renaissance*, Anglistische Forschungen 58 (Heidelberg, 1922), p. 286, calls Gaimar 'eine Hauptquelle des anglo-normannischen Brut und somit des englischen Brute'. See also Bell, *L'Estoire*, pp. lx, lxiii, lxxxvi–lxxxvii; Antonia Gransden, *English Historical Writing c.1307 to the Early Sixteenth Century* (London, 1982), p. 73. Contrast Taylor, *English Historical Literature*, p. 116 and *The Anonimalle Chronicle 1307 to 1334*, ed. Wendy R. Childs and John Taylor (Yorkshire Archaeological Society CXLVII for 1987, 1991), p. 16.

[19] Gaimar, vv. 2312–36. Bell, *L'Estoire*, pp. 237–38 cites the relevant passage from another copy (BL Cotton Domitian X) of the French prose *Brut*.

the story of Buern Butsecarl.[20] This led to the Danish invasions and the heroic resistance of 'good King Alfred' (chapters 104–9). In summing up Alfred's achievement Gaimar includes a passage further re-inforcing the notion of Alfred as the progenitor of the *Anglo-Saxon Chronicle.*

> Nul mieldre clerc de lui n'esteit
> Kar en s'enfance apris l'aveit
> Il fist escrire un livre engleis
> Des aventures e des leis
> E des batailles de la terre
> E des reis ki firent guerre
> E meint livre fist il escrire,
> U li bon clerc vont suvent lire.[21]

Although Alfred's contribution to English literature was well known to scholars at the time – William of Malmesbury, e.g., has much to say on the subject – Gaimar is the first writer to credit the king with a key role in the making of the *Chronicle* itself. Here too he was emphatically followed by the *Brut.*

'The good king Alfred was a good clerk and had many books made. And one book he made of English, of adventures of kings and of battles that had been fought in the land.'[22] When the *Brut* went out of fashion in the later sixteenth century, then out with it went the notion of Alfred as the maker of the *Anglo-Saxon Chronicle.*[23] Not until the later nineteenth century was Gaimar's idea revived – and presumably this was, in part at least, a consequence of the earliest printings of the relevant parts of Gaimar's text, first by Henry Petrie in 1848, then by Thomas Wright in 1850.[24] In 1862 Thomas Hardy argued the case for Alfred, and he was then followed by two of the greatest Victorian scholars, William Stubbs and Charles Plummer. Both Hardy and Plummer acknowledged that in attributing it to Alfred's initiative they were following in Gaimar's footsteps.[25]

---

[20] I shall sometimes confine myself to references to Brie's edition. Since the English version was essentially a translation of the French prose *Brut*, Brie's printed text gives the reader an adequate (for my purposes) indication of the unprinted French. On the story of Buern, see Matter, *Englische Gründungssagen*, pp. 280–97.

[21] Gaimar, vv. 3443–50.

[22] Chapter 109. Cf. BL Cleopatra D VII, f. 127v; BL Add. 18462 (a) f. 49v and (b) f. 158v.

[23] This despite the fact that Alfred continued to be credited with the foundation of just about every institution of which the English were proud, e.g. navy, jury, shire system, common law, the university of Oxford, English monarchy etc. For a typical and immensely influential catalogue of Alfred's achievements see David Hume, *History of England* (London, 1762), vol. 1, chapter 2. See also Louis W. Miles, *King Alfred in Literature* (Baltimore, 1902).

[24] H. Petrie, *Monumenta Historica Britannica* (London, 1848), I; Thomas Wright, *The Anglo-Norman Metrical Chronicle of Geoffrey Gaimar* (Caxton Soc., XI, 1850).

[25] T. D. Hardy, *Catalogue of British History*, I, part 2 (RS, 1862), p. 649; followed by William Stubbs in his introduction to the *Chronica Magistri Rogeri de Hovedene*, vol. 1 (RS, 1868), p. xc; C. Plummer, *Two of the Saxon Chronicles Parallel*, vol. 2 (Oxford, 1899), p. civ n. 4.

Still following Gaimar closely, the *Brut*'s account of Alfred's descendants culminates (chapters 112–13) with the reign of King Edgar. Of Edgar, Gaimar wrote:

> Cil tint la terre cum emperere
> En sun tens amendat la terre,
> Partuit ert pais, n'ert nul guere.
> Il sul regnot sur tuz les reis
> E sur Escoz e sur Gualeis
> Unc puis que Artur s'en fud alez
> Nen ot nul reis tel poestez.[26]

Gaimar was the first, but by no means the last, to mention Edgar in the same breath as Arthur, and it may be significant for the connexion between the two kings which he established that when Arthur's body came to be 'found' later in the twelfth century, it was precisely at Glastonbury where Edgar was, in fact, buried.[27] The *Brut* retained the image of an imperial and Arthur-like Edgar[28] – hardly surprising, given that Gaimar's comparison between Arthur and Edgar in terms of their overlordship over Scotland and Wales would have had an obvious contemporary resonance c.1300 at the time of Edward I's wars against the Welsh and Scots.

The bulk (330 out of 408 lines) of Gaimar's account of Edgar's reign is taken up with something entirely different, the story of the beautiful Elftroed and of the king's love for her. In this story we have what Press characterized as the 'earliest known imaginative realization of a courtly love story', the first French romance, and one in which that notorious troublemaker (the troubadours' bête noire), the *losengier* makes an appearance. When Edgar and Elftroed married it was to the intense disapproval of the most powerful holy man of tenth century England, Saint Dunstan. But their love was such, says Gaimar, followed by the *Brut*, that they cared not a jot.[29]

Gaimar's next subjects were the renewal of the struggle with the Danes in the reign of Aethelred the Unready, then the reigns of King Cnut and his sons. All this, in Gaimar's view, led to a deep hatred between Englishmen and Danes.

---

[26] Gaimar, vv. 3562–68. Translated above p. 96.
[27] See, e.g., Roger of Howden's statement that Edgar was to the English what Arthur was to the Britons, *Chronica*, vol. 1, p. 64.
[28] The French in BL Add. 18462 (a) f. 50r, (b) f. 160r and Cotton Cleopatra DVII f. 128r follows Gaimar very closely.
[29] Gaimar vv. 3595–3960; BL Add. 18462 (a) ff. 50–51, (b) ff. 160–61; Cleopatra DVII, f. 128. Given that Elftroed is later responsible for the murder of her step-son, Edward the Martyr, both Gaimar and the *Brut* treat her strikingly positively. William of Malmesbury had told an almost identical story about the love of Edgar and Elftroed but from a totally different moral standpoint. Whereas Bell, *L'Estoire*, pp. lxix–lxxi, believes it unlikely that either writer knew the other's version, Press, 'The Precocious Courtesy', pp. 270–74, argues plausibly that Gaimar knew, and rejected, William's morality, cf. below, pp. 247, 251–2.

Again the *Brut* (chapters 115–124) simply followed Gaimar in train of thought and language.[30] One of Gaimar's recurring themes is the notion of an ancestral right which the Danish kings claimed to have to the throne of England. It was this theme which lay behind some of his most memorable episodes – the tale of Haveloc, vv. 45–815 (used in chapters 91–2) and the tale of Buern Bocard, Osbright and Aelle, vv. 2593–2829 (used in chapters 103–4).[31] It was this claim to which Gaimar alluded when he introduced the subject of King Swein's invasion:

> En icel tens reis Suain vint
> Pur chalengier e pur cunquerre,

The *Brut* caught the allusion and expanded it.[32] Clearly the notion of a Danish claim to the English throne was one of the most memorable features of Gaimar's history.

Two passages, both written more than a hundred years before the *Brut*, lead to the same conclusion and may enable us to indentify two of Gaimar's earlier readers. The first of these passages takes us to the heart of Henry II's government. According to Richard FitzNigel's account of the origins of Danegeld in the *Dialogue of the Exchequer*, the Danes attacking England came not only to plunder but 'quia aliquid sibi de antiquo iure in eiusdem regni dominatione vendicabunt, sicut Britonum plenius narrat historia'. This allusion to a work in which the Danish claim figured and was known as a 'History of the Britons' suggests that Richard FitzNigel in the 1170s knew Gaimar's history in its original, complete form before its British section was replaced by Wace's version.[33] The second passage was composed in the 1190s by William of Newburgh. It describes how when King Philip Augustus of France married Ingeborg of Denmark what he wanted from her as her dowry was 'antiquum ius regis Dacorum in regno Anglorum'.[34]

The *Brut* (chapters 125–7) continues to follow Gaimar's narrative closely until the reconciliation between earl Godwin and King Edward the Confessor in 1052. Then no more. As already noted, Gaimar's last 1500 lines left no impression on the *Brut*. In consequence the *Brut*'s version of the Norman Conquest is entirely different from Gaimar's. Gaimar emphasises the role of

[30] Compare, for example, Gaimar, vv. 4765–70 with the *Brut*, c. 123.

[31] Matter, *Englische Grundungssagen*, pp. 241–99.

[32] Gaimar, vv. 4136–37; BL Cotton Cleopatra DVII, f. 130r; BL Add. 18462 (a) f. 51v, (b) f. 162r; *The Brut*, cap. 118.

[33] Richard FitzNigel, *Dialogus de Scaccario*, ed. C. Johnson, F. E. L. Carter and D. E. Greenway (Oxford, 1983), p. 55. The editors comment cautiously that this might have been a reference to 'the lost source of Geoffrey of Monmouth and Gaimar'. But there is nothing in Geoffrey to indicate that his lost source – even supposing he had one – supported the idea of a Danish claim to England.

[34] William of Newburgh, *Historia Rerum Anglicarum* in ed. R. Howlett, *Chronicles of the Reigns of Stephen etc.* (RS, 1884–89), vol. i, 368.

Hereward the Wake, criticises William the Conqueror and gives us a remarkable portrait of William II (Rufus) as the model of a chivalrous king, light-hearted, brave and generous. As Sir Richard Southern noted, in Gaimar's version 'the romantic and chivalrous heroes of the story were Anglo-Saxons, who faced their last crafty and treacherous enemy in William I'.[35] The English resistance fighter Hereward the Wake is *un gentilz hom* , his companions are *chevalier* who act *que prodom et que curteis*.[36] Antonia Gransden rightly decribed Gaimar's *Estoire* as a translation of the Anglo-Saxon Chronicle 'filled out with legends with the obvious intention of entertaining the nobility. It presents Anglo-Saxon history seen through the eyes of romance.'[37] But what can we infer about a nobility which was entertained by this kind of romance? Presumably that this was the kind of nobility which found in Gaimar a way of coming to terms with their present situation as a francophone social elite in a country with an old English past. By 1140, in other words, the gentlemen of mid-twelfth century England, and their wives, Gaimar's patrons and his audience, thought of themselves as English, and this despite the fact that they spoke French (as well as English), and despite their French styles and manners.[38] With predecessors as chivalrous and courtly as Hereward and his followers, they could feel at home in England.

In a sense then Gaimar was part of the process by which people in the twelfth century recovered their English past. One part of this movement has been beautifully analysed by Southern. As he pointed out, William of Malmesbury, John of Worcester and Eadmer of Canterbury were Benedictines writing primarily for a learned and monastic audience which wanted to preserve or recover its old places in a new world.[39] But the movement for the recovery of the past was more than just a monastic one. Henry of Huntingdon, archdeacon, canon of Lincoln, dedicated his history to a bishop of Lincoln who was deeply immersed in secular matters.[40] Even more explicitly secular in outlook was Gaimar, writing in the vernacular and for the lay elite, women as well as men. In the remarkable epilogue to his history he tells us that it was commissioned by Constance, wife of Ralf FitzGilbert, and he then mentions seven other contemporaries: King Henry I, Queen Adeliza, Robert earl of Gloucester,

[35] R. W. Southern, *Medieval Humanism and Other Studies* (Oxford, 1970), pp. 154–55. For William's treachery, Gaimar, vv. 5373–98. Only once – when William responds vigorously to the capture of York by Danes – does Gaimar (v. 5415) speak flatteringly of the Conqueror. For Rufus as a model of chivalry see below, pp. 237–45.

[36] Gaimar, vv. 5461, 5500, 5570.

[37] Gransden, *Historical Writing c.550 to c.1307*, p. 210.

[38] Short, 'Patrons and Polyglots', pp. 244–49. For further development of this argument see below, pp. 123–42.

[39] R. W. Southern, 'Aspects of the European tradition of historical writing: 4, the sense of the past', *Transactions of the Royal Historical Society*, 5th ser. 23 (1973), pp. 243–63; Guenée, *Histoire at culture historique*, pp. 313, 320.

[40] See below, pp. 134–5; Campbell, 'Some Twelfth-Century Views', p. 133; Diana Greenway, 'Henry of Huntingdon and Bede' in *L'Historiographie médiévale en Europe*, ed. Jean-Philippe Genet (Paris, 1991), p. 50.

Walter Espec, lord of Helmsley, a poet called David, Walter archdeacon of Oxford, and Nicholas de Trailly, a canon of York.[41] If we consider this list and then add to it an Augustinian canon (William of Newburgh) and a senior government official (Richard FitzNigel, treasurer of England and later bishop of London), it all suggests that Gaimar appealed to a cross-section of landowning society, both lay and clerical, officials, courtiers and magnates.

If this is correct then Gaimar appealed to exactly the same kind of audience as that which was to possess copies and/or read the *Brut*.[42] This is, anyway, one implication of the way the *Brut* responded to Gaimar, took over wholesale so much of Gaimar's text and so many of his value judgements. This means that this kind of audience already existed in England somewhat earlier – perhaps as much as 150 years earlier – than is sometimes supposed or implied by students of the genre of vernacular history.[43] In other respects 1300 was, of course, different. By 1300 the traumas of the Norman Conquest were very ancient history; the need to come to terms with them was long since gone. The *Brut* never even mentions Hereward. It presents the Conqueror in a very positive light, as a lord who treated the English with generosity; by contrast his son Rufus appears as a wicked and destructive king.[44] By 1300 there was evidently no need to challenge what was by then a well-established and venerable monastic view of these two kings.

If we stand back and look at the *Brut*'s Anglo-Saxon history as a whole, we can see that its basic pattern as well as some of its most characteristic touches are derived from Gaimar. Both Gaimar and the *Brut* present the early Anglo-Saxon centuries as an anarchic period of violence and lawlessness. Here, for example, is Gaimar on late eighth and early ninth century conditions.

> En icel tens tel ert la lei
> Ki force aveit si feiseit guerre
> A sun veisin tolit sa terre.[45]

To judge by the language used by William of Malmesbury and Henry of Huntingdon when commenting on early Anglo-Saxon history, Gaimar's was the natural reaction of a twelfth-century reader to some of the early entries in the *Anglo-Saxon Chronicle*.[46] But the *Brut* author had not read the *Chronicle* and his perception of the flavour of those centuries came straight from Gaimar. 'It befell so that all the kings in that time that were in the land ... every one warred upon each other; and they that were mightiest took the land of them who were

[41] Gaimar, vv. 6429–6524. On all this see the fundamental article by Ian Short, 'Gaimar's Epilogue'.
[42] Taylor, *English Historical Literature*, p. 119.
[43] Guenée, *Histoire et culture historique*, pp. 318–20.
[44] *The Brut*, caps. 133–34.
[45] Gaimar, vv. 2016–18. Cf. vv. 2284–86: 'Partuit aveit itels seignurs/ Tresque poeit un poi monter/ Si se faiseit rei appeller.'
[46] See below, p. 228.

most feeble.' Since the *Brut* author used these phrases twice over, once in chapter 96 and then again in chapter 102, Gaimar's perception of early Anglo-Saxon history had clearly made a deep impression.[47] In chapter 102 he used it, as Gaimar had, to introduce the notion of Alfred as the maker of the *Chronicle*, and hence of the principal narrative of English history from the 730s (after Bede) until the mid-twelfth century.

After Alfred's reign, in place of the previous anarchic struggle between a number of small kingdoms, both Gaimar and the *Brut* assume the existence of a united English people, a kingdom of England. Their main theme becomes the struggle for control of that kingdom between Alfred's descendants and the Danes. Thus in a double sense King Alfred is presented as a pivotal figure in the making of English history. This is not how he had been perceived by historians writing before Gaimar. For William of Malmesbury, for example, great though Alfred was, he was neither the maker of the *Chronicle* nor was his reign the pivot of Anglo-Saxon history.[48] But what the *Brut*, the most popular and unreliable of late medieval English histories, read into Gaimar was precisely that: in Anglo-Saxon history, in both senses of the word, Alfred was the key figure. This is also, of course, the basic pattern of Anglo-Saxon history as seen by many of the most reliable of twentieth-century historians! Gaimar and one of his readers have a lot to answer for. Their version of Anglo-Saxon history proved to be one which was found memorable and has been remembered down the centuries.[49] History, after all, in the words of *1066 and All That*, 'is what you can remember. All other history defeats itself.'[50] When the *Brut* was translated into English, it became the first known history to be written in English prose after the mid-twelfth century demise of the *Anglo-Saxon Chronicle*. Since Gaimar's *Estoire* was itself in large part a translation of the *Chronicle*, Gaimar and the French prose *Brut* constitute important links in a remarkable historiographical chain which stretches all the way from the court of King Alfred to the printing shop of William Caxton – and beyond.

---

[47] And compare a similar passage in the text printed by Diana B. Tyson, 'An Early French Prose History of the Kings of England', *Romania* 96 (1975), p. 14.

[48] Since Book I of the *Gesta Regum* ends with the reign of Egbert of Wessex and Book II begins with it, it seems that in William's mind that was the pivotal reign.

[49] This includes their version of the story of Cnut and the waves. Significantly the arrogant attitude attributed to Cnut by the *Brut* is the one which remains proverbial in modern English usage, not the pious and realistic attitude ascribed to him by Henry of Huntingdon and subsequent Latin historians.

[50] W. C. Sellar and R. J. Yeatman, *1066 and All That* (London, 1930), p. v.

8

Henry of Huntingdon and the Twelfth-Century Revival of the English Nation

At what date did the descendants of those newcomers who settled in England in the wake of the Norman Conquest think of themselves as English? Historians have tended to reply, cautiously, 'by the end of the 12th century'.[1] Inevitably and properly they cite the opinion of Richard FitzNigel: 'nowadays when English and Normans live close together and marry and give in marriage to each other, the nations are so mixed that it can scarcely be decided (I mean in the case of freemen) who is of English birth and who of Norman'.[2] If the freemen who lived in England and who spoke English (as well as French or French and Latin) did not see themselves as 'English' until the late twelfth century, then who had they thought they were?[3] Had they continued to think of themselves as Norman

---

* I am particularly grateful to Lesley Johnson and Alan Murray for their immensely helpful comments on a first draft of this paper.

[1] Ralph H. C. Davis, *The Normans and their Myth* (London, 1976), pp. 122, 131; Rodney Hilton, 'Were the English English?' in Raphael Samuel, ed., *Patriotism: The Making and Unmaking of National Identity*, vol. 1 (London, 1989), 40; Ian Short, 'Patrons and Polyglots: French Literature in Twelfth-Century England', *ANS* 14 (1991), 246; Karl Schnith, 'Von Symeon von Durham zu Wilhelm von Newburgh. Wege der englischen "Volksgeschichte" im 12. Jahrhundert' in ed. Clemens Bauer et al., *Speculum Historiale* (Munich, 1965), 243.

[2] Although FitzNigel does not say whether these *permixtae nationes* identified themselves as English or Norman or Anglo-Norman, he does explicitly treat them differently from people of servile condition who are obviously English. Equally obviously English (as Paul Brand reminded me) were those who tried to claim land based on pre-Conquest title. See Richard FitzNigel, *Dialogus de Scaccario*, ed. Charles Johnson (Oxford, 1983), pp. 53–4. Early in Henry II's reign a *statutum* prohibited this, insisting that an Englishman claiming property would have to show an ancestor's seisin on the day Henry I died, R. C. Van Caenegem, *Royal Writs in England from the Conquest to Glanvill* (London, 1958–9), pp. 217–18 and nos. 165, 169, 172, 175, also the discussion in Paul R. Hyams, *King, Lords, and Peasants in Medieval England* (Oxford, 1980), pp. 251–4. There are some indications that this prohibition was aimed at 'rustic' Englishmen. On the other hand Jordan Fantosme, writing – like FitzNigel – in the 1170s, used the term 'Engleis' to refer to those who supported Henry II against the Scots in 1173–4, and presumably he was not thinking of men of servile condition, *Jordan Fantosme's Chronicle*, ed. and trans. R. C. Johnston (Oxford, 1981), v. 631.

[3] On pluri-lingualism see Short, 'Patrons and Polyglots', 229–49 and Cecily Clark, 'Towards a Re-assessment of Anglo-Norman Influence on English Place-names' in eds. P. Sture Ureland and G. Broderick, *Language Contact in the British Isles* (Tubingen, 1991) – a reference I owe to the kindness of Sir James Holt.

French? Or was there an intervening stage when they thought of themselves as Anglo-Normans? Or were they simply confused?[4] Delaying their Englishness until the late twelfth century would seem to allow plenty of room for a generation or two of Anglo-Normans. All the more since it has been powerfully argued that by 1166 a 'hundred years of assimilation had produced a society which in its social structure no less than its art and culture was truly Anglo-Norman'.[5] However although historians and others since the days of David Hume[6] have happily written of 'Anglo-Norman' government, the 'Anglo-Norman' language, 'Anglo-Norman society', 'Anglo-Norman England' and 'the Anglo-Norman realm', they have shied away from the notion of an 'Anglo-Norman' national identity, doubtless for the very natural reason that there is no extant evidence that anyone in the eleventh or twelfth centuries ever used the term 'Anglo-Norman'. In the absence of some such term, it is clearly not easy to argue for the existence of an Anglo-Norman nationality.[7] For, in Robert Bartlett's words, 'nationality is not matter of objective classification at all. It is a matter of identification . . . a social process' in which 'Self-identification exists in a close relationship with identification by others and identification of others.'[8]

[4] 'The whole question of their "Englishness" was in the melting pot as a result of the Norman Conquest . . . Between 1066 and 1200 there were real doubts and some confusion', Geoffrey W. S. Barrow, *The Anglo-Norman Era in Scottish History* (Oxford, 1980), p. 6. For a thoroughly positive view of the cultural and linguistic melting-pot see Short, 'Patrons and Polyglots', 244–9. The whole question has now been re-assessed by Ian Short, '*Tam Angli quam Franci*: Self-definition in Anglo-Norman England', *ANS* 18 (1995), 153–75, who also sees important developments in the 1140s; by Ann Williams, *The English and the Norman Conquest* (Woodbridge, 1995), pp. 155–86; and by Judith Green, *The Aristocracy of Norman England* (Cambridge, 1997), pp. 429–38.

[5] Marjorie Chibnall, *Anglo-Norman England 1066–1166* (Oxford, 1986), pp. 208–20.

[6] David Hume, *The History of England* (London, 1762), vol. 1, pp. 397ff. See now Short, '*Tam Angli quam Franci*', 174, for examples from 1707 onwards.

[7] Thus the phrases 'the "Anglo-Normans" (for want of a better term)' and 'the so-called Anglo-Normans' in Short, 'Patrons and Polyglots', 246. The word *Normanangli* occurs frequently in the work known as the Hyde Chronicle, but in the Appendix I argue that this was written in Normandy. If that argument is accepted then the 'Hyde Chronicle' would be irrelevant to the self-perception of those who lived in England. So, for the same reason, is the work of Orderic Vitalis, nicely characterized as '*The Ecclesiastical History of the Norman gens*' by Ralph H. C. Davis in 'Bede after Bede', *Studies in Medieval History presented to R. Allen Brown*, ed. Christopher Harper-Bill, Christopher Holdsworth and Janet L. Nelson (Woodbridge, 1989), 116.

[8] Robert Bartlett, *Gerald of Wales* (Oxford, 1982), 10. For this reason I am not inclined to place much weight on the English royal chancery practice of continuing to draw up charters addressed to the king's 'faithful subjects both French and English' until the 1170s. On which see Rudiger Fuchs, *Das Domesday Book und sein Umfeld* (Stuttgart, 1987), pp. 361–2, a reference I owe to the kindness of Timothy Reuter. The perceptions of nationality implied by the most formulaic parts of formulaic documents are likely to lag some way behind the perceptions found in those genres where writers enjoyed greater freedom to express both self-identification and identification of others. On this point see below, pp. 153–4. From the perspective of law, George Garnett also regards the address *Francis et Anglis* as 'nothing

Although FitzNigel tells us what he thinks the situation is 'today', i.e. in the late 1170s, he doesn't say how long he thinks it has been so. For at least a generation we might think if we could accept the opinion of one of his exact contemporaries, Walter Map. According to Map, Henry I 'joined both peoples in firm amity, by arranging marriages between them and by all other means he could'.[9] Long ago E. A. Freeman argued that Henry's policy had been successful, but his opinion has generally been discounted, particularly in the light of evidence from the mid twelfth century that the two peoples were neither federated nor firm friends.[10] According to Orderic Vitalis, in 1137 Stephen was informed of a plot 'to kill all the Normans on a fixed day and hand over the government of the kingdom to the Scots'. Twenty years later, in 1157, Richard de Luci, as recalled by the Battle Chronicle, was appealing to the Normans in England to stand fast against the tricks of the English.[11] Thus there has seemed to be good evidence to support the belief that it was not until the end of the twelfth century that 'the Normans in England' claimed identity with the English rather than separateness.

I propose to re-consider the question of English and/or Norman identity in mid twelfth century England, for I find this long delayed Englishness surprising, particularly in the light of recent arguments for the rapid assimilation of even first generation settlers.[12] Since nationality is so subjective a matter, the question is best approached through a study of individual usage and here I shall focus on the sense of identity of one man: Henry of Huntingdon, poet, litterateur and historian, author of a *History of the English* which was to become one of the standard works in the field.[13] Henry, of course, was a member of the only group, the clerical elite, whose voices the surviving evidence allows us to hear. Clearly their education, status and gender means that this is a very restricted group, but

---

more than a standard formula', '"Franci et Angli": the legal distinction between peoples after the Conquest', *ANS* 8 (1985), 135.

[9] Walter Map, *De Nugis Curialium*, ed. Montague R. James, Christopher N. L. Brooke and Roger A. B. Mynors (Oxford, 1983), p. 436. Both FitzNigel and Map were born c.1130.

[10] Edward A. Freeman, *The Reign of William Rufus*, 2 vols. (Oxford, 1882) ii, 455; *The Norman Conquest*, Vol. V, Appendix, Note W, The Fusion of Normans and English (Oxford, 1876), pp. 825–39.

[11] *The Ecclesiastical History of Orderic Vitalis*, ed. Marjorie Chibnall (Oxford, 1969–80), vi. 494; *The Chronicle of Battle Abbey*, ed. Eleanor Searle (Oxford, 1980), p. 182.

[12] Susan J. Ridyard, '*Condigna Veneratio*: Post-Conquest Attitudes to the Saints of the Anglo-Saxons', *ANS* 9 (1987), 179–206; David Rollason, *Saints and Relics in Anglo-Saxon England* (Oxford, 1989), pp. 222–38; Chibnall, *Anglo-Norman England*, pp. 208–10. Indeed since all the settlers, not just the clerics, held their lands as *successores* to Edwardian *antecessores*, they were all under pressure to learn to be 'Englishmen', Garnett, 'Franci et Angli', p. 135.

[13] According to Guenée, c.1300 it was still one of the works which lay 'au fondement même de la culture et de la conscience nationale des Anglais', Bernard Guenée, *Histoire et culture historique dans l'occident médiéval* (Paris, 1980), p. 309. Cf. Felix Liebermann, 'Heinrich von Huntingdon', *Forschungen zur deutschen Geschichte* xviii (1878), 294–5; Antonia Gransden, *Historical Writing in England, c.550 to c.1307* (London, 1974), pp. 194–5; Schnith, 'Von Symeon von Durham', p. 250.

we can do no more than make the best of what we have and, in terms of the questions considered here, Henry of Huntingdon's voice is a highly significant one. At one stage in his history Henry actually refers to the *gens Normannorum et Anglorum* – which is probably as close as we can get to the 'Anglo-Normans'.[14] Moreover R. H. C. Davis identified Henry as a key figure in the development of what he called 'the saga of the Norman race', drawing attention to the speech before the Battle of the Standard (1138) which Henry put into the mouth of Bishop Ralph of Orkney, a speech in which Ralph addresses his audience as *Normannigenae* and reminds them of past Norman victories won by *majores nostri*.[15] This suggests that Henry's use of words denoting nationality is a subject that deserves to be looked at more closely, in particular the way or ways in which he uses the word 'Norman'. Here I shall argue that one of his contexts for 'Norman' is the factional court politics of Stephen's reign and that his usage may lead us to re-assess both Orderic's 1137 plot and de Luci's 1157 speech. Compared with Orderic and William of Malmesbury, Henry remains a neglected figure.[16] In a justly famous article Sir Richard Southern discussed what he called 'the English historical movement', setting it against the cataclysmic political consequences of the Norman Conquest and in terms of an urgently felt 'need to understand and stabilize the present by reviving the experience of the past'.[17] Yet neither Henry nor his History of the English received a mention. This was a pity – partly because, as James Campbell has already pointed out, the omission made the historical movement too exclusively monastic.[18] Certainly Henry, as Nancy Partner has emphasised, was no monk. His son was to succeed him as tenant of the manor of Stukeley (held of Peterborough Abbey), just as he himself had succeeded his own father Nicholas as canon of Lincoln and archdeacon of Huntingdon.[19] Doubtless the omission

[14] *Henry, Archdeacon of Huntingdon: Historia Anglorum*, ed. and trans. Diana Greenway (Oxford Medieval Texts, 1996), p. 716; [Henry of Huntingdon, *Historia Anglorum*, ed. Thomas Arnold (Rolls Series, 1879), p. 264]. Henceforth both editions will be referred to as HH, with page references to Arnold's edition in square brackets.
[15] Davis, *The Normans*, pp. 66, 124; Graham Loud, 'The *Gens Normannorum* – myth or reality?', *ANS* 4 (1982), 105–6.
[16] In part doubtless a consequence of the long-felt need for an edition to match Stubbs on William of Malmesbury and Chibnall on Orderic. Happily Diana Greenway has now supplied this.
[17] Richard W. Southern, 'Aspects of the European tradition of historical writing: 4, the sense of the past', *TRHS*, 5th ser. 23 (1973), 243–63.
[18] James Campbell, 'Some Twelfth-Century Views of the Anglo-Saxon Past', *Peritia* 3 (1984), 133. Southern's omission of Henry might be seen as a consequence of his decision to focus on 'the antiquarian research movement', over – he argues – by 1130, since the turning over of documents in the search for materials of historical interest was certainly not Henry's strong suit. However Henry must have written most of the Anglo-Saxon section of his History, roughly two thirds of the whole, by 1130. On the chronology of composition see now Greenway, *Henry, Archdeacon of Huntingdon*, lxvi–lxxxvii.
[19] Nancy F. Partner, *Serious Entertainments. The Writing of History in Twelfth-Century England* (Chicago, 1977), pp. 14–15, 39–48. Diana Greenway has made a strong case for believing

was partly because, as a historian, is often regarded as a light-weight figure: 'a disappointment, could have done better' was R. R. Darlington's schoolmasterly report on Henry as a contemporary historian.[20] But his approach to writing about his own times stands in sharp contrast to his remarkably systematic treatment of early English history and if he said little about his own times it was not because he was ignorant or uninterested.[21] If he chose to say little then we should weigh his words with care, just as he did. It is not, after all, as though he thought history unimportant. Indeed no one asserted higher claims for history, or did so more emphatically, than did Henry. For him history is 'one of the principal ways of distinguishing between brutes and rational creatures. For brutes whether they be men or animals neither know nor wish to know whence they came, nor their origins nor the events and deeds of their country (*patriae suae casus et gesta*).'[22]

So if, in Henry's mind, the main ingredients of history were *patriae . . . casus et gesta*, then just what was his *patria*? On this opinions have been divided. According to Felix Liebermann, Henry wrote 'vollkommen und nur als englischer Patriot'; more recently Laetitia Boehm expressed the view that he judged the Normans 'aus der normannischen Perspektive'.[23] More recently still David Rollason has observed 'the form almost of an English patriotism' in the writings of Henry of Huntingdon (as well as William of Malmesbury).[24] I have little doubt that Liebermann and Rollason are right. Right from the beginning of his book it is clear that Henry conceived it as a history of England 'the most noble of islands' and of its people from Julius Caesar to the present.[25] Even after 1066 it never became anything remotely approaching a history of the 'Anglo-Norman realm' in the modern sense of England and Normandy combined;

---

that his father Nicholas was a member of the Glanville family, from Glanville in Calvados, who married an Englishwoman, so that Henry's own mother tongue was English, HH, pp. xxiii–xxvi.

[20] Reginald R. Darlington, *Anglo-Norman Historians* (London, 1947), p. 17. Aelred Squire, *Aelred of Rievaulx* (London, 1969), p. 76, dismissed it as 'only in appearance a history'.

[21] On Henry's highly systematic treatment of Anglo-Saxon history see Partner, *Serious Entertainments*, p. 22 and, above all, Campbell 'Some Twelfth-Century Views', 134–5.

[22] HH, pp. 4–5 [2]. Cf. Heinz Richter, *Englische Geschichtschreiber des 12. Jahrhunderts* (Berlin, 1938), p. 172. Antonia Gransden pointed out that he may have been influenced by Sallust, 'Prologues in the Historiography of Twelfth-Century England' in *England in the Twelfth Century*, ed. Daniel Williams (Woodbridge, 1990), p. 64.

[23] Liebermann, 'Heinrich', pp. 291–3. Laetitia Boehm, 'Nomen Gentis Normannorum: Der Aufstieg der Normannen im Spiegel der normannischer Quellen' in *I Normanni e la loro Espansione in Europa nell'alto medioevo*, Settimane di Studio del Centro Italiano di Studi Sull'alto medioevo XVI (Spoleto, 1969), 681.

[24] Rollason, *Saints and Relics*, p. 237. For his 'pride in his country, England' see now Greenway, HH, p. lx.

[25] The island, Henry explains, was first called Albion, then Britannia, now Anglia, HH, 6. See *Aelfric, Lives of the Saints*, ed. and trans. W. W. Skeat, Early English Text Society 76, 82, 2 vols. (Oxford, 1881–5), I, pp. 414–15 for an early example of 'the Englishman's tendency to confuse the identities of "England" and "Britain"', cited by Patrick Wormald, 'The Venerable Bede and the "Church of the English"' in ed. Geoffrey Rowell, *The English Religious Tradition and the Genius of Anglicanism* (Ikon, 1992), note 27.

events that occurred in Normandy are rarely mentioned.[26] This same framework is still in place in the 1150s. The book ends with a poem celebrating England's welcome for Henry II.[27] In other words the book's structure clearly matches its title *The History of the English* – demonstrably Henry's own title for it.[28] Moreover that he identified with the English is suggested by comments such as that English city names were now looked upon as barbarous and ridiculous and that in William I's reign it was an insult to be called English.[29]

At the beginning of Book Seven, entitled 'De regno Normannorum', when he explained that he had reached the point at which he was now dealing with events he himself had seen or heard about from eye-witnesses (though in fact he continued to use an Anglo-Saxon Chronicle related text), he wrote that God had treated the English (*gens anglorum*) as they deserved and had ordered that they were no longer to be a people (*iam populum non esse iusserit*).[30] The devastating experience of 1066 had meant that the correspondence between a kingdom and a people, a community of tradition, custom, law and descent, – a correspondence which, as Susan Reynolds has pointed out, was generally taken for granted as part of the natural order[31] – no longer applied in England. During the composition of the first two versions of his History (both finished soon after October 1131), Henry clearly felt that this disjunction was still a fact of life. Even though the Normans were the legitimate heirs of the kingdom and much less of a scourge than the Danes had been, none the less they had been sent by God to punish the English for their sins.[32] Thus his account of William II's reign has that king summoning the *populus Anglorum* to his aid in 1088, promising them better laws and the restoration of their hunting rights, but then not keeping his promise. Under William Rufus, in Henry's words, 'England had not been able to breathe.'[33] His subsequent narrative of the first twenty-nine years of Henry I's reign is, doubtless prudently, free of critical comments of this kind. But in words composed at some date between c.1123 and c.1132 he noted that

---

[26] Until 1121 Henry's coverage of events in Normandy follows that of the Anglo-Saxon Chronicle. From then on it becomes even thinner; just some lines relating to 1128 – allowing *quidam non indoctus* (probably Henry himself) to display his learning, HH, pp. 478–81 [247–9] – then brief mentions of events in 1137 and 1152.

[27] HH, pp. 776–7 [291–2].

[28] HH, pp. 612–15 [317]. Also the colophon printed and discussed by Diana Greenway, 'Henry of Huntingdon and the Manuscripts of his *Historia Anglorum*', *ANS* 9 (1987), 109–10. *Historia Anglorum* was also one of Henry's titles for Bede's History, HH, 234 [117].

[29] HH, pp. 16–17, 402–3 [9, 208].

[30] HH, pp. 412–13 [213–14].

[31] Susan Reynolds, *Kingdoms and Communities in Western Europe 900–1300* (Oxford, 1984), p. 250.

[32] HH, pp. 14–15, 272–3, 338–9 [8, 138, 173].

[33] HH, pp. 414–15, 448–9 [214, 232]. Cf. the phrase 'dum difficilem futuris temporibus Anglorum previderet respirationem' used of Edward the Confessor's 'green tree' prophecy by Osbert of Clare in the *Vita beati Eadwardi regis Anglorum* completed in 1138; cited in Frank Barlow, *The Life of King Edward*, 2nd edn (Oxford, 1992), pp. 131–2.

the Normans still ruled the English, and he clearly regretted this.[34] Like William of Malmesbury in his *Gesta Regum* (completed by 1125), he still saw England's population as divided into two distinct groups: Norman rulers and English subjects.[35]

But in the continuation and revision of the *History* (Greenway's third version) which Henry wrote in the early 1140s there is no longer any sign of the distinction between Norman rulers and English subjects. Indeed it was at this stage of his writing and in his account of the victory of the northern barons over the Scots at the Battle of the Standard that Henry refers to the *gens Normannorum et Anglorum in una acie*. There can be no doubt that Henry, although not a northerner, identified with this *gens*: *nostri . . . feliciter triumphaverunt*, he wrote.[36] Nowhere else did Henry bring Normans and English together in a single *gens*. (Nor indeed, so far as I can see from the surviving texts, did anyone else.) Presumably at this stage of composition he was keenly aware of the Norman heritage since not only had he just composed the battle oration which he attributed to Ralph of Orkney, but at about the same time (c.1141) he went back to his account of the Battle of Hastings (originally written c.1130) and added to it a speech he put into the mouth of Duke William, an oration similarly full of reminders of earlier Norman triumphs.[37] It was this revision which led Davis to argue that 'the Norman myth' mattered c.1140 in ways that it had not earlier, perhaps – he suggested – because it was now that the Normans in England were becoming English.[38] It is an attractive hypothesis, but it is important to bear in mind that, no matter what Duke William and Bishop Ralph may or may not have said, the author of these Normannising words was Henry, a man whose own sympathies were English rather than Norman. His choice of words to describe the response of the northern troops to Ralph of Orkney's oration is revealing: 'respondit omnis populus Anglorum et resonuerunt montes et colles, Amen,

---

[34] HH, pp. 14–15, 338–9 [8, 173] suggests pessimism, the subjection of the English *in aeternum* and loss of honour *sine termino*. The tone is similar to William of Malmesbury's 'no Englishman today is an earl or bishop or abbot; the newcomers gnaw at the wealth and the guts of England, nor is there any hope of ending this misery', WM c. 227. Since both the old standard edition, *Gesta Regum Anglorum*, ed. William Stubbs, 2 vols. (RS, 1887–9) and the new standard, *Gesta Regum Anglorum*, vol. 1, ed. and trans. R. A. B. Mynors, R. M. Thomson and M. Winterbottom (Oxford, 1998) share the same division into chapters, for simplicity's sake I shall cite the work as WM and by chapter number. Later (c. 419) William expressed the view that the son of Henry I and Margaret represented precisely that hope and although the Atheling's death in 1120 was a blow, the maturing of a new generation of mixed parentage clearly implied that the time for such pessimism was felt – at least when the writer wasn't wallowing rhetorically in gloom – to be coming to an end.

[35] He may have written this as late as c.1130, though conceivably some years earlier if he started writing soon after 1123 – as suggested by Darlington, 'Anglo-Norman Historians', 16. On the dates of the various versions, Greenway, *Henry Archdeacon*, lxvi–lxxvii, making some revisions to the dates in Greenway, 'Henry of Huntingdon'.

[36] HH, pp. 716–19 [264].

[37] HH, pp. 714–17, 388–93 [262–3, 200–2].

[38] Davis, *The Normans*, 66, 124.

Amen'.[39] From his point of view the Standard represented the revival of the English nation, but it was a revival founded upon the appropriation of the military triumphs of the Norman past. In Henry's mind there was a technological side to this. According to him, the victory of 1138 – 'our victory' – was won by the weight of our archery, in other words by precisely that arm which – said Henry – the English had formerly lacked, a lack which explained their defeat at Norman hands in 1066.[40] But 1138 demonstrated that 'we' had now learned how to use that 'Norman' weapon. In this context our victory was both an English and a Norman victory, the triumph of the *gens Normannorum et Anglorum* as well as of the 'English people'. Norman tradition and Norman archery were both assimilated and turned against a newly identified set of outsiders, the barbarous Scots.[41]

Henry was not the only contemporary author whose patriotic feelings were newly stirred by the Standard factor. John of Worcester, for example, uses the word 'nostri' for the first time in his chronicle – and this though the victorious army, mustered by Archbishop Thurstan, also represented the church of York.[42] In Henry's case it looks as though his delight in 'our' victory over King David's barbarous army led him to feel that the English were once again a people – a perception which is then reflected in his account of the remaining years of Stephen's reign, for when decisive swings of the political pendulum occurred it is now the English people (*gens Anglorum*) or the English magnates (*Anglorum proceres*) who are the principal actors.[43]

Yet curiously it is in the third version, precisely when celebrating the triumph of the *gens Normannorum et Anglorum* against the Scots, that Henry also seems to be most anti-Norman. In his introduction to Book Ten he says that no matter how tyrannical Henry I had been, in the light of the atrocious time that followed his death, the result of 'the mad treacheries of the Normans', he seemed in retrospect to have been the best of kings. In his account of 1136, after referring to a rumour that Stephen was dead and to Hugh Bigod's reluctance to yield Norwich Castle, Henry tells us that 'now the aforementioned Norman madness of perjury and treachery began to sprout'.[44] By 1140–1 it is not the oppression of

---

[39]   HH, pp. 716–17 [263].

[40]   HH, pp. 392–3, 716–17 [202, 263–4]. For other evidence of contemporary opinion attributing a decisive role to archery, see above, p. 49.

[41]   If a xenophobic element is needed for an entrenched sense of national identity, then the emergence of the image of the Scots, Irish and Welsh as barbarians in the second quarter of the twelfth century is clearly significant. See pp. 27, 44, 101.

[42]   *The Chronicle of John of Worcester*, ed. John R. H. Weaver (Oxford, 1908), pp. 46, 51. See Donald Nicholl, *Thurstan, Archbishop of York 1114–1140* (York, 1964), p. 21 for the hostility of the monks of Worcester to the church of York. Much less surprising is John of Hexham's assertion that those who mustered around the Standard were determined either to die or to conquer 'pro patria', *The Priory of Hexham*, ed. James Raine, Surtees Society 44 (1863), p. 119.

[43]   HH, pp. 738–41 [275].

[44]   HH, pp. 700–1, 706–7 [256, 259]. The theme of Norman perjury was first touched on in

contemporary Normans that disturbs Henry, it is their perjury and treachery. What can he have had in mind? The 'mad treacheries' must have been something more disturbing than the events of 1136, even if it was then that the first shoots of trouble appeared, since his general reflections on Stephen's early years include the comment that the king's first two years (1136–7) were very propitious, the third (1138) was 'middling with things beginning to fall apart', but the last two (1139–40) were 'pernicious, with everything torn to pieces'.[45] Presumably then the perjury and treachery, the first signs of which had been perceived – retrospectively – as occurring in 1136, were in full bloom in 1139–40.

Given that Henry wrote for a patron, Bishop Alexander of Lincoln, it seems reasonable to consider the possibility that what he had in mind was the disaster that overtook his patron in 1139: Stephen's arrest of the three bishops. Alexander himself, his brother Nigel of Ely, and his uncle Roger of Salisbury, were arrested and their castles seized. The charge against them was treason, plotting on behalf of the empress, a charge they denied. At the council of Winchester (August 1139), Stephen's brother, Henry of Winchester, joined by Theobald of Canterbury and his fellow bishops, went on bended knee to beg the king to restore their possessions. But in vain; Stephen refused 'on the advice of evil men' (*pravorum consilio*). As these words indicate, Henry judged these proceedings harshly. In his mind they deserved to live in infamy (*res infamia notabilis*) and they doomed the house of King Stephen.[46]

There is no doubt that the bishops were the victims of a court intrigue organised by the faction headed by the elder of the Beaumont twins, Waleran of Meulan.[47] According to Robert of Torigny, Waleran 'surpassed all the magnates of Normandy in castles, revenues and connexions'.[48] His estates and career have been well studied by David Crouch. In Crouch's view, as early as the 1120s there was a 'purely Norman nobility of whom Waleran was the acknowledged leader' and it was clearly this group which in the early years of Stephen's reign was acquiring greater influence in England.[49] Yet not only were they the men who accused Alexander of treasonable dealings with the empress in 1139 and so orchestrated the downfall of Henry's patron, they were also the men who in

his account of the revolt of 1088, but he is clearly now very agitated about it. Liebermann, 'Heinrich', 291, used these passages to argue that Henry bitterly hated the Norman oppressors.

[45] HH, 710–11 [260]. See Greenway, HH, p. lxxii, for the significance of this passage in dating Henry's third version.

[46] HH, 718–23 [265–6].

[47] Ralph H. C. Davis, *King Stephen*, 3rd edn (London, 1990), pp. 28–30.

[48] 'qui omnibus Normanniae primatibus et firmitatibus et redditibus et affinibus praestabat', Robert of Torigny, *Chronicles of the Reigns of Stephen, Henry II and Richard I*, vol. 4, ed. Richard Howlett (RS, 1889), p. 142.

[49] David Crouch, *The Beaumont Twins* (Cambridge, 1986), pp. 14, 35–7, 43; cf. the rise of influence of the Cotentin group in the early years of Henry I's reign, Judith Green, *The Government of England under Henry I* (Cambridge, 1986), pp. 146–9.

1141 came to terms with the empress themselves.[50] Hardly surprising if Henry should be enraged by their apparent double-dealing. So I suggest that when, at this stage of the composition of his *History*, he wrote about the 'treacherous Normans', he had in mind not Normans in general, but this court faction in particular. In other words he was here using the word 'Norman' in much the same way as later writers called King John's enemies 'Northerners', referring both to their political stance and to the fact that a significant proportion of them came from a particular region.[51]

There are, indeed, clear indications that Henry had disliked the Beaumonts long before 1139. Even in the first version of his *History* he had criticised – the usually much admired – Count Robert of Meulan, father of the Beaumont twins.[52] In his *De Contemptu Mundi* (on which he had been working since 1134–5) no aristocrat suffered more at Henry's hands than did Count Robert. It is Henry – and no one else – who retailed what may have been no more than malicious court gossip about Robert's marriage and deathbed. True or not, these were stories clearly intended to show that politician in a negative light, as irreligious and rapacious – and to make the explicit point that his twin sons, Waleran and Robert, were no better than their father.[53] By contrast in *De Contemptu Mundi* he characterises Bishop Alexander as both loyal and munificent (*vir fidelis et munificus*).[54] It may also be that Henry had his own personal and local reasons for disliking the Beaumonts. He might have resented the appointment of their protégé Philip of Harcourt as dean of Lincoln c.1133. In 1139 Philip replaced Roger of Salisbury's son as chancellor and then became the Beaumont candidate for the see of Salisbury after Roger had, as it seemed, been hounded to death; this dean can hardly have made himself popular with that part of local society which was attached to the family of Bishop Alexander.[55]

Moreover the 1139 Beaumont coup did not merely mean that one court faction had replaced another. It also involved, as R. H. C. Davis showed, a new political programme. It meant placing the shires in the hands of earls rather than sheriffs, in the hands of the upper nobility rather than the 'bureaucrats whom

[50] By September 1141 Waleran had submitted to the empress following a truce negotiated by his twin brother Robert, earl of Leicester, Crouch, *Beaumont Twins*, p. 51.
[51] James C. Holt, *The Northerners* (Oxford, 1961), pp. 8–16. But not all of Stephen's opponents were based in Normandy, Green, *The Aristocracy of Norman England*, p. 435.
[52] HH, pp. 462–3 [240].
[53] HH, pp. lxxiv–lxxv (dating various versions of *De Contemptu Mundi*) and 598–9, 612–13 [307, 317], where Robert of Meulan is *vir nequissimus* and his sons unjust and unworthy of praise. For a less hostile account of Robert of Meulan's deathbed see the letter discovered and printed by Crouch, *Beaumont Twins*, 216–17.
[54] HH, pp. 612–13 [316].
[55] John Le Neve, *Fasti Ecclesiae Anglicanae 1066–1300, III: Lincoln*, compiled by Diana Greenway (London, 1977), p. 8; Davis, *King Stephen*, pp. 30, 44–5. On the miserable end to Roger of Salisbury's life see HH, pp. 720–23 [266–7].

Henry I and Roger of Salisbury had installed'.[56] Now another characteristic of Henry of Huntingdon's view of history is an unmistakable animus against the great and the powerful. This appears most clearly in his account of the Second Crusade where he contrasts the success of the expedition to Lisbon with the failure of the main crusade against Damascus. Lisbon was captured by a force 'containing no men of rank. Starting out humbly, trusting only in God, not in any great leader, they succeeded. For God resisteth the proud and giveth grace to the humble.'[57] Now one of the great leaders of the Second Crusade was none other than Waieran of Meulan. And who was greater or prouder than he? One of the dedications to Geoffrey of Monmouth's *History of the Kings of Britain* not only shows that Waleran was the equal of Robert of Gloucester but also that he was conscious of his descent from Charlemagne.[58] This maternal lineage gave him not only the proudest ancestry in Europe but also powerful connexions at the French court. The Meulan estates included a considerable part of Paris, 'the bulk of the old Carolingian enceinte on the right bank'; Louis VII, with whom he went on crusade, addressed him as 'our cousin'.[59] In the light of this it is not surprising that Orderic should have portrayed the young Waleran as the leader of those who saw themselves as 'the flower of the knighthood of all France and Normandy' and who at the battle of Bourgtheroulde (1124) sensed an opportunity to thrash those whom they contemptuously dismissed as *pagenses et gregarios* – people whom, for one reason or another, they regarded as their social inferiors. It seems that in their world another label for these country bumpkins and mercenaries was 'the English', for – again according to Orderic – Waleran and his friends had long been seeking an opportunity 'to meet the English in open field'.[60] Perhaps then Waleran and his friends, as they carried out their 1139 coup, as they pushed through their programme of putting English local government into the hands of aristocrats rather than 'bureaucrats', came to be seen – and not only by Henry of Huntingdon – as the Norman faction, an arrogant and snobbish group, conscious of their Frenchness and of their noble chivalry.

[56] Davis, *King Stephen*, pp. 30–1. W. Lewis Warren, *The Governance of Norman and Angevin England 1066–1272* (London, 1987), pp. 92–5.
[57] HH, pp. 752–3 [280–1]. The greatest part of these *pauperes*, he noted, came from England – and they were led by one of his own Glanville kinsmen.
[58] For the clearest discussion of the various dedications see *The Historia Regum Britanniae of Geoffrey of Monmouth I. Bern, Burgerbibliothek, MS 568*, ed. Neil Wright (Cambridge, 1984), pp. xii–xv. Since the dedication to Waleran and Robert of Gloucester clearly pre-dates the dedication to King Stephen and Robert of Gloucester, it presumably pre-dates the negotiations for the exchange of Stephen and Robert in the autumn of 1141 – perhaps the only time when an earl and a king could be described in terms which put them on an equal footing as the two pillars of the kingdom.
[59] Crouch, *Beaumont Twins*, p. 63 for use of the princely formula *dei gratia* in some Meulan charters, including three of Waleran's; 67–8 for Waleran on crusade; 180–1 for his Paris property. Also David Crouch, *The Image of Aristocracy in Britain 1000–1300* (London, 1992), p. 263 for Waleran's Norman 'palace'.
[60] Orderic Vitalis, vi. 350.

Of course Henry's observation on Damascus and Lisbon might have been no more than a fairly conventional comment on the role of the humble in explaining the success or failure of crusades, were it not for the fact that his account of events in England in 1153 reveals a similar distrust of the great. According to Henry, the events of 1153 were determined by the fact that the *proceres immo proditores* 'loved nothing better than discord', and were determined to undermine royal power in the pursuit of their own selfish interests.[61] More than any other chronicler it is Henry who seems to lend substance to that view of the 'medieval baronage' which sees them as 'over-mighty subjects'. Yet Henry's jaundiced play on words, *proceres-proditores*, was the product not of a detached ecclesiastical analysis of the power-play of secular society, but of his own long-held dislike of the court faction which, in 1153 as in 1139, seemed to be gaining the upper hand. For in 1153 the most influential magnate was one who had just decided to switch sides, abandoning Stephen for Henry, none other than Waleran's twin, Robert earl of Leicester.[62]

If they were the 'Normans', then was there a sense in which their opponents could have been identified as the 'English'? Roger of Salisbury himself would seem an improbable Englishman. He was born in Normandy and may never have visted England until 1100. On the other hand his career after 1100 was entirely based in England; indeed he may never have re-visited his 'home'. So far as I know, the birthplaces of his younger relatives, Roger and Adelelm (respectively chancellor and treasurer), and his nephews, Bishops Alexander of Lincoln and Nigel of Ely, are unknown, but their careers were entirely English. Although Alexander and Nigel went to school at Laon, this may not have made them any less or more English than education abroad did for John of Salisbury a generation later.[63] Although modern authors often refer to Alexander as a Norman, the evidence of Henry of Huntingdon rather suggests that he was English. In Henry's prologue he tells us that Alexander – whom he describes as *pater patriae* and 'the flower and pinnacle *regni et gentis*' – had commissioned him to tell the story *hujus regni gesta et nostrae gentis origines*.[64] Conceivably in some contexts by 'our people' Henry might have meant something like 'I and my friends but not necessarily you, bishop' but here the

61   HH, pp. 766–7 [287].
62   HH, pp. 756–7 [283]; his account of the siege of Worcester in 1151 shows that Henry remained critical of Robert Beaumont. Although as earl of Leicester Robert was a great magnate in England – and one who probably stayed in England throughout 1141–53 – both before and after those dates, he was also a Norman landowner on a massive scale (Crouch, *Beaumont Twins*, pp. 79, 87). For his 1153 change of allegiance and his new role as Duke Henry's leading adviser, see *Gesta Stephani*, ed. K. R. Potter and Ralph H. C. Davis (Oxford, 1976), p. 234.
63   Edward J. Kealey, *Roger of Salisbury* (Berkeley, 1972), pp. 150–1, 209–22. Hermann of Tournai, *De Miraculis Sanctae Laudunensis* in J. P. Migne, *Patrologia Latina*, CLVI, col. 983.
64   HH, pp. 4–7 [3]. I have not yet discovered why Bishop Alexander should be called Alexander of Blois by Arnold, p. x in his edition of HH, and by Gransden, *Historical Writing*, p. 193.

pairing of *regnum* and *gens* (twice over) must surely mean that in Henry's eyes Alexander was one of us. Even if Henry's own paternal ancestry was Norman, he identified himself with England and the English; clearly he thought the same could be said of Alexander. Not only did Alexander commission Henry to write a *Historia Anglorum*, two thirds of which deals with the period pre-1066 – *nostrae gentis origines* – but he may also have written, or commissioned the writing of, a collection of Anglo-Saxon law.[65] It was not only in the monasteries but also in the world, the world of the secular aristocracy for which Geoffrey Gaimar's *Estoire des Engleis* was written, as well as the ecclesiastical world of bishops and their clergy, even newly created and non-monastic sees like Lincoln, that the sense of English history was preserved, the Anglo-Saxon Chronicle translated, Bede's Ecclesiastical History of the English People copied and read, and a new English identity created.[66] Not surprising, perhaps, if cathedral clergy were receiving letters like that from Paschal II to York in which the pope referred to Gregory the Great as *gentis vestrae apostolus*.[67]

If in the minds of men increasingly aware of their Englishness, some of the great cross-Channel magnates, Waleran and his friends, had come to be known as 'the Normans', this might make sense of Orderic's report (mentioned above p. 125) of an 1137 plot to kill all the Normans and hand the government over to the Scots.[68] If in 1137 there were already people, or already thought to be people, planning to join the Empress's cause – the accusation made against the three bishops in 1139 – then they would naturally either be looking, or thought to be looking, for support from her uncle, King David of Scotland; and they would see, or would be thought to see, the overthrow of Stephen's powerful aristocratic advisers, the 'Normans', as an essential part of their plot. A hostile reporter could easily refer to anything of this sort as a conspiracy to kill all the Normans and hand the kingdom to the Scots. In other words the rumours which brought down the three bishops in 1139 may already have

---

[65] *Red Book of the Exchequer* III, ccclxii; Green, *Government of Henry I*, p. 162. Patrick Wormald tells me he knows of no reason to doubt this attribution. As diocesan of Lincoln Alexander was involved in the promotion of the only indigenous English monastic order, see A. G. Dyson, 'The Monastic Patronage of Bishop Alexander of Lincoln', *Journal of Ecclesiastical History* 26 (1975), 1–24 and he also assisted in the cult of St Guthlac, *Chronicon Angliae Petriburgense*, ed. J. A. Giles (London, 1845), p. 89. For the early twelfth-century cult of Guthlac at Crowland where, in 1124, an Englishman by descent, Waltheof son of Gospatric, was made abbot, see Orderic Vitalis, ii. pp. xxv–xxix, 322–50.

[66] Davis, 'Bede after Bede', 103–6; Wormald, 'The Venerable Bede', 26–7.

[67] Hugh the Chanter, *The History of the Church of York 1066–1127*, ed. Charles Johnson, 2nd edn (Oxford, 1990), pp. 10, 66, 88–90. See Donald Nicholl, *Thurstan, Archbishop of York 1114–1140* (York, 1964), pp. 5ff for the speed with which those foreign born churchmen, who, like Thomas II of York, grew fat on the wealth of England, came to identify themselves with the ancient rights of their churches. It is worth noting that Nicholas de Trailly, who Gaimar claimed could vouch for the reliability of his *Estoire des Engleis*, was a canon of York.

[68] Orderic, vi. 494. Cf. Crouch, *Beaumont Twins*, p. 37 on 'the feral factions of the royal court' which caused the Beaumont brothers to return to England in 1137.

been circulating two years earlier, probably reaching Orderic in Normandy in the over-dramatised form in which he reported them. Of course if this interpretation is correct, then Orderic's words should not be interpreted to mean that 'native' English resentment against 'Norman' lords was still alive and kicking as late as 1137; what we have instead is language reflecting the struggle for control of the court between two different factions, one of which is identified as being more Norman than the other. Here 'Norman' is not defined in opposition to the English in the sense of an inferior mono-lingual class of natives, but in opposition to the English in the sense of those bi- or tri-lingual members of the elite whose own careers and interests were substantially shaped in England.

If here, as elsewhere in eleventh- and twelfth-century English historical writing, 'Norman' and 'French' were equivalent terms, then this reading of Henry of Huntingdon and Orderic has the further advantage of making sense of some otherwise mysterious chapters in the *Liber Eliensis* – chapters which historians have generally preferred to ignore. Book III chapters 47, 51–53 tell the story of the conspiracy of an ex-monk called Ranulf of Salisbury who allegedly took advantage of the trust placed in him by Bishop Nigel of Ely to cook up a hare-brained scheme to kill all the Frenchmen (*Francigenae*) and take over the kingdom. When the plot was revealed, Nigel hurried back to Ely and had the conspirators tried and punished.[69] E. O. Blake pointed to various discrepancies and improbabilities in the account and offered what he called an 'obvious conjecture'. This is that 'preparations for armed insurrection during 1136 or 1137 had been authorized by Bishop Nigel' and that when reports of the plot brewing at Ely reached Stephen, the bishop reacted by devising a cover story in which his unfortunate clerk had to take the blame. Given the fact that of the three bishops, Nigel was the one most on his guard in 1139, and the fact that he was subsequently one of the Empress's keenest supporters, there is in my view much to support Blake's brilliant conjecture – one that seems to have been undeservedly neglected by historians of Stephen's reign.[70] Indeed it may well be that these four chapters in the *Liber Eliensis*, written in a style unlike the rest of the work, represent the text of the cover story composed in 1137.[71] Interestingly and, I think, significantly they are the only chapters in the whole of the *Book of Ely*'s narrative of twelfth century events where nationality or national nomen-

[69] *Liber Eliensis*, ed. Ernest O. Blake, Camden Soc., 3rd ser. vol. xcii (1962), pp. 286–7, 294–9.

[70] E. O. Blake, 'The *Historia Eliensis* as a Source for Twelfth-Century History', *Bulletin of the John Rylands Library* xli (1959), 318–27. The conjecture was at least mentioned by Kealey, *Roger of Salisbury*, pp. 167–8, and by K. Yoshitake, 'The Arrest of the Three Bishops in 1139 and its Consequences', *Journal of Medieval History* 14 (1988), 111 n. 28.

[71] Perhaps written by the *rhetor quidam Iulianus nomine . . . vir scientia admirabilis, in grammatica nulli secundus* since only in these chapters can we find the sustained use of a classical source, Sallust's *Bellum Catalinae*, *Liber Eliensis*, pp. 287 n. 1, 341–2; Blake, 'The *Historia*', 312 n. 2, 320–1.

clature seems to be at stake.[72] Antagonism between Norman and English had, of course, been central to its coverage of William I's reign, but thereafter – except in these chapters – we hear no more of ethnic tension. The *Book of Ely*'s account of the conquest and of English resistance had been little more than a patchwork of quotations taken from earlier sources, but in one of his own linking phrases the mid twelfth-century compiler decided to explain what he meant by 'Normans': *eorum dico qui utroque parente Normanni et in Normannia sunt educati* – a passage that is interesting both for the way its author defines Normans and for his apparent need to do so.[73] It looks as though when he was writing at least one other meaning of the word 'Norman' was current. Was it 'the Normans' in the sense of a dominant elite of Norman descent? Or was it 'the Normans' in what I suggest was Henry of Huntingdon's new sense, a Normandy-centred court faction (some members of which could even have had one parent of English descent)?

If the Beaumonts had indeed headed a court party known as the 'Normans', then we could anticipate a revival of this party after 1154. By the 1160s Henry II was certainly very conscious of his Norman lineage, patronising Wace's *Roman de Rou* and having the tombs of his ancestors at Fécamp ceremonially re-arranged.[74] Presumably he had felt the same way in the 1150s; after all, when crowned king of England he had already been duke of Normandy for four years. In 1154 his choice as the senior justiciar of England was the politician who was now the greatest of the cross-Channel magnates, Robert Beaumont, earl of Leicester. It is against this background that we should read the Battle Chronicle's account (referred to above, p. 125) of Richard de Luci's May 1157 address to Henry II. 'This church should be famously praised by you, lord king, and by all of us Normans, for it was here that the famous king William, by the will of God, and by the aid and counsel of our kinsmen, defeated his enemies . . . As for us it is by virtue of gifts conferred by William, and by succeeding to our kin, that we possess great estates and riches. Wherefore, my lord, most excellent of kings, all this gathering of Norman nobles asks with fervent prayers that your royal severity maintain that abbey, as the emblem of your – and our – triumph, in its proper privileges and exemptions against all its enemies, and above all against the ambushes (*insidias*) of the English.'[75] Not

---

[72] The last man referred to as a Norman was Picot, William I's sheriff of Cambridgeshire, *Liber Eliensis*, p. 211.

[73] *LE*, 171; cf. *Memorials of St Edmunds Abbey*, ed. Thomas Arnold, 3 vols. (RS, 1890–6), i. 344 for a related passage which does not, however, contain this particular phrase. The compiler evidently identified himself as English, referring to Bede's history both as *historia Anglorum* and as *nostre gentis historia*, pp. 6, 367. Michael Richter suggested that explanation was called for because at that time the usual criterion for calling someone Norman was language, *Sprache und Gesellschaft im Mittelalter* (Stuttgart, 1979), p. 44.

[74] Short, 'Patrons and Polyglots', 238; Robert of Torigny, pp. 212–13.

[75] *Chronicle of Battle Abbey*, pp. 182–3. The deceits of the English is one of the main themes of the speech before Hastings which Wace puts into Duke William's mouth, *Le Roman de Rou de Wace*, ed. A. J. Holden (Paris, 1970–3), ii, vv. 7407–66.

surprisingly these words have been widely used as evidence for the continuing existence – perhaps as late as the 1180s, when the chronicle was written – of a class of great Norman landowners who knew that the native English still had good reason to resent them.

But if we locate Richard de Luci's words both in place and in their immediate political context, then another interpretation becomes possible. There can have been no place in England where the cult of 1066 was more assiduously cherished than the abbey of Battle and where it made more sense to appeal to Norman ancestry. All the more since the abbot of Battle, Walter de Luci – Richard's brother – was a Norman (from Luce, near Lonlay-l'Abbaye), *transmarinus* in the terminology of the English author of the Battle Chronicle. Richard de Luci too could claim to be a Norman, as well as now being a man great enough to take a notoriously condescending view of the pretensions of 'petty knights'.[76] Moreover his speech has to be seen in the context of a dispute between different groups within the ecclesiastical elite. Battle's claim to exemption from diocesan rights had recently been challenged by a new bishop, the prominent lawyer Hilary of Chichester. The abbey's response had been to have a charter forged in the name of William I, giving it the privilege it claimed. When the newly created charter was read out at an assembly at Lambeth in 1155, the crucial phrase containing the exemption caused a storm of protest. In the chronicler's words, 'a shout went up from all sides'. Hilary of Chichester had managed to persuade Archbishop Theobald and the other bishops that the rights of Canterbury, *mater totius Anglie*, and of all of them, would be undermined if 'abbots throughout England were to claim this against their bishops'.[77] Once again, as in 1139, the English bishops were ranged against Normans.[78] Abbot Walter had powerful friends at court, not just his brother but also – as the Battle Chronicle makes plain – his senior colleague, Robert Beaumont.[79] Even so special pleading was needed if Battle was to win its case against the corporate interest of the English episcopate, now headed by the archbishop who had recently crowned Henry. This Richard de Luci supplied with his impassioned appeal to the memories of 1066. More than a century later

---

[76] *Chronicle of Battle Abbey*, pp. 142, 214. See in particular pp. 17–20 for Eleanor Searle's comments on Battle's exploitation of tales of the Conquest in the days of Abbot Walter when *romans de Rou* were court fashion.

[77] *Chronicle of Battle Abbey*, pp. 154, 158. Eleanor Searle 'Battle Abbey and exemption: the forged charters', *EHR* 83 (1968), 449–80.

[78] That prelates of the English church could readily be identified as 'the English' is suggested by Hugh the Chanter's reference to 'Normans and English' meeting the pope in 1119, *The History of the Church of York*, p. 132; also by Beneit of St Albans' reference to Henry II swearing during the Becket dispute that he would not allow his assizes and laws to be put at risk 'on account of the English', *La Vie de Thomas Becket par Beneit*, ed. Borje Schlyter (Lund, 1941), vv. 489–91.

[79] *Chronicle of Battle Abbey*, pp. 180, 196. See also pp. 14–15 for Searle's comments on 'the crucial importance and pervading presence of private alliances' in governing circles.

earls whose privileges were also under threat were to brandish rusty swords in a similar appeal to the memory of 1066.[80]

So far I have touched on three passages in which play was made with notions of *Normanitas*, in all three cases the two authors, Henry of Huntingdon and the Battle Chronicler, were putting words into someone else's mouth. If, as I argue, they were both English then it is plain that we are dealing with highly rhetorical exercises which in no way reflect the self-identification of their authors. This is evidently true also of another well-known speech in which the great deeds of Norman ancestors was emphasised: the pre-Standard speech supposedly spoken by the aged Norman lord, Walter of Espec, but actually composed by the Englishman, Aelred of Rievaulx.[81] Less clear-cut from this point of view is the anonymous and more or less contemporary account of Hervey de Glanvil's speech at Lisbon in 1147.

The author was someone closely associated with Glanvil and therefore with the East Anglian contingent on the Lisbon crusade, but whether he thought of himself as English or Norman is hard to say. The speech itself takes the form of an appeal to Norman courage intended to persuade some reluctant fellow-crusaders to remain with the rest of the army. In the author's narrative of the expedition, he normally refers to the part of the army to which he belonged as *Normanni et Angli*, indeed once as *nostri . . . Normanni scilicet et Angli*.[82] In a more detailed break-down of the Norman and English army group, he listed four constabularies: first, Norfolk and Suffolk, second, the ships of Kent, third, the Londoners, and finally, 'all the rest of the ships'. It later transpires that 'the rest' included eight ships 'of Normans, of Southampton and of Bristol'.[83] Since 'the rest' were the ones who were reluctant to join the siege, it is clear that Hervey de Glanvil's Normanizing speech was chiefly addressed to men at least some of whom were Normans in the straightforward sense that they lived in Normandy. Undeniably, however, as an appeal to solidarity, there is also a sense in which the speech was calculated to embrace the whole Norman and English contingent. Thus Hervey was made to refer to Normandy as the 'mother of our people' (*generis nostri mater Normannia*), clearly playing on the theme of common ancestry.[84] But it does not follow from this that the author identified himself as a Norman any more than late tenth century Normans identified themselves as Danes.[85] Moreover if we take into account not only self-identification but also

[80] Michael T. Clanchy, *From Memory to Written Record. England 1066–1307*, 2nd edn (Oxford, 1993), pp. 35–43.

[81] Chibnall, *Anglo-Norman England*, p. 210; John R. E. Bliese, 'Aelred of Rievaulx's Rhetoric and Morale at the Battle of the Standard, 1138', *Albion* 20 (1988), 543–56.

[82] *De Expugnatione Lyxbonensi*, ed. Charles W. David (New York, 1936), pp. 104–11, 128, 142. And see p. 45 for the charming thought that the author's 'sturdy moral principles and his fair but insular outlook on the continental world were of a quality which may still to this day be properly called English'.

[83] *Ibid.*, pp. 57, 100 for David's discussion of the Caen-Southampton Vitulus family.

[84] *Ibid.*, p. 108.

[85] As Graham Loud pointed out, William of Jumièges believed that the Danish settlers in

identification by others, then the accounts (overlapping but not identical) of the siege written from within the other main army group, comprising Flemings and Lorrainers, are highly significant, for they always referred to their allies – and rivals – simply as 'the English'.[86]

To conclude. In the works of Henry of Huntingdon – as in those of William of Malmesbury – we can trace a developing sense of Englishness. In their early writings in the 1120s it was one which was still shaped by a lingering perception of themselves as a subject population, the down-trodden English oppressed by the French (or Normans). But in what they wrote in the 1140s – and, in Henry's case, in the 1150s – this sense of oppression is absent. At Lincoln he belonged to a society of bishops and cathedral canons, many of them – like Henry himself – family men, a society of landowners and their wives.[87] By 1140 one of his neighbours in this Barsetshire society, Constance, wife of Ralph FitzGilbert, had commissioned Geoffrey Gaimar to compose his vernacular *Estoire des Engleis*. Gaimar not only performed the remarkable feat of rendering the archaic prose of the Anglo-Saxon Chronicle into modern French verse, he also portrayed the tenth-century King Edgar as though he were a figure of twelfth-century romance and presented the eleventh-century resistance fighter Hereward as a courtly gentleman.[88] It looks as though Gaimar was writing for women and men who thought of themselves as English, French-speaking, but English enough to think of the Anglo-Saxon past as their past – even if the *koine* in which the Chronicle was written was probably beyond them. Moreover although a Waleran of Meulan may have sneered at their upstart pretensions and said that they were imagining things, it is also clear that these English men and women felt that they belonged to a Norman-French cultural community, military, secular, and courtly.[89] This is

Neustria became Normans almost at once, Loud, 'The Gens Normannorum', 108–9. William's belief may well have implications for the assumptions of the Norman new-comers to England. Cf. C. Potts, '*Atque unum ex diversis gentibus populum effecit*: historical tradition and the Norman identity', *ANS* 18 (1995), 139–52 for evidence for a mid-eleventh-century Norman belief that they were one people brought together out of several peoples.

[86] *Annales Sancti Disibodi* in *Monumenta Germaniae Historica, Scriptores*, vol. 17, pp. 27–8; *RHF* XIV, pp. 325–7. I have not seen the text of Winand of Cologne's letter (edited and privately printed by Ernst Dümmler, Vienna 1851). According to Helmold of Bosau, *Chronica Slavorum*, ed. Heinz Stoob (Darmstadt, 1963), p. 220, the 'other' part of the army was composed of *Angli et Britanni*.

[87] In Henry's poem 'On Himself' he observed that his verses and house were well-worked, his fields, orchards and marriage bed well-cultivated, see Partner, *Serious Entertainments*, pp. 40–8.

[88] *L'Estoire des Engleis by Geffrei Gaimar*, ed. Alexander Bell (Oxford, 1960). Ian Short, 'Gaimar et les débuts de l'historiographie en langue française' in *Chroniques nationales et chroniques universelles*, ed. Danielle Buschinger (Göppingen, 1960), 155–63; A. R. Press, 'The Precocious Courtesy of Geoffrey Gaimar' in ed. G. S. Burgess, *Court and Poet* (Liverpool, 1981), 267–76.

[89] Richard W. Southern, 'England's First Entry into Europe' in *Medieval Humanism* (Oxford, 1970), 135–57, esp. 137–8, 154–5 (but not 142).

the kind of community to which Henry of Huntingdon belonged and for which he wrote. In Diana Greenway's words, he was 'passionately concerned with the history of secular power – *regnum*'; dynasty, military strength and chivalric ideals were among the major ingredients of this theme.[90] By this date people like Gaimar and Constance FitzGilbert, Henry and Bishop Alexander were at home with the English past. The post-Conquest traumas had faded. Now English history was felt less as a catastrophe and rather more as the history of an increasingly civilised people.[91] As Henry's account of the Battle of the Standard indicates, the self-identification of the English as civilised rested in part upon a negative perception of 'Celtic' society. In other words, Henry – and he was not alone in this – was already writing in terms of the kind of English *Wirgefühl* which Karl Schnith, on the basis of his analysis of William of Newburgh, identified as a late twelfth-century phenomenon.[92] Doubtless these Englishmen and women were often of mixed ancestry – as William of Malmesbury was and Henry of Huntingdon may well have been.[93] They were usually French on their father's side and proud of their forefathers' achievements; and it was, as R. H. C. Davis observed, in about 1140 that the 'saga of the Norman race', the theme of the great deeds of the forefathers, entered historical writing in England.[94] Here it always occurs in a specific rhetorical context: orations designed to strengthen the morale of men who, for one reason or another, were in a tight corner.[95] Outside of this context, on the other hand, when authors writing in England used the word 'Norman', they increasingly came to mean someone thought of as living in, or being based in, Normandy. Analysis of Henry of Huntingdon's usage has also led me to suggest that in the context of a political system focused on a royal court riven by faction – the society of Walter Map's *Courtiers' Trifles*[96] – words like 'Norman' and 'French' could sometimes bear a meaning which was as much political as national. They could be used of cross-Channel magnates like the Beaumonts and their followers, leaders of a court faction labelled 'the Normans' or 'the French' in opposition to a rival faction which was English in the sense that its members, though also francophone, had their lands, interests and careers almost entirely based in England. Moreover the arrival on the scene of a new faction was likely to generate a higher degree of solidarity among those who felt their own interests threatened by the

[90] Diana Greenway, 'Henry of Huntingdon and Bede' in *L'Historiographie médiévale en Europe*, ed. Jean-Philippe Genet (Paris, 1991), p. 50.
[91] See below, p. 228.
[92] Schnith, 'Von Symeon von Durham', pp. 243, 254–6.
[93] Partner, *Serious Entertainments*, p. 11; Campbell, 'Some Twelfth-Century Views', 133.
[94] However the origins of the Norman myth can be traced back to the eleventh century, Loud, 'Gens Normannorum', 104–16.
[95] On this aspect of the orations before Hastings and the Standard see John R. E. Bliese's articles, 'Aelred of Rievaulx's Rhetoric and Morale at the Battle of the Standard, 1138', *Albion* 20 (1988), 543–56 and 'The Battle Rhetoric of Aelred of Rievaulx', *The Haskins Society Journal* 1 (1989), 99–107.
[96] Walter Map, *De Nugis Curialium*, passim.

newcomers. In these circumstances the 'old' Normans were likely to feel more English than ever.[97]

Of course it is also possible that in the mid twelfth century and later there were mono-lingual English *rustici* who continued to think of themselves as the true English and of their lords as both French and foreign. Direct evidence of their views no longer exists, but it is worth noting that John of Worcester's representation of Henry I's nightmare had the king threatened first by *rustici*, then by *milites* and finally by prelates. At least in Johnn of Worcester's imagination the king's worries took shape within the framework of the three orders, not the two nations.[98]

Appendix. The Hyde Chronicle

Although a twelfth-century word for 'Anglo-Norman' does not appear to exist, a similar hybrid term *Normanangli* (and closely related variants of it) appears no less than 23 times in the 36 pages of printed text of the anonymous fragmentary narrative known as the Hyde Chronicle.[99] After careful study David Bates concluded that the word was used to refer to 'the coming together of two peoples under one ruler'.[100] Until recently, however, historians paid little attention to this word, doubtless partly because the author's usage stands alone, and partly because we still lack a decent edition. Recent comment on the chronicle – a history of the Norman dukes from 1035 to 1120 – treats it as a near contemporary source, and I have no quarrel with a dating to the later years of Henry I's reign.[101] Much more doubtful is the question of where it was written. Although the sole surviving manuscript came to be bound up with a thirteenth-century cartulary of Hyde Abbey, Winchester, there is, as Bates observed, actually no reason to assume that the narrative was originally composed there. However his suggestion that the author may have lifted the term *Normanangli* from Anglo-Latin forms such as *Angolsaxonum* or *Anglorum Saxonum* tends to re-inforce the notion that it was written somewhere in England.[102] Warren Hollister pointed to the 'considerable attention that it devotes to the Warenne earls of Surrey' and suggested that it may have been

[97] Fuchs, *Das Domesday Book*, p. 364.
[98] *Chronicle of John of Worcester*, pp. 32–3. And John claimed the authority of Grimbald, one of the king's physicians.
[99] 'Chronicon monasterii de Hyda iuxta Wintoniam' in *Liber Monasterii de Hyda*, ed. E. Edwards (RS, 1886), pp. 284–321.
[100] David Bates, 'Normandy and England after 1066', *English Historical Review*, 104 (1989), pp. 877–80.
[101] Elisabeth van Houts, who is undertaking a new edition, suggests 'probably after 1128 and before 1134' in Christopher P. Lewis, 'The Earldom of Surrey and the date of Domesday Book', *Historical Research* 63 (1990), 330–1.
[102] Bates, 'Normandy and England', p. 878.

produced at the Warenne foundation of St Pancras, Lewes.[103] This suggestion has recently been endorsed and further developed by Christopher Lewis. Certainly, as he points out, 'whoever the author and wherever he wrote, he had no interest in Winchester'.[104] It looks as though the author did not see himself as English since, as Elisabeth van Houts noted, he refers to *Sudsexia* as a name 'in their language'.[105] Nor, when writing about the sons of Henry I and Duke Robert, does he use either the English term Atheling or the Anglo-Latin *Clito*.[106] This, of course, leaves open the possibility that he was a Norman monk of Lewes.

However I am inclined to think that the author, whoever he or she was, was a Norman writing in Normandy. He is at his most 'English' in his evident devotion to the memory of Queen Matilda;[107] but this I do not think this enables us to place him on one side of the Channel or the other. He claims that Harold swore his oath to William on a reliquary of St Pancras and although this might seem to point to Lewes Priory, that saint's role as the punisher of perjurors was better known on the continent.[108] He was certainly very interested in the Warennes; and this would explain his knowledge of Sussex. His sympathy for Frederick Warenne even leads him to take an unusually hostile view of Hereward the Wake.[109] But the more he approaches his own time the more he is interested in the area where the Norman estates of the Warennes lay, the district around Mortemer.[110] The Norman Conquest and therefore English history dominates the earlier part of his narrative. But the English history he does know is demonstrably the kind of history that was known in Normandy, in particular his saga-like stories about the crimes and fall of the house of Godwin. In this and in other respects – for example his account of the execution and cult of Earl Waltheof – he seems to have used sources very similar to those that were available to Orderic at St Evroul.[111] What is most telling, it seems to me, is the fact that after about 1102 he falls silent about events in England and reports only events that occurred in France. He is noticeably interested in the thorny question of the formal relationship between the duke of Normandy and the king

---

[103] This despite the fact that he would have liked to give the form *Normanangli* 'the weight of a calculated political theory' and was therefore attracted by the traditional association with Hyde Abbey 'just across the town wall from Henry's Winchester treasury', C. Warren Hollister, 'Normandy, France and the Anglo-Norman *Regnum*', *Speculum* 51 (1976), 231–2.

[104] Lewis, 'Earldom of Surrey', p. 331.

[105] *Ibid.*, 332 n. 28.

[106] David N. Dumville, 'The Aetheling: a study in Anglo-Saxon constitutional history', *Anglo-Saxon England* 8 (1979), 10.

[107] Chronicon de Hyda, pp. 305, 312–13.

[108] *Ibid.*, p. 290. Moreover, as Lewis points out, the author's term for the reliquary, 'the ox eye' was also known to Wace, 'Earldom of Surrey', 333 – i.e. it was known in Normandy.

[109] Chronicon de Hyda, p. 295.

[110] *Ibid.*, pp. 311, 314.

[111] But his allegiance to the Warennes allowed him to be more critical of Henry I than Orderic ever was, *ibid.*, pp. 313, 320–1. See pp. 287–90, 292–4 for the saga of Godwin and his sons. Cf. Orderic ii. 142, 171 n. 4.

of France as well as more generally in the tense political relationship between them.[112] He continues to be concerned with the Warennes, so deeply indeed as to be almost certainly attached to them in some way, but from now on every event in which they take part – as central figures naturally – takes place in France. It is difficult to explain this narrowing of geographical focus except in terms of an author writing in Normandy.

[112] Chronicon de Hyda, pp. 285, 300, 309, 316.

9

The English Invasion of Ireland

In the history of English attitudes to Ireland the twelfth was the crucially formative century, the period of 'the harsh metamorphosis'.[1] For some centuries before the twelfth the English and Irish inhabited what Denis Bethell called 'a common cultural world in which the Irish could still be teachers'. But, he went on, by the mid twelfth century ' "barbarity" had become, and was to remain, a cliché in describing the Irish – with about as much truth as the previous "sanctity" . . . Even the Old English monastic communities, where the memories of the shared piety and learning of the past were strongest, had come to feel superior, hostile and alien.'[2] No one was to give more memorable expression to this new cliché than Gerald de Barri in his *Topographia Hibernica* and his *Expugnatio Hibernica*, both dating from the late 1180s. As Nicholas Canny has recently written, 'No sixteenth-century Englishman surpassed Gerald in his vituperative dismissal of Gaelic culture.'[3] Since the Welsh and Scots suffered a similar fate at the hands of twelfth-century writers, it is clear that we are faced here by one of the most fundamental ideological shifts in the history of the British Isles.[4] In the case of the Irish, the subsequent history of centuries of half-completed conquest meant that the new attitude of superiority, hostility and alienation was to remain deeply entrenched. English writers of the sixteenth and seventeenth centuries were to do little more than play variations on themes already well and truly established in Gerald's Irish writings. Given the extent to which 'early modern' authors, like their 'late medieval' predecessors, relied heavily and directly upon Gerald for their understanding of Irish history, this is hardly surprising.[5] The degree of dependence upon his supposedly authoritative

---

[1] The phrase is F. X. Martin's, in ed. R. Wall, *Medieval and Modern Ireland* (Totowa, NJ, 1988), 10. I owe this reference to the kindness of John McLoughlin.

[2] D. Bethell, 'English Monks and Irish Reform in the 11th and 12th Centuries', *Historical Studies* viii (1971), 117–18, 125–6.

[3] N. P. Canny, *Kingdom and Colony: Ireland in the Atlantic World, 1560–1800* (Baltimore 1988), 3.

[4] W. R. Jones, 'England against the Celtic Fringe: a Study in Cultural Stereoytpes', *Journal of World History* 13 (1971); R. R. Davies, 'Buchedd a moes y Cymry. The manners and Morals of the Welsh', *Welsh History Review* 12 (1984–5); R. Bartlett, *Gerald of Wales* (Oxford 1982), esp. chapter 6, 'The Face of the Barbarian'. See above, pp. 18, 58.

[5] Particularly important in this regard were Stanihurst's and Hooker's contributions to Holinshed's *Chronicles*. On late medieval use of Gerald see the summary by R. Frame, *The Political Development of the British Isles 1100–1400* (Oxford 1990), 187.

approach comes across very clearly in the words of those seventeenth-century Irish writers who sought to defend the reputation of their own people. According to John Lynch (1662), 'The wild dreams of Giraldus have been taken up by a herd of scribblers. These writers are like a troop which blindly obeys the general without questioning his authority; they follow him . . . animated by the same fell spirit of calumniating the Irish, and, like asps . . . imbibe poison from the viper . . . he has made our name a byword of reproach, in the mouths of mountebanks, in taverns, in club-meetings in private societies . . . I find the calumnies of which he is the author published in the language and writings of every nation, no new geography, no history of the world, no work on the manners and customs of different nations appearing in which his calumnious charges against the Irish are not chronicled as undoubted facts . . . and all these repeated again and again until the heart sickens at the sight.'[6]

The debt to Gerald is perhaps least obvious in the case of the most creative of seventeenth century authors on Ireland, Edmund Spenser. By contrast Spenser himself has contributed to the notion of fundamental change in the 'early modern' period. 'For it is to be thought that the use of all England was in the reign of Henry II, when Ireland was planted with English, very rude and barbarous, . . . for it is but even the other day since England grew civil.'[7] One problem with accepting this kind of expression of opinion as though it were serious evidence of a deep divide between 'medieval' and 'modern' is the fact that similar opinions were a commonplace of twelfth-century thought. William of Malmesbury, for example, believed both that England in his own day was a recently civilised society and that Ireland remained 'rude and barbarous'.[8]

To point out that intelligent men in both centuries took a similarly condescending view of their own past and of their neighbour's present, a view in both cases explicitly based upon perceptions of significant differences, is not, of course, to deny that in other respects there were real differences between the twelfth and sixteenth centuries. The question here is only whether or not such differences had a significant impact upon English perceptions of Ireland. The Reformation, for example, must have done *something* to make Protestant Englishmen hostile to Catholic Irish. But just what? and how significant was it? As Canny pointed out, owing to 'the peculiar nature of Catholicism in Gaelic Ireland', English Protestants 'branded the native Irish as pagan'.[9] Yet seeing the Christian Irish as pagans goes back to the twelfth century, to that confident shaper of European opinion, Bernard of Clairvaux, and to his famous description of the Irish as 'shameless in their customs, uncivilised in their ways, godless in religion, barbarous in their law, obstinate as regards instruction, foul in their lives: Christians in name, pagans in fact'.[10] Gerald's fiercest

---

[6] J. Lynch, *Cambrensis Eversus*, ed. M. Kelly (Dublin 1842), 103, 107.

[7] W. L. Renwick (ed.), *The View of the Present State of Ireland* (Oxford 1970), 67.

[8] See pp. 28–9.

[9] N. Canny, *The Elizabethan Conquest of Ireland* (Hassocks 1976), 123.

[10] Cited together with helpful comment in Bartlett, 38 n. 53, 169 and by F. X. Martin in *A New*

criticisms of the state of religion among the Irish were platitudes of twelfth-century reform.[11]

What important elements did 'the Protestant/Papist complication' add to that devastating judgement? In some contexts this 'complication' may be crucial – the situation of modern Belfast, for example – but it does not follow that it always has been. Doubtless, as Karl Bottigheimer put it, 'the religious difference reinforced at every point older conflicts of a political and cultural nature'.[12] The fundamental point surely remains the one made by Denis Bethell: that it was in the twelfth century that the hitherto dominant view, an essentially positive one, was replaced by a new, hostile and condescending one. Gerald tells a story of sailors storm-driven onto the coast of Ireland and scarcely able to believe the primitiveness of the native inhabitants. Those sailors of the Spanish Armada washed up on the Irish coast four hundred years later were to experience exactly similar feelings. They clearly felt they had more in common with their Protestant English enemies than with the Catholic 'savages' amongst whom they had to seek refuge.[13]

In this same context I find difficulties with the notion that Gerald represented a 'medieval' as opposed to a 'Renaissance' view of the world. Indeed I confess to finding difficulties with the frequently re-iterated belief that 'Renaissance man' was significantly different from 'medieval man'. I do so because when scholars give examples of such differences, I find their evidence unconvincing. It has, for example, been claimed that by the sixteenth century,

> we can state confidently that the old concept of the Irish as being socially inferior to the English had been replaced with the idea that they were anthropologically inferior and were further behind the English on the ladder of development. The old world had lacked a sense of history and hence a concept of social process and development, but the widening horizons of the articulate citizen of sixteenth-century England, both intellectually and geographically, slowly eroded the old idea of a static world.[14]

But Gerald had noted that 'the Irish have not progressed at all from the primitive habits of pastoral farming. For while mankind usually progresses from the woods to the fields, and then from the fields to settlements and communities of citizens, this people despises work on the land, has little use

---

History of Ireland. II. Medieval Ireland, ed. A. Cosgrove (Oxford 1987), 59–60. For one modern response to Bernard's words see F. X. Martin, *No Hero in the House* (Dublin 1976), 5.

[11] Gerald, *The History and Topography of Ireland*, ed. J. J. O'Meara (Harmondsworth 1982), 106, 111.

[12] K. Bottigheimer, 'Kingdom and Colony: Ireland in the Westward Enterprise, 1536–1660' in *The Westward Enterprise*, ed. K. R. Andrews, N. P. Canny, P. E. H. Hair (Detroit 1979), 55.

[13] Gerald, *Topography*, 110–11; *God's Obvious Design*, ed. P. Gallagher and D. W. Cruickshank (London 1990), 223–47. I owe this reference to the letter of Francisco de Cuellar to the kindness of Mia Rodriguez-Salgado.

[14] Canny, *Elizabethan Conquest*, 128–31.

for the money-making of towns and condemns the rights and privileges of civil life.' As Gerald's biographer has observed, 'the concepts behind this passage – the ladder of evolution of human societies and the persistence of primitive survivals – would not be out of place in nineteenth century anthropological thought'. And Gerald was not 'ahead of his time'. These sorts of ideas were taken for granted by other twelfth-century historians such as William of Malmesbury and William of Newburgh.[15]

Another example. When in 1572 Lord Deputy Fitzwilliam wrote, 'Till the sword have thoroughly and universally tamed . . . them in vain is law brought amongst them', he is said to have been acting as spokesman for 'the aggressive young men influenced by the ideas of the Renaissance'.[16] But Gerald long before this had advocated a similar policy. 'First tame them, then govern them', was his line. 'If their innate fickleness leads them to presume to break the peace then, dissembling any feelings of compassion we may have, they must be punished at once.' Not surprisingly Gerald envisaged a drastically curtailed future for the Irish. They were to be 'either disabled or destroyed'. Those that survived were to be reduced to the status of second class citizens, whose function was to obey and to serve. They were to be forbidden all use of arms and they were to be made to pay an annual tribute in perpetuity.[17]

It has been suggested that seeing the Irish as barbarians allowed sixteenth-century English commanders to make war 'absolved from all normal ethical restraints' and that atrocities of the sort committed by Sir Humphrey Gilbert in Munster in the 1570s had not been perpetrated by 'Norman lords'.[18] But they had. In 1185 'when the Irish insolently invaded Meath, they together with their chief were put to the sword and one hundred heads were sent to Dublin'. At Waterford in 1170 some seventy prisoners were slaughtered and their bodies thrown over the cliff. This time Gerald felt that the newcomers had gone too far and had 'displayed intolerable and inhuman brutality'. None the less in speeches put into the mouths of the victors he rehearses the arguments for and against this sort of treatment of prisoners, concluding with what he believed was the argument that won the day: 'they should be killed in order to inspire fear, so that

[15] Bartlett, *Gerald of Wales*, 159, 176.
[16] Canny, *Conquest*, 128. However Canny later described the English of the late sixteenth century as 'reverting to the notion that change could only be effected by force which had inspired all English thinking on the reform of the Gaelic population ever since Giraldus Cambrensis had first addressed himself to that subject in the twelfth century', *Kingdom and Colony*, 32.
[17] For these themes see *Expugnatio Hibernica*, ed. and trans. A. B. Scott and F. X. Martin (Dublin 1978), 244–53. For some early thirteenth century elaborations of these ideas see R. R. Davies, *Domination and Conquest* (Cambridge 1990), 117. In the seventeenth century some Protestants took a more optimistic line. Sir William Petty, for example, believed that though an Irish Catholic was at present worth no more than a negro or a slave (£15), it might be possible to raise his value to that of an Englishman (£70), cited Canny, *Kingdom and Colony*, 110–12.
[18] Canny, *Conquest*, 122.

as a result of the example we make of them this lawless and rebellious people may shrink from engaging our forces in future'. As Gerald knew perfectly well, in acting thus the invaders were behaving in Ireland differently from the way they would have behaved in contemporary 'civilised Europe'. One of their excuses was that this was how the 'barbarous Irish' themselves behaved and so they had to be treated in ways they would understand.[19] These same lines of argument were to be employed in Thomas Churchyard's justification of Humphrey Gilbert's policy of terror.[20]

'Once persuaded', we have been assured, 'that the Irish were barbarians' then the 'aggressive young men' of the Renaissance 'were able to produce a moral and civil justification for their conquest of Ireland'.[21] So too in the twelfth century. The moral justification, set out in *Laudabiliter* as well as in forged papal privileges, was that since the Irish were a barbarous and sinful people, it was right that Henry II should be set as a reforming ruler over them. There was a civil law justification in what Gerald termed the *ius irrefragabile* created by the 'voluntary' submission of the Irish kings to Henry II. Gerald also offered a justification based upon 'history'. Since the Irish were descended from the Basques, a people whose modern capital – Bayonne – already lay within Henry II's dominions, it followed that they ought to acknowledge his rule elsewhere.[22] This view of Irish ancestry derived from the work of another twelfth-century writer, Geoffrey of Monmouth, and it marked a significant variation on the traditional belief that the Irish came from Spain. This is because twelfth-century opinion was in no doubt that the Basques – unlike the Spanish – were barbarians.[23] Thus Geoffrey of Monmouth, writing in the late 1130s, took it for granted that the Irish were an uncivilised people. And it was Geoffrey, of course, who invented the story that King Arthur had conquered Ireland – the story with which Hakluyt began his *Principal Navigations*.[24]

Already in the twelfth century there were worries that the newcomers were running the risk of being infected by the barbarous Irish, by being, as Gerald put

---

[19] *Expugnatio*, 58–65, 234, 246. See also *The Song of Dermot and the Earl*, ed. G. H. Orpen (Oxford 1892), 110–11, for further details of this atrocity narrated in a neutral tone and explaining that it was done in order to shame the Irish. See above, pp. 41–2.

[20] Thomas Churchyard, *A Generall Rehearsall of Warres* (London 1579), Qi–Qiii, e.g. 'that he did but then begin that order with them, which they had in effect ever tofore used toward the English'.

[21] Canny, *Conquest*, 128.

[22] *Topography*, 99–100; *Expugnatio*, 144–8, 230–2.

[23] *History of the Kings of Britain*, trans. L. Thorpe (Harmondsworth 1966), 101. On the barbarous manners and morals of the Basques see ed. J. Vielliard, *Le Guide du Pèlerin de Saint-Jacques de Compostelle* (Macon 1938), 20–31, where the author was aware of the kinship between them and 'Scots', still the normal continental term for Irish. Henry of Huntingdon, writing in the 1120s, still held to the traditional view of Irish origins, *Henry, Archdeacon of Huntingdon, Historia Anglorum*, ed. and trans. D. Greenway (Oxford 1996), 28–31; pp. 14–15 in Arnold's Rolls Series edition (London 1879).

[24] *History of the Kings of Britain*, 219, 222. Unfortunately on p. 219 Thorpe translated *barbari* as 'pagans'.

it, defiled by the pitch they touched.[25] When the English court chronicler, Roger of Howden, reported Hugh de Lacy's marriage to a daughter of the king of Connaught in 1181, he observed that it was done 'according to the custom of that country' – an intriguing comment in the light of Howden's condemnation of the Irish on the grounds that many of them 'had as many wives as they wanted'.[26] It seems that a violent and instinctive antipathy to Irish marriage law which, like Irish dress, was believed to lead to sexual sinfulness on a massive scale was central to both twelfth- and sixteenth-century perceptions of the Irish. Indeed the earliest signs of the approach of 'the harsh metamorphosis' are to be found in the hostile comments made on Irish marriage law by late eleventh century church 'reformers'; what was presumably divorce they construed as deserting or even selling wives.[27] Similarly when another English chronicler, Ralph of Diceto, envisaged the Irish clergy agreeing in 1172 to embrace English norms, it was, in his words, 'above all in matters relating to marriage'.[28] Similarly when Camden, in his *Britannia*, arrives at last at Ireland and the Irish, he very early on (though not without having already mentioned Gerald more than any other author) promises that 'in the end of this book we shall treat more largely of their customs' – but then cannot resist an immediate reference to the 'amours . . . among the wilder sort'.[29] In my view those who believe in fundamental shifts in European modes of perception are more likely to find what they are looking for in the twelfth century than in the sixteenth. On the whole – and unlike scholars of the Italian Renaissance – medievalists have been far too modest in the claims they have made for the 'Twelfth Century Renaissance'.

If, as I believe, students of anti-Irish opinion in early modern literature sometimes underestimate the extent to which these attitudes were shaped by twelfth-century writers, above all Gerald, the fault lies at least in part with medieval historians and with the ways in which medieval studies have developed since the mid nineteenth century. 'For centuries', as F. X. Martin has observed, 'historians and political writers, English and Irish, nationalist and unionist, were content to speak of the "English Conquest" of Ireland'.[30] But then the word 'English' went out of favour and a period of fluctuating terminology set in. Nowadays if modern scholars wish to inform themselves about the twelfth-century invasion of Ireland, they find themselves reading not about the English but the Normans, or Anglo-Normans or Anglo-French or Cambro-Normans. Inevitably one side-effect of this new nomenclature is to break a continuity

[25] *Topography*, 109.
[26] *Gesta Henrici Secundi*, ed. W. Stubbs (London RS 1867) i, 28, 270. On Howden's knowledge of Ireland see above, pp. 84–6.
[27] *The Letters of Lanfranc Archbishop of Canterbury*, ed. and trans. H. Clover and M. Gibson (Oxford 1979), 66–71. Significantly these letters were printed by James Ussher in his *Veterum Epistolarum Hibernicarum Sylloge* (Dublin 1632).
[28] *Historical Works of Ralph of Diceto*, ed. W. Stubbs (London RS 1876) ii, 350–1.
[29] Camden's *Britannia*, col. 966, from 1695 edn.
[30] *New History of Ireland*, vol. II, l.

which earlier generations had taken for granted, to create instead a presumption that the 'English' thought-world of the sixteenth and seventeenth centuries may have been significantly different from the now differently labelled thought-world of the twelfth. Questions of terminology are therefore important and it is to these that I now turn.[31]

In the earlier part of this century 'Norman' became standard form, perhaps under the influence of G. H. Orpen's four volumes, *Ireland under the Normans* (1911–20). The sheer weight of academic respectability behind the term 'Norman' seems to have persuaded even 'nationalist' historians who had long regarded Henry II's intervention in Ireland as English malevolence that if they wanted to be regarded as serious students of the past then they had better abjure 'English' and adopt 'Norman'. More recently academic historians when giving some thought to the matter of nomenclature have tended to shy away from 'Norman' – though often continuing to use it casually and in passing. For example in an important and strategically-sited discussion, F. X. Martin argues against use of the terms 'Norman invasion' or 'Norman conquest', not however – as he might have done – on grounds of lack of contemporary warrant for them, but on grounds that they 'endowed a political event with racial overtones, in keeping with the concept of the Normans as a Herrenvolk'. Thus he prefers the more anodyne Anglo-Norman or Cambro-Norman. Others have suggested Anglo-French or Anglo-Continental. If, as many historians believe, these hybrid terms at least reflect inconsistencies and ambiguities in contemporary usage, then even if none of them is entirely satisfactory, it doubtless makes sense to prefer one without resonance in contemporary political debate.[32] However if there is a satisfactory term it does not help historical understanding to avoid it. And in my view there is such a term, the old-fashioned one: English. This is what Michael Richter has been arguing for some time, though he has also, in my view, clouded the issue by basing his case in part on the dubious proposition that *lingua materna* can be taken as the criterion of nationality.[33]

The best reason for saying that the invaders were English is that this is what contemporary narrative sources say they were. Obviously they do not say that every single one of them was English. Occasionally we hear of men with names like 'Gualensis' of 'le Flemmeng'.[34] But this usage itself makes clear that

---

[31] As recognised by D. Cairns and S. Richards, 'Righting Willy', *Textual Practice* 4 (1990), 103–4.

[32] F. X. Martin, 'Introduction' in *New History of Ireland*, II, l–lii; R. Frame, *Colonial Ireland, 1169–1369* (Dublin 1981), vi–vii; R. Frame, *Political Development*, 52; R. R. Davies, *Domination and Conquest*, x.

[33] M. Richter 'Giraldiana', *Irish Historical Studies* 21 (1981); 'The Interpretation of Irish History', *Irish Historical Studies* 24, 1985; *Medieval Ireland. The Enduring Tradition* (London 1988), 130. It is not easy, in any case, to be certain of the mother tongue of Dermot's principal allies in the late 1160s and early 1170s. See I. Short, 'On Bilingualism in Anglo-Norman England', *Romance Philology* 33 (1980), 467–79. Whether their first vernacular was French or English, the essential point is that by then they thought themselves to be Anglais/English.

[34] E.g. *Expugnatio*, 136, 194; *Song of Dermot*, vv. 3112, 3175. Clearly the name 'Gualensis'

Welshmen and Flemings were not often to be found amongst 'those that counted'.[35] Gerald's basic usage is clear. In the *Expugnatio* he almost always uses the word English. In his *Topography* the term he uses as an era in Irish history is 'adventus Anglorum'; he uses phrases like 'before the coming of the English' and refers to the modern population of the island as 'Irish and English'.[36] If we turn to the verse history known as *The Song of Dermot and the Earl* the evidence is equally clear-cut. Here the newcomers are referred to as 'English' on about eighty occasions; there is just one line where, instead, we hear of 'French, Flemings and Normans'.[37]

Irish sources point in the same direction. Unfortunately only one set of twelfth century annals survives in a contemporary manuscript, the Annals of Inisfallen, of Munster provenance.[38] These consistently refer to the newcomers as either 'the foreigners' or the 'grey foreigners'. Clearly this usage, which continues right through the thirteenth century and beyond, doesn't help us to discover where the foreigners were thought to come from. The other sets of annals are much more informative. Although the Annals of Tigernach (the house chronicle of Connaught) generally refer to the newcomers as 'foreigners', they sometimes call them 'Saxons', as in 1167, 1170, 1171, 1172, 1176, 1177 and 1178.[39] The Annals of Ulster and the – for most of this period almost identical – Annals of Loch Cé also usually say 'foreigners' but occasionally, as in 1172 and 1176 (and in 1185 in Loch Cé) refer to Saxons.[40] Mac Carthaigh's Book normally uses the word Saxon up until 1185, though the word 'foreigner' starts to be used in 1176 and becomes standard usage from 1192.[41] There are, of course, problems with annals which survive only in later copies. We have to bear in mind the possibility that the entries 'may have been altered – reworded, expanded, shortened, suppressed – on each subsequent occasion when the annals were recopied'.[42] However it is hard to see any evidence of such tampering in the fluctuating terminology of the annals, or indeed any motive for it. Even the seventeenth-century *Annals of the Four Masters* may be

could – perhaps generally did – mean 'of Welsh blood' or 'having Welsh kin' since in one case, *Expugnatio*, 150, Gerald explained that it didn't.

[35] I put it like this because no doubt many of the humbler soldiers, especially the vital archers, were Welsh. *Expugnatio*, 30, 140.

[36] *Topography*, 52, 65, 74, 85, 93, 108. It would be tedious to do this for the *Expugnatio*, so frequently is the word 'English' used. See Richter, 'Giraldiana', 429.

[37] I deal with this one line later and in n. 46. Although the surviving text of the *Song of Dermot* may date from c.1230, there is good reason for thinking that the poet had access to an earlier written text. See D. Crouch, *William Marshal* (London 1990) 95–6.

[38] *The Annals of Inisfallen*, ed. S. Mac Airt (Dublin 1951); M. T. Flanagan, *Irish Society, Anglo-Norman Settlers, Angevin Kingship* (Oxford 1989), 174.

[39] 'The Annals of Tigernach', ed. W. Stokes, *Revue Celtique* 18 (1897), reprinted by Llanerch Press (Felinfach, Lampeter, 1993); see Flanagan, *Irish Society*, 233, 248, and 246 n. 53.

[40] *Annals of Ulster*, ed. W. M. Hennessy and B. MacCarthy (Dublin 1887–1901); *Annals of Loch Cé*, ed. W. M. Hennessy (London 1871).

[41] *Miscellaneous Irish Annals*, ed. S. Ó hInnse (Dublin 1947).

[42] Flanagan, *Irish Society*, 173.

trustworthy in this respect. Whereas in 1170 and 1171 they call the invaders Saxons in order to distinguish them from the Galls of Dublin, under the year 1169 they refer to Flemings. Gerald too had distinguished between those who went over in 1169, whom he calls the men of St David's, and those who went over in 1170, the men of Llandaff. Since the Flemings were still an identifiable and influential group in Pembrokeshire (i.e. St David's) in the late twelfth century, the usage of the *Four Masters* appears remarkably precise. In the *Expugnatio* Gerald used the non-ethnically specific term *advenae* (newcomers) to refer to the earliest invaders; only after the arrival of Maurice FitzGerald in the autumn of 1169 does he adopt – and retain – the term 'English'.[43] Taking Irish usage in conjunction with Gerald and *The Song of Dermot*, and given the fact that the Irish annalists often refer to Henry II as the 'king of the Saxons' – with the probable implication that in their eyes his subjects were primarily Saxons – it seems difficult not to agree with the conclusion of Marie Therese Flanagan. 'How', she asks, 'did the Irish perceive them (the incomers)? The answer is as *Saxain*, as *Sassanaig*, or English.'[44]

In view of the overwhelming evidence of contemporary narrative sources that the invaders were perceived as 'English', the question naturally arises as to why, in the nineteenth century, the habit of centuries was broken and the use of the word 'English' dropped. Presumably in part because a preference for terms which were not part of the vocabulary of fierce contemporary political debate was felt, consciously or unconsciously, to permit calmer and more scholarly discussion of aspects of twelfth-century history. This is fair enough – except, of course, when the aspect which is being discussed is precisely the question of the identity of the invaders. Another reason for questioning the use of 'English' in this context may well have derived from the characteristic tendency of nineteenth-century scholarship to distrust chroniclers' tales, to publish record evidence and to regard it as being much more reliable than narrative sources. Undoubtedly if we turn from chronicles to charters then any idea that the 'adventus' was purely an English phenomenon disappears at once. For example in a charter of c.1176 Strongbow addresses 'his men French, English and Irish'. A charter issued by Strongbow's constable, Raymond le Gros (d.1188), was addressed to 'French, English, Flemings, Welsh and Irish'. King John was to address 'all his faithful subjects, French and English and Irish of Ireland'.[45] The

[43] *Annals of the Four Masters*, ed. J. O'Donovan (Dublin 1851), vol. 2, p. 1173. *Expugnatio*, 30ff, 262.

[44] M. T. Flanagan, 'The Normans in Ireland' in *Irish History in the Classroom: Seminar held at Cultra Manor, Holywood, Co. Down* (Belfast 1987), 23–32. I am very grateful to Marie Therese Flanagan for sending me a copy of this article. As she points out there, the Irish annals never refer to 'Normans' in Ireland, even though earlier in the twelfth century they had used the term *Frainc* to describe Norman activity outside Ireland.

[45] These examples are cited by Bartlett, *Gerald*, 14 and by James Lydon, 'The Middle Nation' in *The English in Medieval Ireland*, ed. J. Lydon (Dublin 1984), 12. But note the absence of any reference to Normans. A poem which has been dated to the early 1190s and which compares the invasion from the east to shoals of coarse fish assailing the bright salmon

nomenclature in these and many other charters is clearly important. It demonstrates that Frenchmen, Englishmen, Welsh and Flemings participated. It shows that a man with legal training, drafting a charter, may well have chosen his words with care so as to be deliberately all-inclusive, to allow no category of persons to be able to claim that the terms of the charter were of no concern to them. The one reference to 'French, Flemings and Normans' in the *Song of Dermot* (line 2647) is a revealing one. It occurs when Robert FitzStephen offers to stand trial before Henry II, and his peers, French, Fleming and Norman, go bail for him. Here too we are in the world of lawyers' terms.[46]

But this kind of evidence tells us nothing about the relative numbers of French, Welsh and English engaged in the enterprise of Ireland. Such formulas, in other words, tell us very little about the overall character of the invasion and virtually nothing about the perception of it by contemporaries. This is where the narrative sources come in. Their stories may be inaccurate in detail, but the words in which they are framed give us a much better idea about such perceptions. Occasionally even charters may do this – not in the formulae of the address but in the language of the body of the charter. Thus one Irish charter referred to land 'long held by our predecessors before the conquest of Ireland by the English' (*predecessores nostri diu ante conquisitionem Hibernie ab Anglicis*).[47]

There is, however, one chronicler who presents complications of a kind which may well have helped to reassure nineteenth-century scholars that they were on the right track when they began to steer clear of the word 'English'. This is Gerald. For example his remark that 'the English are the most worthless of all peoples under heaven . . . in their own land they are slaves to the Normans' has often been quoted and interpreted to show that Gerald had a low opinion of the English – not the sort of people, therefore, who could have embarked on the conquest of Ireland.[48] But Gerald was a complicated man with a complicated career. His scornful remarks about the English were written in 1201, in his account of a speech he claims to have made in a consistory court in Rome, i.e. at a time when he had became a 'Welshman' and was acting as a

(i.e. the Irish) identifies the ugly fish as British (i.e. Welsh), English and French, B. Ó'Cuív, 'A poem for Cathal Croibhdhearg Ó Conchobair', *Ériu* xxxiv (1983), 157–74. I owe my knowledge of this poem to the kindness of Katharine Simms. It seems unlikely that in ordinary conversation the poet would normally have used so cumbrous a formula as the 'Welsh, English and French' invasion.

[46] As J. H. Round observed, the writer of the poem seems to have had special knowledge of legal formulas, *The Commune of London* (London 1899), 153–4.

[47] The *'Dignitas Decani' of St Patrick's Cathedral, Dublin*, ed. N. B. White (Dublin 1957), no. 111. However a charter of King John, extant in an *inspeximus* of 1237, refers to the *adventum Francorum in Hiberniam, Calendar of Charter Rolls*, pp. 230–1. One explanation for this might be that the original charter of 1 April 1203 was issued in France (at Rouen). For another reference to the French in Ireland in a document of John's reign, *Rot. Chart.*, 78.

[48] *Giraldus Cambrensis: De Invectionibus*, ed. W. S. Davies in *Y Cymmrodor* 30 (1920), 93; F. X. Martin, *New History*, II, li.

mouthpiece for grievances which the Welsh had against the English.[49] But by this date his views had changed radically and we cannot safely use words written at this stage of his career in order to throw light on his attitudes at an earlier stage. Up until the mid 1190s, when he himself was probably in his fifties, Gerald identified himself with the English, hoped for a career and a bishopric in England. Thus in 1188 he actively supported Canterbury's rights over the Welsh church. His Irish writings belong to this stage of his career. In the *Topography* he refers to 'we English people'; after 1200 he will write of 'we Welsh'.[50] Similarly the fact that for a while Gerald espoused a Welsh cause should not make us call him Giraldus Cambrensis, no matter whether we translate it 'Gerald of Wales' or 'Gerald the Welshman'. Either way it tends to identify him too emphatically with just one stage of a career which, roughly speaking, began as pro-English, went first pro-Welsh, then pro-French.[51] Although he may have seen to it that rubrics to manuscripts produced under his auspices after 1200 referred to him as 'Giraldus Kambrensis', it is surely better to call him Gerald de Barri since 'de Barri' or 'Barrensis' is how he referred to his own brother and this is a form which does not, as it were, identify the whole man with just one stage in his career.[52] Although he sometimes referred to himself as 'the archdeacon' or as 'master Gerald', neither of these forms helps to pinpoint him at all precisely; on the other hand a contemporary poem does suggest that quite early in his career he was known as 'de Barri'.[53]

Naming him Gerald of Wales is just one of the ways in which this great writer has been misinterpreted; another is the result of mistranslation. One such mistranslation is of a passage which, in this context, is highly significant. Whether historians refer to Normans, Anglo-Normans or Cambro-Normans the impression created by this kind of usage is that the invasion of Ireland was, in some sense and in large part, a Norman enterprise. Phrases and titles like 'pre-Norman Ireland' or 'Ireland before the Normans' remain standard. But contemporary sources virtually never use the word 'Norman' in an Irish connexion and Gerald himself does so in one context only: Prince John's expedition to Ireland in 1185. In Book II chapter 36 of the *Expugnatio* he refers to the Irish being treated with contempt 'by our newly arrived Normans'. In the next chapter, entitled *Tripertita Familia*, he writes – I leave this in Latin because the translation is crucial – *Denique tripertita nobis in primis familia fuerat; Normanni, Angli, nostri in Hibernia reperti. In summa familiaritate primos habuimus, in minori medios,*

[49] Bartlett, *Gerald*, 50–7.
[50] *Topographia*, 119 'noster Anglorum populus'; contrast 'gens noster Britannica', *De Invectionibus*, 93. For the end of Gerald's hope of promotion within English court circles, see above, chapter 4 n. 57.
[51] Bartlett, *Gerald*, 9, 94–8.
[52] *Expugnatio*, 32, 116 and esp. 188; also *De Rebus a se Gestis* (*Opera*, vol. 1, ed. J. S. Brewer, London RS 1861), 56. On the rubric 'Kambrensis' see Y. Wada, 'Gerald on Gerald: Self-presentation by Giraldus Cambrensis', *ANS* 20 (1997), 223–46, esp. 242.
[53] *De Rebus*, 58, 61. The poem is printed in Brewer, *Opera*, vol. 1, 386.

in nulla postremos. A. B. Scott translated this as: 'One final point. Men of three races formed the greater part of our garrison, for Normans, English and men of our race were all to be found in Ireland. I have been best acquainted with the first mentioned, less so with the second, and not at all with the third group.' This translation creates a nonsense in giving the impression that the people whom Gerald knew least well were his own kindred! No wonder the author of the notes and historical commentary, F. X. Martin, drew the conclusion that in this passage Gerald's Latin was confused, possibly written in haste.[54] More serious is the fact that Scott's translation creates the impression that Gerald was making a statement about the occupying forces in general. He was not. *Familia* here refers not to 'the garrison of Ireland' but to John's household – to which Gerald himself had been attached. Gerald is making two points. First, that in 1185 there were three household factions vying for influence over John: one, Normans, i.e. new arrivals who had come from Normandy; two, English, i.e. those who, whatever their ancestry, were now primarily based in England; three, *nostri in Hibernia reperti*, i.e. those of us who were now based in Ireland – these, of course, were primarily Gerald's own kindred.[55] Secondly, that 'we', i.e. John and his advisers, paid most attention to the Normans, some attention to the English and none at all to 'us'. That *habuimus* did not refer to an authorial 'we' but to the most influential voices around John is plain from a sentence just a few lines later. 'Those who had long served in Ireland and whose initiative had opened up a way into the island for us, came under suspicion and were rejected, while we shared our counsel only with the new arrivals.' Unfortunately by mistranslating *habuimus* as 'I have been' and the chapter heading *Tripertita Familia* as 'The Garrison made up of Three Different Races', Scott seemed to lend credence to the notion of a Norman or Anglo-Norman invasion.[56] In fact the 'Normans' in Gerald's book were an identifiable – and powerful – group during John's expedition of 1185, but no more than that.

But we have still not reached the end of the complexities of Gerald. Even if we translate this chapter correctly we are still left with the fact that Gerald was here making a distinction between 'us' and 'the English'. By 'us' Gerald means the frontiersmen, the adventurer-settlers, men like John de Courcy and Hugh de Lacy, but first and foremost his own family, the FitzGeralds.[57] What then were the FitzGeralds? Who did they think they were? F. X. Martin has suggested they should rather be called 'Nestines', emphasising their descent from Nest, the extra-ordinary and splendid Welsh princess.[58] To emphasise her eponymous role

---

[54] *Expugnatio*, 244–5 and n. 497. Yet see *ibid.*, xxx and n. 496. Ironically at this point the old translation by Thomas Forester in Bohn's Antiquarian Library is distinctly better.
[55] *Expugnatio*, 244–5.
[56] Cf. Bartlett, *Gerald*, 24.
[57] Flanagan, *Irish Society*, 299; Bartlett, *Gerald*, 22; *Expugnatio*, 156, 168–70; a good genealogy of Gerald's family is provided by I. W. Rowlands, 'The Making of the March', *ANS* 3 (1981), 142–57.
[58] *NHI*, 68–9.

is to emphasise the Welsh side of Gerald's family – which is what Gerald himself did during his Welsh period.[59] Earlier, however, Gerald had preferred a different emphasis. Then he tells us that his descent was 'three parts English and Norman' and 'one part Welsh'. This is the sort of passage which has been adduced as evidence by those who wish to call the earliest invaders Cambro-Norman or Anglo-Welsh. But a statement of ancestry is not quite the same thing as a statement of perception of present identity. By the late twelfth century there were many who were conscious of Norman ancestry but who now thought of themselves as English. After describing his ancestry, Gerald tells us that all his upbringing had been among the English.[60] In the context of Ireland the most telling evidence for the self-perception of the FitzGeralds is a passage from a speech which Gerald puts into the mouth of Maurice FitzGerald. In 1171, besieged in Dublin, and telling his men not to look for outside help, they must save themselves, Maurice says, 'What are we waiting for? Surely we are not looking to our own people for help? For we are caught in a bind. Just as we are English to the Irish, so we are Irish to the English.'[61] As Martin, one of the editors of the *Expugnatio*, pointed out, this is the most frequently cited sentence in the whole work, yet though the Latin says *Anglos* and their translation says 'English', he goes on to refer at least a dozen times on the same page to the Normans at Dublin, and not once to the English. Similarly Bartlett, who observes that 'the speech expresses the dilemma of all colonial societies in a nutshell', refers to it as 'put into the mouth of one of the earliest Norman invaders'.[62] Their treatment of this passage illustrates, it seems to me, the extraordinary reluctance of modern historians to use the word 'English' even when it is staring them in the face. If, as this suggests, the FitzGeralds saw themselves as English, then presumably we should understand the distinction of 1185 as being between 'us the frontiersmen' and 'those other Englishmen who had as yet no real experience of the Irish frontier'. This is all the more apparent if we recall that 'us' included men like De Courcy, from Cumbria and the English north-west, and Hugh, head of the Herefordshire branch of the de Lacy family.[63]

---

[59]   In his *De Rebus a se Gestis* written c.1208.

[60]   *De principis Instructione, Giraldi . . . Opera*, vol. 8, ed. G. F. Warner, p. lviii, first preface, mid 1190s. Discussed by Bartlett, *Gerald*, 17–18. The theme of mixed descent appears also in a speech put into the mouth of Gerald's kinsman, Robert FitzStephen, *Expugnatio*, 48, cf. 156. Although Gerald was to describe FitzStephen as 'natione Kambrensis' in a later version of his *Expugnatio* (*Exp.*, p. xxxvi) presumably because FitzStephen was born in Wales, he had earlier made the point that it was thanks to his own family that the coast of South Wales had been held 'for the English'. *Itinerarium Kambriae, Giraldi Opera*, vol. 6, p. 91 (I, 12) – i.e. here too we have a shift from an English to a Welsh perspective.

[61]   *Expugnatio*, 80.

[62]   *Expugnatio*, 307 n. 122; Bartlett, *Gerald*, 18. But the most recent history has resolutely adopted the form 'the English invasion of Ireland', S. Duffy, *Ireland in the Middle Ages* (Dublin 1997), 56–81. And see also the entries 'Anglo-Norman invasion' (signed MTF) and 'Normans' (signed RFF) in ed. S. J. Connolly, *The Oxford Companion to Irish History* (Oxford 1998).

[63]   On Hugh see W. E. Wightman, *The Lacy Family* (Oxford 1966), 16; on De Courcy,

Just as there has been a reluctance to use the word 'English', so also there has been a reluctance to see what happened in Henry II's reign as a dramatic turning point in Irish history. This indeed is one of the principal arguments of Michael Richter's recent book *The Enduring Tradition*, and a similar emphasis is implicit in W. L. Warren's insistence that we shall misread Henry's and John's 'dealings with Ireland unless we see that it had parallels in Aquitaine and Brittany'.[64] Obviously it is right to adopt a comparative approach and there are parallels between Ireland and Brittany – both suffered under Henry II's readiness to attack his neighbours' lands.[65] None the less in crucial respects Ireland was different. Henry's aggressions were normally justified by a claim to have hereditary rights to or over the territory in question. But he had no hope of making such a claim to Ireland with the slightest shred of plausibility.[66] It is this which explains Gerald's observation that Irish 'high-kings' 'achieved the king-ship of the whole island not through any ceremony of coronation or rite of anointing, or even right of heredity or order of succession, but only by force and arms'.[67] But for a king who saw himself as a civilised ruler of a civilised world, brute force alone was not enough. Henry therefore had to fall back on the highly unusual sorts of justification enshrined in Laudabiliter and in what Gerald called 'the five-fold right'.[68] Not all, however, were persuaded that Henry's claim was a just one.[69] Much more importantly Ireland was different because, as J. A. Watt has put it, it

> became a country to which Englishmen of all levels of society, save the very highest, emigrated and settled in large numbers, expropriating the lands and towns of the indigenous population, building a new society in the image of the one they had left. It was also a society which the home government retained and maintained as a dependency, exercising firm control over the policies and personnel of the overseas administration it had established and

overturning the previous view that his primary connexions were with Somerset, see S. Duffy, 'The First Ulster Plantation: John de Courcy and the Men of Cumbria' in eds. T. Barry, R. Frame and K. Simms, *Colony and Frontier in Medieval Ireland. Essays presented to J. F. Lydon* (London 1995), 1–27.

[64] Warren, 'King John in Ireland' in *Essays presented to Michael Roberts*, ed. J. Bossy and P. Jupp (1976), 11.

[65] No view of Henry II in the first half of his reign is more misleading than one which sees him as a peace-loving, stay-at-home king. See J. Gillingham, 'Conquering Kings: Some Twelfth-Century Reflections on Henry II and Richard I' in *Warriors and Churchmen in the High Middle Ages: Essays presented to Karl Leyser*, ed. T. Reuter (London 1992), reprinted in *Richard Coeur de Lion*.

[66] I am not persuaded by Walter Ullmann's suggestion that Henry II claimed a hereditary right based upon King Arthur's supposed conquest of Ireland. See above, p. 23 n. 20.

[67] *Topographia*, 123.

[68] *Expugnatio*, 148.

[69] See, e.g., *The Chronicle of Ralph Niger*, ed. R. Anstruther (London 1851), 92 and William of Canterbury in *Materials for the History of Thomas Becket*, ed. J. C. Robertson (RS 1875–85), 2, 364.

continued to develop. Thus medieval Ireland fulfils the strictest criteria semantics can impose on the word 'colony' as Gascony . . . which did not receive substantial emigration from England or know dispossession of its native ruling class, did not.[70]

In recent years historians of medieval Ireland have tended to emphasise the ways in which pre-1160s Irish society was changing and was open to outside influences: 'Despite the oft-repeated cliché that twelfth-century Ireland was a highly conservative, anarchic, and isolated society, twelfth-century Ireland was not like eighth-century Ireland.'[71] Whether intentionally or not, one effect of this approach is to undermine the cataclysmic interpretation which sees 1169 as the year of destiny. As Richter has put it, the 'English intervention in Ireland in the late twelfth century merely accelerated a process which had started long before'. He has suggested that the arrival of the English was like the arrival of the Scandinavians, the only important difference being that we have a great deal more source material for the twelfth-century arrival than for the ninth. 'For the Irish it can have made little difference whether Dublin and its hinterland were held by the Hiberno-Norse or by the English.'[72] But did the Scandinavians regard the Irish as barbarians? And although Irish society was undoubtedly changing in the twelfth century, one area in which it was not was in marriage law. This led to the Irish being judged and found wanting by ecclesiastical reformers – an articulate body of men who were all too certain of their own moral rectitude and were very ready to condemn as uncivilised values which they did not share.[73] The emphasis on Ireland as just one of Henry's dominions, the parallel with the coming of the Scandinavians, the emphasis on the openness of twelfth-century Ireland to outside influences – three different points but they have this in commmon. They tend to obscure the emergence of one devastating phenomenon: the idea that the Irish were an inferior and barbarous people.

One late twelfth-century writer who shared to the full the by now common-place view of Irish barbarity was the Yorkshire chronicler William of Newburgh. Newburgh enjoys a high reputation for the breadth and geographical range of his interests, for the judiciousness of his approach, most famously for holding some sort of balance between Becket and Henry II, and for his critical sense of history – most famously in his dismissal of Geoffrey of Monmouth. His judgement on Henry II's expedition to Ireland in 1171–2 was that it marked the end of Irish freedom. That it meant that a people who had been free since time immemorial, unconquered even by the Romans, a people for whom liberty

---

[70] J. A. Watt, *NHI*, 313. The whole chapter, much more wide-ranging than its title – 'Approaches to the history of fourteenth-century Ireland' – suggests, is essential reading.
[71] Flanagan, *Irish Society*, 2.
[72] M. Richter, *Medieval Ireland. The Enduring Tradition* (London 1988); M. Richter, 'The interpretation of medieval Irish history', *Irish Historical Studies* 24 (1985), 177.
[73] F. J. Byrne in *NHI*, 41–2; Bartlett, *Gerald*, 43; K. Hughes, *The Church in Early Irish Society* (London 1966), 260–5.

seemed, as he put it, an inborn right, were now fallen into the power of the king of England. William expounded this view of the significance of 'the eighteenth year of the reign of King Henry' in a chapter which he entitled 'The Conquest of the Irish by the English'.[74]

[74] William of Newburgh, *Historia Rerum Anglicarum*, ed. R. Howlett in *Chronicles of the Reigns of Stephen etc.* (RS 1884), 16, 165–6, 168.

Part Three. Values and Structures

10

Thegns and Knights in Eleventh-Century England: Who was then the gentleman?

I shall be considering England during the long eleventh century – from the 990s, the Battle of Maldon and Byrhtferth of Ramsey's 'Life of Oswald', to the 1130s, the world of Geoffrey Gaimar. I shall do so in the light of a situation where, on the one hand, historians of Anglo-Saxon England commonly refer to gentlemen and gentry in their period but do so casually, as though their presence there is something to be taken for granted, and, on the other, where scholars who regard themselves as historians of the gentry seem reluctant to admit that the phenomenon they study can have existed much before 1200, if then.[1] In the first part of this paper I shall argue that there was a gentry in eleventh-century England, that below the great lords there were many layers of society whose members shared the interests and pursuits of the great, i.e. we should accept the terminology of historians of Anglo-Saxon England from Sir Frank Stenton onwards.[2] I shall also argue that in all probability many vigorous members of the Anglo-Saxon gentry were knights, using the word 'knight' to mean the kind of person whom, in the late twelfth century, Richard FitzNigel described as an active knight (*strenuus miles*), i.e. someone whose characteristic and indispensable possessions were his body armour and the requisite horses.[3] Because from about 1200 the term 'knight' came to be used in an increasingly exclusive way, applied to increasingly restricted and elevated sections of the 'gentle' elite, historians have often written of the 'rise of the knight' and have suggested that this 'rise'

---

[1] For example in a book sub-titled 'The Gentry of Angevin Yorkshire, 1154–1216' Hugh M. Thomas refers to that period not only as 'the earliest period in which sufficient information survives for a detailed regional study of the gentry' – which it may well be – but also as 'a time when the gentry in some ways were first beginning to emerge as an independent force in English history', *Vassals, Heiresses, Crusaders and Thugs* (Philadelphia, 1993), 3. According to a recent article, 'Henry II was the gentry's midwife', Jean Scammell, 'The Formation of the English Social Structure: Freedom, Knights, and Gentry, 1066–1300', *Speculum* 68 (1993), 618.

[2] E.g. Sir Frank Stenton, *The First Century of English Feudalism 1066–1166* (Oxford, 2nd edn 1961), 23, 120.

[3] Richard Fitz Nigel, *Dialogus de Scaccario*, ed. and trans. C. Johnson, F. E. L. Carter and D. E. Greenway (Oxford, 1983), 111. I assume here that wealthy men owned expensive horses and that training for war was only one of the factors that made some horses more expensive than others.

should be seen in terms of the spiralling costs of knightly equipment. However I shall argue that in the eleventh century the active knight (in Richard FitzNigel's sense) rose (in the sense of becoming more numerous) as a consequence of the diminishing cost of military equipment. I shall argue this in the context of an England characterised by rapid economic growth and a powerful monarchy: 'Campbell's kingdom'. I shall also argue that in these respects the Norman Conquest made little difference. In the second part of this paper I shall focus on the 'honour of arms', the political and military values of the secular elite. Here, by contrast, I shall argue that '1066 and All That' led to important changes.

I begin with what John Blair has called the new landscape of late Anglo-Saxon England, the result, in his words, of 'drastic changes in the structure of local economy and society, the same changes which produced stable nucleated villages and common field-systems. Great estates broke up into small ones, of the same order of magnitude as a typical high medieval parish and village territory, which provided the economic base for a new extensive class of country gentry. Just as a great lord in the eighth century had his proprietary minster, so a modest local thegn in the late tenth had his manorial church.'[4] This same period saw the emergence of that other familar feature of the English landscape: the market town. Recently Robin Fleming has emphasised the urban as well as the rural setting within which the landowners of Domesday England moved.[5] Presumably many of the four or five thousand secular English landlords whose existence in 1066 is indicated by Domesday Book, belonged to a category of 'middling landowners', even though identifying them with precision (e.g. distinguishing between separate individuals with common names) is notoriously difficult. This has not prevented local historians such as Alan Everitt from identifying regions (e.g. the Kentish Downland) in which lesser landowners were particularly numerous; nor others, such as John Blair, from using words like 'country gentry' on the basis of their own study of a particular locality.[6] Here then, both in town and country, there appears to be the economic base for a gentry – the sort of people who could 'live idly and without manual labour' and were thus able to 'bear the port, charge and countenance of a gentleman'.[7] One eleventh-century Hampshire thegn able to bear such 'port, charge and countenance' was Alvric. When he had a church built at Milford, it was stipulated that the 'priest should wait for Alvric before beginning the service'.[8]

---

[4] John Blair, 'The Making of the English Parish', *Medieval History* 2.2 (1992), 15.
[5] Robin Fleming, 'Rural Elites and Urban Communities in Late-Saxon England', *Past and Present* 141 (1993), 3–37.
[6] Alan Everitt, *Continuity and Colonization: the evolution of Kentish settlement* (Leicester, 1986), 175–80; John Blair, *Early Medieval Surrey* (Stroud, 1991), 160–61.
[7] Sir Thomas Smith, *De Republica Anglorum: a discourse on the Commonwealth of England*, ed. L. Alston (Cambridge, 1906), 39–40.
[8] Also that the priest who was sent to Milford from Christchurch should be fed at Alvric's table whenever he was at Milford. P. H. Hase, 'The Mother Churches of Hampshire' in ed. John Blair, *Minsters and Parish Churches. The Local Church in Transition 950–1200* (Oxford, 1988), 60.

But most historians of the gentry would probably wish to argue that more than an economic base is required before they would be willing to concede the existence of a gentry. Three criteria widely regarded as crucial are first, the participation by local landowners in local public office; second, the existence of county solidarities; and third, the participation by some local landowners in national assemblies.[9] It seems to have been the perceived absence of this combination of criteria that led many of the contributors to a volume on *Gentry and Lesser Nobility in Late Medieval Europe* to decide that in 'their' countries they could see no real equivalent of the English gentry.[10] But by precisely these criteria it seems to me more probable than not, that the peculiarly English brand of the lesser nobility existed before 1066 and, in some respects at least, was re-created after it.

Recent trends portray Anglo-Saxon England as a much-administered land. As James Campbell has put it, it was 'one in which the connections between the central authority and the localities mattered very much and one in which the number of men, below the level of sheriff, who were in some sense agents of government, was very large'.[11] Between village reeves and sheriffs there were the hundred reeves, responsible for chairing meetings of the hundred courts every three or four weeks ; some of these reeves also managed royal manors, holding them at farm from sheriffs. By the tenth century public concern about levels of crime had led to a number of men in each hundred being made responsible for policing, for keeping the peace and for managing the suretyship system.[12] The evidence for this is nearly all in the form of legislation, reasonable enough as evidence for concern but obviously a poor guide to practice. In two other spheres of government, however, the evidence is much better. First, the evidence of geld rolls and geld accounts demonstrates the presence of collectors working within an effective taxation system. Secondly, the evidence of surviving coins shows a considerable number of moneyers active in the localities and operating within a centrally controlled currency system. In the light of the workings of late Anglo-Saxon public finance it seems reasonable to believe in the real existence of a law enforcement and peace-keeping system based upon the shire, the hundred and the vill. As Ann Williams has put it, 'However powerful the earls and king's thegns, or for that matter, the bishops and abbots

[9] For the clearest exposition of this view of the gentry see Peter Coss, *Lordship, Knighthood and Locality. A Study in English Society c.1180–c.1280* (Cambridge, 1991), 307–10. I am also much indebted to Peter Coss's kindness in helping me to clarify my thoughts by sending me an as yet unpublished discussion of these issues.

[10] Very much the consensus of the contributors to the volume on *Gentry and Lesser Nobility in Late Medieval Europe*, ed. M. Jones (Gloucester, 1986). For a particularly clear statement of this see F. R. H. Du Boulay's contribution, 'Was there a German Gentry?', 119–32, esp. 124.

[11] James Campbell, 'Some Agents and Agencies of the Late Anglo-Saxon State' in ed. J. C. Holt, *Domesday Studies* (Woodbridge, 1987), 201–18, esp. 205.

[12] For a convenient summary of the policing and pledging system see Helen M. Jewell, *English Local Administration in the Middle Ages* (Newton Abbot, 1972), 159–68.

might be, they were not allowed to slip through this net.'[13] As long ago as 1612 the first great historian of medieval England, Samuel Daniel, was led to observe that 'these links thus intermutually fastened, made so strong a chaine to hold the whole frame of the State together in peace and order, as all the most politique regiments upon earth, all the interleagued societies of men, cannot shew us a streighter forme of combination'. He then went on to wonder whether the existence of this strong chain might not answer the question of 'how so great a kingdome as England then was, could with one blow be subdued by so small a province as Normandy'. 'For', he suggested, 'this might make the Conqueror, coming upon a people thus law-bound hand and foot, to establish him so soone and easily as he did.'[14]

Like many of those who held local office later the agents of the late Anglo-Saxon state could be described as part-time and unpaid, though some of them evidently and sometimes legitimately found some of the profits of the system sticking to their hands.[15] That these men met together frequently at either hundred or shire level or both seems reasonably certain. That they met together often enough to form local solidarities, articulated at the shire level, is implied by the comment of the Anglo-Saxon Chronicle on the breakdown at the end of Aethelred's reign. 'In the end no shire would even help the next.'[16] In J. R. Maddicott's opinion, 'the county community, where the gentry found a voice, predated the Conquest'.[17] At this level numerous English landowners must have survived the conquest and although many traditional solidarities must have been overthrown, the continued functioning of shire and hundredal institutions would surely have led to the re-emergence of new local solidarities. Of course those who doubt the usefulness of the term 'county community' when applied to the fourteenth and fifteenth centuries will doubtless doubt that it should be applied to the eleventh century either. My concern here is merely to point to respects in which there is much similarity – though not a simple continuity – between these two periods.[18]

That some of these men also met regularly at national level is stated firmly for William I's reign by the author of the Anglo-Saxon Chronicle. In his words, the Easter, Whitsun and Christmas crown-wearings were attended by 'all the powerful men over all England, archbishops and bishops, abbots and earls,

---

[13] Ann Williams, 'A Bell-house and a Burh-geat: Lordly Residences in England before the Norman Conquest' in ed. R. Harvey and C. Harper-Bill, *The Ideals and Practice of Medieval Knighthood IV* (Woodbridge, 1992), 240. I am deeply indebted to Ann Williams' kindness in reading a draft of this paper and suggesting many references.

[14] Samuel Daniel, *The First Part of the Historie of England* (London, 1612), 69, 128–30.

[15] Campbell, 'Agents and Agencies', 208–9, 216.

[16] ASC, 1010.

[17] J. R. Madicott, 'Magna Carta and the Local Community 1215–59', *Past and Present* 102 (1984), 25.

[18] In Freeman's opinion the late medieval shire was 'ruled by an assembly not so very unlike what the gathering of the thegns of Herefordshire must have been in the days of Cnut', E. A. Freeman, *The History of the Norman Conquest*, vol. 5 (Oxford, 1876), 449–50.

thegns and knights (*cnihtas*)'.[19] Did men below the level of earl and thegn manage to make their opinions heard? As is well known Henry I's Coronation Charter shows that by 1100 it was well worth offering concessions to the *milites . . . per loricas*. Certainly contemporaries believed that on occasions the *milites gregarii* or the *milites pagenses* were able to give Henry significant support.[20] Such men were not always followers of fashion. According to William of Malmesbury, a fashion – albeit a shortlived one – for having short hair was started by a *miles provincialis*.[21] Consider the 'deep speech' which began four days after the Christmas festivites of 1085 and ended with the decision to launch the Domesday inquiry. I find it hard to believe that this was not discussed in an informal way over Christmas and that the cnihts who had turned up for the Christmas crown-wearing had not expressed their views, particularly no doubt on the subject of how they had suffered during the quartering of the great army on their estates.[22] Paucity of evidence makes parallels for the pre-conquest period harder to find – though we should certainly remember James Campbell's question: Whom was the Confessor seeking to please when he abandoned the *heregeld* in 1051?[23] In Byrhtferth's *Life of Oswald* there is an account of a stormy general assembly in which the forces of righteousness were hard put to it to win the day against pressure from the 'unworthy crowd' (*indignus vulgus*). At this meeting the last speech, by Byrhtnoth, addressed *ad exercitum*, begins with the words: 'Listen to me, *seniores et juniores*' – for which I suggest we consider the translation 'thegns and cnihts'.[24]

In eleventh and early twelfth century England then we find a local elite, a broad land-owning class with urban connections, many of them holding public office in a part-time and unpaid fashion, exercising social control over the populace, attending meetings both locally and nationally. All this suggests that there is a strong prima facie case for believing that historians of Anglo-Saxon and Anglo-Norman England are justified in using the term 'gentry'. After all in a kingdom which enjoyed remarkable territorial stability from the tenth century onwards, in terms of its frontiers as well as its internal boundaries, the distances

[19] ASC, 1087.
[20] Florence of Worcester, *Chronicon ex chronicis*, ed. B. Thorpe, 2 vols. (London, 1848–49), ii.49; *The Ecclesiatical History of Orderic Vitalis*, ed. M. Chibnall, 6 vols. (Oxford, 1969–80), vi.206; W. Stubbs, *Select Charters* 3rd edn (Oxford, 1876), 101.
[21] William of Malmesbury, *De Gestis regum Anglorum*, ed. W. Stubbs, 2 vols. (RS, 1887–89), ii.531.
[22] ASC, 1085. The Worcester chronicler believed that, as well as barons and sheriffs, the *praepositi regis* were among those required to share the burden, FW ii.18.
[23] James Campbell, *The Anglo-Saxons* (London, 1982), 244.
[24] *Historians of the Church of York*, ed. J. Raine, vol. 1 (RS, 1879), 444–46. Whitelock translated *seniores et juniores* as 'veterans and young men', *English Historical Documents*, 2nd edn (London, 1979), i.914. However we translate *juniores* (bearing in mind the range of meanings of 'iuvenis') it is clear that Byrhtferth saw the *vulgus* as well as the nobles as capable of political action, ibid., 444. On this meeting see also the details in ed. E. O. Blake, *Liber Eliensis* (Camden Soc., 1962), 85.

to be covered in moving between centre and locality differed hardly at all between the early and later middle ages; between these periods, even though horse-drawn transport may have improved, there was nothing approaching a communications revolution.[25]

Yet it is widely believed by historians of the gentry that there was no gentry in England until, at the earliest, the late twelfth century. How can this be? Partly, I think, because seduced by the proliferation of administrative records from the end of the twelfth century onwards they have not taken sufficient account of the power of the crown in earlier centuries, nor of the number of local offices involved in the policing and pledging system. And partly because they have tended to see early medieval society as a two-tier system with a huge gulf between the nobles and all the rest.[26] In consequence they have seen some of the non-nobles, the knights for instance, as rather more humble than they were. It is true that before 1200 the word *miles* was used in a less exclusive fashion than it was later. But it certainly does not follow that, as has recently been claimed, until the late twelfth century knights 'were not clearly distinguished from the cultivators from whom they were drawn'.[27] Indeed there can be no doubt whatever that by the 1130s, at the very latest, *chevaliers* were *gentil hommes* and in absolutely no danger of being confused with 'cultivators'. On this point the evidence of Geoffrey Gaimar's *Estoire* is decisive. Written for the wife – 'dame Custance la gentil' – of a Lincolnshire landowner it is a work of immense significance, the earliest extant history composed for the serious entertainment of the lesser nobility.[28] In Gaimar great nobles admired for their military skills such as Robert of Bellême or Gilbert Fitz Richard are referred to as *chevaliers*, so too are the 1,700 men attached to King William II's household. We are told that many a *gentil home* was dubbed (*adubat*) at Rufus's great feast which is the climax

[25] As Christine Carpenter has observed of the later medieval and early modern periods, 'fundamental conditions remain in outline to a large degree constant: a more or less centralised monarchy lacking a large bureaucracy, standing army or police force, and an absence of modern technology to transmit and enforce orders on the ground', in 'Who ruled the Midlands in the later Middle Ages?', *Midland History* 19 (1994), 5.

[26] For an eloquent protest against this view of Anglo-Saxon society see Campbell, *The Anglo-Saxons*, 244.

[27] Scammell, 'The Formation', 591, 597, 604. On p. 593 the argument that the same person could be at once cultivator and knight and in both capacities dependent is supported by quoting from the early eleventh century text in which, allegedly, Hugh of Lusignan was told by his lord, William of Aquitaine, 'You must obey my will because you are mine. If I tell you to work as a peasant (*rusticus*), you must do it.' But this text (ed. J. Martindale, 'Conventum inter Guillelmum Aquitanorum comes et Hugonem Chiliarchum', *EHR* 84 (1969), 542–48) is, of course, anything but a matter of fact statement of the rights of a lord. See Stephen D. White, 'Stratégie rhétorique dans la *Conventio* de Hugues de Lusignan' in *Mélanges offerts à Georges Duby* (Publications de l'université de Provence, Aix en Provence, 1993), vol. 2, 147–57.

[28] On the milieu in which Gaimar wrote see Ian Short, 'Gaimar's Epilogue and Geoffrey of Monmouth's *Liber Vetustissimus*', *Speculum* 69 (1994), 323–43. Gaimar's values are discussed below, pp. 233–58.

of Gaimar's courtly history. Hereward the Wake and his companions were both *chevaliers* and *gentil hommes*; their enemies were French *chevaliers*. In Gaimar's mind such men existed both before and after 1066. In the wars between Cnut and Edmund Ironside 'many a *gentil home*' lost his life. During Earl Siward's 1053 expedition against Macbeth among the English casualties was 'un des chevaliers le rei/ E les huscherles qu'il menat'. When Godwin was put on trial for the murder of Alfred, a *chevalier* called Merleswein spoke, characterised just two lines later as 'riche barun'. Earlier King Edgar treated a *chevalier* as his most confidential advisor and when he spoke to him addressed him as 'brother'. Earlier still King Alfred summoned *chevaliers*, sergeants and archers to the siege of London.[29] Although Gaimar's history has been very little taken into account in the discussion of knighthood and the rise of the gentry, as evidence for the varying ways in which 'gentil hommes' and 'chevaliers' were perceived in the England of the 1130s it could not be bettered, composed as it was within and for a society of *chevaliers*, *gentil hommes* and gentle ladies, and in their language.

But how seriously can we take Gaimar's view of earlier generations, of the 'gentil hommes' of Domesday Book and beyond? It is at this point that Sir Frank Stenton's views have cast a long shadow. It was Stenton's contention that 'The ordinary knight of the eleventh century was a person of small means and insignificant condition.'[30] When Sally Harvey, in a justly famous article, referred to Domesday *milites* as 'men of low social status' and as 'humble people no better off than prosperous peasants', she was retaining Stenton's tone and doing so on the back of statistical evidence showing that in terms of income from land some of them may indeed have been no better off than rich farmers (*villani*).[31] But this does not automatically mean that they were 'humble' or 'of low social status'. In whose eyes? To my eye even if some *milites* were not richer than farmers, they none the less lived in much closer association with their lords than did farmers, and they therefore belonged to a different social group.[32] Of course a great and snobbish aristocrat like Waleran of Meulan who saw himself as 'the flower of knighthood of all France and Normandy' looked at them with condescending eyes. According to Orderic, he dismissed even knights attached to the king's military household as 'country bumpkins' (*pagenses et gregarios*).[33] It

---

[29] Geffrei Gaimar, *L'Estoire des Engleis*, ed. A. Bell, Anglo-Norman Text Society (Oxford, 1960), lines 3359–60, 3627–31, 4232, 4930–32, 5051–52, 5462, 5568–71, 5835–37, 5882, 6076.

[30] Sir Frank Stenton, *Anglo-Saxon England*, 3rd edn (Oxford, 1971), 636.

[31] Sally Harvey, 'The Knight and the Knight's Fee in England', *Past and Present* 49 (1970), 3–43. Careful reconsideration of her statistics still leaves room for the contention that 'many of the smallholdings assigned to Domesday *milites* were insufficient for the support of a heavy cavalryman', Donald Fleming, 'Landholding by *Milites* in Domesday Book: a Revision', *Anglo-Norman Studies* xiii, ed. M. Chibnall (Woodbridge, 1990), 97.

[32] J. Gillingham, 'The Early Middle Ages' in ed. K. O. Morgan, *The Oxford Illustrated History of Britain* (Oxford, 1986), 158.

[33] OV, vi.350–51. Not that Orderic alleges that Waleran called them peasants. In Orderic's

may well be that in the eleventh and twelfth centuries many well armed and armoured men were of lower status than such men had been in earlier centuries, because all the evidence suggests that armour and weapons were being produced on a bigger scale than ever before, were becoming more widely available, and hence cheaper – just as the 'Great Re-Building' of c.1050–c.1150 (the age of the mass-produced church) meant that stone churches were becoming cheaper.[34] In earlier centuries, say the seventh to ninth centuries, the increasing availability of armour had been on a scale sufficient to create an aristocratic class of heavily armed wariors, and thus to create a gulf between them and the ordinary warrior equipped with spear and shield.[35] But by the eleventh century the further increase in manufacture, itself partly a result of an English government initiative, was such that now it was not only aristocrats who could afford decent armour. As James Campbell put it, 'A countryside whose economy was developing . . . could support more gentlemen of the horse and hauberk owning kind than heretofore.'[36] This development may help to explain why it was that in Aethelred's reign ealdormen and king's thegns came to owe heriots higher than previously. For once high-quality wargear was more widely available, heriots at the traditional levels may no longer have seemed appropriate to men of the highest rank.[37] Indeed the very number of eleventh-century texts on status might be thought to indicate a new level of contemporary concern with social mobility. Hence the eleventh-century legal text which insisted that a ceorl remained a ceorl – a 'mere' freeman – even though 'he possesses a helmet and a coat of mail and a gold-plated sword'.[38]

But this free man with his helmet, sword and hauberk who was not a thegn, should he be thought of as a cultivator, a peasant, albeit a prosperous one? Or, given the emphasis on his military equipment, would it not seem more appropriate to think of him as a knight – even, to use a contemporary English term, as a *cniht*? And if he was a *cniht*, what would this tell us about his status? It has often been claimed to be significant that the English word 'knight' is derived from 'cniht'. Those who downgrade the *miles* similarly downgrade the *cniht*. According to Stenton, 'the Old English *cniht* was essentially the retainer of some greater man' and he noted that the word 'cnihtas' could be used, as in the Anglo-

eyes a *pagensis eques* was quite capable of finer feelings and of meeting the cost of transporting William I's abandoned corpse from Rouen to Caen. Ibid., iv.104.

[34] Blair, *Minsters and Parish Churches*, 9–10.

[35] See e.g. Josef Fleckenstein, 'Zur Frage der Abgrenzung von Bauer und Ritter' in his *Ordnungen und formende Kräfte des Mittelalters* (Göttingen, 1989), 307–14.

[36] James Campbell, 'Was it Infancy in England? Some Questions of Comparison' in *England and her Neighbours, 1066–1453. Essays in honour of Pierre Chaplais*, ed. M. Jones and M. Vale (London, 1989), 12–14.

[37] This, of course, is not to deny that the defence needs of Aethelred's government also acted as a stimulus to change. On the whole subject see N. P. Brooks, 'Arms, Status and Warfare in Late Saxon England' in *Ethelred the Unready*, ed. D. Hill (Oxford, 1978), 81–103.

[38] The *Northleoda laga* cited by Richard Abels, *Lordship and Military Obligation in Anglo-Saxon England* (London, 1988), 165.

Saxon Chronicle entry for 1083, of 'any miscellaneous body of armed French-men'. Stenton clearly found, as he himself acknowledged, the status of the cniht a difficult question and his discussion of it in *The First Century of English Feudalism* is uncharacteristically opaque and ambiguous. Thus although he acknowledged that the Anglo-Saxon cniht was a retainer attached to the personal service of a nobleman, that his service might well require him to fight by his lord's side, mounted and otherwise equipped for war, and that his service might be so highly regarded that 'more than one man of this class acquired property which must have given him an important place among the landed gentry of his shire' – none the less, despite all this, Stenton gave no indication that a *cniht* might be a man of aristocratic or gentle birth. Indeed he refers to one group of *cnihts* as 'a group of hunt servants'.[39] This treatment of the *cniht* allowed Sally Harvey, explicitly referring back to Stenton, to describe the cniht as the 'unheralded serving retainer'. Similarly David Crouch, while pointing to the similarity between OE *cniht* and 'another French word for knight, *bacheler*,' chose to emphasise the word's 'servile' and 'grubby' associations.[40]

But Stenton's analysis of the Old English cniht is, I think, flawed and this is, in part at least, a consequence of his – equally flawed – belief in 1066 to 1166 being 'The First Century of English Feudalism'. This pushed him into believing that Anglo-Saxon cnihts could not be 'proper' knights, knights in what he called 'the technical sense of the word', because it was an article of faith for him that knights in the technical sense of the word could only exist after feudalism began, i.e. only after 1066. Indeed he suggested that after 1066 the word 'cniht' was sometimes – but only sometimes – used in what he called 'the Norman sense of the word' and as such referring to men of significantly higher status than when used in its old English sense. Thus, he claimed, even an Englishman like the author of the Anglo-Saxon Chronicle was using the word in its 'Norman' sense when he listed *cnihtas* as being among those 'powerful men' who attended the Conqueror's crown-wearings.[41] Clearly if only Stenton could have accepted that cniht in the 'Old English' sense carried the same range of meanings as in the allegedly new Norman sense then his analysis would have been much less tangled. He could have returned to Maitland's position, that the difference between the cniht of the tenth century and the knight of the twelfth is one of military tactics.[42] Certainly the word cniht has strong overtones of service and

---

[39] Stenton, *First Century*, 132–36. Even in the third edition of his *Anglo-Saxon England* (Oxford, 1971), 527, he contented himself with the observation that 'the position of the Old English cniht is a difficult question' and a reference to these pages in his earlier work.

[40] Harvey, 'The Knight and the Knight's Fee', 4; David Crouch, *The Image of Aristocracy in Britain 1000–1300* (London, 1992), 130.

[41] Stenton, *First Century*, 132–33, esp. n. 3, for his assertion that post 1066 the word embraced both 'knights in the strict sense and sergeants'.

[42] F. W. Maitland, *Domesday Book and Beyond* (Fontana edn, 1960), 363. As Abels pointed out, Aelfric of Eynsham's choice of the word *cniht* to translate *miles* in the phrase *miles portat gladium* is very striking, *Lordship and Military Obligation*, 138.

this may have made the chronicler prefer to say 'ridere' rather than cniht when referring to the dubbing of a king's son in 1086. Even so, in preferring 'ridere', the chronicler was not choosing a word that clearly indicated a man of higher status than cniht.[43] The crucial point is that although the Old English cniht served, the service he characteristically rendered was noble service. Indeed the cniht was often a nobleman, a young noble in the service of another lord. The two cnihts (Wulfstan's son and Offa's kinsman) who figure in the *Battle of Maldon* both clearly belong to this category of cniht as young noblemen.[44]

One noble landowner explicitly referred to as a cniht in an Anglo-Saxon charter was Osulf, a kinsman of Bishop Oswald, who was leased an estate in two manors and for several lives by the bishop of Worcester.[45] This brings me to Oswald's famous letter to King Edgar in which he set out the terms on which he had leased estates, beginning with the requirement that they should perform the *omnis lex equitandi . . . quae ad equites pertinent* and continuing with payment of church dues, the obligation to provide horses, to be responsible for building work on bridges and the church, and for helping with the bishop's hunt by erecting hedges and providing spears. Attention has focused on the 'lex equitandi' ever since Maitland wrote, 'For a moment we are tempted to say the law of chivalry.' Although he rejected the temptation he did not unwrite it, and he concluded his discussion of the subject with the comment that 'the day for heavy cavalry and professional militancy was fast approaching when Oswald subjected his tenants to the lex equitandi'.[46]

However, against Maitland, Stenton showed that the law of riding more probably referred not to military service but to the duty of escorting the lord from place to place, and he summed up the services set out by Oswald as a 'very incoherent series of obligations. They range from hunting service to bridge-building and at many times resemble the miscellaneous duties of the 11th century geneat.' (In Stenton's view, the geneat 'was a peasant with some of the characteristics of a mounted retainer'.)[47] Stenton's dismissive tone may have influenced Christopher Dyer's comment on Oswald's memorandum. 'The services owed to the bishop were confined to escort duties, assistance with hunting, administrative work and so on. Had the bishops really given up hundreds of hides of land in the form of about seventy substantial holdings merely to obtain such relatively minor services?'[48] Escort duty, assistance with

---

43 Thus in the chronicler's account of Rufus's 1092 campaign in Normandy we hear of one castle being garrisoned with cnihts and others with 'ridere', ASC, 1086, 1092.

44 *Battle of Maldon*, lines 9 and 153.

45 A. J. Robertson, *Anglo-Saxon Charters* (Cambridge, 1939), no. 46.

46 Maitland, *Domesday Book and Beyond*, 358–63.

47 Stenton, *First Century*, 125, 129–30. In a footnote, 127 n. 2, he acknowledged that 'the persons who received Oswald's leases form a somewhat aristocratic body' – though without then reconsidering his comparison of the services they owed with those owed by the geneat. For his assessment of the geneat's status, *Anglo-Saxon England*, 473.

48 Christopher Dyer, *Lords and Peasants in a Changing Society. The Estates of the Bishopric of Worcester 680–1540* (Cambridge, 1980), 43.

hunting and administrative work. Minor services! Of course if we assume that tenth century England was quintessentially a military society, and in consequence all that really mattered were military values and obligations, then all other services are by definition minor. My impression is that most historians of Anglo-Saxon England acknowledge the importance of escort and hunting services but take them for granted, and quickly pass on to discuss – and at some length – the question of whether or not the memorandum deals with military service, and if so, in what form. Since most recent discussions of the memorandum and the *lex equitandi* have been in books on military obligation and organisation, this focus has been entirely justified. But intentionally or not, this approach has inevitably tended to reinforce the assumption that in Anglo-Saxon society all that really mattered was war. So in the hope of restoring a balance I shall spend a little time elaborating what has been taken for granted.

Richard Abels has already pointed out that the services owed by Bishop Oswald's tenants recall not only, as Stenton had observed, what the author of the eleventh-century treatise known as the *Rectitudines* had to say about the 'geneat's law', but also what he had to say about 'thegn's law'.[49] According to this author, a thegn's services included responsibility for the deer fence at the king's residence and for guarding his lord. According to another eleventh-century text on status, the 'promotion law', characteristic of the prospering thegn was that he rode in the king's household band on his *radstefn* – an unusual term meaning, according to Dorothy Whitelock, that as well as serving in the king's bodyguard he was expected to undertake important errands as a mounted messenger. According to the *Rectitudines* the geneat's obligations varied from estate to estate but characteristic were paying rent, riding and performing carrying services, entertaining his lord, reaping and mowing, cutting deer hedges and maintaining places from which deer may be shot, building and fencing the lord's house, bringing strangers to the village, acting as guard to his lord, taking care of the horses and carrying messages far and near wheresoever he was directed.[50] Clearly there is a core of services common to Oswald's memorandum and to the law of thegns and geneats: these are escort and bodyguard duties, messenger and hunting services. What they have in common is that they bring the person who performs them into close proximity to his lord, and it is this proximity, of course, which was the key to advancement. These, I suggest, were the sorts of services the cniht owed.[51] Who could not see the advantages of owing escort services, of having to be attached, at least for a while, to a lord's riding household? Being at the bottom of this particular laddder of service, the geneat's obligations included the more menial ones of reaping and mowing, although whether the prospering geneat performed these services in person or whether

[49] Abels, *Lordship*, 153.
[50] *EHD*, i.468; ii.875.
[51] This point was made by Peter Coss, *The Knight in Medieval England 1000–1400* (Stroud, 1993), 12.

he merely took responsibility for getting them done, while giving his personal attention to those duties which brought him closer to his lord, is another matter.[52] The important point here is that some of the services he owed his lord were precisely the kinds of service which the highest in the land owed to the king. According to the Kent Domesday when the king came to Canterbury or Sandwich he was obliged to provide food and drink for the members of a bodyguard provided for him by Alnoth Cild and his like. Alnoth was one of the magnates of Kent, important enough to be taken to Normandy as a hostage in 1067.[53]

Since effective political and military action depended upon the rapid reception and distribution of accurate information, reliable envoys were absolutely vital. One of the scenes in the remarkable South German eleventh-century poem *Ruodlieb* describes this very well and makes it clear that the envoy, when surrounded by a large and excited crowd, had to be sufficiently at ease to be able to address a king directly and deliver his message accurately.[54] This is the thegn acting as envoy, the thegn who, in the words of the promotion law, went on his lord's errand to the king.[55] In all manner of circumstances a lord needed men who could speak on his behalf. Thus one of the obligations laid upon Alvric's priest at Milford was that 'he should accompany Alvric to the Hundred whenever he went there'.[56] The geneat, on the bottom rung of this ladder, presumably carried only messages for lesser lords or just routine ones for greater lords.

The tendency for scholarly literature to concentrate on military matters can also be seen in the attention it has given to the Berkshire customs in Domesday Book – an almost exclusive focus on the so-called 5 hide system. But these customs contain other passages which suggest that hunting services were also amongst the characteristic duties of the Berkshire 'tainus vel miles regis dominicus'. His heriot, here referred to as 'relief', could include dogs and hawks as well as arms and horses. These customs also contain the provision that a man who failed to respond to the royal summons to assist at a hunt had to pay a 50 shilling fine.[57] We have here a package of duties, escort and bodyguard,

---

[52]   As Abels, *Lordship*, 144, suggests, some of the services owed by sokemen may have been performed by their dependants.

[53]   *Domesday Book. Kent*, ed. P. Morgan (Chichester, 1983), 1b, a reference I owe to the kindness of Ann Williams.

[54]   *Ruodlieb*, ed. F. P. Knapp (Stuttgart, 1977), III, lines 31–70. This envoy is variously referred to in the poem as *missus, nuntius, iuvenis* and *legatus*. The king called him 'Friend' and rewarded him with 3 marks of gold. In terms of the useful distinction made by Mary C. Hill, *The King's Messengers 1199–1377* (London, 1961), 6–7, between 'messengers' and 'envoys', he was clearly an envoy. See also the discussion of *legati regis* by Campbell, 'Some Agents', 212–14.

[55]   *EHD*, i.468; for an example of the importance of such men see the events of 1065 as described by both the DE version of the Anglo-Saxon Chronicle and the *Life of King Edward*, ed. F. Barlow (2nd edn Oxford, 1992), 78–81.

[56]   Hase, 'The Mother Churches of Hampshire', 60.

[57]   *Domesday Book. Berkshire*, ed. P. Morgan (Chichester, 1979), 56c.

messenger and hunting services; those who perform them are on the inside track. If we wish to see the 'lex equitandi' in operation in the eleventh century then we need do no more than look again at a very familiar image – the second scene of the Bayeux Tapestry: Harold in the company of his milites, with his hawk and his hounds, and the legend 'Harold dux Anglorum et sui milites equitant ad Bosham'.

The people who perform these kinds of service are not peasants. The eleventh century tract on the reeve sets out in mind-boggling detail the work of villagers, but contains not a word about helping with the hunt.[58] Those who are involved with hunting are associated with their lords, and with the life-style of lords. Hunting was central to the gentle life-style. Thus Offa's kinsman on the eve of Maldon released his hawk only when battle was imminent.[59] Even at his most forlorn the noble travelled with his hunting dog.[60] When one eleventh century author, Andrew of Fleury, described a man as born into rustic ignobility but who rose to higher things and lived nobly to such effect that he was able to marry a wife from a noble family, then the attributes of the parvenu on which he dwelt were his stables, his kennels and his mews.[61] This story is located in Burgundy and told at Fleury, but it is hard not to think that in these respects England and the continent were alike. Living like an earl rather than a monk meant, in Eadmer of Canterbury's words, keeping horses and going hunting with hounds and hawks.[62] As Asser had observed, the 'ars venatoriae' was one of the skills appropriate to noblemen, and the whole art of hunting was, for a model king, second in importance only to the art of governing his realm.[63] The author of the *Life of King Edward*, of course, gives the impression that for Edward the Confessor it was hunting that took precedence. Moreover this author tells us that although in public Edward carried himself as a king and lord, in private and with his followers he behaved as one of them (*ut consocium*). And where if not out hunting – as was his wont, for in the woods and glades with his hawks and hounds were, we are told, his only worldly pleasures – can King Edward have been most typically in private?[64] At least in this respect the Confessor conformed to the conduct of the great king in *Ruodlieb*, who at feasts preferred to talk and joke with fellow huntsmen rather than with rich counts. Mastery of the special skills and language of the hunting field quite as much as

---

[58] *Anglo-Saxon Prose*, ed. M. Swanton (London, 1975), 25–27. However one of the reeve's many springtime duties might include seeing to the cutting of a deer-fence.

[59] *Battle of Maldon*, lines 5–8; and see Gale R. Owen-Crocker, 'Hawks and Horse-trappings: the Insignia of Rank' in ed. Donald Scragg, *The Battle of Maldon AD 991* (Oxford, 1991), 220–37.

[60] *Ruodlieb*, I, lines 44–47.

[61] *Les Miracles de Saint Benoit*, ed. E. De Certain (Paris, 1858), 218.

[62] *Memorials of St Dunstan*, ed. W. Stubbs (RS, 1874), 238.

[63] *Asser's Life of King Alfred*, ed. W. H. Stevenson (Oxford, 1959), chapters 75–76. On the centrality of hunting for the ninth century aristocracy see Janet L. Nelson, *Charles the Bald* (London, 1992), 68–69.

[64] *Life of King Edward*, 18, 62, 78.

great wealth or high birth could take you into the inner circle. This is how the young Ruodlieb won his access to the court of the great king, in a passage strikingly reminiscent of the way Gottfried von Strassburg's Tristan, incognito, won his entrée into the court of King Mark.[65] To hunt with a lord was to serve and accompany him in his pleasures. But to share the pleasures of hunting was also to share the dangers. When he was out hunting a lord was at risk, whether from accidents, from the over-boisterous humour of young men at play, or from ambush – as Tristan ambushed and killed Duke Morgan of Brittany.[66] Those who went hunting with their lord had his life in their hands. As a 'iuvenis', Ruodlieb had, the poet claimed, served his lords supremely well, risking his life for them both in war and in the hunt.[67] Those who hunted with the king guarded the king and they were appropriately rewarded. According to the *Constitutio Domus Regis* of c.1136 knight-huntsmen ('milites venatores') were paid 8 pence a day and other huntsmen (*catatores*) 5 pence a day, eight or five times as much as the sergeants who received 1 penny a day. Also attached to the hunting staff of the king's 'domus' were archers; those who carried the king's bow were paid 5 pence a day.[68] It was believed that Nigel d'Albini began his illustrious career by carrying the king's bow.[69] Hunting and shooting were central to the interests of the gentlemen of that time. Fishing too? Ruodlieb made a great impression – and more than once – by his knowledge of how to catch lots of fish and make a game of it.[70] In the seventh century Wilfrid had impressed the South Saxons by his fishing expertise, but had not – not at any rate to judge from Bede's earnest phrases – treated it as a sport. Many centuries later, William of Malmesbury believed that the same Sussex coast witnessed a light-hearted fishing trip which ended in disaster when the fisherman, Duke Harold, was storm-driven to Ponthieu.[71]

In the eleventh century hunting became a political issue. Cnut's law – 'It is my

---

[65]   *Ruodlieb*, I, lines 92–141, II, lines 1–48. Gottfried von Strassburg, *Tristan*, trans. A. T. Hatto (Harmondsworth, 1960), 78ff.

[66]   *Tristan*, pp. 114–16. Cf. Nelson, *Charles the Bald*, 68, 256.

[67]   *Ruodlieb*, I, lines 9–10.

[68]   *Dialogus*, 135. The best discussion of the hunting establishment of the Anglo-Norman kings is F. Barlow, *William Rufus* (London, 1983), 122–29.

[69]   J. O. Prestwich, 'The military household of the Norman kings', *EHR* 96 (1981), 24–25.

[70]   *Ruodlieb*, fragments II and X, esp. II, line 16 'Sic piscando sibi ludum fecitque sodali.' Perhaps Chrétien's Fisher King was playing a different game; none the less when Perceval encountered him he was fishing mid-stream with hook and line, *Chrétien de Troyes, Arthurian Romances* (Harmondsworth, 1991), 424. At Avignon, in Clement VI's bed-chamber, at Runkelstein and in the Louvre there are fourteenth and fifteenth century paintings showing angling as an aristocratic pursuit for both sexes. My knowledge of these scenes I owe to the kindness of Andrew and Jane Martindale.

[71]   Bede, *Historia Ecclesiastica*, iv.13. 'Ibi, ut animum oblectaret suum, piscatorium conscendit navigium, et interim quidem longiusculo ludo in altum proceditur', WM c. 228, cited thus as the most economical way of referring to both Stubbs's edition (see above, n. 21) and *William of Malmesbury Gesta Regun Anglorum Vol. 1*, ed. and trans. R. A. B. Mynors, R. M. Thomson and M. Winterbottom (Oxford, 1998).

will that every man is to be entitled to his hunting in wood and field on his own land' – anodyne though it sounds, may none the less be evidence that hunting rights had become a cause for concern.[72] Were a disturbingly large number of people now joining in the exclusive game, e.g. by keeping staghounds or hawks, the sorts of animals a thegn might, as we know from one surviving will, bequeathe to a king?[73] Serious efforts were made, above all by William the Conqueror in England, to stop people hunting who wanted to do so. According to the Anglo-Saxon Chronicle, when Rufus was facing difficulties at the start of his reign, he tried to attract the English to his cause; he promised to forbid unjust taxes 'and granted people their woods and hunting rights'.[74] Loss of status was reflected in loss of hunting rights. If the numbers of English who survived the Conquest were to play a crucial role in ensuring the continuation of English government, there may none the less have been a period – a generation or two – when for some of them the loss of their hunting rights meant a loss of gentility.[75]

Below the great lords, the earls and king's thegns, there were many layers of society – lesser thegns and the thriving freemen, cnihts and geneats – who shared common interests and pursuits. In the context of a comment on cnihts and milites, Peter Coss has recently observed that English society on the eve of the Norman Conquest 'was very little different from that which prevailed in France'.[76] This I think is right. But at this point we have to add in the ingredient that was different – the institutions of a powerful royal government in England.[77] It is certainly arguable that for a generation or two after 1066 great landowners had more power over their major tenants than had been the case at the end of the Anglo-Saxon era, none the less in the continuing network of shires and hundreds we have an institutional framework which allows us to see the 'lesser nobility' as a gentry – both before and after 1066.[78]

II

I turn to the word 'gentleman' in the sense of someone who accepts a code of honour. It was to this code that Edward duke of York appealed when he swore

[72] *EHD*, i.467.
[73] D. Whitelock, *Anglo-Saxon Wills* , no. XI. Cf. above, n. 56.
[74] ASC, 1087, 1088, followed by William of Malmesbury, c. 306.
[75] Although Oliver Rackham, *The History of the Countryside* (London, 1986), 49, 223, believes that in England interest in deer husbandry began with that blessedly familiar landmark, 1066, there seems to be some evidence for both fallow-deer and deer parks before that date.
[76] Coss, *The Knight*, 18. It is worth noting that no eleventh century French or Flemish author, whether writing in England or about England, appears to feel any need to comment on differences between continental and insular *milites*.
[77] Campbell, *The Anglo-Saxons*, 244.
[78] See John Hudson, *Land, Law, and Lordship in Anglo-Norman England* (Oxford, 1994), 4, 48–60, 227–29, 279, for the county court and tenants' rights after 1066.

'on my trouthe and as y am trewe gentilman' and in the light of it that Henry duke of Somerset was accused of lacking 'verray gentilness and the noble honoiur that oweth to be grounded in every gentilman'.[79] Given the common interests and pursuits of the upper reaches of Anglo-Saxon society we might reasonably expect to find them accepting a code of behaviour, if not yet a code of chivalry, none the less a code of the kind described by Karl Leyser:

> a brotherhood in arms which bound together men of high birth, great wealth and assured positions with much more modest warrors, often their vassals, with whom they shared certain fundamental values and rituals. A modern simile might be that of an officers' mess, where there is a common bond between all members, regardless of rank. It would indeed be unwise were the most junior second lieutenant to presume on this and occupy habitually his colonel's favourite armchair but the community of attitudes and status is there none the less.[80]

Obviously values like loyalty and courage and prowess – the values usually called 'heroic' or 'the traditional military values' – are explicitly articulated in many eleventh century sources, the Song of Maldon and the *Encomium Emmae* to name but two. Courage should not lead to rashness. Although it is certainly arguable that Byrhtnoth made a strategically defensible decision when he allowed the Vikings to cross the causeway, the poet clearly disapproved. 'Because of his pride the earl set about allowing the hateful race too much land.'[81] In the Bayeux Tapestry William exhorts his milites to prepare themselves for battle *sapienter* as well as *viriliter*. In the *Battle of Maldon* those who stood and fought, of whatever rank, were said to be acting 'in a thegnly fashion'.[82] Kings too were expected to act in a thegnly fashion, displaying the prowess of the warrior as well as of the huntsman. As Karl Leyser pointed out, the Sallustian topos, the *officium militis et imperatoris*, was used by both the Worcester Chronicle and William of Malmesbury in order to praise Edmund Ironside and King Harold.[83] A king like Aethelred the Unready who consistently absented himself from campaigns was likely to find himself in serious political trouble.

How far down society were men expected to live up to these military values? Ann Williams has pointed out that each of the five men who utter words of

---

[79] Cited by D. A. L. Morgan, 'The Individual Style of the English Gentleman' in ed. Jones, *Gentry and Lesser Nobility*, 17.

[80] Karl Leyser, 'Early Medieval Canon Law and the Beginning of Knighthood' in his *Communications and Power in Medieval Europe. The Carolingian and Ottonian Centuries*, ed. T. Reuter (London, 1994), 51–52.

[81] *Battle of Maldon*, lines 89–90. The author of the account of the battle contained in the *Liber Eliensis* (p. 135) also felt that Byrhtnoth set out to challenge the Vikings *nimia animositate*.

[82] *Battle of Maldon*, lines 232, 294. In twelfth century French those who fought courageously, of whatever rank, were said to be acting like *chevaliers*, *Jordan of Fantosme's Chronicle*, ed. R. C. Johnston (Oxford, 1981), lines 865, 1233.

[83] Leyser, 'Early Medieval Canon Law', 54.

encouragement in the *Battle of Maldon* belong to different ranks of society and has suggested that they speak not as individuals but on behalf of the social groups to which they belong: three for the aristocrats (the earls, king's thegns and median thegns) and two for the freemen, or at any rate for their upper ranks, the geneats and the thriving ceorls. All five share the same sentiments and all share the same fate, dying on the field of battle. Of course this is a poem, a poem with a message, that loyalty, fidelity of lord and man and of both to the king, is what upholds land and people, and if Ann Williams is right, it is a message which is suspiciously neatly arranged, a kind of propaganda.[84] On the other hand there is evidence to suggest that these values were felt as well as encouraged. The majority of the Englishmen mentioned in Domesday Book as having fought at Hastings were freemen.[85] According to the Anglo-Saxon Chronicle there were many from South Eastern England who willing to live and die with Godwin in 1052.[86] According to Orderic, at Bourgtheroulde in 1124 one of the aristocratic rebels observed: 'Odo Borleng and his men have dismounted. A mounted soldier who has dismounted with his men will not fly from the field. He will either die or conquer.' Here the men who had chosen to stand and fight were precisely those whom Waleran labelled 'the country bumpkins'.[87]

There were words for those who lived and fought close by their lord's side. One such word was *commilitones*, to which Karl Leyser drew attention in the writings of Widukind.[88] According to Gilbert Crispin, Herluin was outstanding among the *domi ac militiae commilitones* of Count Gilbert.[89] Those who dismounted with Odo were his *commilitones*.[90] In the *Life of Oswald*'s account of Maldon we hear of Byrhtnoth's *commilitones*.[91] According to the twelfth-century story — which there are reasons to believe may go back to a contemporary or near-contemporary version — as Byrhtnoth en route to challenge the Vikings

---

[84] Ann Williams, 'The battle of Maldon and "The Battle of Maldon": History, poetry and propaganda', *Medieval History* 2 (1992), 41–44.

[85] Abels, *Lordship*, 143–44. Doubtless, as Abels has emphasised, we should resist the old idea that Harold's army had been based on a general levy of all able-bodied freemen. The freemen named in Domesday Book would have been lords in their own right, gentleman farmers rather than peasants, and presumably owing honourable services to their own lords.

[86] ASC, CD; however the Worcester Latin version makes it sound as though it was the lithsmen rather than all the good men and true of the south-eastern counties who were willing to commit themselves to Godwin's cause. Cf. *Life of King Edward*, 40.

[87] OV, vi.350–51.

[88] Leyser, 'Early Medieval Canon Law', 54.

[89] *Vita Herluini*, ed. J. A. Robinson, in *Gilbert Crispin, Abbot of Westminster* (Cambridge, 1911), 87. Cf. Leyser, 'Early Medieval Canon Law', 50.

[90] OV, vi.350. Orderic emphasises how much Odo was loved by his men. Cf. Ralph of Caen's characterisation of the relationship between Tancred and his *commilitones*. 'Ita enim dicebat in corde suo: "Thesaurus meus sint milites mei." ' Ralph of Caen, *Gesta Tancredi in expeditione Hierosolymitana*, c. 51.

[91] *Vita Oswaldi*, p. 456. Translated as 'fellow-soldiers' by Whitelock (*EHD*, i.917) and as 'personal retinue' by Lapidge in ed. Scragg, *The Battle of Maldon*, 54.

approached the abbey of Ramsey and sought hospitality and provisions from Abbot Wulfsige for him and for his men, he was told that the place would not suffice for such a great multitude, but that provision could be made for him and seven of his men. To this he is said to have replied courteously (*eleganter*): 'The lord abbot knows that just as I have no desire to fight without them so I will not dine without them.'

At Ely he and his men received a better reception and in consequence the estates once destined for Ramsey were granted instead to Ely.[92] In any case whatever may have happened and whatever Byrhtnoth may – or may not have – said, the attitude the story enshrines was well known in Anglo-Saxon England, being attributed to Alexander the Great in both Old English and Latin versions of the apocryphal *Letter of Alexander to Aristotle*.[93] Another word for these men was *socii*. According to the Abingdon Chronicle, at Hastings Harold and his *socii* were killed.[94] The same term was applied by the Worcester chronicle to the men who came to England with Alfred in 1036, and with both Duke William and Count Eustace in 1051.[95] In the Anglo-Saxon Chronicle they are *geferan*.[96] In Gaimar's French, the word is *cumpaignon*. Where their lord went, his companions went too, in one case even remaining in the chamber with a king as he carried out an act of rape.[97]

But it seems to me that the model of conduct to be followed by nobles and their companions in eleventh century England did not involve only the 'heroic' virtues. The word 'thegnly' could also be applied to honourable behaviour at a meeting of the shire, as is clear from the account of a Herefordshire lawsuit in Cnut's time.[98] At such meetings, as well as on the eve of battle, eloquence was clearly regarded as an admirable quality. For example, one of the speakers at the great assembly described in Byrhtferth of Ramsey's 'Life of Oswald' is the *intrepidus miles Alfwoldus*, praised amongst other things as *affabilis eloquio*. Alfwold was brother of the powerful ealdorman Aethelwine, and son of Athelstan Half-King. Very strikingly, in a long passage which was a conscious digression from his main subject, Byrhtferth portrayed the sons of Athelstan as the model aristocratic family, and he explicitly picked out Aethelwine as the best of the brothers. He prasised Aethelwine's urbane eloquence, his upright conduct and his fine appearance. But the quality which Byrhtferth praised above all others was Aethewine's *mansuetudo*, his gentleness of spirit.[99]

---

[92] *Liber Eliensis*, ed. Blake, Book II, Chap. 62.

[93] Alan Kennedy, 'Byrhtnoth's Obits and Twelfth-Century Accounts of the Battle of Maldon' in ed. Scragg, *Maldon*, 73.

[94] *Chronicon Monasterii de Abingdon*, ed. J. Stevenson (RS, 1858), i.483.

[95] *The Chronicle of John of Worcester Vol. II*, ed. and trans. R. R. Darlington and P. McGurk (Oxford, 1995), 522, 558, 562; and in these contexts *milites* was evidently a natural equivalent.

[96] *Two of the Saxon Chronicles Parallel*, ed. C. Plummer and J. Earle, i.158–59, 172–73, 176.

[97] Gaimar, *Estoire*, lines 1090, 1525, 1891, 2623–24, 3217, 3227, 5515, 5541, 5549.

[98] Robertson, *Anglo-Saxon Charters*, no. LXXXVIII.

[99] *Vita Oswaldi*, 428–29, 445–46, 465, 467.

It is worth recalling here what Stephen Jaeger writes on the subject of *mansuetudo* in his 'The Origins of Courtliness'. He calls it 'the civic virtue par excellence' and claims that its gradual filtering through the ranks of the lay nobility marks nothing less than the civilising of Europe. 'Mansuetudo is one of the dominant themes of medieval ethical writings: be slow to anger, tolerate wrongs for the sake of a more distant goal, do not seek revenge.' 'Its opposite vices, wrathfulness and vengefulness, entangle societies and social groups in destructive networks of conflict and make impossible the peace and tolerance necessary for civilized interaction.' Of course showing a calm benevolence to friends and enemies alike involves a degree of dissimulation and in analysing 'mansuetudo', Jaeger quotes Proust's contrast between 'the great gentleman' and the 'smart and wealthy man of the world of finance or big business'. 'Where one of the latter would have thought he was giving proof of his exclusiveness by adopting a sharp, haughty tone in speaking to an inferior', the former, 'affable, pleasant, smiling' practised 'an affectation of humility and patience, a pretence of being just one of the audience, as a privilege of his good breeding'. Jaeger argues that this affectation of affability was immensely valuable in the inner circle of advisors and ministers to a king, a situation where a group of ambitious, talented and proud men was thrown together in direct competition with each other for favour.[100]

Byrhtferth of Ramsey was not exactly writing from within the world of the secular aristocracy. Indeed Jaeger – had he analysed any tenth and eleventh century authors writing in England – would probably have said that here was an ecclesiastical author seeking to educate lay society.[101] None the less Jaeger's view of court politics is, it seems to me, entirely applicable to English politics in the crises of 975–78, 1035–36, and 1051–52. As Campbell has pointed out, in the last two centuries of its existence, the nearest Anglo-Saxon England 'seems to have come to civil war was in the crisis of 1051–52; and in that crisis war was avoided'. He emphasises the role of royal violence in maintaining that peace.[102] No doubt. But perhaps a code of aristocratic restraint also played a part in the avoidance of war. In the *Life of King Edward*, the family which dominated the last thirty years of Anglo-Saxon England was praised in terms strikingly similar to those used of Aethelwine by Byrhtferth of Ramsey. Godwin, we are told, was notable for

> his equable temperament . . . with pleasing and ready courtesy, polite to all (*iocunda et promta affabilitate omnibus affabilis*) . . . He did not discard the gentleness (*mansuetudo*) he had learnt from boyhood but as though it was natural to him (my italics), took infinite trouble to cultivate it in all his dealings with inferiors and among equals.[103]

---

[100] C. Stephen Jaeger, *The Origins of Courtliness. Civilizing Trends and the Formation of Courtly Ideals 939–1210* (Philadelphia, 1985), 36–38.

[101] Given his argument that this set of ideals was first developed in tenth century Germany, he might also have pointed to Byrhtferth's interest in matters German.

[102] Campbell, 'Was it Infancy?', 5–6. However there were elements of civil war in 1014–16.

[103] *Life of King Edward*, 8–9, especially 'quamque a puero addidicerat mentis mansuetudinem

Harold too 'walked in his father's ways, that is to say, in patience and mercy and with kindness to men of good will. . . . he was endowed with mildness of temper. He could bear contradiction well, not readily revealing or retaliating – never, I think, on a fellow-citizen or compatriot.' Moreover both Harold and Tostig are described as having 'at times so cleverly disguised their intentions that one who did not know them was in doubt what to think'.[104] In the context of the praise for the courtly and gentle behaviour of Aethelwine and Godwin, it is interesting to note that in the crises in which they were involved, men could be killed and yet that violence was not allowed to escalate into civil war. In 978 King Edward the Martyr was murdered – 'yet' in the words of the Anglo-Saxon Chronicle, 'his earthly kinsmen would not avenge him'.[105] Aethelwine's brother Alfwold had one of those trying to recover property from Peterborough Abbey put to death, and in consequence went to Winchester as a penitent. But Bishop Aethelwold ordered him to be given a magnificent reception and treated as a *miles Christi*.[106] Godwin's involvement in the murder of the atheling Alfred in 1036 may have incurred some ecclesiastical censure, but not until fiften years later was it dragged up to threaten his career. Killing, it seems, was still an acceptable continuation of politics.[107] And yet, despite the killings, civil war was averted – at any rate until the trouble in Northumbria in 1065 with its consequences for the catastrophe of 1066.[108] Of course it may also be that the relative peacefulness of England meant that in 1066 its soldiers were relatively inexperienced in the exercise and wiles of war when compared with their Norman enemies. Despite the existence of Old English maxims such as 'a mounted troop must ride in regular array', the author of the *Carmen de Hastingae Proelio* clearly regarded the English as naive in miltary matters.[109]

This brings me to the recent and important paper by Matthew Strickland in which he suggests that 1066 led to the introduction of 'differing conceptions and conventions of warfare'. He argues on the basis of passages from William of Poitiers and Orderic that in mid-eleventh century France there existed a convention of taking prisoners for ransom in battle and that this operated as a mechanism offering both financial gain and mutual protection to aristocratic

non exuit, verum hanc, ut naturaliter sibi inditam, erga subditos et inter pares eterna assiduitate excoluit'. See pp. 32 and 42 (also ASC E) for his restraint in 1052. In Cicero's, *De Officiis*, Ulysses is represented as a model of affability, tolerating insults in order to achieve his ultimate ends, Jaeger, *Origins of Courtliness*, 36.

[104] *Life of King Edward*, 48–51, 78–80.
[105] ASC, 978.
[106] *Vita Oswaldi*, 446; Blake, *Liber Eliensis*, xii–xiii.
[107] Below, pp. 215–16.
[108] See the explicit comments on the avoidance of civil war in ASC D for 1051, CD for 1052 and in the *Life of King Edward*, 80.
[109] Maxims I, from the Exeter Book, in S. A. J. Bradley, *Anglo-Saxon Poetry* (London, 1982), 347; *The Carmen de Hastingae Proelio*, ed. C. Morton and H. Muntz (Oxford, 1972) where the English 'Nescia gens belli solamina spernit equorum' (line 369) are contrasted with the French 'Artibus instructi, Franci, bellare periti' (line 423).

opponents. Where private war was endemic, where the dominance of the castle led to protracted campaigns, war – he suggests – became such an integral part of the warrior's existence that such conventions were likely to develop. Thus 'for the Norman knighthood of 1066, killing on the scale habitually seen in Anglo-Scandinavian warfare had become a remote phenomenon'. In Anglo-Saxon sources by contrast he found no examples of warriors being spared in pitched battle. Vikings often took prisoners, of course, but only during the course of raids; they did not look to do so – as, he argues, the French did – in battle. In battle they preferred to kill. Thus the English experience of war – raiding and slaving on an ocasional basis from a distant kingdom, rather than the endemic local warfare of France – meant there was no call for such chivalrous conventions. Paradoxically the very peacefulness of England inhibited their development.[110]

Similarly I have argued that whereas in England before 1066 aristocrats who found themselves at the mercy of their enemies had to reckon with the real possibility that they might suffer death or mutilation, the influence of French conventions in the generations after the Norman Conquest meant that similarly placed nobles could be increasingly confident that life and limb would be spared.[111] As Henry of Huntingdon put it, there was a sense in which the Norman Conquest had been less cruel than the Danish because – in stark contrast to the bloodbath among the English upper aristocracy which accompanied Cnut's victory in 1016–17 – the Normans granted life to the defeated.[112] It is easy to write of 'traditional military values' as though they were timeless and unchanging. Doubtless some of them such as loyalty, courage, and prowess were. But in other literally vital ways, matters of life and death, the honour of arms was changing. I have called this change the introduction of chivalry. Was it a change of which contemporaries were aware? Orderic thought so. According to him the matter was debated in 1088 when the rebels in Rochester Castle were on the verge of surrender. On one side William II, urged on by his loyal English subjects, wanted to put the 'traitors' to death. On the other many of the great men in William's army argued that he should temper his royal rigour with mercy; having overcome them by his strength, he should spare them by his graciousness (*mansuetudine*).[113] Orderic is late evidence for attitudes in 1088. On the other hand if he is right that the difference between Norman and English law regarding traitors helps to explain the contrasting fates of Earls Roger and Waltheof in 1075–6, then it does seem probable that the difference would have been observed and debated at the time.[114] That such matters were

---

[110] Matthew Strickland, 'Slaughter, Slavery or Ransom: the Impact of the Conquest on Conduct in Warfare' in ed. C. Hicks, *England in the Eleventh Century* (Stamford, 1992), 41–60.

[111] Below, pp. 209–29.

[112] Henry of Huntingdon, *Historia Anglorum*, ed. T. Arnold (RS, 1879), 138; *Henry, Archdeacon of Huntingdon, Historia Anglorum*, ed. and trans. D. Greenway (Oxford, 1996), 272.

[113] OV, iv.126–35.

[114] OV, ii.314, 318. Both William of Jumièges and William of Poitiers felt that English political mores were more bloodthirsty than Norman ones.

indeed debated, if not in England, at any rate in the eleventh century, is clear from the *Ruodlieb*. Much of the early part of that remarkable work takes the form of an insistent argument against hanging high status prisoners of war. Ruodlieb told a count that he deserved to be hanged from a tree by the calves of his legs, – at which point everyone shouted 'Get on with it then!' – but instead the hero advocated mercy. 'Be a lion in battle but like a lamb when taking vengeance.' Mercy, he advises the king, is the best policy. 'You conquer with lamblike clemency and wisdom better than another could conquer by the sword.'[115]

If the eleventh and early twelfth centuries witnessed changes in the ways in which aristocrats treated each other, it saw also changes in the way they treated 'ordinary soldiers'. The demise of slavery meant that ordinary soldiers who could not afford ransoms were no longer a potential source of profit and in consequence, especially in the closing stages of a combat, were now more likely to be killed than captured. On the other hand once non-combatants were no longer the targets of the slave-raid, with all its attendant terrors and massacres – as they still had been, according to Wulfstan, at the time of Danish conquest – then they were distinctly better placed than in earlier centuries. In this respect too the Norman Conquest marked, as Marjorie Chibnall observed, a real watershed in English history, 'the first conquest that did not lead to an increase in the number of slaves'.[116]

By way of conclusion I shall try to locate these developments within a much longer chronological perspective. In many respects the secular values of the late Anglo-Saxon period still seem to be those of the eighth century. Take Bede's story of the Northumbrian noble Imma who was knocked unconscious in a battle against the Mercians. The next day when he was taken prisoner he was afraid to admit that he was a *miles* and passed himself off as a poor peasant (*rusticus pauper*). In consequence he was thrown into chains but, much to his captor's astonishment, the fetters kept falling off. Eventually the Mercian lord whose prisoner he was questioned him, promising not to harm him if he told the truth about his identity. Imma then confessed to being one of the king's thegns (*ministrum regis*). 'Then', said the Mercian, 'you ought to die because all my brothers and kinsmen were killed in the battle. But I shall not break my sworn promise and so I shall not kill you.' Instead Imma was taken to London, presumably to a slave-market, and sold to a Frisian. Naturally his new master had no better luck with manacles. Eventually the Frisian allowed Imma to go to the royal court of Kent in return for his promise to raise the money for his redemption or return to his master (*dominus*), if he couldn't. In fact he raised the money – apparently he had old connections at the Kentish court – and sent it as promised.[117] The assumptions behind this story are many and all of them, in this

---

[115] *Ruodlieb*, III, lines 5–14; IV, lines 86–87.
[116] Marjorie Chibnall, *Anglo-Norman England* (Oxford, 1986), 187–88. For further development of this point, above, pp. 45–8.
[117] Bede, *HE*, iv.22.

context, important. That a noble keeps his promises, even when given to a slave dealer and his owner, even when to do so conflicts with other obligations such as that to seek vengeance for the blood of kinsmen. It shows that battles could result in many high-status casualties. On the Northumbrian side a king was killed; on the Mercian, all the brothers and kinsmen of Imma's aristocratic captor. In consequence a high-status prisoner was likely to be put to death, while a commoner involved in supplying the 'milites' would be spared and sold into slavery.[118] So also in the late Anglo-Saxon period – in which, of course, Bede continued to be read, and in English as well as in Latin – we see a world in which men of high status still had reason to fear violent death, a world of slaving and of a sense of honour, the honour of vengeance and of keeping promises. On the other hand, although it was a world which accepted assassination, it had become one in which internal war was avoided remarkably successfully. I have suggested that the courtly and restrained aristocratic values espoused in the 'Vita Oswaldi' and the 'Vita Edwardi' may have had something to do with this – though Northumbrian society probably remained untouched by them. After 1066 the nobles and gentry of England were much more willing to take up arms and go to war against each other than they had been during the last century of Anglo-Saxon England. But after 1066 wars were no longer slave hunts nor did the victors slaughter their high-status enemies in battle, not at any rate until the battle of Evesham in 1265. Nor indeed did they put them to death after battle, not at any rate until after Boroughbridge in 1322. From then on, of course, in what Maitland called 'the ages of blood', we see, in essence, a reversion to pre-Conquest Anglo-Scandinavian practice, different only in that the influence of professional lawyers in the later period meant that when the fighting was over there was usually a rather more elaborate parade of judicial process before the killing began.[119] In these variations in the prevailing ethic of the secular elite over many centuries there is little room for the notion of a straightforward advance from bloodier to more peaceful or humane values.

[118] In this context it is worth reading the scene in *Beowulf* where the Swedish king Ongentheow besieged his mortal enemies. All night long he repeatedly threatened them, saying that in the morning he would dispatch them, some by the sword's edge, some on the gallows-trees, for the birds' entertainment. Although such threats were also made in the twelfth century they cannot have sent shivers down the spine of a besieged nobleman in quite the same way as they must have done earlier.

[119] Below, pp. 209–29.

11

The Introduction of Knight Service into England

I begin with naming of parts, with definition of terms. By 'knight' I mean a well-armed soldier, a man who possessed horse, hauberk, sword and helmet. It is clear from, for example, the Bayeux Tapestry that, so far as equipment is concerned, there was no significant difference between Englishman and Norman.[1] Both of them, by this definition, were knights. I have adopted this definition partly because it was equipment, not battle tactics, which determined cost. It was equipment therefore, not battle tactics, which might conceivably have had some consequences for the organisation of the society which had to bear that cost.[2]

By 'knight service' I mean service performed by well-armed soldiers of this type and owed to a lord (in this case the king) in return for land held from that lord. This I take to be what many historians refer to as feudal service.

As is well-known, J. H. Round in a famous essay argued that it was William the Conqueror who was responsible for the introduction of knight service into England,[3] and for some sixty years it was generally held that Round was right.[4]

---

[1] N. P. Brooks, 'Arms, Status and Warfare in Late-Saxon England' in *Ethelred the Unready: Papers from the Millenary Conference*, ed. D. Hill, British Archaeological Reports, British Series, 59, 1978.

[2] Presumably the frequency with which men went to war in England and Normandy would also have had a bearing on the matter. On this question, see above, pp. 182–3. On the training of the cavalryman see C. Gillmor, 'Practical Chivalry: the Training of Horses for Tournaments and Warfare', *Studies in Medieval and Renaissance History* 13, 1992, 7–29. From the late 1980s onwards much important work has been done on horses in warfare, e.g. B. S. Bachrach, 'Caballus et Caballarius in Medieval Warfare' in ed. H. Chickering and T. H. Seiler, *The Study of Chivalry*, Kalamazoo 1988; R. H. C. Davis, *The Medieval Warhorse: Origin, Development and Redevelopment*, London 1989. Lack of evidence means that for the eleventh and twelfth centuries there is no chance of emulating Andrew Ayton's fine study, *Knights and Warhorses. Military Service and the English Aristocracy under Edward III*, Woodbridge 1994, but on mounted troops in England before 1066 see A. Hyland, *The Medieval Warhorse from Byzantium to the Crusades*, Stroud 1994, 71–79. For a brief overview which entertainingly dispels some myths, M. Bennett, 'The Medieval Warhorse Reconsidered', *Medieval Knighthood V*, ed. S. Church and R. Harvey, Woodbridge 1995.

[3] J. H. Round, 'The Introduction of Knight Service into England' in *Feudal England*, London 1895.

[4] D. C. Douglas, *The Norman Conquest and British Historians* (David Murray Lecture), Glasgow 1946; 'The Norman Conquest and English Feudalism', *Economic History Review* ix, 1939; both reprinted in *Time and the Hour. Some Collected Papers of David C. Douglas*, London 1977.

Then, in the early 1960s there was a period of lively debate. Eric John, Richardson and Sayles and D. J. A. Matthew led the attack on Round's doctrines[5] while, in their different ways, Powicke, Prestwich, Hollister and Holt all contributed to the controversy.[6] But when, at the end of the decade, the dust eventually settled down, it seemed that most people were still inclined to accept Round's thesis.[7]

In this paper I propose to look more closely at Round's arguments than has been done hitherto, but before turning to the evidence it might help to try to clarify some of the issues at stake. First, it is necessary to distinguish between knight service and the knightly quota (the *servicium debitum*). In theory at least it would have been possible for William to have introduced knight service but to have imposed no quotas, simply to have demanded for each campaign as much as he could get.[8] This is a scenario which might have appealed to someone, like Round, who believed in the arbitrary character of William I's power since quotas tend to set an upper limit to service (though they do not have to) and, as is clear from thirteenth-century history, there is a tendency for quotas to be re-negotiated downwards.[9] In theory equally possible would be a scenario which envisages William modifying a pre-existing framework of knight service by introducing quotas. This, it seems, was the position which Maitland adopted after reading what he called 'Mr Round's convincing papers'.[10] But what Round

---

[5] The first shots were fired by Marjorie Hollings, 'The Survival of the Five Hide Unit in the Western Midlands', *EHR* 63 (1948), but it was in 1960 that the main barrage began: E. John, *Land Tenure in Early England*, Leicester 1960; H. G. Richardson and G. O. Sayles, *The Governance of Medieval England*, London 1963; D. J. A. Matthew, *The Norman Conquest*, London 1966; E. John, *Orbis Britanniae*, Leicester 1966. By contrast Barlow registered his dissent from orthodoxy almost casually, in a passing reference to abbots conducting their quotas of thegns to Hastings, Frank Barlow, *The English Church 1000–1066*, London 1963, 170. Note also his omission of any reference to the 'introduction of knight service' in Frank Barlow, *The English Church 1066–1154*, London 1979.

[6] J. C. Holt, 'Feudalism Revisited', *Economic History Review*, 2nd ser. 14, 1961; Michael Powicke, *Military Obligation in Medieval England*, 1962; C. Warren Hollister, *Anglo-Saxon Military Institutions*, Oxford 1962; J. O. Prestwich, 'Anglo-Norman Feudalism and the Problem of Continuity', *Past and Present* 26, 1963; C. Warren Hollister, *The Military Organization of Norman England*, Oxford 1965.

[7] Thus R. Allen Brown, *The Normans and the Norman Conquest*, London 1969, 219 was right to maintain that Round's thesis was 'untouched though not unchallenged'. See also C. Warren Hollister, '1066: The "Feudal Revolution"', *American Historical Review* 73, 1968, 708–23; the passing reference in John Le Patourel, *The Norman Empire*, Oxford 1976, 252; also J. Boussard, 'Services féodaux, milices et mercenaires dans les armées en France aux XC et XL siècles', *Ordinamenti Militari in Occidente nell'alto medioevo*, Centro Italiano di Studi sull' Alto Medioevo, Settimana XV, Spoleto 1968, 136. I owe this reference to the kindness of David Bates.

[8] Among the writs of summons issued by Henry II's government, those demanding a tenant's *servitium debitum* (or a proportion of it) were outnumbered by vaguer writs which asked him to serve either *cum toto posse* or in such a manner as would cause the King to be grateful to him. Powicke 65–67.

[9] I. J. Sanders, *Feudal Military Service*, Oxford 1956.

[10] Pollock and Maitland, *The History of English Law*, Cambridge 1968, i, 259.

was arguing for was something different. For him the introduction of knight service meant *both* the introduction of a new kind of military tenure *and* the imposition of quotas by which each of William's tenants-in-chief knew just how much he owed in return for his holding. Round believed that these quotas were established in 1070 and that, once fixed, they remained in force until Henry II's reign. More widely held today, however, is a modified version of his thesis, a version which would regard the quotas as being imposed piecemeal throughout William's reign, as new fiefs were distributed and as the numerous soldiers brought over to England to cope with the turbulent events of the Conqueror's reign were gradually accommodated within the landed resources of English society. In this modified version the quotas, once fixed, do not necessarily have to remain static. There is room for a continuing process of re-negotiation between king and individual tenant-in-chief – and undoubtedly the evidence for the reigns of William II and Henry I seems to require a modification of the thesis along these lines.[11] But common to both the strict Round thesis and to its modification is the view that quotas were a consequence of a new type of tenure; and that neither the tenure nor the quota had existed in pre-conquest England. When Round first put forward this view he was, of course, well aware that it overturned the conventional wisdom of his own day. What then was the evidence which he cited to justify his self-consciously revolutionary assertion?

His starting point was his observation that the larger *servicia debita* of Henry II's reign were almost invariably reckoned in multiples of five or ten. From this it followed that these knight-service quotas could not represent the number of five-hide units contained in the fief and since Round, like his opponents, believed that the Anglo-Saxon system of military obligation was the 'five hide-system' it followed that knight service could not be a continuation of pre-conquest arrangements. Moreover the number of different sized fiefs assessed at precisely the same figure proved that the assessment was wholly arbitrary. Round, of course, believed that behind these arbitrary assessments lay what he described as 'the unit of the feudal host', the *constabularia* of ten knights.[12] On the whole the constabulary part of Round's theory has been discarded but the rest of it has been retained – and this even though for Round himself the rest of it was a consequence of the *constabularia*.[13] Thus for Hollister the strikingly symmetrical structure of feudal quotas suggested that 'a single assessor was evidently responsible' and he confidently identified that assessor as being William the Conqueror.[14] It seems to me, however, that a tendency to deal in round numbers is so widespread a human habit that a long drawn-out process of bargaining and re-assessment is also likely to end up in multiples of five and ten.

[11] Richardson and Sayles, 85–88.
[12] Round, 258–61.
[13] Contrast Round, 261, with Hollister, *Military Organisation*, 33–34, and the more cautious note in Brown, *The Normans*, 220 n. 75.
[14] Hollister, '1066', 721.

In one sense, Round was bound to be right. Since the fiefs acquired by the Norman lay aristocracy after 1066 were 'wholly new creations, constructed from the scattered fragments of Anglo-Saxon estates'[15] any quotas imposed on them had to be new ones, different from the hypothetical quotas that might have existed on the estates of their English *antecessores*. But this, of course, was not what Round was getting at. For him the establishment of knight-service quotas meant the introduction of a type of tenure new to English society. Thus in the end it was the evidence concerning ecclesiastical estates, where there was substantial continuity of land holding across the divide of 1066, which came to be of crucial importance. Indeed, as Knowles observed, 'almost all the proofs he offered were drawn from monastic sources'.[16]

His proofs were one writ and the words of three chronicles. The writ was the famous writ addressed to Aethelwig of Evesham in which William I summoned 'those five knights whom you owe me from your abbey' – the writ generally thought of as the earliest surviving writ of summons to the feudal host. The chroniclers on whom Round relied were Roger of Wendover (though he mistakenly referred to Matthew Paris), the *Liber Eliensis* and the Abingdon Chronicle.[17] I now propose to examine these items of evidence one by one.

Roger of Wendover

According to Roger of Wendover in the year 1070 William imposed military servitude on bishoprics and abbacies which had, up to then, been free from all secular service. And he adds that William had these arbitrarily assessed quotas noted down in the rolls.[18]

Now Roger of Wendover's version of other happenings in 1070 is so wildly inaccurate that many historians have doubted whether anything he said about this year's events can be taken seriously.[19] But for Round and his followers this particular passage represents St Albans tradition, the tradition, it may be, of a well-informed house. 'Tradition' is a usefully vague word. Is it possible to pin it down in any way? I think we can at least try. The most obvious place to look for the local tradition of a religious community is in its *Gesta Abbatum*. Now although the St Albans *Gesta Abbatum* was compiled by Matthew Paris, it has been plausibly argued that for the earlier section he relied upon an 'ancient roll' written by Adam, cellarer of St Albans c.1140–c.1170.[20] Reading the *Gesta*

---

[15] Round, 260.

[16] D. Knowles, *The Monastic Order in England*, Cambridge 1963, 608, where Round's marshalling of the evidence is described as 'complete and masterly'.

[17] Round, 298–305. In reality, as Richardson and Sayles pointed out, the words which Round attributed to Matthew Paris were originally written by Roger of Wendover.

[18] The most useful edition of Roger's *Flores Historiarum* is contained within Matthew Paris, *C[hronica] M[ajora]*, ed. H. R. Luard, RS 1872–84. This passage is at ii, 6.

[19] Above all Richardson and Sayles, 62–63.

[20] Richard Vaughan, *Matthew Paris*, Cambridge 1958, 182–84.

Abbatum we do unquestionably find some very vivid memories of the losses suffered by the house in the Conqueror's reign, but of the imposition of knight service there is not a word.[21]

There is nothing here then to suggest that at this point Wendover was using St Albans tradition to supplement his well-known sources: among them William of Malmesbury, Henry of Huntingdon, Ralph of Diceto, Robert of Torigny and John of Worcester. On the other hand his account of the siege of Ely in 1071 does contain some details about Hereward's castle and about a castle built by William at Wisbech which suggest some confused awareness of Ely tradition.[22] If the *Liber Eliensis is* anything to go by, then at Ely in the late twelfth century men did indeed talk about *servitium debitum* as an objectionable burden newly imposed by the Conqueror. At any rate whether or not it was gossip from Ely which lay behind Wendover's account it is clear that my next step must be to assess the value of the Ely evidence.[23]

Liber Eliensis

The account of William's reign comes towards the end of Book II of the *Liber Eliensis* (chapters 101–34). We know that Book III was completed between 1169 and 1174. Book II is not so easy to date, but it may have been written not much earlier. It contains, for example, some references to Bishop Nigel of Ely as a despoiler of the church's treasure, and allusions of this kind may have come more easily after Nigel's death, i.e. after 1169. Two things, however, are certain. First: the passages in question were written after 1154 and before 1174.[24] Second: the compiler of the *Liber Eliensis* only had a very confused notion of events in the generation after the conquest. We can identify some of his sources. As well as tradition, what he called the *pia fidelium relatio*, they included an Ely cartulary (or cartularies), a version of the *Gesta Herewardi*, John of Worcester and William of Poitiers. But copies of undated royal writs taken from the cartularies did not help the compiler to establish an exact sequence of events, and he was quite happy to insert extracts from William of Poitiers and John out of context

---

[21] *Gesta Abbatum Monasterii Sancti Albani*, ed. H. T. Riley, RS 1867, i, 41–51, though it may be that the anecdote about the confrontation between William I and Abbot Frederick (pp. 49–50) is one of Matthew's interpolations. What we do find is a tradition of a pre-Conquest tenant of St Albans, Turnothus, *miles strenuissimus*, who held the manor of Flamstude on terms which included the defence of the abbey in the event of war.

[22] Paris, *CM*, ii, 7. Luard indeed believed that Wendover had access to the *Liber Eliensis* (in which case the source of his knight service story would be plain) but the verbal parallels which he cites – i, 503 (actually based on John of Worcester) and ii, 7 – are insufficient.

[23] A task which is considerably simplified by the existence of an excellent edition: *L[iber] E[liensis]*, ed. E. O. Blake, Camden Society 1962.

[24] On the problem of dating see *LE*, xxiii, xlviii and Book II chapters 54, 61 and 98.

and regardless of chronology.[25] The following summary of the contents of chapter 104 (itself undated) will give some idea of his methods.

Having settled matters abroad King William collected a multitude of warriors and returned to England, sending ahead instructions to ensure that his fortresses were properly defended against Hereward and the others in the Isle of Ely (a clear reference to the events of 1070–71, though the multitude of warriors has overtones of 1085). The king then imposed an intolerable tribute (this is a quotation from John's annal for 1067) and in the same year ordered a survey of the whole of England, how much land each of his barons possessed etc. (i.e. here quoting John's account of Domesday). In other words the compiler has welded together into a single episode events dated 1070, 1067 and 1085/86. Not surprisingly Dr Blake's conclusion is that the compiler's 'treatment of narrative sources . . . deprives the information tendered on general English history of most of its value'.[26]

Bearing this in mind I now turn to what the *Liber Eliensis* has to say about knight service. This is in chapter 134, the last of the chapters dealing with William I's reign and, as it would seem, set in the time of Abbot Simeon. Simeon was abbot from 1082 to 1093.[27] But when the compiler says that the king demanded *debita militie obsequia* from the bishops and abbots of all England he links it with a Scottish campaign; indeed he quotes (though without giving the date) John of Worcester's annal for 1072. The abbot went to William to complain about this new and intolerable imposition, but the king only added to the burden by requiring him to keep a garrison of forty knights in the Isle. In consequence in the next chapter (chapter 135) we hear that William Rufus wants a *servitium debitum* of eighty knights.

What can we conclude from this? Obviously that in the second half of the twelfth century the community of Ely was agitated about knight service, and about its alarming fluctuations. Here the problems of the late 1160s spring to mind.[28] Also that the community believed that William had introduced it. But it is clear that they had no documentary proof of this. In a chronicle which has been described as 'little more than an inflated cartulary',[29] this section is written in a lively anecdotal style. Nor I think, in view of the compiler's historical method, can we assume that Ely tradition linked the king's demand with the year 1072. The compiler used John's reference to the Scottish campaign simply as a peg on which to hang his story about Abbot Simeon's visit to the royal

---

[25] See, for example, Dr Blake's analysis of the account of the siege of Ely, *LE*, liv–lvii.

[26] *LE* II c.104, and p. lviii. Note that John's account of the Domesday Inquest included the question: *Quot feudatos milites?*

[27] For the writer's mistakes on the periods of rule of the abbots of Ely see *LE*, 410–14, and ed. D. Knowles, C. N. L. Brooke and Vera London, *The Heads of Religious Houses. England and Wales 940–1216*, Cambridge 1972, 44–45.

[28] See W. L. Warren, *Henry II*, London 1973, 275–81; R. Hühn, *Das Königtum Heinrichs II von England*, Erlangen 1968, 44–49.

[29] Antonia Gransden, *Historical Writing in England c.550–c.1307*, London 1974, 272.

court. At Ely the introduction of knight service was just something that was thought to have happened some time in William's reign and was associated with the rule of Abbot Simeon (1082–93).

To believe that it happened in William's reign was only natural. After all there were many lay tenants whose obligations did date back to the Conqueror's reign – as they well knew.[30] If the neighbours and kinsmen of the monks traced the origins of their own *servitia debita* back to the conquest it would not be very surprising if, one hundred years after the event, the monks themselves came to do the same – particularly in view of the very widely held belief that the church had suffered grave material damage as a result of the conquest.

An alternative, and possibly mutually reinforcing, source for this late twelfth-century Ely tradition can be found in another set of traditions – the traditions of the Exchequer. According to Alexander of Swereford, writing in 1230, Exchequer tradition held that at the conquest William I had enfeoffed the services of 32,000 knights and although Alexander doubted the number he probably accepted the date.[31] Now it is interesting to note just how close were the links between Ely and the Exchequer. As he himself tells us Alexander of Swereford had discussed these matters with William of Ely, Treasurer of the Exchequer under Richard I and John,[32] and William had referred back to the opinions of his predecessors and kinsmen, Richard FitzNigel, author of the Dialogue of the Exchequer and archdeacon of Ely, as well as to Richard's father, Bishop Nigel of Ely. But if Ely tradition could have been, in some sense, official tradition, just how good was official tradition? The author of the Dialogue of the Exchequer is notoriously not the best source for William the Conqueror's reign.[33] As Alexander of Swereford pointed out, apart from Domesday Book, there was nothing from William's reign among the records of the Exchequer and though he had looked through a few rolls for Henry I's reign he had found no references to scutage. In consequence no one in the Exchequer knew anything for certain about the *debita servitia militaria*.[34]

For the moment we might do well to remain cautiously sceptical about Ely traditions, even if they did derive from official sources.

---

[30] See, for example, the *carta* of Robert Foliot in ed. H. Hall, *R[ed] B[ook of the] E[xchequer]*, RS 1896, i, 332 – and Foliot was one of Ely's tenants, *RBE*, i, 364. For other examples see Round, 295–6.

[31] Swereford's phrase was 'illud commune verbum in ore singulorum tune temporis divulgatum', *RBE*, i, 4.

[32] H. G. Richardson, 'William of Ely, the King's Treasurer (?1195–1215)', *TRHS*, 4th ser. xv, 1932, 45–90.

[33] *Dialogus de Scaccario*, ed. C. Johnson, F. E. L. Carter and D. Greenway, London 1983, xx, 55–56. See J. Hudson, 'Administration, Family and Perceptions of the Past in Late Twelfth-Century England: Richard FitzNigel and the Dialogue of the Exchequer' in ed. P. Magdalino, *The Perception of the Past in Twelfth-Century Europe*, London 1992.

[34] *RBE*, i, 4–6. In view of Matthew Paris's own links with Alexander Swereford (Vaughan, 14) it may be that Roger of Wendover was also aware of Exchequer gossip.

The Abingdon Chronicle

The Abingdon Chronicle is rather different. In the first place a new edition of the chronicle to match Dr Blake's study of the *Liber Eliensis* is badly needed. Doubtless it records 'Abingdon tradition', but when and how? Stenton has argued, and persuasively, that it was written 'towards the middle of the twelfth century' by an unknown monk who had joined the community by 1117 at the latest. It is also, I think, fair to say, as Stenton said, that the 'author shows himself remarkably well informed about the history of the monastery in the Norman period'.[35] The Abingdon Chronicle, then, is indeed different from the *Liber Eliensis* or Roger of Wendover and we should do well to look closely at what it has to say. Now, in fact, the chronicle does *not* tell us that William imposed a new burden, merely that 'by the king's command it was noted in the rolls how many knights were required from the bishoprics and abbeys'.[36] This could be correct, or it may be that the author, at this point, is simply reflecting mid twelfth-century practice.[37] He then goes on to tell us that Abbot Athelhelm assigned manors from the church's possessions to his kinsmen, in each case stating the terms of service. These, or course, were the estates which had once been held by thegns killed at Hastings.[38] In other words, although the Abingdon Chronicle reports the granting out of knights' fees, it may not be reporting the initial establishment of the *servitium debitum*, merely its writing down.[39] But I shall return later to the Abingdon Chronicle.

---

[35] F. M. Stenton, *Early History of the Abbey of Abingdon*, Oxford 1913, 4–8, and F. M. Stenton, *The First Century of English Feudalism 1066–1166*, Oxford 1961, 213 n. 4. See also M. Biddle, H. T. Lambrick and J. N. L. Myres, 'The Early History of Abingdon, Berkshire, and its Abbey', *Medieval Archaeology* 12, 1969, 68. For the suggestion that it was originally compiled in the 1130s, S. Keynes, *The Diplomas of King Aethelred 'the Unready'*, Cambridge 1980, 10. The editor-designate of the new edition adopts Stenton's dating, J. Hudson, 'The Abbey of Abingdon and its Chronicle', *ANS* 19, 1995, 184–85.

[36] *Chronicon [monasteri de Abingdon]*, ed. J. Stevenson, RS 1858, ii, 3. The phrase 'cum iam regis edicto in annalibus annotaretur' should be translated 'in the rolls', not 'in the annals'. See Richardson and Sayles, 63, and, in addition to the references they give, *Dialogus*, 97 and *RBE* i, 4.

[37] The *servitia debita* could have been noted either in the 'rotulus qui exactorius dicitur quem quidem nominant breve de firmis', *Dialogus*, 62, or perhaps more likely, in the Danegeld Roll which Swereford refers to (*RBE*, ii, 659) but which he had never seen. The first reference to scutage in the Dialogue links it with Danegeld (*Dialogus*, 52). In any event, as Round noted, 'the officials of the exchequer were well aware of the amount of *servitium debitum* from every fief', Round, 285.

[38] *Chronicon*, ii, 3–4. Later Abingdon tradition was less kindly disposed towards Abbot Athelhelm, ibid., ii, 283–84.

[39] Compare the tradition that William I introduced written law into England, *Dialogus*, 63.

The Evesham Writ

Now I come to Round's last proof, the writ addressed to Aethelwig of Evesham.[40] This is evidence for some sort of quota at Evesham[41] but were Aethelwig's knights being summoned to do campaign service? Perhaps they were being called to Clarendon to swear an oath similar to the 1086 oath of Salisbury.[42] Perhaps they were being summoned to a feast: in the 1090s Abbot Aldwin of Ramsey was released from the duty of supplying ten knights *in festis*,[43] but the day for which they were summoned, *ad octavas Pentecostes*, is an unlikely day for a feast,[44] while the requirement that they were to come 'prepared' echoes such phrases as *cum equis et armis parati*: prepared for war.[45]

If this *is* Evesham's feudal quota being summoned to war, can we say when and where? Abbot Aethelwig died in February 1077; the writ must be dated to 1076 or earlier. It was issued at Winchester, presumably in the spring. William seems to have been abroad in the spring of 1067, 1073, 1074, and 1075. This leaves the years 1068–72 and 1076. Round opted for 1072, to link the writ with the Ely Chronicler's reference to *debita militie obsequia* for a Scottish campaign. But Clarendon is a strange place to muster an army for Scotland; and the date (a week after Whitsun) does not fit a campaign which John of Worcester dated to after 15 August. In 1072 Aethelwig was probably already with the king at Winchester at Easter and then at Whitsun at Westminster, so he is unlikely to have required a summons by writ.[46] William was at Winchester in April in 1068, 1069 and 1070; his whereabouts in April 1071 is unknown. Any of these years are possible, but 1068 or 1069 seem most likely, because we hear of military

---

[40] Round, 303–304. Translated in *English Historical Documents*, ii, 960. See now the better text printed as no. 131 in the new edition by David Bates of *Regesta Regum Anglo-Normannorum: The Acta of William I, 1066–1087*, Oxford 1998. I am very grateful to David Bates for his kindness in sending me a copy of his text and note in advance of publication, in which he concludes that 'some doubts must remain about whether this is an authentic writ of summons of William I's reign'.

[41] Though it was not always a quota of five knights. See H. M. Chew, *The Ecclesiastical Tenants-in-Chief and Knight Service*, London 1932, 9.

[42] Matthew, *The Norman Conquest*, 117–20. This is a valuable discussion of the writ, though the suggestion that *omnes illos qui sub ballia et iustitia tua sunt* were Aethelwig's vassals is probably overshooting the mark. It is worth noting that Henry II, in 1166, was also concerned with oaths of allegiance, *RBE*, i, 412.

[43] *Regesta Regum Anglo-Normannorum*, i, ed. H. W. C. Davis, Oxford 1913, n. 462; *Chronicon Abbatiae Rameseiensis*, ed. W. D. Macray, RS 1886, 212.

[44] Though the consecration of Walkelin as bishop of Winchester on the octave of Pentecost 1070 (31 May) would presumably have called for some solemn celebration.

[45] This was the formula used by Richard I in 1196, *The Historical Works of Master Ralph de Diceto*, ed. W. Stubbs, RS 1876, ii, lxxx. Compare the phrase used in Henry I's Coronation Charter, 'ita se equis et armis bene instruant, ut apti et parati sint ad servitium meum'. Stubbs's *Charters* (9th edn) 119. I owe this point and the references to John Prestwich's kindness and critical scrutiny.

[46] *The Heads of Religious Houses*, 47; Round, 304; Worcester, ii, 9 (see below n. 58); while the suggestion about Aethelwig's movements in 1072 is based on *Lanfranc's Letters*, 45–49.

activities in the west, undertaken by Harold's sons from their Irish base. The muster at Clarendon might have been intended for the south-west, but was then perhaps switched to meet a greater danger in the north.[47]

The earlier we date the writ the less the time available to William to carry through a major re-organisation, but even if 1072 is correct, is it reasonable to assume that Evesham had only recently been subjected to such a quota? The writ summoning these five knights survives in a copy in an Evesham cartulary.[48] Another writ copied on the same page of the same cartulary contains the following words. 'Know that I have confirmed to Abbot Aethelwig his abbey of Evesham and whatever belongs to it, with its lands, men, its custom, law and liberty . . . as fully as in the time of my kinsman King Edward or before.'[49] Was this writ issued *before* William introduced knight service?[50] Or are we to accept the words of one writ but not of the other? Was William's constant repetition, not just in the case of Evesham but in document after document, that he asked only for the old services, simply not true? Or would it make life simpler if, as a working hypothesis, we assumed that the Evesham quota pre-dated 1066?

This has brought me to the end of this consideration of Round's marshalling of the evidence. It does indeed show that there was a late twelfth-century tradition that William introduced knight service, but that, I think, is all. Since Round wrote, however, one more chronicler has been brought into the debate and it is to his evidence that I shall now turn.

Orderic Vitalis

According to Orderic 'William distributed lands to knights and ordered their ranks in such a way as to ensure that he would have 60,000 knights always ready at his command.'[51] Is this the language of someone who thought that William was an innovator? Or is this how a chronicler might have described Cnut's grants to his men? I do not think that Orderic's sentence, taken in isolation, is unambiguous. It is clearly important to set it in context. Up to this point Orderic has been following the sequence of events as outlined by William of Poitiers, and this has taken him up to 1070.[52] Only after a long digression does he pick up

[47] For William's itinerary see Bates, *The Acta*, 76–84. To judge from the language of the Anglo-Saxon Chronicle in 1068 it was actually at or immediately after a Whitsun court that William received the news that forced him to go north. Against so early a date is the point that writs usually seem to have been written in Old English before 1070, Bates, *The Acta*, no. 131. If genuine he is inclined to favour 1076.

[48] BL Cotton MS Vespasian B xxiv, fol. 18. For a brief description of the book see P. H. Sawyer, 'Evesham A, a Domesday Text', *Worcester Historical Society*, 1960, *Miscellany* 1.

[49] Bates, *The Acta*, no. 133.

[50] If authentic it can be dated to between 1070 and 1078. Its authenticity is, however, questionable, Bates, *The Acta*, 455.

[51] Orderic Vitalis, *Historia Ecclesiastica*, ed. M. Chibnall, 6 vols., Oxford 1969–80, ii, 266–67.

[52] Orderic, ii, 258–59.

the chronological thread again with an account of the year 1071.[53] For Orderic this digression had served as a general summing up of William's treatment of England. On this basis there is no justification for dating the distribution of lands to knights to 1070–71. In the immediately preceding sentence Orderic had referred to the Domesday Survey; in the one before that, he gave us an estimate – *ut fertur* – of the revenues which William derived from England. He goes on to say that the Normans became corrupted by greed and abused their authority. It is at this point that he puts a famous speech into the mouth of a monk called Guitmund, criticising the Conqueror for his oppressive treatment of the English church. In this context if Orderic actually had thought that William's distribution of lands to knights created new obligations would he have chosen such neutral words? It is worth noting that in Guitmund's long speech there is nowhere a reference to novel military burdens.[54]

What then did Orderic have in mind when he talked about distributing lands to knights? Two other passages from the *Historia Ecclesiastica* are perhaps worth mentioning. The first is taken from his account of William's deathbed speech. We hear that William has imposed a *militare servitium* of one hundred knights on Count Guy of Ponthieu.[55] Did Orderic intend his readers to understand that this involved a tenurial revolution in Ponthieu? I wonder. In the second passage (iv, 7) Orderic writes, 'His temporibus militiam Anglici regni rex Willelmus conscribi fecit et lx millia militum invenit.'[56] Comparing this sentence with the earlier juxtaposition of two sentences, one about Domesday, the other about 60,000 knights, I would suggest that in both places Orderic had the same thing in mind. In Orderic's eyes these 60,000 knights are there not as a result of a series of arbitrary assessments made by the king but as a consequence of the kinds of arrangement visible in Domesday Book.

We know that Orderic visited Worcester in about 1115. He reports that he found a monk called John writing a chronicle which had started at Wulfstan's command.[57] Since this is obviously a reference to the text formerly attributed to Florence of Worcester, it may well be significant that, according to 'Florence', among the questions which the Domesday Inquest was designed to answer was: *quot feudatos milites*, 'how many enfeoffed knights'.[58] I would suggest therefore that although Hollister believed that Orderic was referring to 'a revolution in military tenures',[59] it is clear that Orderic himself thought he was speaking of a Domesday-related system – speaking perhaps of something that Hollister would have called a five-hide system. It may be a warning to us that the two things

---

[53] Orderic, ii, 280–81.
[54] Orderic, ii, 266–79.
[55] Orderic, iv, 88–89.
[56] Orderic, iv, 52–53.
[57] Orderic, ii, 158–61.
[58] Florence of Worcester, *Chronicon ex chronicis*, ed. B. Thorpe, 2 vols., London 1848–49, ii, 18–19.
[59] Hollister, '1066', 718–19.

were not quite as distinct as Hollister would have us believe, but that quota and five-hide system were inter-related. In conclusion, the evidence of Orderic Vitalis cannot be said to give any support to the Round Thesis.

The Argument from Silence

Now for the arguments of Round's critics. Essentially their main argument is Freeman's old argument, the argument from silence. If indeed the introduction of knight service had meant the imposition of a new and heavy burden, as the language of Wendover and the *Liber Eliensis* undoubtedly indicates, then one might expect some kind of an outcry to be reflected in the sources. It is true that William I's reign is a period particularly devoid of exactly contemporary chroniclers. But surely somewhere there would be some reminiscence of the outcry in that very considerable amount of material that was written before the mid-twelfth century. After all for this purpose we do not need chroniclers of the calibre of Orderic Vitalis or William of Malmesbury; a writer of limited horizons, concerned only with the affairs of his own church, is quite sufficient; especially indeed since most of these local writers are chiefly concerned with the material well-being of their house.[60]

I have counted no less than sixteen Anglo-Norman authors who dealt, in one way or another, with the aftermath of 1066. Six of these authors are anonymous. Three of them wrote local history, one at Durham, one at Evesham and one at York.[61] The other three are compilers of versions of the Anglo-Saxon Chronicle, D, E and the other Peterborough version used in the later twelfth century by Hugh Candidus.[62] The ten authors to whom names can be given are Symeon of

[60] The method followed here is merely an extension of that sketched out by John, *Land Tenure*, 142–43. Without the aid of Antonia Gransden's admirable survey, *Historical Writing in England*, it would have been an arduous task indeed.

[61] *Cronica monasterii Dunelmensis*, printed in E. Craster, 'The Red Book of Durham', *EHR*, 40, 1925, 523–9. The author of this short history, written between 1072 and 1083, saw in William I a king who confirmed everything that the church possessed *in terris et legibus et libertate et quietudine*. The *History of the Church of Evesham* (in *Chronicon Abbatiae de Evesham*, ed. W. D. Macray, RS 1863, 77–98) was probably composed shortly after the death, in 1077, of Abbot Aethelwig, but in its present form dates from the beginning of the twelfth century. Its author was concerned for the liberties as well as for the estates of the church and he believed that, in both spheres, Evesham had emerged unscathed from the troubles of William's reign. The author of *Chronica Pontificum ecclesiae Eboracensis* (*Historians of the Church of York and its archbishops*, 3 vols, ed. J. Raine, RS, 1879–94) had nothing to say about the imposition of a new form of military obligation despite his view that under the Norman kings the *status regni* was transformed and the peace of the church disturbed, ii. 354.

[62] Scholars continue to discuss the provenance of the D text. York, Worcester and Evesham have all been suggested. For a plausible argument linking it with Ealdred of Worcester and York, see P. Wormald, *How do we know so much about Anglo-Saxon Deerhurst?* Deerhurst Lecture, 1991. The E version is thought to have been compiled at St Augustine's, Canterbury, though in its extant form it contains interpolated Peterborough material.

Durham,[63] Giso bishop of Wells[64] Hermann of Bury St Edmunds,[65] Goscelin of St Bertin,[66] Eadmer of Canterbury,[67] Heming,[68] Colman[69] and John[70] at Worcester, Hugh the Chanter[71] and, finally William of Malmesbury.[72] These sixteen authors

Further Peterborough tradition emerges in *The Peterborough Chronicle of Hugh Candidus*, ed. W. T. Mellows, London 1949.

[63] Symeon has now been very plausibly identified as the author of the work formerly known as *Historia Dunelmensis Ecclesiae* (printed in *Symeonis Monachi Opera Omnia*, ed. T. Arnold, RS, 1, 1882) and soon to be edited by David Rollason under a new title, *Libellus de exordio atque procursu istius hoc est Dunelmensis ecclesie*. See ed. D. Rollason, *Symeon of Durham. Historian of Durham and the North*, Stamford, 1998. In this work, probably written c.1105 (see W. M. Aird, 'The Political Context of the *Libellus de Exordio*' in Rollason, *Symeon*, 32–45), we are told that the Conqueror planned to impose new customs on the church, but this refers to *tributum*, not knight service. In any event both the tax-gatherer, Ranulf, and William himself were miraculously persuaded by St Cuthbert that it would be wiser to leave the lands, laws and customs of the saint unimpaired (ed. Arnold, 107–8).

[64] Giso's memorandum is printed in J. Hunter, *Ecclesiastical Documents*, London, Camden Soc., 1840, 15–20. It is evident that Giso (bishop from 1060 to 1088) believed that he had successfully preserved the *summa libertas* of his church.

[65] Hermann's *De Miraculis sancti Edmundi*, written soon after 1095, is printed in *Memorials of St Edmund's Abbey*, i, ed. T. Arnold, RS 1890.

[66] C. H. Talbot, 'The Liber Confortatorius of Goscelin of St Bertin', *Studia Anselmiana* 37, *Analecta Monastica* 3rd ser., Rome 1955. But since Goscelin's allusions to the aftermath of 1066 deal with individual human tragedies rather than with institutional problems, it would be unwise to put much weight on his silence on this score.

[67] In describing the 1097 quarrel between William II and Anselm about the knights which Canterbury owed to the king, Eadmer makes not the slightest suggestion that the obligation itself was regarded as either unjust or novel. See Eadmer, 40, 78–79 and *The Life of St Anselm by Eadmer*, ed. R. W. Southern, London 1962, 88. Moreover, although in his *Miracles of St Dunstan* (in *Memorials of St Dunstan*, ed. W. Stubbs, RS 1874) Eadmer enumerates the tribulations which befell his church in the aftermath of 1066, the imposition of a new *servitium debitum* is not among them. Equally there is nothing is Osbern's *Miracles of St Dunstan*, but the latter's allusion to the Norman Conquest is so brief and discreet that his silence can hardly count.

[68] *Hemingi Chartularium Ecclesiae Wigornensis*, ed. T. Hearne, Oxford 1723, ii, 405–408 contains a brief account of Wulfstan's career.

[69] *The Vita Wulfstani of William of Malmesbury*, ed. R. R. Darlington, London 1928. On the assumption that William was following Colman's English Life very closely indeed, I have credited it to the latter. Although we hear of the number of knights whom Wulfstan kept in his household at the king's command (ibid., 55–56) – clearly with the events of 1085–86 in mind – there is no mention of a recently imposed knightly quota.

[70] *The Chronicle of John of Worcester*, vol. 2, ed. R. R. Darlington and P. McGurk, Oxford 1995, xvii–xviii, explains why this is no longer attributed to Florence.

[71] Ed. C. Johnson, *Hugh the Chanter, The History of the Church of York 1066–1127*, 2nd edn, Oxford 1990. Written in the 1120s, it is also silent on this subject, though it begins with a summary of the damage done to the town and church of York as a result of the Norman Conquest.

[72] William is an important source for the history of two churches: Malmesbury in Book 5 of *De Gestis Pontificum* and Glastonbury in his *De antiquitate Glastoniensis ecclesiae* in *Adami de Domerham, Historia de rebus gestis Glastoniensis*, ed. T. Hearne, Oxford 1727, i, 1–122. In the case of Glastonbury, he puts the damage done by the Normans on a par with that done by the Danes (ibid., 110). Moreover there is no mention of the introduction of knight service

represent at least a dozen Anglo-Norman churches. Very different though they are in some ways, common to all of them is a belief that in William I's reign their church had gone through a period of either trial or tribulation. Sometimes they reckoned that their church had emerged unscathed thanks either to the intervention of a saint, like St Cuthbert at Durham, or to the prudence of a prelate, like Aethelwig at Evesham. But where churches did suffer, it is clear that the memory of that suffering lingered on and was later recorded. Within the general tale of woe it is possible to isolate five main themes: (1) estates were devastated; (2) treasure and ecclesiastical ornaments were carried off; (3) oppressive tribute was imposed; (4) estates were lost owing to the reckless generosity of new Norman prelates; (5) estates were lost owing to the need to provide for knights. Although the last of these themes is obviously linked with the turbulent history of the Conqueror's reign it is not, equally obviously, a complaint about the introduction of a novel form of military obligation. Nowhere in the Anglo-Norman literature do we find any such complaint – and this despite the fact that everyone of these dozen churches appears in Round's list of those owing the *servitium debitum*. The earliest source to add this particular complaint to the list is the *Liber Eliensis* and I, at least, would be inclined to give more weight to the silence of sixteen more nearly contemporary writers than to the lively but muddled assertions of the Book of Ely and Roger of Wendover.

Taking the argument from silence a stage further, there is no mention of the imposition of knight service in the letter collections of Lanfranc, Anselm and Herbert Losinga – though Anselm indeed does refer to English knights holding land of the church of Canterbury before 1066.[73] Nor did Pope Gregory VII, not the most mealy-mouthed of men, accuse William of having made any such attack on the liberties of the church during the course of their disagreement in 1079–80.[74] But there is still more to be said about the argument *e silentio*. Documentary sources, as well as literary ones, are silent. Round, of course, had great fun with Freeman's reliance on the silence of Domesday Book. 'Wonderful are the things that people look for in the pages of that great survey; I am always reminded of Mr Secretary Pepys' writing for information as to what it contained 'concerning the sea and the dominion thereof'.[75] But if the silence of Domesday Book is fairly unremarkable, what is surely well worth remarking upon is the silence of all the 211 writs and charters of William I extant for English beneficiaries. Consider, for example, the reaction of Bishop Herbert of

anywhere in the whole of William's guided tour of English churches (i.e. the *De Gestis Pontificum*) – hardly a fact which suggests that it loomed large in the collective memory of the English church.

[73] *The Letters of Lanfranc, Archbishop of Canterbury*, ed. H. Clover and M. Gibson, Oxford 1979; *Anselmi opera omnia*, ed. F. S. Schmitt, Edinburgh 1946–52, vols. ii–v (especially iv, n. 176); *Epistolae Herberti de Losinga, Osberti de Clara, et Elmeri*, ed. R. Anstruther, Brussels 1846.

[74] In this context it might be observed that had William ever introduced knight service, 1070 would have been a most unlikely date for any such action since it was precisely in that year that papal legates were in England. M. Gibson, *Lanfranc of Bec*, Oxford 1978, 131–40.

[75] Round, 229–30.

Norwich to Henry I's *aide pour fille marier* in 1110, the first known case of this aid in English history. He took the trouble to get a writ of exemption for one of the manors of his church. It was not to be subject to any new custom on account of this *aide pour fille marier*. At least two other prelates obtained similar writs.[76] It seems to me curious, to say the least, that if William I had introduced a burdensome new custom on no less than thirty-nine churches, that not one of them should have succeeded in either buying or preserving some such writ.[77] After all some of the men who ruled their communities both before and after 1070, abbots like Aethelwig of Evesham and Baldwin of Bury St Edmunds, were men high in William's favour. If the Norman Conquest and settlement was 'a joint stock enterprise' these were shareholders whose vote William needed. Or, to put it another way, it seems equally curious that not one of the churches on which William did not impose knight service, for some arbitrary reason or another, troubled to get some documentary proof of their fortunate exemption. Yet further, if churchmen at the end of the eleventh century had known that William had at some stage in his reign, introduced knight service then it strikes me as being curious that there are no forged or interpolated charters exempting churches from this new burden. I shall return later to the question of forgery, but would like first to draw together the threads of this argument from silence. Some silences speak louder than others. A very considerable number of documentary, epistolary and narrative sources all have nothing to say on the subject. This surely is a resounding silence.

Five-hide system or knightly quota?

But where do we go from here? Even if, as I have argued, the evidence, both direct and indirect, in favour of Round's thesis is late, fragmentary and extremely fragile, may it not still be true that the undoubted existence of quotas in the reign of Henry II suggests that by that date somehow or other, whether suddenly or gradually, there had been profound changes in military organisation since Anglo-Saxon times. For all parties to the dispute are agreed that Anglo-Saxon military organisation was based on the five-hide system and that this is very different from the knightly quota.[78] Again definition is necessary. By the five-hide system I refer to a 'standardized recruitment arrangement based on the hide'. In this

---

[76] *Regesta*, ii, nn. 946, 963, 968.

[77] Compare V. H. Galbraith's comment that the 'absence of any outcry against the use of the sworn inquest is a warning not to accept the common assumption that it was introduced by William I'. V. H. Galbraith, *The Making of Domesday Book*, Oxford 1961, 53.

[78] That all parties to the debate make this same basic assumption has been pointed out by G. W. S. Barrow, *The Anglo-Norman Era in Scottish History*, Oxford 1980, 162–63, 166. Though Aethelred II's demand for a helmet and byrnie from every eight hides may, if it is not simply a way of solving 'acute problems in supplying expensive equipment' (Brooks, 89), imply a select fyrd quota of one well-armed soldier from every eight hides. *ASC* s.a. 1008.

system the amount of service owed could always be calculated by dividing the total number of hides by five, the result being what Hollister called 'the select fyrd quota'. But the knightly quota is the result of an individual and arbitrary bargain made between lord (in this case the king) and tenant.[79] What the advocates of continuity argue is that the Anglo-Saxon five-hide system evolved into the twelfth-century knightly quota system. For the advocates of the Norman revolution on the other hand the Anglo-Saxon system was so utterly different from the feudal quota that no such evolution was possible; either the hidage system came to an abrupt end with the conquest, or it survived for a while but was supplemented by the radically new burden of knight service.

But can we really take it for granted that in Anglo-Saxon England military obligation was based on the five-hide system? Leaving aside for one moment the military households of king and earls – though the implication of John Prestwich's recent paper is that, in so doing, we are leaving out the single most important element in the whole politico-military system[80] – are we saying that when a rather reluctant Anglo-Saxon landowner answered his king's summons to war by bringing with him only the minimum allowable force, he was always supposed to find out what that minimum was by dividing the number of hides he held by five? Or is it conceivable that, as the result of an earlier agreement made between this reluctant landowner and the king – or between his father and the king, or the king's father – he would be entitled to bring some other acceptable number of well-armed men to the muster? If the latter were the case then, by my definition, he would be bringing his quota of knights to the muster. In this case we would have to admit that Anglo-Saxon England knew more than one form of military obligation. If this were the case, it should surely not be very surprising.

Given the perennial pressures of politics and patronage, the concept of a uniformly administered national system simply does not make much sense. Powerful men and royal servants always hoped to be able to come to some favourable arrangement.[81] Moreover as soon as we turn our attention to later and better documented periods it becomes clear that armies were normally recruited not under any one system of obligation but under a combination of systems.[82] Nor can we argue that the cavalry was recruited under one system and the infantry under another. Edward I's cavalry force, for example, might be composed of men who served for pay (including the knights of the royal household) and of men who served at their own expense (including both those

---

[79] Hollister, '1066', 717.

[80] J. O. Prestwich, 'The Military Household of the Norman Kings', *EHR* 96, 1981. Note, in particular, what Prestwich says about 'the feudal system', ibid., 31–32.

[81] For the effects of politics and patronage on the 'national' administration of Danegeld in the eleventh and twelfth centuries see Judith Green, 'The last century of Danegeld', *EHR* 96, 1981.

[82] Powicke, chapters 3–7 passim. This was also the case in thirteenth-century Scotland, see G. W. S. Barrow, *The Anglo-Norman Era in Scottish History*, 164–66.

who were fulfilling a strict feudal obligation and those who had been summoned by virtue of the fealty and esteem they owed to the king).[83] And, after all, much of Hollister's work was intended to demonstrate that five-hide system and knightly quota existed side by side *after* 1066, so why should they not have co-existed *before* 1066?[84] The evidence of Berkshire Domesday can perhaps be used to suggest that the five-hide system existed in pre-conquest England, but can it be used as evidence that it was *the* Anglo-Saxon system? We might just as well argue on the basis of a single piece of evidence like King John's levy of troops in 1205 that military obligation in Angevin England was organised nationally not feudally.[85] No historian does in fact draw this conclusion from the writ of summons of 1205 because, for the early thirteenth century, we have plenty of other evidence and we know that different systems existed side by side. Indeed, eight years later, the writ summoning the levy of 1213 shows us how the two systems could interact – with men summoned under a national obligation being expected to go with their lords to the muster exactly as Maitland had envisaged the Anglo-Saxon hidage system operating in practice.[86]

But my argument so far has been entirely hypothetical. Plausible it may be that more than one system of obligation should exist in Anglo-Saxon England – but is there any evidence for it? Is there, in short, any evidence for the quota before 1066? I think that perhaps there is.

In a grant of immunity drawn up on the dorse of a charter of King Offa c.800 Cenwulf of Mercia reserved the three public burdens on an estate of thirty or thirty-six hides with a special proviso concerning army service: 'verum etiam in expeditionis necessitatem vires v tantum modo mittantur'.[87] Since as a rule pre-conquest diplomas do not specify the number of men, this is undoubtedly an exceptional document. But just how exceptional were the circumstances to which it refers? Even if this endorsement were a unique document – and it has been so described[88] – it should at least give us pause.[89] Is it likely that the beneficiary in this case, a layman named Pilheard, was the only landowner to secure favourable terms for himself in the whole of Anglo-Saxon

---

[83] M. Prestwich, *War, Politics and Finance under Edward I*, London 1972, 67–91.

[84] Though I would envisage them as *alternative* forms of service, not as a *double* burden imposed upon each important landholder as Hoyt and Hollister seem to think. See Hollister, '1066', 720–21.

[85] The writ is printed in Stubbs's *Charters*, 276–77.

[86] Matthew Paris, *CM* ii, 538–39; F. W. Maitland, *Domesday Book and Beyond*, Fontana paperback 1960, 196.

[87] *Cartularium Saxonicum*, ed. W. de Gray Birch, London 1885–93, n. 201.

[88] N. Brooks, 'The development of military obligations in eighth- and ninth-century England' in P. Clemoes and K. Hughes (eds.), *England before the Conquest*, Cambridge 1971, 70 n. 2. As Brooks points out, the obligation 'is compulsory upon *tota gens*, yet is done by each from his hereditary lands'.

[89] Indeed it has provoked some discussion. See H. M. Chadwick, *The Origin of the English Nation*, Cambridge 1924, 151; Hollings, 'The Survival of the Five Hide Unit in the Western Midlands', 476; Hollister, *Anglo-Saxon Military Institutions*, 61–62.

history? Other quotas may have been arranged by means of purely verbal agreements – as indeed most if not all the quotas of William I's reign must have been.

But the Pilheard endorsement is not quite a unique document. Curiously enough another quota is fixed in another charter also attributed to Cenwulf of Mercia. In a grant dated 821 in favour of the abbey of Abingdon, Cenwulf allowed that the abbey should perform 'expeditio' *cum xii vassallis et cum tantum scutis.*[90] Since the list of estates whose possession Cenwulf confirms comes to a total of very much more than sixty hides, this is clearly an arbitrary quota. Yet, so far as I can see, the terms of this charter have not been quoted in the debate about *servitium debitum*, not at any rate since Maitland.[91] And for this there is a reason. When I said the charter fixed the quota, I used the word 'fixed' advisedly. The charter is, of course, a forgery and Sir Frank Stenton rightly dismissed it as such. When he used the charter, he was interested in the extent of Mercian rule in ninth-century Berkshire and he wanted better evidence than an Anglo-Norman fake. For in Stenton's view the forged charters in the Abingdon Chronicle were not fabricated by the mid twelfth-century compiler but by an unknown earlier hand. They 'bear the known characteristics of Early Norman work'.[92] More precisely he was inclined to link them with the period when Faricius was abbot.

But what does this tell us about Abingdon tradition on the subject of knight service? It tells us that early in the twelfth century it was believed not that quotas had been imposed by the Conqueror, but that they had existed centuries earlier. Moreover since the very next sentence in the Abingdon charter deals with bridge-work and burh-work, it suggests that our twelfth-century forger looked upon the quota as a modification of one of the three ancient public burdens, not as something radically new and different. Further, the monks of Abingdon presumably believed that if they produced their book at a meeting of the shire court then it would not be greeted by a howl of laughter and derision – which might well have been its fate if the quota had actually been introduced within the memory of some of those attending that court.

Finally, it would be strange if quotas did not exist before 1066. In recent years we have learnt more and more about the value of placing England in a wider

---

[90] *Chronicon*, i, 25–27. But by contrast there is no good evidence for a pre-conquest quota at Worcester. The tenth-century 'shipful' of sixty men due from the triple hundred of Oswaldslow was not the same thing as the Worcester twelfth-century *servicium debitum* of 60. This has frequently been pointed out, for example by C. Dyer, *Lords and Peasants in a Changing Society. The Estates of the Bishopric of Worcester, 680–1540*, Cambridge 1980, 39–50. It remains possible, however, that the 'shipful' served as the base on which a quota was later negotiated.

[91] Maitland, *Domesday Book and Beyond*, 348.

[92] Faricius was abbot 1100–1117. See Stenton, *Early History*, 9–23. I owe Pauline Stafford a debt of thanks for her help with the problems posed by the chronicle and its charters. For further clarification we must await John Hudson's forthcoming edition.

European context.[93] That quotas existed in Normandy before the accession of Duke William has been accepted ever since Haskins wrote and both Jean Yver and Donald Matthew have suggested that the military obligations underlying these quotas should be connected with Carolingian practice.[94] The full force of their arguments can best be appreciated if we turn from West to East Francia. In the Ottonian *indiculus loricatorum* of 980/81 we actually possess a list of quotas. To compare this list with the quotas which Round calculated from the pipe rolls of the 1160s is an instructive exercise. All the East Frankish bishoprics and some of the royal abbeys and nunneries owed service. Why some royal abbeys and nunneries were exempt it is hard to know but those which owed service were generally the richest and most venerable. This exactly describes the characteristics of Round's list. The numbers on the 980/81 list are all round numbers, multiples of ten, and this of course was precisely the feature of his list which first set Round's mind working. In a significant number of cases the Ottonian quota still seems to have been in force two hundred years later: the bishop of Augsburg, for example, who owed one hundred loricati in 980/81, turned up to witness the Treaty of Venice in 1177 accompanied by a retinue of one hundred knights.[95] It is also, I think, clear that in tenth-century East Francia bishops performed homage to the king but that in the twelfth century a learned German ecclesiastic like Gerhoh of Reichersberg believed that they had not done homage. In part it is a question of words. *Hominium* was a twelfth-century term; in the tenth century men talked of *manus dare*.[96] In part, of course, it is also a question of the change in attitude brought about by the Investiture Contest. Churches and new religious orders founded in the twelfth century could not be pressed into service in the way that their pre-Gregorian predecessors had been.[97]

Equally in recent years we have learnt more and more about English society before 1066. It was a society ruled by a military aristocracy; a society where if you failed to perform military service your lord might confiscate the estate

---

[93] See, in particular, J. Campbell, 'Observations on English Government from the Tenth to the Twelfth Century', *TRHS*, 5th ser. 25, 1975; J. Campbell, 'England, France, Flanders and Germany: some comparisons and connections' in *Ethelred the Unready*; J. Campbell, 'Was it Infancy in England? Some Questions of Comparison' in *England and her Neighbours, 1066–1453. Essays in honour of Pierre Chaplais*, eds. M. Jones and M. Vale, London 1989.

[94] Matthew, *The Norman Conquest*, 60–62; J. Yver, 'Les premières institutions du duché de Normandie' in *I Normanni e la loro espansione in Europa nell'alto medioevo*, Centro Italiano di Studi sull' Alto Medioevo; Settimana XVI, Spoleto 1969, 336–37.

[95] The many problems surrounding the *indiculus* have been discussed by K. F. Werner, 'Heeresorganisation and Kriegführung im deutschen Königreich des 10. und 11. Jahrhunderts', *Ordinamenti Militari*, 791–843 (reprinted in Werner, *Structures politiques du monde franc*, London 1979) and by L. Auer, 'Der Kriegsdienst des Clerus unter den sächsischen Kaisern', *Mitteilungen des Instituts für Österreichische Geschichtsforschung* 79, 1971, and 80, 1972.

[96] P. Classen, 'Das Wormser Kondordat in der deutschen Verfassungsgeschichte' in *Investiturstreit und Reichsverfassung, Vorträge und Forschungen* 17, Sigmaringen 1973, 422–31.

[97] As is well known, abbeys and bishoprics founded after 1066 do not appear in the list of *servicia debita* of Henry II's reign, Sanders, *Feudal Military Service*, 17 n. 4. And see note 74.

which you held from him; a society where lords demanded reliefs (though they called them heriots); a society where lords expected to control the marriages of the widows and daughters of their tenants:[98] in short precisely the kind of society in which a king might issue a Coronation Charter – indeed in all probability pre-conquest kings did go in for such publicity stunts.[99] This is the kind of Germanic society in which the aristocracy, both the secular and ecclesiastical aristocracy, might expect to perform royal military service and where, at times, kings might be persuaded to set a limit to the amount of service they could demand by agreeing to fix a quota. When that happened is anybody's guess. Most likely it occurred as part of a continuing process of individual bargains struck over a very long period of time. It may be that in that bargaining process rules of thumb like 'five hides make a knight' had some sort of rôle to play.[100] But what almost certainly did not happen is that knight service and knightly quotas were both introduced during the course of a revolutionary military re-organisation carried out by William the Conqueror. This is not to argue that the direct political and social consequences of the conquest were not massive. They were. But a new royal family, a new ruling class, a new language and a new culture could all be imposed without the introduction of any new principle of military tenure.

POSTSCRIPT

This paper was originally given at Battle in 1981, i.e. at an early meeting of the series of conferences established by the late Allen Brown. It was character-istically kind of Allen that he should have allowed views which were anathema to him to be ventilated at what was then very much his own conference. Since then – somewhat to my surprise and even chagrin – I have failed to notice any detailed rebuttal. Of course this may have been primarily because sensible people were weary of the old debate. The paper given by J. C. Holt at Battle in 1983, entitled 'The Introduction of Knight-Service in England' (*Anglo-Norman Studies* 6, 1983; reprinted in J. C. Holt, *Colonial England 1066–1215*, London 1997), concentrated on developments during the century following the conquest and left untouched the question of whether or not there had been quotas before 1066. Marjorie Chibnall remained convinced that in pre-conquest England 'the basis for calculating obligations remained territorial rather than personal' and that a post-conquest imposition of knight service 'introduced new concepts as

---

[98] Brooks, 'Arms, Status', 81–97; Maitland, *Domesday Book and Beyond*, 348–49, 360, 364–65, 369.
[99] See the ingenious piece of detective work by P. Stafford, 'The laws of Cnut and the history of Anglo-Saxon royal promises', *Anglo-Saxon England* 10, 1981.
[100] On this and similar rules of thumb see J. C. Holt, 'The Carta of Richard de la Haye, 1166: a note on "continuity" in Anglo-Norman feudalism', *EHR* 84, 1969.

well as new men' (*Anglo-Norman England 1066–1166*, Oxford 1986, pp. 29, 33). However in a book on post-conquest England there had been no room for detailed consideration of the evidence relating to earlier centuries. Soon afterwards this was provided in the full-length study by Richard Abels, who shared my doubts about the universality of the five-hide unit before 1066 and concluded that 'throughout the Anglo-Saxon period each warrior fought not as a freeman defending the nation or the "folk", as many have assumed, but as a commended man serving his lord. Land entered into this system only obliquely', *Lordship and Military Obligation in Anglo-Saxon England*, London 1988, 184, 253. Most recent work has been strongly influenced by Abels' analysis of the pre-1066 material, see, e.g., the discussion by Stephen Morillo, *Warfare under the Anglo-Norman Kings 1066–1135*, Woodbridge 1994, 22–28, 55. Thus Brian Golding, considering the case of 'those pre-conquest abbeys which had settled thegns on estates in return for service' accepts that 'it is likely, to put it no more strongly, that they knew a quota' , *Conquest and Colonisation. The Normans in Britain 1066–1100*, London 1994, 135–36. As Michael Prestwich noted, 'the topic of military obligation in the Anglo-Saxon period is a topic more prickly than the spears of a fourteenth-century Scotttish schiltrom' but he concluded 'that a lord in receipt of an individual summons would most probably have attended the king with an armed following appropriate to his rank, rather than one carefully calculated at one fifth of the number of hides he held. If Anglo-Saxon armies are thought of in this way, then there was not perhaps so much of a contrast with the methods introduced by the Normans after the conquest', *Armies and Warfare in the Middle Ages: the English Experience*, New Haven 1996, 58–62. Most recently Judith Green has observed 'Quotas may not have been novel: there may well have been similar bargains between kings and leading laymen and ecclesiastics about the numbers of men to be provided before 1066', *The Aristocracy of Norman England*, Cambridge 1997, 225.

In looking at 1066 and the question of 'the introduction of feudalism' in the context of an immensely wide-ranging comparative study Susan Reynolds came to the conclusion that 'the chief reason for looking for immediate and systematic change is the difficulty of abandoning a long and learned historio-graphical tradition', *Fiefs and Vassals*, Oxford 1994, 350–51. The traditional view continues to be upheld by George Garnett, though with a new twist. For him it is an essential part of his theory that the concept of the 'crown' was first used soon after the conquest and not, as one might have thought, to refer to royal authority in *all* its elements, but to 'encapsulate the innovations in royal power introduced at the Conquest'. His belief that these innovations included a new form of tenure which meant that from then on men became bishops and abbots only after they had done homage to the king is a belief which requires that *servitia debita* should be a post-conquest phenomenon, Garnett, 'The Origins of the Crown' in ed. J. Hudson, *The History of English Law. Centenary Essays on 'Pollock and Maitland'*, *Proceedings of the British Academy* 89, 1996, 173–80.

There is no doubt that Round's argument is further weakened by the doubts

– unresolved, and probably unresolvable (see above, p. 195 n. 40) – now surrounding the Evesham writ on which he placed so much weight. In view of all this it speaks volumes for Yorkshire grit that in a paper first published in 1997 J. C. Holt can retain both Round's doctrine and its date in stating that, 'the church was subjected to the new burden of knight-service within six years of the conquest', *Colonial England, 1066–1215*, 5.

12

1066 and the Introduction of Chivalry into England

J. C. Holt began his first presidential address to the Royal Historical Society, a paper on 'The Revolution of 1066', with the chivalrous tale of how King Stephen spared the life of young William Marshal.[1] Stephen was undoubtedly a chivalrous king. As Samuel Daniel, the first great English historian of the middle ages observed with the astonishment natural to an observer looking back from the standpoint of the early seventeenth century, his reign was remarkable for the fact that though he 'had his sword continually out, and so many defections and rebellions against him, he never put any great man to death'.[2] Indeed it was chivalry which made the civil war virtually unwinnable for Stephen since it meant that he was unable to treat his female rival in the way he would have dealt with a man. When the Empress was within his grasp as she was at Arundel in 1139, instead of imprisoning her, he let her go. But, as Marjorie Chibnall pointed out, Stephen's action was far from being either a 'mistake' or the quirky behaviour of an amiable individual.[3] Not even the ruthless Henry I had been able to bring himself to keep a child in prison, despite the eminently foreseeable problems which would – and did – arise when William Clito grew up. In the early twelfth century there were conventions of chivalrous conduct which prudent kings dared not flout.

In this paper I propose to argue that a little noticed aspect of the revolution of 1066 was the introduction of chivalry into England. So I had better say at once that what I mean by chivalry is not what twelfth century authors meant by 'chevalerie', i.e. I do not mean either a company of knights, or the hard-won skills of a warrior on horseback. What I have in mind is chivalry in the sense of a secular code of values, and – more precisely – a code in which a key element was the attempt to limit the brutality of conflict by treating prisoners, at any rate when they were men of 'gentle' birth, in a relatively humane fashion. I suggest that the compassionate

---

[1] J. C. Holt, 'Feudal Society and the Family in Early Medieval England: I. The Revolution of 1066', *TRHS*, 5th series XXXII (1982), 193.

I owe a considerable debt of thanks to the Leverhulme Trust for providing the time for what thought lies behind this paper; I am also very grateful to Jinty Nelson and the members of our seminar at the Institute of Historical Research for their helpful comments on an earlier version of this paper.
[2] Samuel Daniel, *The Collection of the Historie of England* (London, 1618), p. 67.
[3] M. Chibnall, *The Empress Matilda* (Oxford, 1991), p. 81.

treatment of defeated high-status enemies is a defining characteristic of chivalry –
and entirely compatible with very different treatment being meted out to people
regarded as low-status.[4] After all, in all societies dominated by military aristocracies and in which army commanders were expected to lead from the front, there
was bound to be a certain camaraderie and a code of values common to the great
aristocrats and their armed companions: values such as admiration for courage,
loyalty, largesse and for prowess both on foot and on horseback. The sense of
honour which linked men who shared these values can be seen, for example, as
early as the days of Bede. I think of Imma, *de militia iuvenis*, a prisoner freed so that
he could arrange for his ransom and who swore to return to captivity if he failed to
raise the money.[5] So it is certainly not surprising that ideologies of knighthood
have been found in ninth century Francia.[6] But it is my contention that these age-
old value systems became a code of chivalry when kings and aristocrats came to
place a high value on the merciful treatment of those of their fellows who were at
their mercy. A new reluctance to kill or mutilate each other would suggest that
nobles were beginning to value their bodies in new ways. So also, from a very
different angle, would the chivalrous notion, inconceivable – as is often said – in
the world of *Beowulf*, that the state of being in love was likely to make a knight more
valiant and more courteous.[7]

I shall consider two separate, but potentially related, spheres of conflict: the
blood feud and the rebellion (the latter commonly either a succession dispute or
closely linked with one). Societies in which secular nobles regarded the blood
feud as acceptable were, on my definition, unchivalrous since the conventions
governing the blood feud seem to have allowed protagonists to seize their
enemies unarmed and unawares, for example when asleep or at mealtimes, and
then to kill or mutilate them.[8] Equally unchivalrous were those societies in

---

[4] There was, in Hollister's words, 'a pervasive . . . sense of class distinction: to mutilate poor
thieves was a very different matter than to blind the count of Mortain'. C. W. Hollister,
'Royal Acts of Mutilation: the Case against Henry I', *Albion* X (1978), 338.

[5] Bede, *Ecclesiastical History of the English People*, ed. B. Colgrave and R. A. B. Mynors (Oxford,
1969) IV, c. 22, pp. 400–404.

[6] Notably by two authors who both chose the word 'knighthood', not 'chivalry', to indicate
the phenomenon they were observing: K. Leyser, 'Early Medieval Canon Law and the
Beginnings of Knighthood' in *Institutionen, Kultur und Gesellschaft im Mittelalter. Festschrift für
Josef Fleckenstein*, ed. L. Fenske, W. Rösener and T. Zotz (Sigmaringen, 1984), pp. 549–66,
and by J. L. Nelson, 'Ninth-century Knighthood: the Evidence of Nithard' in *Studies in
Medieval History Presented to R. Allen Brown*, ed. C. Harper-Bill, C. Holdsworth and J. L.
Nelson (Woodbridge, 1989), pp. 255–66.

[7] M. Keen, *Chivalry* (New Haven, 1984), pp. 13, 30–31, 116–17. For some comments on
developments which may have led to a heightened awareness of sex amongst the
aristocracy of this period, J. Gillingham, 'Love, Marriage and Politics in the Twelfth
Century', *Forum for Modern Language Studies* XXV (1989), 292–303; reprinted in Gillingham,
Richard Coeur de Lion (London, 1994).

[8] For a twentieth-century example of an 'honourable' but apparently underhand vengeance
killing see J. K. Campbell, *Honour, Family and Patronage. A Study of Institutions and Moral Values
in a Greek Mountain Community* (Oxford, 1964), p. 196. The discussion by P. H. Sawyer, 'The

which kings, would-be kings and their aristocratic supporters were executed, murdered or mutilated. Although the evidence suggests that such conduct was frowned on by some people, notably churchmen, it also suggests that such conduct could bring significant political gains, in other words was regarded as acceptable by men of the world. Thus cults of murdered royal saints existed precisely because it had been left up to God to prosecute the feud on their behalf; in this world their killers had reaped the rewards.[9] A further advantage of emphasising the humane treatment of rebels as a critically important ingredient of chivalry is that this definition, as will become plain, creates room for an old chestnut which has been in danger of being discarded, the notion of a late medieval 'decline of chivalry'. However, setting such speculative matters aside for now, in this paper I wish to do no more than show first, that the Normandy of 1066 was a more chivalrous society than late Anglo-Saxon England, and second, that after the conquest political mores in England came to be distinctly more chivalrous than they had been before 1066.[10]

To start with Normandy. In the twenty years or so after c.1025 we know – if we can trust Orderic Vitalis – of at least eight named men who were murdered and one who was mutilated. Gouhier de Bellême was taken unawares and decapitated; Walter de Surdon and two of his sons were taken prisoner and hanged by William fitzGiroie; in revenge his surviving sons took axes to Giroie's lord, Robert de Bellême, and butchered him 'like a pig'. Robert's brother, William de Bellême, subsequently invited William fitzGiroie to his wedding, where he cropped his ears, blinded and castrated him. Then there were the conflicts which seem to have focused around control of the boy duke. Count Gilbert de Brionne, Turold, and Osbern were assassinated. Osbern's steward, Barno de Glos, then took revenge on his master's murderers, William of Montgomery and his accomplices, by killing them while they were asleep.[11]

The standard view of Norman history is that the 'anarchy' of William's minority was followed by a period of good order imposed by the stern rule of the adult duke, but that after his death Normandy relapsed into anarchy again. This is how Orderic describes the duchy under the rule of Robert Curthose:

Bloodfeud in Fact and Fiction' in *Tradition og Historie-Skrivining*, Acta Jutlandica LXIII:2, Humanistik serie 61 (Aarhus, n.d.), seems to me at times to distinguish too sharply between a bloodfeud and a political dispute. For elaboration of this see the Postscript to this essay.
[9] D. W. Rollason, 'The Cults of Murdered Royal Saints in Anglo-Saxon England', *ASE* XI (1983), 14. Presumably a similar explanation lies behind the early take-off of the cults of Simon de Montfort and Thomas of Lancaster.
[10] In similar fashion Matthew Strickland argues that the Norman Conquest witnessed the introduction of conventions which avoided killing in battle on the scale which had been habitual in Anglo-Scandinavian warfare. 'Slaughter, Slavery or Ransom: the Impact of the Conquest on Conduct in Warfare' in *England in the Eleventh Century*, ed. C. Hicks (Stamford, 1992), pp. 41–59.
[11] *Orderic* II, 14, 28, 120; III, 88; IV, 82; VI, 396–98. Also Orderic's interpolations in *GND* VI c. 7, VII c. 10 – cited in this manner to facilitate reference to both *Guillaume de Jumièges, Gesta Normannorum Ducum*, ed. J. Marx (Rouen, 1914) and *The Gesta Normannorum Ducum of William of Jumièges, Orderic Vitalis and Robert of Torigni*, ed. and trans. E. Van Houts (Oxford, 1992–95).

The whole province was in disorder; troops of bandits were at large in the villages and all over the countryside, and robber bands pillaged the weak mercilessly. Duke Robert made no attempt to bring the malefactors to justice, and for eight years under the weak duke scoundrels were free to treat the innocent with the utmost brutality. . . . As these outrages spread like a plague no honour or reverence was shown to consecrated persons or things. Crimes of arson, rapine and murder were committed daily and the wretched population bewailed its unspeakable misfortunes. Sons of iniquity rose to power in Normandy, ready and eager for all evil-doing, and cruelly devoured the bowels of their mother . . . want, disorder and shame abounded.[12]

I might have quoted any one of a dozen other passages to the same effect for the disorder in Normandy after 1087 is one of Orderic's main themes. In several passages he heightens the impression of savagery by heated condemnation of Robert de Bellême as a sadistic torturer.[13] Yet if we look to see what facts Orderic adduces in support of his rhetoric, then it becomes clear that he has very few concrete details or names to report. What we are given is propaganda – propaganda needed to justify a whole series of dishonourable actions on Henry's part: for example, the arrest of his brother during the latter's visit to the English court in 1103[14]; the attack on Normandy (undeniably his brother's

[12] *Orderic* IV, 146–8. This theme which runs through volumes IV (especially pp. 110–286) and VI (especially pp. 24–96) can also be found in III, 106 and V, 24, 300–302. It has been claimed that Orderic's rhetoric is 'amply proved by the more prosaic narrative of the nuns of La Trinité of Caen', C. W. David, *Robert Curthose* (Cambridge, Mass., 1920), p. 79, following C. H. Haskins, *Norman Institutions* (New York, 1918), pp. 62f. But for a very favourable view of Robert as a good lord and a model of *chevalerie*, see Geffrei Gaimar, *L'Estoire des Engleis*, ed. A. Bell (Oxford, 1960), lines 5737–44. Some popular support for Robert is implied by the name given, according to Orderic, to the reward received by those who 'betrayed' Caen to Henry I in 1105: 'Traitors' manor', *Orderic* VI, 78. See also *Le Roman de Rou de Wace*, ed. A. J. Holden (Paris, 1971) II, 303 and the observation by David Bates that although no modern commentator has dissented from Orderic's judgement on Robert's character, the duke's real problem may have been that he was severely outweighed financially, 'Normandy and England after 1066', *EHR* CIV (1989), 868.
[13] *Orderic* IV, 158–60, 170, 226, 298; V, 226, 234, 300; VI, 30, 34, 62. For a different view of Robert of Bellême see 'Co ert le meillur chevaler, Ke l'em seust pur guerreier', Gaimar, lines 5881–2, and below, p. 249. For a more detached view, K. Thompson, 'Robert of Bellême Reconsidered', *ANS* XIII (1991), 263–84; also idem, 'Orderic Vitalis and Robert of Bellême', *JMH* 20 (1994), 133–41.
[14] David, *Curthose*, p. 148 and *Le Roman de Rou* II, 277–83. In this respect modern historians have treated Henry I very kindly, especially compared with their censure of Stephen – such are the penalties of failure. But it is clear that Henry had no compunction about arresting people at court, 'multos proditione cepit', as Henry of Huntingdon put it, *Henry Archdeacon of Huntingdon, Historia Anglorum*, ed. D. Greenway (Oxford, 1996), pp. 604–5 [311] – the page number in square brackets refers to Arnold's 1879 RS edition. For one such case see *Liber monasterii de Hyda*, ed. E. Edwards (RS, 1886), p. 313; comparison of this account with *Orderic* VI, 190 shows how much Orderic favoured Henry.

patrimony); the life-long imprisonment of Curthose[15]; and the arrest of Robert de Bellême while the latter was under safe-conduct. This was conduct which drew down upon Henry criticism from both the pope and the king of France.[16] Essentially Orderic was accepting Henry I's defence to the case against him.

But for all the troubles which Orderic insists beset Normandy between 1087 and 1106, and in sharp contrast to the outbreak of vendetta killings early in the 11th century, not a single aristocrat was murdered during this 'second anarchy'. Some were certainly killed during the course of feuding – Orderic names six – but to judge fron his own account, they were all killed in combat.[17] Orderic's comments on two of the deaths are especially interesting. Of Richard de Montfort he says that his killing (c.1091) was 'greatly mourned by men on both sides'. Of the killing of Gilbert fitzEngenulf (probably 1091), he says that it was 'to the great grief even of those who had done the deed' and that their lord, Geoffrey count of Mortagne 'considering that his men had committed a serious crime' made peace and 'with the sweetness of a marriage alliance stifled the evil that had been sown'. These feuds were property disputes waged with violence, but violence controlled so as not to escalate into the blood feud. Between these two twenty year periods of political anarchy aristocratic opinion in Normandy had turned against the blood feud.[18] This development has been obscured by the resounding phrases of Orderic's anti-Curthose rhetoric. In this context a decree issued by William in 1075, limiting the vendetta by proclaiming that only a father or a son of the victim was entitled to take vengeance, was clearly a milestone along the way.[19]

[15] When William of Malmesbury completed the first version of his *Gesta Regum* he was left wondering whether or not Robert would ever be released, but as Stubbs pointed out, there was little that it was safe to say about Henry I during his lifetime. It is clear, for example, that when William began writing he was not at all sure how emphatically he could condemn kings for murdering their kin, William of Malmesbury, *De Gestis Regum Anglorum*, ed. W. Stubbs, 2 vols. (RS, 1887–9) i. xxxvi. The relevant passages are in cc. 12 and 39. I shall cite this work as WM and by chapter number as the most economical way of referring to both Stubbs's edition and to the *Gesta Regum Anglorum* vol. 1, ed. and trans. R. A. B. Mynors, R. M. Thomson and M. Winterbottom (Oxford, 1998).

[16] *Orderic* VI, 256; WM c. 406. See above p. 52. According to Suger when Louis VI was on his death-bed he made his heir promise not to arrest at court. However when Louis attacked his own brother Philip, it is noticeable that Suger justified this by employing themes similar to Orderic's. Suger, *Vie de Louis VI le Gros*, ed. and trans. H. Waquet (Paris, 1929), pp. 124, 274.

[17] *Orderic* IV, 200–202 (Amaury de Montfort and Gilbert fitzEngenulf), 210 (Gilbert du Pin), 214–16 (Richard de Montfort), 232 (Theobald son of Waleran and Guy the Red). The unnamed defenders of an unnamed castle were slaughtered by Reginald de Grancey, *Orderic* VI, 44. Reginald, however, had taken the castle by storm, see below, n. 72.

[18] As things turned out, even the c.1077 murder of Mabel Talvas precipitated not a vengeance killing but a trial by ordeal – though Orderic believed the desire for vengeance was still there and portrays it as a close-run thing, hardly surprising in the circumstances. He also believed that Richard de Montfort had wanted to avenge Amaury's death and asserted that, in Stephen's reign, a revenge killing followed the death of Roger le vicomte. *Orderic* III, 136, 160–62, IV, 200, VI, 512–14.

[19] Haskins, *Norman Institutions*, p. 278. D. Bates, *William the Conqueror* (London, 1989), p. 154,

Just conceivably aristocratic society in early eleventh century Normandy was not so vendetta-bound as Orderic makes it appear. He may have been exaggerating. Long ago social anthropologists identified 'the peace in the feud' and argued that many such bloodcurdling stories were not so much about actual feuds in the past as about keeping the peace in the present. 'We must not take sagas and tales of feuding as evidence, for they may, like the tales of the Nuer "man of the earth's" curse, stand as warnings.'[20] All we know from William of Jumièges is that Gilbert, Turold and Osbern were killed, not how they were killed.[21] However, if Orderic was exaggerating, this would mean that eleventh century aristocratic Normandy was more peaceful than I have indicated, and though this would necessitate some changes to the argument, they are changes which would strengthen it by heightening the contrast between England and Normandy.

Although Orderic generally presents William as an awesomely stern and ruthless ruler, he occasionally shows him in more merciful mood. If we believe William of Poitiers, this is how he was all the time, and never more so than in his treatment of rebels. When Guy de Brionne submitted, William did not punish him as severely as he could have – says William of Poitiers –, nor did he sentence any of Guy's fellow conspirators to death as they deserved. During his account of the rebellion of William of Arques, he pauses to assert that the duke did not behave like other princes in killing prisoners of war or exacting the death penalty even when entitled to do so by custom or established law (*iuxta ritum sive legum instituta*). When the count of Arques surrendered, he was accordingly treated with what William of Poitiers calls 'praiseworthy clemency'.[22] William's determination to praise the duke to the skies probably accounts for the fact that he nowhere gives any sign of acknowledging that previous dukes of Normandy, Richard II, Richard III and Robert, also seem to have treated rebels in similar fashion.[23] By the time William became duke, it was already Norman custom that,

links it with the policy begun with the Truce of God promulgated in 1047. Although violence between aristocrat and aristocrat does not appear to come very high on the agenda of the promoters of the peace movement, Glaber did perceive the Truce as an attempt to limit *ultionis vindictam*, *Rodulfus Glaber Opera*, ed. J. France et al. (Oxford, 1989), pp. 236–8.

[20] M. Gluckman, *Custom and Conflict in Africa* (Oxford, 1965), p. 22. But, he continues, stories of real feuds such as that between the Hatfields and McCoys in the Kentucky and Virginia hills may have been better warnings.

[21] *GND*, VII c. 1. But it is clear that William, writing probably in the 1050s (see Van Houts, xxxii–xxxv), felt the need to be discreet. This suggests deeds of which he at least could not approve.

[22] WP I cc. 9, 25, 28 – citation by Book and chapter as the most economical way of referring to both *Guillaume de Poitiers, Histoire de Guillaume le Conquérant*, ed. R. Foreville (Paris, 1952), and *The Gesta Guillelmi of William of Poitiers*, ed. and trans. R. H. C. Davis and M. Chibnall (Oxford, 1998); cf. *GND*, VII c. 7.

[23] *GND*, V c. 3, VI cc. 2–4. *GND*, V c. 14 could be read to suggest that William believed that if not dukes then at least kings should hang traitors – and their wives. But in this case the traitors had refused to surrender Melun when called upon to do so, see below, p. 225. Duke

although aristocratic rebels might be exiled or have their estates confiscated, their lives and limbs were spared. In the context of 1066 it is clearly important to consider William's first conquest, the conquest of Maine. Here too the duke's enemies were regarded as rebels, at least according to William of Poitiers. Even so, the panegyrist assures us, William adopted a strategy of conquest which was intended not to punish them, but to minimise bloodshed; throughout the war for Maine he was satisfied by the submission of his opponents.[24]

Turning to England before 1066, it is clear that here high-status political opponents who fell into the king's hands were not always so lucky. According to the *Vita Edwardi*, had Godwin and his sons been caught in 1051, they would have been killed.[25] That this was not merely a rhetorical flight on the part of the *Vita's* author is suggested by the following cases. In 1016 Earl Uhtred of Northumbria submitted to Cnut and gave hostages; he was none the less killed.[26] John of Worcester gives a vivid picture of the frenzy of intrigue, murders and executions that followed the death of Edmund Ironside; in 1017 at least five members of the highest nobility were put to death.[27] In 1036 the atheling Alfred was so badly mutilated that he soon died.[28] In 1041 Hardacnut 'betrayed Earl Eadwulf under his safe-conduct' and the earl was killed. In December 1064 Queen Edith had Gospatric, one of Tostig's enemies, tricked and killed at court.[29] Similarly the record of Æthelred's reign, even setting aside the uncertain dimensions of the massacre of St Brice's day, had been a bloody one. In 993 Æthelred blinded Ælfgar. In 1006 he had Ælfhelm's sons blinded after Ælfhelm himself had been put to death by his new chief minister Eadric Streona; and in 1015 king and minister again co-operated in 'basely' killing the 'chief thegns of the Seven Boroughs'.[30] The history of Æthelred's reign does not suggest that

---

William 'the Great' of Aquitaine was also praised for sparing life and limb, Adémar de Chabannes, *Chronique*, ed. J. Chavanon (Paris, 1897), p. 208.

[24] WP I cc. 38–40, including clemency shown to Geoffrey de Mayenne, and followed in WM c. 232.

[25] *The Life of King Edward the Confessor*, ed. F. Barlow, 2nd edn (London, 1992), p. 36. Cf. *vix evadentes* of the outlaws of 1052, *The Chronicle of John of Worcester*, vol. 2, ed. and trans. R. R. Darlington and P. McGurk (Oxford, 1995), p. 570.

[26] JW, 482; *Symeonis Monachi Opera Omnia*, ed. T. Arnold, 2 vols. (RS, 1882–5), I, 218 (henceforth SD); F. M. Stenton, *Anglo-Saxon England*, 3rd edn (Oxford, 1971), p. 390; W. E. Kapelle, *The Norman Conquest of the North* (London, 1979), pp. 17–20.

[27] JW, 494, 502–5. See R. Fleming, *Kings and Lords in Conquest England* (Cambridge, 1991), chapter 2, entitled 'Cnut's Conquest and the Destruction of the Royal Kindred'. But there were limits. The author of the *Encomium* as well as John of Worcester believed that Cnut wanted Edmund's young sons eliminated but sent them abroad so as to avoid being branded a child murderer, *Encomium Emmae*, ed. A. Campbell, Camden Society, 3rd ser. LXXII (1949), p. 30.

[28] *ASC*, s.a. 1036; *Encomium*, p. 43. See S. Keynes, 'The Aethelings in Normandy', *ANS* XIII (1991), 195–6.

[29] *ASC*, s.a. 1041; SD II, 198; JW, 598.

[30] *ASC*, s.a. 993, 1002, 1006, 1015. John of Worcester blames the 'treacherous' Eadric for the murders of 1006 and 1015, JW, 456–8, 478–80. See S. Keynes, 'A Tale of Two Kings',

lamentations over the murder of King Edward in 978 led to any diminution of political bloodshed. Late Anglo-Saxon England was still a society in which the power struggles between royal dynasties often ended bloodily, both for the royals themselves and for their aristocratic companions. Clearly the creation of a single English kingdom diminished the number of potential succession disputes. But there is some evidence that Athelstan may have shed royal blood in establishing himself on the throne and there can be no doubt at all that two kings, Edmund and Edward the Martyr, were murdered during the course of the tenth century.[31] Despite many important changes since the seventh and eighth centuries, the 'barbarian, iron-age strain' which Geoffrey Barrow observed in the monarchies of Scandinavia and the British Isles was still there in pre-conquest England.[32]

What is important in this context is that both William of Jumièges and William of Poitiers perceived English politics as peculiarly savage. In one highly rhetorical passage the latter addresses England directly: *tu Anglica terra*. 'Did not Cnut most cruelly slaughter your noblest sons, both young and old, in order to force you to submit to him and his sons?'[33] They exploited this perception in order to explain or justify invasion. William of Jumièges envisaged Swein's invasion of England as revenge for the massacre of St Brice's day.[34] 1066 was explicitly presented as due retribution for the shedding of innocent blood in 1036 when, to secure the throne for Cnut's son Harold, Godwin had committed that most foul of deeds, the betrayal, murder and mutilation of Alfred and his followers.[35] Like his father, Harold Godwinsson was portrayed by William of Poitiers as a cruel killer (*truculentus homicida*). In the oration to his troops before Hastings, William tells his men that if defeated they will either be slaughtered or at the mercy of the cruellest of enemies.[36]

TRHS, 5th ser. XXXVI (1986), 211–16. Although the extant narrative sources critical of the king and his minister were composed after the reign's catastrophic end, it is certainly possible that a reputation for cruelty had contributed to Æthelred's problems.

[31] SD II, 124, Athelstan ordered his brother to be drowned; but see Stenton, *ASE*, pp. 355–6. For the moment William of Malmesbury's account of Athelstan's reign remains out of bounds, D. Dumville, *Wessex and England from Alfred to Edgar* (Woodbridge, 1992), pp. 142, 146, 150, 168.

[32] G. W. S. Barrow, *Kingship and Unity. Scotland 1000–1306* (London, 1981), p. 24. If the killing of Rufus was another of Henry I's misdeeds, then the development I am sketching here would have to be modified, but in outline would still stand.

[33] WP I c. 2, II c. 32.

[34] *GND* V, 6; cf. WM c. 177

[35] WP I cc. 3–4; *GND* VII, cc. 6, 16. If WJ and WP used a common source, as suggested by R. H. C. Davis, 'William of Poitiers and his History of William the Conqueror' in *The Writing of History in the Middle Ages*, ed. R. H. C. Davis and J. M. Wallace-Hadrill (Oxford, 1981), p. 79, then, as Foreville showed (*Guillaume de Poitiers*, pp. xxxi–xxxv), it would have included an account of Alfred's ill-fated expedition. Was this drafted by Lanfranc? See G. Garnett, 'Coronation and Propaganda: some Implications of the Norman Claim to the Throne of England in 1066', *TRHS*, 5th ser. XXXVI (1986), 111.

[36] WP II cc. 8, 15; cf. Strickland, 'Slaughter, Slavery or Ransom', p. 59. Orderic presents

William the Conqueror, of course, behaved very differently – or so his panegyrist insists on telling us. Although the English who supported Harold were, like the men of Maine, rebels and therefore deserved death, they were, he says, treated mercifully. Having won the battle of Hastings, William was entitled to slaughter and exile the defeated magnates (*potentes*) and to licence his soldiers to loot the country. But he preferred to move with greater moderation and to impose his rule more mercifully (*clementius dominari*).[37] Much of this is patently untrue. The land was plundered and many of the English elite were driven into exile. On the other hand William does seem to have pursued a policy of sparing the lives and limbs of the leaders of the English resistance movement. It would be naive in the extreme to believe this simply on the strength of the word of an author as sycophantic as William of Poitiers. But the famous character sketch of the Conqueror contained in the Peterborough Chronicle's entry for 1087 tells us, not once but twice, how stern he was to those who resisted his will. According to the longer of these passages: 'He was a very stern and violent man, so that no one dared do anything contrary to his will. He had earls in his fetters who acted against his will. He expelled bishops from their sees, and abbots from their abbacies, and put thegns in prison.'[38] Given the impression this author intended to convey, it is clear that English aristocrats did not pay for their opposition with either life or limb. It seems indeed that William was willing to be reconciled even with guerilla leaders like Eadric the Wild and possibly Hereward.[39] Still more striking is the degree of freedom he allowed his principal rival for the throne, Edgar the Atheling. However young Edgar was in 1066, by 1069 certainly, and by 1068 probably, he was old enough to be making trouble. Yet in 1075, after years of fomenting rebellion, he was again received at court and remained there, if without much honour, until 1086.[40] Here there is a

---

Harold as a fratricide, as does the author of the 'Hyde' chronicle, also, I suspect, writing in Normandy, *Orderic* II, 170, Hyde, pp. 291–3.

[37] WP II cc. 18, 26; and cc. 33–5 for further instances of William's merciful treatment of the English. Cf. WM c. 254, contrast *Orderic* IV, 94.

[38] *ASC*, s.a. 1087. On date and authorship see C. Clark, *The Peterborough Chronicle 1070–1154*, 2nd edn (Oxford, 1970), pp. xxii–xxiv. Orderic regards the imprisonment of Morcar as unjust, IV, 96, while Gaimar (lines 5695–5704) expresses the view that he, and others, would have been better off if they had been killed.

[39] Florence of Worcester, *Chronicon ex Chronicis*, ed. B. Thorpe, 2 vols. (London, 1848–9) II, 7 (henceforth FW). According to the *Gesta Herwardi*, William himself was very happy to be reconciled with Hereward – unlike some of his followers, *Lestorie des Engleis*, ed. T. D. Hardy and C. T. Martin (RS, 1888) I, 397–9, 403–4. Cf. Gaimar, lines 5598–5630. For comment see J. Hayward, 'Hereward the Outlaw', *JMH* XIV (1988), 301, and D. Rollason, *Saints and Relics in Anglo-Saxon England* (Oxford, 1989), p. 220. For an important study of the *Gesta Herewardi* as a text showing just how chivalrous the English were, see Hugh Thomas, 'The *Gesta Herwardi*, the English, and their Conquerors', *ANS* 21 (1999).

[40] N. Hooper, 'Edgar the Aetheling: Anglo-Saxon prince, rebel and crusader', *ASE* XIV (1986), 197–214. William's biographers have generally been content to observe that his treatment of Edgar shows that he 'could be forgiving towards defeated enemies', D. C. Douglas, *William the Conqueror* (London, 1964), p. 375, Bates, *William the Conqueror*, p. 95.

contrast not only with Cnut's treatment of rival claimants but with all previous Anglo-Saxon practice.

The one exception to William's policy of clemency is the execution of Earl Waltheof. Conceivably William of Poitiers was writing before Waltheof's death in 1076[41], but even if he had known of it he could easily have explained it in terms which exonerated his hero. For, as Orderic puts it when recounting this episode, 'The law of England punishes the traitor (*traditorem*) by beheading.' The leading Norman in the 1075 rebellion, Roger of Hereford, was not executed but condemned to prison and this, Orderic says, was 'according to the laws of the Normans'.[42] Thus William would doubtless have explained that as an Englishman Waltheof was punished by the cruel English law imposed against his natural and better instincts by a soft-hearted Norman ruler. Waltheof, after all, had submitted in 1066 and been recognised as earl; had rebelled in 1069, apparently distinguishing himself by the number of Normans he killed at York, then submitted again in 1070 and was given William's niece in marriage as well as being made earl of Northumbria. When Waltheof got involved in the revolt of 1075, the king had reason to think that his generosity had been abused.[43]

Moreover there was another way in which by 1075 Waltheof's record might have been perceived as a bad one. In 1073 he had dispatched a band of his lads (*iuvenes*) to Settrington near York and there they killed the sons and grandsons of Carl while the latter were sitting down to a meal. Waltheof was avenging the death of his grandfather, Ealdred, killed by Carl.[44] It was the last act in the most famous blood feud in Anglo-Saxon history – atrocious behaviour by the standards of the civilised Frenchmen of the 1070s. Other actions of the natives which the conquerors might well have thought barbarous were the 1067 attack on Copsige, attacked by Oswulf while feasting, and decapitated.[45] Also the death

---

Chibnall has suggested that sparing Edgar was – as it may have been – an astonishingly astute tactical move, *Anglo-Norman England 1066–1166* (Oxford, 1986), pp. 18–19. Whatever William's motives in this particular case may have been, my point is that his treatment of Edgar fits into a Norman pattern of politics which is about to become an English one.

[41] Davis, 'William of Poitiers', p. 74.

[42] *Orderic* II, 314, 318. Other unnamed rebels were mutilated, II, 316, as also in 1071, II, 228.

[43] WM c. 253 on Waltheof's prowess at York. Despite this, in Orderic's and John of Worcester's eyes he was unjustly executed, *Orderic* II, 344, FW II, 12. B. J. Levy's interpretation of the Hyde chronicler's account of Waltheof – 'a second Absalom' – and of his execution is based on the unlikely assumption that it was written at Hyde Abbey, 'Waltheof "Earl" de Huntingdon et de Northampton: la naissance d'un heros anglo-normand', *Cahiers de Civilisation Médiévale* XVIII (1975), 190. For the argument that it was written in Normandy see above, pp. 142–4. For other interpretations of Waltheof in 1073–76, see F. S. Scott, 'Earl Waltheof of Northumbria', *Archaeologia Aeliana*, 4th ser. XXX (1952), 193–212 and Kapelle, pp. 134–7.

[44] SD I, 219. On this see C. R. Hart, *The Early Charters of Northern England and the North Midlands* (Leicester, 1975), pp. 143–50. D. Whitelock, *The Beginnings of English Society* (Harmondsworth, 1952), pp. 44–5.

[45] WP II c. 48. According to the *Historia Regum*, Copsige was forced out of a church by fire

of Earl Edwin in 1071, killed according to the D and E chronicles, 'by his own men'. According to Orderic, here presumably following William of Poitiers, when the traitors brought Edwin's head to William, he was moved to tears and, instead of rewarding them, he exiled them.[46] Perhaps Edwin's killers had been expecting the kind of reward presumably given by Edward the Confessor to those who brought him the head of the Welsh prince Rhys in 1053 and the head of king Griffith in 1063.[47] It is clear that by the third quarter of the eleventh century English politics was a much rougher game than contemporary Norman politics. Conceivably the perception that this was so may have contributed to the notion, held by a number of French and Italian authors, that the English were barbarians.[48]

Whatever the doubtless complex mixture of reasons for the different treatment of an English and a Norman rebel in 1075–6, the fact remains that all the other aristocratic leaders of the English revolts against the conqueror received much gentler treatment than did Waltheof, i.e. were dealt with as though they were Norman. Thus it seemed to Henry of Huntingdon that the Norman conquest had been less cruel than the Danish because, amongst other reasons, the Normans granted life to the defeated.[49] If William on being elevated to a royal throne felt more godlike than when he was a mere count or duke, then he only once expressed his newly acquired majesty by ordering the execution of a high-status rebel.

There are signs that for a generation or so after the conquest the native English continued to take a more robust attitude towards rebels. That Orderic saw things in these terms is clear from his account of the 1088 rebellion. According to this, William II, urged on by his loyal English subjects, believed that the *perfidos traditores* should be hanged or otherwise put to death. But William's army contained many friends and relatives of the rebels, who pleaded on their behalf. 'You have defeated them by your strength; now spare them by your magnanimity. Temper royal rigour with clemency.' In the end after prolonged debate, the king was persuaded, and he guaranteed life and limb to

and beheaded, SD II, 198. Cf. the killing of Walcher of Durham in similar circumstances in 1080. By contrast Rufus's men captured Robert of Mowbray when they forced him out of the church in which he was trapped, FW II, 38 – and this even though king and *optimates* may have looked askance at the way he killed Malcolm *inermis*, Orderic IV, 270, see below, pp. 234–4.

[46] *ASC*, s.a. 1071; FW II, 9; *Orderic* II, 258 has him killed by Normans after betrayal by his *familiares praecipuique satellites*. Malmesbury, also presumably following WP, likewise has William in tears, WM c. 252.

[47] *ASC*, s.a. 1053, 1063. See K. L. Maund, *Ireland, Wales and England in the Eleventh Century* (Woodbridge, 1991), pp. 138–9; also idem, 'Cynan ab Iago and the Killing of Gruffudd ap Llywelyn', *Cambridge Medieval Celtic Studies* X (1985), 57–65.

[48] Among such authors were Lanfranc, William of Poitiers, John of Tours, Paschal II, Anselm, and Ivo of Chartres; see above, p. 57.

[49] HH, 272–3 [138]. By contrast William of Malmesbury pointed out that Cnut, unlike William, restored *honores integros* to the defeated, WM c. 254.

the rebels if they surrendered – which they then did. As they emerged from Rochester Castle, the English shouted 'string them up, string them up'. But Rufus kept his word and their only punishment was the loss of their estates in England.[50]

The events of 1075 and 1088 marked the early stages of a new pattern of English politics, and a very important one. For the next two centuries the kings of England chose not to execute aristocratic rebels – though they had no hesitation about calling them traitors.[51] In this regard the Norman and Angevin kings behaved more like French dukes than Anglo-Saxon kings. Thus the sense of shock and outrage which can be heard in contemporary narratives of Edward II's reign when once again, after so long an interval, captured enemies of the king were put to death.[52] As Maitland put it, 'For two centuries after the Conquest, the frank, open rebellions of the great folk were treated with a clemency which, when we look back to it through intervening ages of blood, seems wonderful.'[53]

One of Maitland's comments on the execution of Waltheof was that it reflected the 'idea of personal law' – one law for the English, another for the Norman.[54] The French legal historian Jean le Foyer disputed this, on the grounds that Norman law also insisted on the death penalty for treason. In support he cited the Norman *Très Ancien Coutumier* and the case of Conan, the citizen of Rouen whose involvement in the 1090 revolt against Robert Curthose was punished by him being pushed by Henry from the top of the great tower of Rouen.[55] But le Foyer's arguments do not convince. For one thing he failed to

---

[50] *Orderic* IV, 126–34. Orderic's final comment, that the further some of them had gone in their treachery the greater the devotion with which they subsequently served Rufus, suggests he saw the cogency of the 'Norman' argument. F. Barlow, *William Rufus* (London, 1983), pp. 89–93. Orderic envisaged similar tension between 'soft' magnates and 'hard' *pagenses milites* in 1102, *Orderic* VI, 26. But in the *Chanson de Roland* debate on how to deal with a traitor, the 'hard men' won in the end. Ganelon was condemned to death despite the barons' argument that 'molt es gentilz hom' and that if pardoned he would serve the king faithfully, lines 3800–3811.

[51] See, amongst countless other examples, Roger of Howden's frequent references to *nefanda proditorum rabies* when dealing with the revolt of 1173–4, 'Benedict', *Gesta Regis Henrici Secundi*, ed. W. Stubbs, 2 vols. (RS, 1867), I, 42–7. Despite such passages, Maitland believed that before 1300 'men would not have been brought up to admit in perfectly general terms that the subject who levies war against the king is a traitor', F. Pollock and F. W. Maitland, *The History of English Law*, 2 vols. (1968 edn), II, 505; and, following Maitland, J. G. Bellamy, *The Law of Treason in England in the Later Middle Ages* (Cambridge, 1970), p. 23.

[52] See N. Fryde, *The Tyranny and Fall of Edward II 1321–1326* (Cambridge, 1979), pp. 58–62. And, for a chronicle edited since then, *The Anonimalle Chronicle 1307–1334*, ed. W. R. Childs and J. Taylor, Yorkshire Archaeological Society CXLVII (1991), pp. 106–10.

[53] Pollock and Maitland, II, 506. It was, perhaps, the collapse – and not only in England – of real chivalry in relations between kings and aristocrats that lay behind the institution of formal orders of chivalry in the second quarter of the fourteenth century.

[54] Ibid. I, 50.

[55] J. le Foyer, *Exposé du droit pénal normand au XIIIe siècle* (Paris, 1931), p. 124; *Orderic* IV, 224–6; Barlow, *Rufus*, pp. 274–5.

take account of Conan's status. Conan was a bourgeois and different rules clearly applied. In twelfth century England, for example, although no nobles were executed for political offences, the Londoner William fitzOsbert was drawn and hanged as 'an enemy of the king and kingdom'.[56] The passage le Foyer cites from the *Très Ancien Coutumier* – even accepting the possibility that this later treatise can be used in evidence for Orderic's lifetime – states that the proper penalty for a number of crimes, including *traditio*, is hanging and that neither the duke nor his judges are to dare to accept money.[57] But the implication of this last clause is surely precisely that they were sometimes bought off. In any case, if we want to know what the law really was, we should pay less attention to what the authors of legal treatises said ought to happen, and more, where it can be ascertained, to what did happen. In the case of aristocratic rebellion, it can be ascertained. As Orderic's chronicle shows beyond all doubt, aristocratic Norman rebels were not hanged.

Turning to the English law of treason, from Alfred's reign onwards it prescribes the death penalty for plotting against the life of the king. According to Alfred, 'If anyone plots against the king's life, by himself or by means of the harbouring of fugitives or his men, he is to be liable for his life and all that he possesses.'[58] In practice this laid down the death penalty for rebellion since all rebellions/succession disputes threatened the life of the king, at any rate until kings, or would-be kings, could be defeated and allowed to live. In this sense, i.e. in reality, levying war against the king had been treated as treason centuries before Edward I's reign – the date conventionally given for the introduction of this notion into English law.

In English history Edgar Atheling is, I think, the first clear case of a defeated claimant who survived the struggle for the throne without having to flee the realm or be tonsured to do so. Then come the imprisonments of Robert Curthose and of Stephen. This development meant that it became possible to be accused of rebellion without necessarily being accused of plotting against the king's life.[59] For attempts to assassinate the king, the death penalty continued to

---

[56] Roger of Howden, *Chronica*, ed. W. Stubbs, 4 vols. (RS, 1868–71), IV, 6.

[57] *Le Très Ancien Coutumier de Normandie*, ed. E.-J. Tardif (Rouen, 1881), cap. 36, 2. See also Foreville, *Guillaume de Poitiers*, p. 64 n. 3.

[58] Cited from S. Keynes and M. Lapidge, *Alfred the Great* (Harmondsworth, 1983), pp. 163–5. The capitulary issued by papal legates in 786 suggests that sentiments of this kind existed long before Alfred's reign. See P. Wormald, 'In Search of King Offa's "Lawcode"' in *People and Places in Northern Europe 500–1600. Essays in honour of P. H. Sawyer*, ed. I. Wood and N. Lund (Woodbridge, 1991), pp. 30–34.

[59] It is probably impossible to discover the real intentions of rebels. Although chroniclers seem to have been clear that the rebels of 1095 intended to kill Rufus (FW II, 38; *Orderic* IV, 280; Gaimar, lines 6134ff), when the accounts of 1075 (*ASC*, s.a. 1075; *Orderic* II, 312–14, 320; WM c.255) and 1088 (FW II, 21; *Orderic* IV, 122) do ascribe intentions, they leave room for the possibility that all that was intended was 'to drive their royal lord out of his kingdom'. In the *De Injusta Vexatione* – which may take us closer to an actual treason trial in the king's presence than any other account, see F. Barlow, *The English Church 1066–1154* (London, 1979), pp. 281ff; M. Philpott, 'The *De iniusta vexacione Willelmi episcopi primi* and Canon Law in

be applied – even to men of high-status, as is clear from the 1242 case of William Marsh, hanged, drawn and quartered for allegedly instigating a 1238 attempt to murder Henry III.[60] Indeed murdering one's lord continued to be ferociously punished – as is clear not only from the *Leges Henrici Primi* but also from the fate of those involved in the 1127 murder of Charles the Good.[61] It is in this context that we should understand Suger's comment that a chamberlain who plotted against Henry I deserved death (and therefore got off lightly when blinded and castrated).[62] But once rebels were no longer automatically regarded as threats to the king's life, then more lenient punishment of rebellion became possible. Law-books, *Glanvill* for example, retained the provision that the life and limbs of a convicted traitor were at the king's mercy, but in practice the kings of the twelfth and thirteenth centuries consistently displayed clemency.[63] Rebellion was always treason. Before 1066 high-status rebels had cause to fear death if they were defeated and captured; as they did again after 1300. It is just that the clement treatment of rebel traitors became the norm during the chivalrous centuries which started with the reign of William the Bastard.[64]

Anglo-Norman Durham' in eds. D. Rollason, M. Harvey and M. Prestwich, *Anglo-Norman Durham 1093–1193* (Woodbridge, 1994) – the charge laid against the bishop of Durham by Hugh of Beaumont *ex precepto regis* in 1088 was that his treachery occurred when the king's enemies 'regnum suum pariter sibi et coronam auferre volebant', SD I, 181.

[60] Matthew Paris, *CM* IV, 193–6; also III, 497–8. See F. M. Powicke, *King Henry III and the Lord Edward* (Oxford, 1947), pp. 751–4.

[61] According to the *Leges Henrici Primi*, ed. and trans. L. J. Downer (Oxford, 1972), c. 75, 1, the guilty man was to be 'condemned to scalping or disembowelling or to human punishment so harsh that while enduring the dreadful agonies of his tortures . . . he may declare, if it were possible, that he had found more mercy in hell than had been shown to him on earth'. Cf. *Materials for the History of Thomas Becket*, ed. J. C. Robertson, 7 vols. (RS, 1875–85), I, 128. Whatever their ancestry, many of those put to death for the murder of Charles the Good were wealthy and powerful lords, Galbert of Bruges, *The Murder of Charles the Good*, trans. and ed. J. B. Ross (New York, 1967), cc. 29, 56–7, 81, 84.

[62] Suger, *Vie de Louis VI*, p. 190.

[63] *Tractatus de Legibus et Consuetudinibus Regni Anglie qui Glanvilla vocatur*, ed. G. D. G. Hall (Edinburgh, 1965), XIV, I. Although Henry II commonly treated his enemies mercifully – and was praised for doing so, e.g. *Radulfi de Diceto Decani Londiniensis Opera Historica*, ed. W. Stubbs (RS, 1876), I, 434; William of Newburgh, *Historia Rerum Anglicarum*, ed. R. Howlett in *Chronicles of the Reigns of Stephen, Henry II and Richard I* (RS, 1884), I, 176; Giraldus Cambrensis, *Expugnatio Hibernica*, ed. and trans. A. B. Scott and F. X. Martin (Dublin, 1978), pp. 122–4, 128, – his clemency did not extend to barbarians beyond the realms of chivalry; see Howden, I, 240 and above, p. 58.

[64] The failure to recognise rebellion as treason partly accounts for E. J. Mickel's view, *Ganelon, Treason and the 'Chanson de Roland'* (London, 1989), p. 147, 'that the treatment of traitors became harsher in the late 12th and 13th centuries'. Mickel follows many legal historians in associating increasing severity with an increasing influence of Roman law. However, although legal historians commonly discuss treason in terms of a distinction between Roman and Germanic elements, it is not an approach which I have found in the least helpful. Even in Anglo-Saxon England, as Bellamy pointed out, 'pure Germanic treason, wherein loyalty to the lord was all and there were no special sanctions against hostility directed towards the king, can hardly ever have existed'. Bellamy, *Law of Treason*, pp. 1–6.

The last aristocrat to suffer death for rebellion at the hands of a Norman king was William de Alderie. He was involved in the 1095 revolt against Rufus and was hanged, but that the climate of opinion was changing is perhaps suggested by the comments of the Hyde chronicler and William of Malmesbury, both of whom insist that de Alderie was unjustly done to death.[65] Undoubtedly more significant of the new attitude is the fact that of the various nobles involved in the 1095 rebellion, de Alderie was the only one to lose his life. William of Eu was blinded and castrated; and Robert de Mowbray was imprisoned. Orderic's belief that Rufus wanted to deal more severely with the rebels but concealed his real wishes 'out of respect for their exalted kinfolk who might have sought vengeance in Normandy', highlights an element of political calculation which must have had extra force during those periods when England and Normandy were under different rulers.[66] But this is a shift in opinion and practice which both pre- and post-dates those fairly short periods. It is, in any case, a development much too fundamental to be explained simply in such local and limited terms – above all because it is a development with a parallel history, if an as yet insufficiently investigated one, common to much of Western Europe.

The last men of note to be mutilated for rebellion were probably Luke of La Barre, Geoffrey of Tourville and Odard of Le Pin, blinded on Henry I's orders in 1124. Although according to Orderic, Henry I was able to justify this punishment, the fact that Orderic – and probably therefore also Henry – felt forced to do this is another indication of the way opinion was moving.[67] Even more revealing is the fate of another of Henry I's enemies, William count of Mortain. He was captured at Tinchebrai and imprisoned. According to the obituary of Henry I which Henry of Huntingdon wrote c.1140, one of the king's three vices was cruelty, as exemplified by his blinding of the captive count, his kinsman. So horrible a crime, Huntingdon says, was kept secret during the king's lifetime and only came out after his death. When the historian revised this obituary soon after the accession of Henry II in 1154, he allowed some of his criticisms of the new king's grandfather to stand, but he decided to delete this accusation altogether.[68] Whether or not Henry I really did blind William of Mortain, Henry of Huntingdon's treatment of the story reveals just how appalling such an accusation was thought to be in the mid twelfth century.

Once kings found themselves constrained by aristocratic opinion to treat rebels more mercifully, then it began to be possible for would-be rebels to consider whether or not they might make an 'honourable' or 'chivalrous' announcement of their intentions. Thus what Round called 'the famous *diffidatio*'

---

[65] *Hyde*, p. 301; WM c. 319.

[66] *Orderic* IV, 284.

[67] *Orderic* VI, 352–4.

[68] HH, pp. 698–701 [255–6]. D. E. Greenway, 'Henry of Huntingdon and the Manuscripts of his *Historia Anglorum*', *ANS* IX (1987), 121, 126. See p. 120 n. 91 for the accusation (also later suppressed) that Henry had kept his brother in chains. I am indebted to Diana Greenway for further advice on the manuscripts.

may have been not some ancient Germanic custom, but a relatively recent practice first recorded in England in 1138. According to William of Malmesbury, Robert of Gloucester sent envoys to Stephen and 'more majorum amicitiam et fidem interdixit, homagio etiam abdicato' and so, *rege . . . diffidato*, he was entitled to help his sister the Empress, despite his earlier oath of allegiance to Stephen.[69] The terms in which William then criticised Stephen's conduct at Lincoln in 1141, – *nec modo more majorum amicitiam suam eis interdixerat, quod diffidiare dicunt* – implies that the verb *diffidiare* (presumably a Latinisation of a French word) was an unfamiliar one in Anglo-Latin literature. If the word itself could have entered Anglo-Latin vocabulary only after 1066, it may be that the action it signified only did so then as well.[70] Did William of Malmesbury, creative as always, find himself inventing a new political language, partly to justify Robert of Gloucester's conduct (oath-breaking in 1138; giving battle against an anointed king in 1141), but partly also as a way of describing a new reality, a new perception of revolt, declared in a new way? And did he therefore, in his patron's cause, hope that readers would be hoodwinked by his assertion that it was all done in traditional fashion (*more majorum*)? Or was this no more than a way of saying that this is what Robert's French ancestors would have done?

By Stephen's reign the new pattern of politics was clearly established. Geoffrey de Mandeville and Ranulf of Chester were arrested for treason, and then released.[71] Samuel Daniel was not, however, quite right to claim that

---

[69] William of Malmesbury, *Historia Novella*, in ed. Stubbs, *Gesta Regum* II, 545. I leave aside the question of whether *diffidatio* was, as Round believed, an 'essential feature of continental feudalism', *Geoffrey de Mandeville* (London, 1892), pp. 27–8. However, as Jane Martindale kindly pointed out, my discussion of *diffidatio* in the original version of this article clearly overestimated the extent of William of Malmesbury's originality as a consequence of my forgetting the use of the verb *defidavit* in Hugh of Lusignan's *conventum* (see above, p. 168 n. 27). The word also occurs in the Durham tract *De Injusta Vexatione*, formerly dated 1125–50, but now more generally seen as late 11th century, see above n. 59 and M. Strickland, *War and Chivalry* (Cambridge, 1996), 40 n. 47. Fortunately although this weakens the case for William's originality, it simultaneously strengthens the case for the influence of French political mores and vocabulary in post-conquest England. For further cogent discussion of *diffidatio* see David Carpenter, 'From King John to the first English duke: 1215–1337' in eds. R. Smith and J. S. Moore, *The House of Lords, a thousand years of British tradition* (London, 1994), 28–38.

[70] Stubbs, *Gesta Regum* II, 569. John and Richard of Hexham and Ailred of Rievaulx all assert that Robert de Brus formally broke off his ties to David of Scotland in 1138 – without, however, using William's word, *The Priory of Hexham*, ed. J. Raine, Surtees Society XLIV (1863), p. 119; *Chronicles of the Reigns* III, 162, 195. It may be significant that the next use of a 'diffidatio' verb, – and in a slightly different form *defida*– occurs in the treaty between Ranulf of Chester and Robert of Leicester, Stenton, *English Feudalism*, pp. 250–53, 286–8. Cf. *Dictionary of Medieval Latin from British Sources*, prepared by R. E. Latham et al., Fasc. III (London, 1986). However in what is the earliest instance of the vernacular form (also c.1140) cited in the *Anglo-Norman Dictionary*, ed. L. W. Stone et al. Fasc. II (London, 1981), it clearly refers to a subject renouncing his allegiance to a king, in this case a king who has raped his wife, Gaimar, lines 2678–82.

[71] J. O. Prestwich, 'The Treason of Geoffrey de Mandeville', *EHR* CIII (1988), 294–8.

Stephen 'never put any great man to death'. In 1138 he hanged Arnulf de Hesdin at Shrewsbury. However Arnulf was hanged not just because he was in revolt against Stephen, but because his refusal to surrender Shrewsbury castle when called upon to do so, meant that the king ordered his men to risk their lives in an assault. Under the customs of war this meant that the lives of the defenders were forfeit.[72] Moreover in 1140 Robert of Gloucester hanged Robert fitz Hubert, a notoriously treacherous Flemish commander of mercenaries whose death pleased the chroniclers on both sides.[73] These cases apart, neither Stephen nor the Empress executed their opponents. The political morality of the twelfth century aristocracy is well expressed in Geoffrey Gaimar's vernacular *History of the English* of c.1140. On the one hand we have the – presumably proverbial – sentiment, 'Home ke traist, nad nul lei' (the man who betrays has no right to law). On the other the conduct of the legendary hero-king Haveloc the Dane. According to Gaimar, the usurper who deprived the young Haveloc of his throne was a traitrous felon. None the less once Haveloc had recovered his right, he pardoned his enemy's high-ranking supporters. Haveloc's clemency, says Gaimar, was founded on the advice of his barons.[74]

To put these developments into perspective it may help to look at practice in contemporary Celtic societies. Madog ap Meredith, for example, emerged as ruler of Powys in 1132 after two of his uncles and four cousins had been either murdered or mutilated. Consider the entry for 1130 in the *Brut y Tywysogyon*: 'Iorwerth ap Llywarch was slain by Llywelyn ap Owain in Powys. Soon after that, Llywelyn ap Owain was deprived of his eyes and his testicles by Maredudd ap Bleddyn. In that year Ieuf ap Owain was slain by the sons of Llywarch ab Owain, his first cousins. At the close of the year Madog ap llywarch was slain by Meurig, his first cousin, son of Rhiddid.'[75] Similarly in Ireland and Scotland. In 1141 Diarmait Mac Murchada killed or blinded seventeen members of the royal families of Leinster. It was by killing and mutilating rivals that the line of David secured its hold on the throne of Scotland in the twelfth and thirteenth centuries.[76] Contrast this with what happened when King John tried to secure his hold on Anjou and Normandy by murdering Arthur of Brittany.[77] To an observer like Gerald de Barri who in his early writings saw himself as a representative of English civilisation, this aspect of Celtic politics was all very distressing. When a prince died, he noted, 'the most frightful disturbances occur

---

[72] *Orderic* VI, 520–2; HH, pp. 712–13 [261]. Matthew Strickland, *War and Chivalry. The Conduct and Perception of War in England and Normandy, 1066–1217* (Cambridge, 1996), 222–4; J. Bradbury, *The Medieval Siege* (Woodbridge, 1992), pp. 317–24.

[73] *Gesta Stephani*, ed. and trans. K. R. Potter and R. H. C. Davis (Oxford, 1976), p. 92; *Gesta Regum* II, 563–4; *The Chronicle of John of Worcester*, ed. J. R. H. Weaver (Oxford, 1908), pp. 61–3.

[74] Gaimar, lines 517, 743–50, 3717.

[75] *Brut y Tywysogyon. Red Book of Hergest Version*, ed. T. Jones (Cardiff, 1955), pp. 112–13.

[76] *A New History of Ireland, II, 1169–1534*, ed. A. Cosgrove (Oxford, 1987), pp. 26–7; A. A. M. Duncan, *Scotland. The Making of the Kingdom* (Edinburgh, 1975), pp. 166, 196–7, 529, 546.

[77] J. Gillingham, *The Angevin Empire* (London, 1984), 69.

. . . people being murdered, brothers killing each other or putting each other's eyes out. As everyone knows from experience, it is very difficult to settle disputes of this sort.'[78] And indeed this is not how succession disputes were handled in twelfth century England. In England disputes over succession to high office, or succession to great estates, certainly involved violence, but it was violence which was controlled so as to spare the lives – and limbs – of the royals and aristocrats who engaged in it. Compared with contemporary Celtic politics the so-called 'anarchy of Stephen's reign' was a very chivalrous affair.

Chivalry was essentially an aristocratic business. Non-noble rebels continued to be punished by death or mutilation when the bodies of their noble leaders were spared.[79] Similarly in chivalrous warfare the lives of noble captives were spared while low-born prisoners might be summarily put to death – especially if they were archers or crossbowmen.[80] On the other hand it was not just aristocrats who had reason to feel safer in the 'age of chivalry'. Even the vast majority of commoners, the non-combatants, were now much less likely to become casualties of war, since they were no longer in danger of being caught up in slave-raiding campaigns and, in consequence, being either massacred or captured and sold as slaves – a danger that, to judge from Wulfstan's lament, still seems to have been very real at the time of the Danish Conquest.[81] In this sense too the 1066 campaign was the first new-style invasion of England; it did not result in an increased supply of slaves to the market.[82] The slave market at Rouen probably no longer existed and the acquisition of slaves was no longer one of the main purposes of Norman warfare.[83] Indeed one of the many ways in which William of Poitiers demonstrated Duke William's superiority to Julius Caesar was by pointing out that William's invasion of

---

[78] *Descriptio Kambriae* in *Giraldi Cambrensis Opera*, ed. J. S. Brewer et al., VI, 211–12. Cf. *Topographia Hibernica*, ibid., V, 167–8. On the English stage of Gerald's career, see R. Bartlett, *Gerald of Wales* (Oxford, 1982), pp. 15–16, and above, pp. 155–7.

[79] Hollister, 'Royal Acts of Mutilation', 330–38. For some examples see *ASC*, s.a. 1075; FW II, 11; *Orderic* II, 228, 316 (unnamed, despite the 'of whatever rank'). In 1136 Stephen hanged one of Henry I's doorkeepers, a man 'of humble rank', for pillaging, *GS*, pp. 6–8. A doubtful case is the castellan whom Curthose, applauded by Orderic, blinded in 1088; as Chibnall noted, his name, Robert Quadrellus, suggests he may have been a crossbow-man, *Orderic* IV, 154.

[80] Strickland, *War and Chivalry*, pp. 176–81, 223.

[81] 'Often two seamen, or maybe three, drive the droves of Christian men from sea to sea, out through this people, huddled together as a public shame to us all', *Sermo Lupi ad Anglos*, trans. in *EHD* I, no. 240. *ASC*, s.a. 1036. On the ferocity of war as slave-hunt see above, pp. 45–9, 102.

[82] M. Chibnall, *Anglo-Norman England 1066–1166*, pp. 187–8.

[83] On the last references to Rouen as a slave market, D. Pelteret, 'Slave raiding and slave trading in early England', *ASE* IX (1981), 108–109, esp. n. 85. William of Malmesbury believed that William I was brought to view the slave trade in a light different from that in which it had been seen by the Anglo-Danish royal house, WM cc. 200, 269 (despite the translation of *mancipia* as 'serfs'). However Patrick Wormald points out that the laws of Cnut and William take a similar line on slaves.

Britain did not result, as the Roman's had, in shiploads of prisoners being transported to the continent.[84]

I have argued elsewhere that chivalry was a code appropriate to a certain stage of socio-economic development, that conventions which made for the merciful treatment of aristocratic prisoners could operate more readily and effectively in societies where there were plenty of political and strategic assets, above all towns and castles, which could be exchanged in return for sparing life and limb.[85] Given the relative absence of towns and castles from the Celtic landscape, it is not surprising that prisoners there got comparatively short shrift. As Gerald de Barri observed, 'In France, knights are held in captivity; here (he was writing of Ireland and Wales) they are decapitated. There they are ransomed; here killed.'[86] Seen in this light it is not at all surprising that the lives and limbs of royals and their aristocratic followers should be at risk in conflict during the early Anglo-Saxon centuries. As Bede's story of Imma shows, captive nobles could expect death and captive commoners could expect enslavement.[87] On the other hand, given the socio-economic developments in the later centuries of Anglo-Saxon England it is surprising that the dark age barbarian strain should still be so evident on the eve of the Norman Conquest. A partial explanation may lie in two considerations. One is that in socio-economic terms the northern part of the English kingdom was markedly different from the rest. As Robin Frame has observed there is 'a broad distinction . . . between southern and midland England on the one hand and the remainder of the British Isles on the other'.[88] It is noticeable that a high proportion of the political savagery in eleventh century England involved Northumbrian politics even when, as in 1064, the bloodshed itself took place at the royal court. The second is the possibility that a movement towards an increasingly chivalrous political style occurred in, roughly, the ninth and tenth centuries, but was then reversed, first by confrontation with, then by take-over by the 'barbarous' Danes.[89] But it remains

---

[84] WP II c. 40. William I took hostages to Normandy, not slaves to the market.

[85] Above, pp. 53–4. By 'appropriate to' I do not, of course, mean 'determined by'. However in a very wide-ranging survey, O. Patterson, *Slavery and Social Death* (Cambridge, Mass., 1982), pp. 106–107, noted that upper class captives were usually ransomed 'among all the advanced states of Africa, Asia and Europe'.

[86] Gerald, *Expugnatio*, p. 246, repeated in *Descriptio* VI, 220. In relatively unindustrialised societies a higher proportion of warriors, lacking good body armour, were exposed to lethal blows – especially from arrows – as contemporaries were well aware, above, pp. 49–50.

[87] Bede IV c. 22.

[88] R. Frame, *The Political Development of the British Isles 1100–1400*, p. 13. It is clear that the killing of Bishop Walcher in 1080 inclined both Henry of Huntingdon and William of Malmesbury to take a stern view of Northumbrians throughout their history, HH, pp. 268–9 [136], 282–3 [143], 316–17 [163], 400–401 [207]; WM cc. 72–3, 271 (though see c. 200 for 'their' claim that, well-treated, they could behave nicely – *dulciter*).

[89] William's overview of Anglo-Saxon history (see below, n. 91), including his comments on Cenwulf of Mercia and Egbert of Wessex, suggests that he had a sense of 'improvement' in the ninth century followed by 'decline' beginning in Æthelred's reign, WM cc. 95, 106,

true, of course, that so far as observers like William of Jumièges and William of Poitiers were concerned, both Northumbria and Danish kings were integral aspects of the eleventh century English political system – as indeed they were.[90] Moreover twelfth century English historians, notably William of Malmesbury, Henry of Huntingdon and Geoffrey Gaimar, all looked back at the Anglo-Saxon period and saw it as less peaceful, less well-organised and less humane than their own times.[91] They saw the history of their own country as a history of progress, of civilising progress.

Less important, though perhaps of some interest, are the implications of this subject for our assessment of the character of William the Bastard. It is not customary to think of him as a chivalrous king – though his most recent biographer, David Bates, does allow that William 'practised a primitive kind of chivalry' on the grounds that 'he had a code of correct behaviour for the battlefield' and because he punished the soldier who hacked at Harold's corpse as well as the murderers of Earl Edwin.[92] But probably most historians would concur with the judgment implied by the concluding words of Bates's biography, a final reminder of William's 'savage and pitiless career'.[93] Savage and pitiless by whose standards? If we put his management of the conquest of England into the context of mid-eleventh-century England, then there is much to be said for the view that he was the first chivalrous ruler in English history. Clearly he was capable of conduct which some contemporaries regarded as atrocious – the mutilation of the defenders of Alençon would be an obvious example.[94] Orderic was surely right when, looking back from the 1120s and

---

165, 180. Henry of Huntingdon also regarded Æthelred's style of government as unusually cruel and violent, HH, pp. 328–9 [168–9]; like William he believed that Edmund Ironside was murdered.

[90] So was Cornwall, also the scene of a notorious vengeance-killing, see O. J. Padel, 'Geoffrey of Monmouth and Cornwall', *Cambridge Medieval Celtic Studies* VIII (1984), 20–7.

[91] HH, pp. 260–61 [131], 338–9 [173]; Gaimar, lines 2016–18, 2283–6, 2313–16; WM cc. 4, 245. On William's views see above, pp. 5, 28. I am reminded of the seventeenth-century Edinburgh lawyer-administrators living in 'a new milieu . . . in which men thought with pride of their modern civilized society and looked back with horror to the barbarities of the past . . . And not only back; . . . men looked sideways to the highland area of their country, without understanding, but with embarrassment, fear and violent hostility', J. Wormald, 'Bloodfeud, Kindred and Government in early modern Scotland', *Past and Present* LXXXVII (1980), 96–7.

[92] Bates, *William the Conqueror*, p. 94, in effect following William of Malmesbury's account of his 'correct code of behaviour for the battlefield' and his stories of how the king punished those who broke the code, WM cc. 234, 243, 252. Malmesbury's view clearly derived from his reading of William of Poitiers, where what Davis ('William of Poitiers', p. 82) called 'the commonplaces of chivalric literature' could already be found.

[93] Bates, *William the Conqueror*, p. 186.

[94] F. Barlow, *William I and the Norman Conquest* (London, 1965), p. 20; J. Gillingham, 'William the Bastard at War' in *Studies for R. Allen Brown*, pp. 150–51; reprinted in ed. M. Strickland, *Anglo-Norman Warfare* (Woodbridge, 1992) and in ed. S. Morillo, *The Battle of Hastings* (Woodbridge, 1996).

later, he saw the harrying of the north as massacre by famine.[95] But so far as I can see those who were mutilated or who died in these two episodes were non-nobles – and chivalry was essentially an aristocratic preserve. By the standards of this privileged class, Guibert de Nogent's comment that William kept prisoners – like Guibert's father – in prison for too long was a more serious criticism of his chivalrous credentials.[96] The judgment of Samuel Daniel, himself a member of the household of James I's queen, is an intriguing one: that William's greatest virtues were 'devotion and mercy, the brightest stars in the sphere of majesty'. And that the Conqueror's mercy could be 'seene in the often pardoning and receiving into grace, those who rebelled against him as if he held their submission satisfactory for the greatest offence, and fought not to defeat men but their enterprises: For we find but one Noble man executed in all his Raigne, and that was the earle Waltheof, who had twice falsified his faith before'. Daniel then went on to describe William's treatment of Edgar the Atheling as 'an especial note of his magnanimity'. Even more striking is Samuel Daniel's conclusion that 'these may be as well vertues of the Time, as of Men, and so the age must have part of this commendation'.[97]

A final twist. If you lived in a chivalrous society in which it was no longer thought decent to kill or mutilate aristocratic enemies openly, then there were ways round this – perhaps. David Douglas in an appendix to his *William the Conqueror* drew attention to the number of allegations of secret poisoning in eleventh-century Normandy and to the contrast with England, where despite the sudden deaths of Hardacnut (1042), Godwin (1053) and Edward Atheling (1057), this accusation is noticeable by its absence.[98] Orderic repeats rumours that William himself poisoned three of his most important enemies.[99] But in eleventh-century England, where other options were known to be available to the man determined to get rid of his enemies, there was no call for allegations of this kind.

---

[95] See e.g. *Orderic* II, 230–32; IV, 94.

[96] *Self and Society in Medieval France. The Memoirs of Guibert de Nogent*, ed J. F. Benton (New York, 1970), p. 69, and n. 2. A dubious case, given the uncertain status of the unfortunate prisoner, is provided by Anselm's letter asking Lanfranc to intercede on behalf of 'a certain man' whom William intended to maim, *Sancti Anselmi Opera Omnia*, ed. F. S. Schmitt (Edinburgh, 1946–61), III, letter 27. I owe this reference to the kindness of David Bates. On the practice of threatening to maltreat prisoners of war see Strickland, *War and Chivalry*, 198–9.

[97] S. Daniel, *The First Part of the Historie of England* (London, 1612), p. 146 and, as a further indication of his quality as a historian, pp. 128–30. See also J. Hayward, *The Lives of the III Normans, Kings of England* (London, 1613), pp. 90–91, 103–105.

[98] Douglas, *William the Conqueror*, 408–14.

[99] *Orderic* II, 312.

POSTSCRIPT

In the original version of this paper I made the mistake of assuming that what I meant by the terms 'feud' and 'blood feud' would 'emerge' from the material presented there. But comments by more than one author in the recent collection of essays edited by Guy Halsall, *Violence and Society in the Early Medieval West* (Woodbridge, 1998), make it plain that this was very naïve of me.

By 'feud' I mean publicly acceptable 'private war'; by 'blood feud' I mean a 'private war' pursued with the publicly acceptable intention of shedding blood. (This formulation is meant to exclude the situation where, as in Robert Curthose's period of rule in Normandy, deaths in war were unintended and regretted.) By 'private war' I mean what later theorists would call 'guerre couverte' as opposed to the 'guerre ouverte' waged by public authorities, the kind of people whom Christine de Pisan called 'sovereign princes such as emperors, kings, dukes and other secular lords who are lords principal of secular jurisdiction'. For this distinction, in Latin sometimes indicated by the words *werra* and *bellum*, as early as the ninth century, see the essay by Janet Nelson on 'Violence in the Carolingian world and the ritualization of ninth-century warfare' in that collection (p. 93).

Later medieval evidence suggests that it was expected – or hoped – that private war would be waged according to rules which were different from those which applied in public war. Thus in a case before the parlement of Paris in 1361 William de Ferté argued that he had fought fairly because, amongst other things, though he had ravaged his opponent's (in this case his lord's) estates, he had taken neither prisoners nor plunder, nor had he burned the land, i.e. he had not employed the usages of public war (M. H. Keen, *The Laws of War in the Late Middle Ages*, London, 1965, 79–80). There are evident parallels between the restraint which William de Ferté claimed he exercised and the prohibitions against capturing men, money, arms and horses *pro guerra* in the fourteenth clause of the Norman *Consuetudines et Justicie* of 1091 (Haskins, *Norman Institutions*, 284). This kind of thinking explains, I suggest, Orderic's account of the fate of Ivo de Grandmesnil, punished by Henry I because he had waged war in England and had burned the crops of his neighbours (*quia guerram in Anglia ceperat, et vicinorum rura suorum incendio combusserat*) vi.18 – perhaps early twelfth-century Norman custom regarded crop-burning as an acceptable means of fighting a feud. For evidence that private war as such was acceptable in England see Glanvil IX.1 and 8 (cf. Maitland, *History of English Law*, i.302), and also the account in *The Chronicle of Jocelin of Brakelond*, ed. and trans. H. E. Butler (Edinburgh, 1949), 133–4, of how Abbot Samson of Bury St Edmunds 'prosecuted a feud' (J. Gillingham, *The Angevin Empire*, p. 43) by organising a night-raid to carry off his adversary's cattle – but not, be it noted, to burn his crops.

Why do I use the word 'feud' rather than 'publicly acceptable private war'? I suppose because 'feud' is much less cumbersome and because long, long ago I read the chapter on 'Friede und Fehde' in Otto Brunner's *Land und Herrschaft*. Moreover my understanding of feud is based upon ordinary English usage. According to *The Chambers Dictionary* (1993 edition) feud is 'a war waged by private individuals, families or clans against one another on their own account; a bloody strife; a persistent state of private enmity'. (I use feud/bloodfeud to distinguish between the first and second of those definitions.)

But in a situation where so many academics believe that there has to be a series of tit-for-tat killings for a state of feud to exist and who even argue that violence for political ends is not feud, it was foolish of me not to explain my reasons for dissenting from that distinction between bloodfeud and political dispute which I recorded in note 8. When, as nearly always in this period of history, we are dealing with high-status families, the idea of a distinction between private/familial hostility on the one hand, and 'political' hostility on the other, seems to me both inappropriate and, in practice, given the state of the evidence, impossible to demonstrate even if it were appropriate. In other words a pretty useless distinction. We can, of course, swap definitions of feud – whether from dictionaries or not – in a persistently tit-for-tat fashion. All I claim for my use of the word 'feud' is that it corresponds reasonably well to a contemporary term – *guerra* – and all I claim for my distinction between 'feud' and 'bloodfeud' is that it is analytically useful, as – for example – in the contrast between the 'anarchies' of Duke William's minority and of King Stephen's reign.

13

Kingship, Chivalry and Love

Political and cultural values in the earliest history written in French: Geoffrey Gaimar's *Estoire des Engleis*

On many counts Geoffrey Gaimar's *Estoire des Engleis* is a remarkable work. Written in England in the late 1130s, it is the earliest extant history in the French language.[1] What still survives, covering the period from the fifth century AD onwards in some 6,600 lines of French verse, is merely the rump of an astonishingly ambitious historical enterprise – a history that began with Jason and the Golden Fleece and ended with the death of Rufus in 1100. As these terminal dates suggest Gaimar's interests were secular rather than religious. Ecclesiastical matters are dealt with in a fairly perfunctory fashion. His major themes were the stuff of secular politics: kingship, war and marriage. One of the principal features of the 'twelfth century renaissance' is the increasing visibility of lay culture, thanks to the survival of an increasing number of works written not in Latin but in a vernacular, above all in French, the most cosmopolitan of vernaculars. Thus Gaimar's history is potentially a text of enormous importance. It significantly pre-dates the works of, for example, Wace, Chrétien of Troyes and Wolfram of Eschenbach. It offers us an unparalleled insight into the thought-world of the secular aristocracy of the early twelfth century.

Indeed, as is well-known, the genesis of Gaimar's work is explicitly associated with the cultural interests of two of the period's outstanding noblemen: Walter Espec and Robert of Gloucester. He claims to have used a work which he calls 'Walter Espec's book' and which the lord of Helmsley had himself obtained from Robert of Gloucester.[2] This confirms Ailred of Rievaulx's characterisation of Walter, founder of fashionable Rievaulx, one of the heroes of the Battle of the Standard, as a man who occupied himself with reading histories or who, as

---

[1] Ian Short, 'Gaimar et les débuts de l'historigraphie en langue française' in ed. D. Buschinger, *Chroniques Nationales et Chroniques Universelles* (Göppingen, 1990), 155–63. On the date see the full discussion in Ian Short, 'Gaimar's Epilogue and Geoffrey of Monmouth's *Liber vetustissimus*', *Speculum* 69 (1994), 323–43. The footnotes which follow reflect only very inadequately how much this paper owes to Ian Short's help, advice and encouragement.
[2] Geffrei Gaimar, *Estoire des Engleis*, ed. A. Bell (Oxford, 1960), lines 6441–50.

233

was his custom, listened attentively to those who tell the deeds of our ancestors.[3] Robert of Gloucester, illegitimate son of Henry I and patron of both William of Malmesbury and Geoffrey of Monmouth, was of course an even greater figure at court and in the court culture of the day.[4] Two noble and courtly women are also closely associated with Gaimar's history: first, Henry I's widow, Adeliza, 'la reine de Luvain' as Gaimar refers to her, the patron of his friend and rival author, David; and second, but in this context a more important lady, Gaimar's own patron, 'dame Custance la gentil', Constance, wife of the Lincolnshire landowner, Ralf FitzGilbert.[5] That Gaimar's work can be located so precisely in so powerful, cultivated and courtly a milieu makes it even more extra-ordinary that it has been so neglected.

As a verse history it has been better appreciated – or, rather, parts of it have been – by scholars of language and literature than by prosaic historians.[6] More than 30 years ago Dominica Legge observed that Gaimar was a writer with ideas and that his achievement both in form and content was magnificent.[7] Gaimar's modern editor recognised him as a pioneer exponent of octosyllabic couplets, the classic verse form of Wace, Benoit of Sainte-Maure and Chrétien of Troyes.[8] Specialists in the medieval English romance have long been interested in some of Gaimar's stories – above all the tales of Haveloc and Buern Butsecarle. As for Gaimar's story of King Edgar and Aelfthryth, A. R. Press described this as 'the earliest known imaginative realization of a courtly love story'.[9] Gaimar's epilogue contains an offer to write a history of Henry I's reign including those parts which a rival, David, had allegedly failed to reach: the king's 'famous exploits' – 'the love affairs and the courting, the hunting and the drinking, the festivities and the pomp and ceremony, the acts of generosity and the displays of wealth, the entourage of noble and valiant knights that the king maintained, and the generous presents that he distributed'.[10] According to Press, these few lines

---

[3] In the speech with which he encouraged the English army before the Battle of the Standard, Walter is made to speak of himself 'legendis historiis operam darem vel more meo veterum gesta narranti aurem attentius commodarem', Ailred, *Relatio de Standardo*, ed. R. Howlett, *Chronicles of the Reigns of Stephen, Henry II and Richard I*, 4 vols. (RS, 1884–9), iii.185.

[4] D. Crouch, 'Robert, earl of Gloucester, and the daughters of Zelophehad', *JMH* 11 (1985), 227–43; and see above, pp. 36–7.

[5] Gaimar, lines 6431, 6451, 6483, and see also p. 207 for a second reference to 'Aeliz la bone reine' in manuscript D. On all this, see Short, 'Gaimar's Epilogue', passim.

[6] 'The poem adds little that is of value to the historian, and its interest lies mainly in the language in which it was written', R. R. Darlington, *Anglo-Norman Historians* (London, 1947), 6. Contrast Gaimar's presentation of himself as a serious and scholarly historian, P. Damian-Grint, '*Estoire* as word and genre: meaning and literary usage in the twelfth century', *Medium Aevum* LXVI (1997), 190–5.

[7] M. Dominica Legge, *Anglo-Norman Literature and its Background* (Oxford, 1963), 27–36.

[8] A. Bell, 'Gaimar as Pioneer', *Romania* 97 (1976), 462–80.

[9] A. R. Press, 'The Precocious Courtesy of Geoffrey Gaimar' in ed. G. S. Burgess, *Court and Poet* (Liverpool, 1981), 267–76, 273; cf. Legge, 'Anglo-Norman Literature', 36.

[10] Gaimar, lines 6504–10.

on Henry I's court amounted to 'the earliest known and quite explicit formulation of an entirely new historiographical concept . . . a wholly secular and superbly self-possessed celebration of the world's delights, values and activities'.[11]

But set these few lines and the romantic episodes aside and what is left? First, a French verse translation of the prose annals of the *Anglo-Saxon Chronicle* from 495 until 959, a *tour de force* in its way, but tedious reading and hardly adding any reliable information; then a history of the years between 959 and 1100 which is generally regarded as deserving Antonia Gransden's comment: 'history seen through the eyes of romance. . . . The value of his work as a historical source is small. . . . even when not led astray by his love of legends and eulogy, he is an inaccurate writer.'[12] Thus Gaimar hardly figures as a source for historians of the 11th century.[13] Gransden allows for his potential significance as a source for the values of his own day since she emphasises that his work reflects what she identifies as 'the most significant historiographical trend' of the time, 'the increasing influence of romance literature', but by confining her comments to Gaimar as a source for the years before 1100, she effectively sidelined this.[14] A few historians have looked to Gaimar's history as a source for attitudes in the 1130s. They have generally done so in the context of the question of cultural and ethnic identity in early twelfth century England. Thus for R. W. Southern it showed how the conquerors, beginning to deplore 'their lack of French freedom . . . took refuge in English history and found in the imagined liberties of a distant past a source of present hope'. Less complicatedly R. H. C. Davis suggested that 'it helped the Normans to become English'.[15] This kind of interpretation has also made sense to the specialists in literature such as Rosalind Field, Susan Crane and Ian Short.[16]

Despite being conventionally regarded as a precociously courtly work, Gaimar's history remains in many ways a neglected subject. Few literary scholars have looked beyond his romantic tales, though in 1975 Maria Luisa Meneghetti analysed the text as a whole in terms of what she called its 'courtly and chivalric

---

11 Press, 'The Precocious Courtesy', 268–9.

12 Antonia Gransden, *Historical Writing in England c.550 to c.1307* (London, 1974), 209–12. Cf. 'Gaimar's extant work has little value as history', Legge, *Anglo-Norman Literature*, 31.

13 Mostly they adopt Ken Lawson's Stentonian approach, sifting it for a few small 'grains of truth', M. K. Lawson, *Cnut* (London, 1993), 77–9. Cf. F. M. Stenton, *Anglo-Saxon England* (4th edn, Oxford, 1971), 699.

14 Gransden, *Historical Writing in England*, 210, 212. Cf. B. Golding, *Conquest and Colonisation. The Normans in Britain* (London, 1994), 8–9.

15 R. W. Southern, *Medieval Humanism* (Oxford, 1970), 154–5; R. H. C. Davis, *The Normans and their Myth* (London, 1976), 126–7. See also above, pp. 6, 140.

16 Rosalind Field, 'Romance as history, history as romance' in ed. Maldwyn Mills, Jennifer Fellows and Carol M. Meale, *Romance in Medieval England* (Cambridge, 1991), 163–73; Susan Crane, *Insular Romance* (Berkeley, 1986), 14–15; Short, 'Gaimar's Epilogue', 323. See also Ian Short, 'Patrons and Polyglots: French Literature in Twelfth Century England', *ANS* XIV (1991), 229–49.

ideology' and a recent study of twelfth century historical writing in French and Latin includes a brief discussion of Gaimar's portrayal of 'real' as well as of 'fictional' characters.[17] Strangely enough even historians of chivalry have hitherto ignored Gaimar – and this though they commonly use courtly romances in an attempt to work their way, in Maurice Keen's words, 'towards a definition of chivalry's elusive ethical implications'.[18] Nor is Gaimar mentioned anywhere in Stephen Jaeger's study of the formation of courtly ideals.[19] Given the fact that in Gaimar's history we have a work which is secular in tone, written in the vernacular of chivalry and yet is not – for the most part at any rate – quite so obviously fiction as the early vernacular sources traditionally turned to by historians of chivalry, the *chansons de geste* and the works of authors such as Marie de France or Chrétien de Troyes, the decision to ignore Gaimar – if decision it is – is an intriguing one. All the more so since, given all the uncertainties surrounding the dating of the earliest surviving texts of *chansons* such as Roland, Gormont or the *Coronnement de Louis*, Gaimar's history is the earliest firmly datable extant work with a claim to be considered as chivalric literature.[20]

Of course in form it is a work of English, mainly Anglo-Saxon, history – at first sight unpromising ground for a social and cultural phenomenon as quintessentially French as chivalry.[21] None the less it is in French and as part of a history of Britain and England in French verse it belongs to a genre that was, in Marjorie Chibnall's phrase, only 'a short step' away from the *chansons de geste*.[22] Indeed, according to Legge, part of Gaimar's pioneering achievement was to create the genre.[23] Yet although it is the earliest surviving French history

---

[17] Maria Luisa Meneghetti, 'L'Estoire des Engleis de Geffrei Gaimar. Fra Cronaca Genealogica e Romanzo Cortese', *Medioevo Romanzo* 2 (1975), 232–46. Unfortunately she also sees the work as the product of feudal anarchy, the reign of Stephen, when monarchy was weak and barons relatively strong. In this she may have been misled by Legge dealing with Gaimar in a chapter entitled 'Stephen and the Anarchy'. I owe to the kindness of Henrietta Leyser my knowledge of Jean Blacker, *The Faces of Time* (Austin, 1994), a work that deals with William of Malmesbury, Orderic, Geoffrey of Monmouth, Wace and Benoit de Sainte-Maure as well as Gaimar.

[18] Maurice Keen, *Chivalry* (New Haven and London, 1984), 2.

[19] C. S. Jaeger, *The Origins of Courtliness* (Philadelphia, 1985).

[20] Gaimar himself claimed to have used now lost books in French, *en romanz*, as well as in English and Latin (lines 6435–8). For a full discussion of his sources real and imagined see Short, 'Gaimar's Epilogue'. For a discussion of the date of the *Chanson de Roland* see J. F. Benton, ' "Nostre Franceis n'unt talent de fuir": the Song of Roland and the Enculturation of a Warrior Class', *Olifant* 6 (1979), 237–58, reprinted in his *Culture, Power and Personality in Medieval France*, ed. T. N. Bisson (London, 1991).

[21] Although in Gaimar, as Southern noted, 'the romantic and chivalrous heroes of the story were Anglo-Saxons', *Medieval Humanism*, 155. The essential Frenchness of chivalry is beautifully stated in Keen, *Chivalry*, 33, 42, 105, 238.

[22] M. Chibnall, *The World of Orderic Vitalis* (Oxford, 1984), 204.

[23] In her words, 'Gaimar set the pattern of popular history for something like three centuries', Legge, *Anglo-Norman Literature*, 29. The pattern emerges when we put Gaimar together with works which are bound up with his history in the four surviving

dealing with war, love and kingship – the very stuff of chivalry – so far as I know only one historian, Warren Hollister, has highlighted the chivalric quality of Gaimar's work. He took Gaimar's lines on Henry I's court, described them as painting a 'chivalric picture' and used them to clinch his argument that 'during the years between the reign of William the Conqueror and the death of Henry I, the age of chivalry dawned in the Anglo-Norman world'.[24] My aim in this paper is simply to offer some further elaboration of this point and to do so in the most straightforward way possible by describing in a more extended way the values contained within Gaimar's *Estoire des Engleis*. I shall consider Gaimar's values and assumptions under four headings: chivalry, kingship, nobles and finally, love and marriage, before ending with a few implications and questions.

I. *Chivalry*

For a start Gaimar uses the word *chevalerie*. I quote his description of Robert Curthose.

> Under heaven there was no better lord
> Much goodness and much valour
> Did this duke of Normandy and much wondrous service
> And much fair chivalry (*bele chevalerie*).[25]

Much more important are the lines which describe how Rufus first dubbed (*adubat*) 'many a *gentil home*' and then, on a second occasion, *aduba* the thirty young men whom Giffard the Poitevin brought to court.[26] In view of the fact that historians of chivalry have always regarded dubbing as central, it is astonishing that, so far as I can discover, not one of them has ever cited Gaimar's account, especially in view of the attention given to the various shades of meaning of the word *adouber* by Jean Flori.[27] *adoubet* in the sense of being equipped for war is to be found in Gaimar when he describes how Cnut and Edmund Ironside are armed for the duel that is to settle matters between them.[28] There can, however, be no doubt whatever that the dubbing which took place at the magnificent court which

manuscripts, Wace's *Roman de Brut*, Jordan Fantosme's *Chronicle*, the *lai d'Haveloc* and Langtoft's history, Bell, Gaimar, *Estoire*, xv–xviii.
[24] C. Warren Hollister, 'Courtly Culture and Courtly Style in the Anglo-Norman World', *Albion* 20 (1988), 1–17.
[25] Gaimar, lines 5738–44. On the word 'chevalerie' see Jean Flori, 'La notion de Chevalerie dans les Chansons de Geste du XII siècle. Étude historique de vocabulaire', *Le Moyen Âge* 81 (1975), 215–18; J. Flori, 'Seigneurie, Noblesse et Chevalerie dans les *Lais* de Marie de France', *Romania* 108 (1987), 183–206; J. Flori, 'La notion de chevalerie dans les romans de Chrétien de Troyes', *Romania* 114 (1996), 289–315. For drawing the last two to my attention I am much indebted to the kindness of the author.
[26] Gaimar, lines 6076, 6099.
[27] Jean Flori, 'Sémantique et Société Médiévale. Le Verbe Adouber et son Evolution au XIIe Siècle', *Annales* 31 (1976), 915–40.
[28] Gaimar, lines 4256–90.

Rufus held in his new hall at Westminster was a ceremonial entry into chivalry, not a mere arming. According to Flori's chronology of knighthood, however, it was not until the later twelfth century that the knightly order was formed and that dubbing became a favour to be solicited from kings and princes. The ritual grants of arms referred to in pre-c.1180 Latin sources should all be interpreted, he argues, in one of two ways. Some, such as the ceremony undergone by the king's son Henry at Westminster in 1086, marked a princely or baronial entry into authority. Others, such as cases reported by early twelfth-century historians like Fulcher of Chartres and Orderic Vitalis, did indeed mark the arming of men (squires) to make them knights – but knights only in the sense of well-equipped soldiers, not in the sense of knights as members of 'Chivalry', a social elite, with its distinctive ethic, ideology, rites and customs.[29] Flori argues that in the earlier, pre-1180 *chansons de geste*, there are no certain cases where *adouber* means knighting, and only four possible ones.[30] But it seems clear that the ceremony which Gaimar visualised Giffard the Poitevin as soliciting was a knightly dubbing. On the one hand, Giffard cannot possibly have had the heirs to thirty baronies as his squires (*vadlez*), all coincidentally just at this stage in their careers.[31] On the other hand it was not a simple arming of thirty young men, but a splendid and fashionable courtly occasion. Giffard and his followers had to stage a demonstration – they all turned up at court with their hair cut unfashionably short[32] – before Rufus would dub them. When he did, in Gaimar's words, 'the knighting was so splendid an affair (*Si richement les aduba*) that people will talk of it for ever'.[33] In the light of Gaimar's usage, Flori's four 'possible cases' should become probable ones. In any event all four occur in *chansons* normally dated later than 1138, the *Charroi de Nîmes*, the *Chanson de Guillaume* and the *Moniage de Guillaume*.[34] In other words the earliest

[29] J. Flori, 'Les origines de l'adoubement chevaleresque: Etude des remises d'armes et du vocabulaire qui les exprime dans les sources historiques latines jusqu'au début du XIIIe siècle', *Traditio* 35 (1979), 209–72; J. Flori, *L'Essor de la Chevalerie* (Paris, 1986), 59–61. The whole of the first part of this book, to p. 115, is on dubbing. See also J. M. Van Winter, '*Cingulum Militiae*: Schwertleite en *Miles*-Terminologie als Spiegel van veranderend Menselijk Gedrag', *Tijdschrift voor Rechtsgeschiedenis* 44 (1976), 1–92 (I owe my copy of this to the kindness of Richard Barber); and Alessandro Barbero, *L'Aristocrazia nella società francese del medioevo* (Bologna, 1987).

[30] Flori, 'Semantique et société médiévale', 918, 923–7, 930–2.

[31] Gaimar, lines 6079, 6087, 6092.

[32] For another demonstration hair cut – though this time a demonstration of pleasure rather than protest – see Joinville's *Life of Saint Louis* in trans. M. R. B. Shaw, *Chronicles of the Crusades* (Harmondsworth, 1963), 189. Cf. the suggestion that the tenth century Byzantine nobility turned up at court in old clothes as a demonstration of opposition, Karl Leyser, *Communications and Power in Medieval Europe. The Carolingian and Ottonian Centuries*, ed. T. Reuter (London, 1994), 138.

[33] Gaimar, lines 6099–6100. On the subject of the diffusion of ritual and newly-coined phrases see David Crouch, *The Image of Aristocracy in Britain 1000–1300* (London, 1992), 136–8, 155–6.

[34] On the dating of these chansons see, e.g., D. J. A. Ross, 'Old French' in *Traditions of Heroic and Epic Poetry* (London, 1980), 103, 105, 116.

instances of the word *adouber* in the full 'chivalrous' sense all occur in Gaimar's English history. Although strictly speaking this is evidence only for the outlook and vocabulary of the late 1130s, the fact that Gaimar placed the 'dubbing of the thirty' in the 1090s might even encourage us to interpret the *Anglo-Saxon Chronicle*'s account of Henry's 1086 knighting in a more chivalrous fashion than Flori would like.[35]

In the light of his account of dubbing, we might well suspect that Gaimar used the word *chevaler* rather more chivalrously than is sometimes thought. According to Meneghetti, Gaimar used the word *chevaler* fairly frequently and with a similar semantic range to the Latin *milites*.[36] Occasionally *chevalers* means no more than soldiers. When Havelocs's ally Sigar summoned an army by the fifth day an army of 30,000 *chevalers* had mustered.[37] Viking armies could be composed of *chevalers bons e provez*, just as Saracen armies are in the chansons.[38] Sometimes the word means cavalry in opposition to infantry – Sigar summoning his knights, spearmen and footmen to a meeting in his hall which was then attended by 'li chevalier e le serjant'.[39] More often it means elite warriors, for example in opposition to sergeants and townspeople. Rufus was informed that the Angevins besieging his garrison in Le Mans had erected a gallows on which they planned to hang 'li chevalier e li sergant e li burgeis'. When the victorious Haveloc is recognised as lord and king it is by the 'chevaliers, li prodom e li burgeis'.[40] Great nobles admired for their military skills, such as Robert of Bellême or Gilbert FitzRichard, are referred to as *chevalers*. Naturally English warriors, Hereward the Wake and his companions, are just as much *chevalers* as their French enemies.[41] One of those whose voice was listened to at the trial of

---

[35] Flori's interpretation of 1086 is chiefly based on Orderic's account (Orderic, iv.120). But although Orderic with hindsight may have seen the ceremony as a pre-figuration of Henry's coronation, can this have been so clear to the author of the Anglo-Saxon Chronicle who wrote that William 'dubbade his sunu Henric to ridere'? Besides making too much of the choice of the word 'ridere' rather than 'cniht', Flori dates its composition to post-1127, but see Cecily Clark, *The Peterborough Chronicle 1070–1154* (Oxford, 1970), xxi–xxiii for the view that most of the annals were composed soon after the events they described, and those for 1083–88 by a man who knew the royal court.

[36] Meneghetti, 'L'estoire des Engleis', 236–8. On the semantic range of the word 'chevalier' see Flori, 'La Notion de chevalerie', 219–44, 407–45. Less helpful is Bell's comment that the word 'chevalier is frequently used but without clear definition', A. Bell, 'Notes on Gaimar's Military Vocabulary', *Medium Aevum* XL (1971), 96, a remark which may reflect the orthodox view that 'proper' *chevalers* could not have existed in Anglo-Saxon England given the authority of Stenton's opinion that not until after 1066 was there a feudal society in England and hence only then a creature worthy of being called a knight 'in the technical sense of the word', F. M. Stenton, *The First Century of English Feudalism 1066–1166* (Oxford, 2nd edn 1961), 132–3. On this view see above, pp. 169–72.

[37] Gaimar, lines 735–6.
[38] Gaimar, line 2986.
[39] Gaimar, lines 645–6, 695.
[40] Gaimar, lines 752–3, 5808–9.
[41] Gaimar, lines 5519, 5568–71.

Godwin was a *chevaler* called Merleswein, referred to just two lines later as *riche barun*.[42] Not all the 1,700 men attached to William II's household can have been of baronial rank. None the less they are all 'powerful knights whom the king retained and held most dear'.[43] A particularly striking illustration of the brotherhood of arms is the case of the *chevaler* called Ethelwold whom King Edgar held dear, whom at times he called 'brother' or 'friend'.[44] In turbulent times a *chevaler* could be made a king; presumably here *chevaler* means noble.[45] For Gaimar then, although *chevaler* could mean just a soldier, it usually refers to an elite warrior, the kind of man who waited on kings and lived in the society of courts.[46]

If there were dubbed knights in Gaimar's world, then was there also a code of chivalrous behaviour? He clearly has views on the rules of war to be followed by all good knights. The king's men should not attack a man under the king's protection as Hereward was when Norman knights surprised him at his meal.[47] By contrast Hereward, when an outlaw at war with William, was fully entitled to surprise Norman knights while they were eating and kill twenty-six of them.[48] Some wars Gaimar describes as *guerre mult male*. One such was waged by Cadwalla and Mul of Wessex in 686. This, Gaimar explained, elaborating the laconic phrases of the *Anglo-Saxon Chronicle*, involved burning, plundering and robbing.[49] Even worse had been the conduct of the Scots in 684. 'The Scots cruelly wrought havoc; no church found any protection against them; they burned churches and chapels; violated married women and young girls.'[50] Thus there is unmistakably a critical edge when Gaimar says of William the Conqueror that, having tricked the northern thegns of their inheritances, he then marched south plundering and burning towns.[51]

From Sidney Painter to Jean Flori, historians of chivalry have seen in some of

---

[42] Gaimar, lines 4930–3, 5882, 6346.
[43] Gaimar, lines 5835–9, 5783, 5799, 5814 for the king's household knights as the garrison of Le Mans.
[44] Gaimar, lines 3627, 3631, 3705.
[45] Gaimar, line 2698, here elaborating the *ASC*'s 'not of royal birth'.
[46] If this is so then Gaimar's usage differed somewhat from Geoffrey of Monmouth's, at any rate if Tatlock is right in thinking that for Geoffrey the word *miles* 'implied not a rank but a function with little of the chivalric about it', J. P. S. Tatlock, *The Legendary History of Britain* (Berkeley, 1950), 332. However see *The History of the Kings of Britain*, vi.2, trans. L. Thorpe (Harmondsworth, 1966), 146.
[47] Gaimar, lines 5598, 5610, 5630–3.
[48] Gaimar, lines 5461–5, 5519–29.
[49] Gaimar, lines 1513–22, elaborating *ASC*'s statement that they 'ravaged Kent and the Isle of Wight'.
[50] Gaimar, lines 1478–82. I am grateful to Ian Short for confirming that Gaimar blamed the Scots, though the corresponding passage in the *Anglo-Saxon Chronicle* had referred – admittedly in easily misunderstood terms – to the conduct of the Northumbrian forces against the Scots in Ireland. Gaimar's words probably reflect the anti-Scottish feeling common in late 1130s England. On this see above, pp. 47–9, 101–2.
[51] Gaimar, lines 5377–98.

Orderic's stories about William Rufus the first clear evidence of a chivalric code of honour: fighting according to rules and sparing the lives of defeated enemies.[52] Orderic was writing in Latin in the early 1130s. Just a few years later Geoffrey Gaimar produced his own account of Rufus's reign and did so in French, the vernacular of chivalry. Despite this historians of chivalry have not looked at Gaimar on Rufus. Why not? I suppose because historians in general have been dismissive of Gaimar's account of the the reign, regarding its chronology as hopelessly muddled and conflated.[53] Of course in a sense it is, but in this context that is beside the point – that is to say, beside Gaimar's point. He was no longer turning annals into French verse; he was producing a brilliant portrait of a chivalrous king and shaping his material to this end.

It is surely not accidental nor muddled thinking on Gaimar's part that he begins his account of Rufus with the war against Maine, even though it actually occurred during 1098–1100, i.e. at the end of the reign, causing Barlow to comment, 'Gaimar devotes lines 5784–974 to the king's four expeditions to Maine, which he conflates, and produces scarcely a detail which can be trusted.'[54] It is precisely this anti-chronological ordering of the material which allows him to begin with those stories which, as we know from the accounts written by monks such as Orderic and William of Malmesbury, were the ones which made the deepest impression on contemporaries – the king's bravura crossing of the Channel in a storm and then his release of his prisoner, Elie of La Flèche, count of Maine. As told by Gaimar, these stories reveal a dauntless, good-humoured and generous king, one who spectacularly treats his enemies in conformity with one of the central planks of the chivalric code. Moreover, in Gaimar's eyes, the generosity worked to William's political advantage. After Count Elie had been released, his barons advised him to submit to Rufus, and he did.[55] It was exactly this episode which had led William of Malmesbury, much as on other counts he disapproved of Rufus, to write eloquently of the king's *magnanimitas* and to wonder if in him the soul of Julius Caesar had been re-incarnated.[56] According to Gaimar's rather less heretical

---

[52] Sidney Painter, *French Chivalry* (Baltimore, 1940), 33–4, 44–5; Flori, *L'Essor*, 271–4; see also Chibnall, *The World of Orderic*, 136–45.

[53] Although Freeman often cites Gaimar, he has no doubt that other writers were 'of much higher authority', E. A. Freeman, *The Reign of William Rufus* (Oxford, 1882), ii.600. On the other hand although Gaimar only figures on about twenty pages of Barlow's biography, since the relevant entry in his index reads 'Gaimar, passim', it seems likely that Gaimar helped to shape Barlow's judgement that 'Rufus undoubtedly played a part in developing the knightly code which became known as chivalry.' Frank Barlow, *William Rufus* (London, 1983), 118.

[54] Barlow, *Rufus*, 381 n. 179.

[55] Gaimar, lines 5921–50.

[56] WM c. 320. Since both standard editions of William's *Gesta regum*, William of Malmesbury, *Gesta Regum Anglorum*, vol. 1, ed. and trans. R. A. B. Mynors, R. M. Thomson and M. Winterbottom (Oxford, 1998), and ed. W. Stubbs, 2 vols. (RS, 1887–9), divide the work into identical chapters, I cite it in this fashion for simplicity's sake. Cf. c. 309 where he

version, Elie's submission so enhanced William's reputation that he could have advanced to Rome in pursuit of the claim once made by Brennius and Belinus. Here Rufus is explicitly associated with the heroic world of Geoffrey of Monmouth's great British kings.[57] But, in Gaimar's version of events, Rufus chose not to. Instead he returned to England and with his lands at peace he held court in his magnificent new hall at Westminster.

. In so far as historians of the Norman period have been able to bring themselves to make much use of the 'unreliable' Gaimar, it has been for his account of that court.[58] Usually when he used the word *curteis* it was in a military context. We see Rufus *cume prodom e cume curteis* riding to war in the company of 1,700 knights *de privee maisnie*.[59] He used the identical formula – *prodom e curteis* – to praise a fisherman who gave his former lord, Hereward, vital help in his struggle against the Normans.[60] Although this suggests that *curteis* had the warlike sense which Glyn Burgess has attributed to it in what he termed 'pre-courtly literature',[61] none the less there can be no doubt that Rufus holding court at Westminster is portrayed as a very courtly king. He was not to be ruffled by the Giffard hair-cut. Instead he laughed and in a splendidly courteous gesture he got twenty of his own squires to chop off their hair too. In Gaimar's words, 'A curtesie le lur turnat.'[62] One of the key symbols of courtly society, the 'self-consciously youthful, lay, aristocratic and curial' 1090s cult of long hair which monastic authors associated with 'the youth of the court' and which they fiercely condemned,[63] is handled by Gaimar in a way which reveals his indifference to monastic values. He betrays not the slightest sympathy for those monks who wanted to impose puritanical standards on the world outside the monastery.[64]

When at this Westminster court, Earl Hugh of Chester got on his high horse and 'announced that he was not prepared to act as anyone's servant', it was once again Rufus's good humour and generosity of spirit which turned to his own advantage what could have been an ugly incident. The outcome was that the earl

compared the king's magnanimity to Alexander's. John of Salisbury was also impressed, *Policraticus*, ed. C. J. J. Webb (Oxford, 1909), ii.613–14; so too was Henry of Huntingdon, *Historia Anglorum*, ed. T. Arnold (RS, 1879), 231; ed. D. Greenway (Oxford, 1996), 446–7.

[57] Gaimar, lines 5957–68. Apart from Rufus, Edgar is the only king of England whom Gaimar associated with the world of Geoffrey of Monmouth.

[58] Crouch, *Image of Aristocracy*, makes good use of this episode in Gaimar. So also does Blacker, *Faces of Time*, 93–5.

[59] Gaimar, lines 5823–44. See Barlow, *Rufus*, 385 n. 191.

[60] Gaimar, lines 5500, 5518, 5844.

[61] G. S. Burgess, *Contribution a l'étude du vocabulaire précourtois* (Geneva, 1970), 21–2.

[62] Gaimar, lines 6089–93.

[63] Robert Bartlett, 'Symbolic Meanings of Hair in the Middle Ages', *TRHS*, 6th ser. 4 (1994), 50–2, 58–9.

[64] Cf. Gaimar on Dunstan's attempted interference with Edgar's love marriage (below, p. 251). But there is no doubting his piety and reverence for saints – when kept in their proper place, in shrines.

willingly volunteered to serve the king and in return was given high authority in
North Wales. In Gaimar's words, 'And this act of liberality (*bonté*) by the king
will evermore be to his credit, and people will always talk of the great act of
nobility (*barnage*) that he performed.'[65] The jokiness which so offended monks
appears in a totally different light in this secular history. Indeed Rufus's handling
of the situations created by Earl Hugh's pride and the Giffard hair-cut
demonstrates that he possessed to the full two of those qualities which Stephen
Jaeger has highlighted as key components of the courtly ideal: restraint of
passion and witty good humour.[66] In Gaimar's words William 'was joyful and
merry all his days' and 'never was a king so well loved nor so honoured by his
people'.[67] Throughout William II is presented as a model king, a fine warrior, a
lion feared by his neighbours and also a ruler who did much for the internal
well-being of his kingdom, both by a conscious policy of encouraging the great
virtue of hospitality and by ruling strongly and keeping the peace. Indeed the
theme of Rufus's peace and justice is almost as central as the theme of his good
humour.[68] A lion of justice with a smile?[69]

It was after this court, to continue with Gaimar's narrative, that Rufus heard
that his enemy Malcolm of Scotland had been killed.[70] But instead of
immediately rewarding Robert of Mowbray, the man responsible for Malcolm's
death, he summoned him to court in order to investigate and determine whether
he has done well or not. In the very next lines Mowbray is accused of treason.
Gaimar himself explicitly leaves open whether or not the killing of Malcolm was
right or wrong (*u dreit u tort*).[71] Whatever really happened, there was undoubtedly, as Barlow put it, 'more than a whiff of dishonour in the air'.[72]
Orderic believed that Malcom was murdered while *inermis* and returning to
Scotland under safe-conduct, and that in consequence 'king and magnates felt
deep shame that such a disgraceful and cruel deed had been perpetrated by
Normans'.[73] Killing a noble, let alone a king, unarmed and in such circumstances
was certainly against the rules. If a row over this helped to precipitate the
rebellion of Robert Mowbray, he would not be the last earl of Northumbria to
rebel believing that he had received scant justice after performing a signal

[65] Gaimar, lines 6011–46.
[66] Jaeger, *Origins of Courtliness*, 116, 162–75, 238, 246, 258–61.
[67] Gaimar, lines 6239, 5917–18, and for the laughter of Rufus, 5929, 5937–8, 6012, 6039, 6089, 6299.
[68] Gaimar, lines 5775–7, 5869, 6173, 6206–7.
[69] By contrast with Rufus, Henry I's relative lack of a sense of humour, his notorious inability to take a joke and his economical court style (in comparison with that of his first wife as well as with that of his predecesssor) may mean that Gaimar's allusion to the jokes and feasting at Henry's court was intended ironically. For an example of Gaimar's humour see below, p. 247.
[70] In fact Malcolm had been killed in 1093.
[71] Gaimar, lines 6106–28.
[72] Barlow, *Rufus*, 316–17.
[73] Orderic, iv.270.

service against the Scots. In Gaimar's version, after Mowbray has been accused of treason, Rufus marches against him and defeats him. But then, and this is emphasised, Rufus neither mutilated him nor put him to death, even though he had wanted to kill the king and was guilty of that same treason 'for which', in Gaimar's words, 'Waltheof had been killed'.[74] The explicit parallel between Mowbray and Waltheof means that Gaimar is comparing William II with his father, on whose orders the English earl had been executed in 1076. It is a comparison entirely to the advantage of the more chivalrous Rufus. He spared life and limb, whereas William the Conqueror had put an innocent man to death.[75] After noting the miracles at Crowland Abbey attributed to the presence there of the body of William I's victim, Gaimar writes simply 'A little later the king died.'[76]

This icy brevity stands in marked contrast to Gaimar's extra-ordinary treatment of Rufus's death, with its lengthy description of the outpouring of grief by worthy knights and noble barons. Moreover he insists that Rufus made a good end. At least three times the dying king asks for the *Corpus domini*, but he is 'in the forest far from any church'. A huntsman gives him communion in the form of some herbs in flower and gets the king to eat a little. This and the fact that he had taken consecrated bread the previous Sunday 'should be a good warrant for him'.[77] Other versions of Rufus's death have him die at once, without a word. As Eadmer made explicit this meant that he died unrepentant and unshriven.[78] Obviously Gaimar's insistence that the king begged for communion and possessed 'good warrant', is evidence that he was well aware that many people, ecclesiastics in particular, took a very different view of Rufus's fate. As Antonia Gransden observed, 'this reads like a conscious refutation of contemporary accounts'.[79] But what is it that Gaimar is insisting on throughout his account of Rufus's life and death? That what the king obtained was what Geoffrey de Charny, who wrote about chivalry from the

---

[74] Gaimar, lines 6128–36, 6168. For a discussion of the rebellion of 1095 and the treatment of the rebels see Barlow, *Rufus*, 346–59. In the light of Gaimar's favourable portrait of Rufus, it is worth noting that he did not mention the fate of William of Alderie, widely believed, according to William of Malmesbury, to have been unjustly punished by Rufus, WM c. 319. On the subject of the appropriate penalty for rebellion, see above, pp. 209–29.

[75] Gaimar, lines 5721–2 and p. 271 for the editor's comment on the translation of *surdit* as 'calumny'.

[76] Gaimar, lines 5718–32.

[77] Gaimar, lines 6329–408. Moreover he is careful to insist that the bishop and monks of Winchester prayed and sang so well for Rufus 'that never till the day of judgement will there be such masses and such service for any one king as they did for him', lines 6411–23. The fact that Gaimar refers to 'good bishop Walkelin' is beside the point. There was no consecrated bishop of Winchester when Rufus was buried there. And the cathedral at Winchester which Gaimar knew, see lines 2329–36, was the one built by Walkelin.

[78] Eadmer, *Historia Novorum*, ed. M. Rule (RS, 1884), 116; Orderic, v.290; WM c. 333; *ASC* ad annum 1100, 'impenitent'.

[79] Gransden, *Historical Writing*, 211. Gaimar, lxxiii–iv for Bell's suggestion that Gaimar's account might derive 'from an eye-witness of the fatal scene'.

inside, said was the highest honour in chivalry, 'honour in this world and the repose of paradise hereafter'.[80]

II. *Kingship*

Obviously I have already said much about 'chivalric kingship'. In this part I shall focus on other aspects. Gaimar's history was explicitly inspired by the *History of the Kings of Britain* and like Geoffrey of Monmouth he used the reigns of kings to organise his material. This is king-centred and court-centred history. It ends with Rufus as a model of chivalrous kingship. It had begun with Haveloc, on whom Gaimar lavishes more than 700 lines. When we are first introduced to this bold and handsome young man (*bel vadletun*), with the beautiful body and joyous (*liez*, one of the words used of Rufus) countenance,[81] he is a servant in a king's *maison*, receiving cake and simnels. At once we are in the world of the *Domus Regis* as described in the *Constitutio* (a document thought to be precisely contemporary with Gaimar).[82] No sooner has the scullion received his cake and simnels, than he gives them away. 'He would give away whatever he had, that was his way, and if he had nothing to give then he would borrow in order to be able to give.' Of course we – the author and his readers – know that although Haveloc, the male Cinderella, is working in the kitchen and is ignorant of his real *lignage*, he is in fact a king's son, *de gentil lit*.[83] We are in a society of largesse and lineage.[84] This sets the tone for the whole history. From now on the virtues which will be praised are the classic virtues: prowess, largesse, *franchise*. Thus Haveloc displays both prowess and a generous spirit. Young Haveloc is bold and strong enough to deal with any one who pesters him by beating and binding them; but he is also so *francs* that he is quick to release them and be reconciled.[85] Later when he recovered his father's throne by defeating the usurper Odulf in battle, he alone killed more than twenty.[86] After his victory 'two princes who were his enemies and had supported Odulf came and asked for mercy as also did the *menue gent* of the land. Taking the counsel of his barons Haveloc pardoned them.'[87]

[80] 'très-haute honneur en ce siècle et à la fin l'âme en paradis', Geofrey de Charny, *Livre de Chevalerie* in Froissart, *Oeuvres*, ed. Kervyn de Lettenhove (Brussels, 1875), i. part 3, 511.
[81] Gaimar, lines 104–11.
[82] *Constitutio Domus Regis*, in Richard Fitz Nigel, *Dialogus de Scaccario*, ed. C. Johnson, F. E. L. Carter, D. Greenway (Oxford, 1983), 129–35, esp. 131–2.
[83] Gaimar, lines 103–60.
[84] On largesse as the supreme virtue, see Chrétien, *Cligés*, lines 175–213.
[85] Gaimar, lines 109–24.
[86] And he was a dab hand with an axe, Gaimar, lines 537–52, 741–2.
[87] Gaimar, lines 743–50. Meneghetti interpreted this passage as a sign of the weak monarchy of Stephen's reign, 'L'Estoire des Engleis', 244–5; but see above, p. 225. In Gaimar, and in the somewhat later Lai of Haveloc, there is nothing remotely resembling the savage punishment (typically fourteenth century) meted out to Odulf in the Middle English *Havelock the Dane*. See W. R. J. Barron, 'The penalties for treason in medieval life and literature', *Journal of Medieval History* 7 (1981), 187–201.

After using the tale of Haveloc to engage his reader's interest, Gaimar confines himself for the next 1,800 lines or so to a remarkably close version of the laconic annals of the *Anglo-Saxon Chronicle*, often doing little more than adding an adjective here and there. Since this is all very basic, this scamper through the early centuries – although tedious reading – does have the advantage of highlighting the most basic terms in Gaimar's vocabulary of kingship. Exactly as we would anticipate kings are 'valiant': Aethelric son of Ida, Oswald, Ceolred of Mercia. Aethelfrith, the victor at Chester, is noble and mighty. Eanfrith of Bernicia and Offa of Essex are *gentil*. Anna is noble; Cwichelm and Aethelheard of Wessex are wise. Cenwalh was *prodom*, so too Aethelred of Mercia; Hlothere of Kent was *prodom e noble*; Nothumbrian Osric is *fort*.[88] The first king of whom a little more is said, and the first to be called *li bon reis*, is Oswy. He 'established laws and loved peace'.[89]

Then, after inserting another tale, the story of Buern Butsecarle, Gaimar arrives at the life and times of King Alfred, on which he has a great deal to say. Indeed in the longer term his 600 line account of Alfred was to be the most influential part of his entire history. At times Gaimar presents Alfred in entirely coventional terms as a ruler 'who well knew how to give counsel/ And order a battle/ And well he knew how to make war.'[90] Like Rufus and Haveloc, Alfred demonstrated mercy and generosity, this time after his victory over the heathen Danes in 878. Here Gaimar is elaborating the account in the Anglo-Saxon Chronicle.[91] But Gaimar also emphasises what was exceptional about Alfred, his learning and his concern for history; he identifies him as the brain behind the *Anglo-Saxon Chronicle*.[92] Since he praises no other king in similar terms, it is clear that Gaimar recognised Alfred for the exceptional ruler he was. By contrast, with Alfred's son, Edward the Elder, we are back in the realm of the conventional: 'li proz, li sages, li gentilz'.[93]

On his next good king, Edgar, Gaimar devotes about 400 lines. He was more powerful than any king since Arthur.[94] Edgar indeed is the one king to be explicitly compared with Arthur – though only, it should be noted, in terms of

[88] Gaimar, lines 1005, 1079, 1255, 1280, 1287, 1301, 1360, 1423, 1517, 1610, 1648, 1711, 1722.

[89] Gaimar, lines 1308, 1389.

[90] Gaimar, lines 2845–7, 3381, 3441–2.

[91] Gaimar, lines 3190–228. Though Gaimar does not go to the extent Asser does in elaborating both the desperate straits to which the Danes were reduced and the extent of Alfred's mercy, *Asser's Life of King Alfred*, ed. W. H. Stevenson (Oxford, 1959), 46.

[92] 'He was a clerk and a good astronomer'; 'no better clerk there was than he'. Gaimar, lines 2848, 3443. Although admiration for Alfed's learning was commonplace, no other historian, until the author of the prose *Brut* – who was copying Gaimar – does what Gaimar does, i.e. credits Alfred with responsibility for the *Anglo-Saxon Chronicle*, lines 2329–36, 3445–50. See above, pp. 113–22.

[93] Gaimar, line 3454.

[94] Gaimar, lines 3562–8. On the association between Edgar and Arthur see above, pp. 23, 96.

power. Otherwise he treats Edgar far more positively than he does the tyrannical Arthur. Edgar is given the qualities of the chivalrous/courtly king. Although all too fond of women, he is *francs e debonaire*, wise and valiant, *francs e gentilz*.[95] By far the greater part of Gaimar's version of Edgar's reign is taken up with the story of the king's love for Elftroed, a story to which I shall return. Here I simply emphasise that it is a story of treachery and vengeance. Edgar's trusted friend, the knight Ethelwold, was sent to see Elftroed but fell for her himself, and so he became a deceiver (*losengier* – the bête noire of the troubadours), betraying both her father and his own lord. When Edgar eventually discovered the treachery, he had Ethelwold covertly killed. This, Gaimar wryly observes, meant that Edgar could not avenge his man's death because no one could tell him who killed him.[96] Although Gaimar very sensibly makes no attempt to portray Edward the Confessor as a knight, he does praise him highly, above all as a law-giver and as peace-keeper.[97] The one episode in his reign which he narrates at length is the trial of Godwin. Here we are shown an angry king accusing Godwin of betraying and murdering his brother. But at the end of the trial Edward very properly accepts the advice of his magnates in the formal shape of an award of the court; he is then reconciled with Godwin and his family, treats them generously and Godwin serves him well. On this episode, Gaimar's last words are 'And Edward reigned in great honour.'[98] That forgiveness and reconciliation may lead to good service from those forgiven, and from their kin and friends, is one of the arguments put both at the trial of Ganelon and in the Rochester debate about what Rufus should do with the rebels of 1088.[99] As literary scholars have pointed out, in several respects the trial in Gaimar is like the trial in Marie de France's *Lanval*.[100] An angry king brings charges against an accused whom he wishes to see dead. The defendant denies the charge *de mot en mot* – how else? – and there then ensues a debate as to whether a king's word is alone sufficient. In the end the barons give their decision and the king accepts it. But unlike Marie, Gaimar emphasises what the king wins, good service and honour.

Cnut and William I – the two great conquerors of English history – are two kings about whom Gaimar writes much but about whom he remains ambivalent.[101] At times, notably in the legendary context of his single combat with Edmund Ironside and in punishing Eadric Streona for his murder of Edmund, Cnut is treated very favourably. It is worth noting that in this version the murderous traitor was executed only after Cnut had summoned the barons and

---

[95] Gaimar, lines 3572, 3583, 3592, 3737.
[96] Gaimar, lines 3664–856.
[97] Gaimar, lines 4855–60, 5133–4.
[98] Gaimar, lines 4861–5028.
[99] Orderic, iv.126–35. Cf. above, pp. 219–20.
[100] Bell, Gaimar, *Estoire*, lxxv.
[101] Gaimar, line 5421, refers to William as 'li bons reis', but otherwise, as already noted, he takes a critical view.

formally recounted and proved his offence before them.[102] On the other hand, Cnut kills Olaf, explicitly referred to as the rightful king of Norway, and when Edmund's sons are grown-up enough to pose a threat to him, he plotted to have them put to death. This was on the advice of his queen, and Gaimar clearly disapproved.[103] It may have been this ambiguity in Gaimar's treatment of Cnut which allowed later readers of Gaimar's version of the story of King Canute and the waves to read a negative view of the king into it, and thus help to establish the popular image of the ruler who was arrogant rather than the humble king portrayed by Henry of Huntingdon.[104]

For Gaimar's perception of the characteristic qualities of 'bad kings', there is one generalisation to the effect that such rulers fail to do right and torment their serfs.[105] Otherwise we are almost entirely dependent upon his portrayals of three villains in the tales of Haveloc and Buern Butsecarl.[106] The first such *feluns reis* is Edelsi, the fifth century British king who, in order to seize his niece's inheritance, disparages her by marrying her to his scullion Haveloc and then jokes nastily about their plight.[107] The second is Odulf, *traitre e fel*, who betrayed his lord, Haveloc's father, and then got the conquering King Arthur *le fort* to install him on the throne of Denmark.[108] The third is Osbrith of Northumbria, *li fel*, who raped Buern's wife, left her weeping and afterwards joked about it with his *privez* (two of whom had been in the room when he carried out the rape).[109]

III. *Nobles*

The dramatic incidents of these two tales also enable us to see what qualities Gaimar admired in men not of royal birth.[110] In the first tale we see Sigar, the good seneschal and justiciar who recognises Haveloc as the true heir and raises

[102] Gaimar, lines 4301, 4343, 4389–92, 4447–78.
[103] Gaimar, lines 4535–64, 4688.
[104] Gaimar, lines 4689–718. Whatever moral Gaimar intended, he did not spell it out in the explicit manner of a Henry of Huntingdon.
[105] Gaimar, lines 1441–2.
[106] Apart from a brief reference to the heathen Cubba as 'un tirant' there are virtually no clear-cut cases of 'bad kings' in Gaimar's real history. Even Aethelred the Unready escapes fairly lightly despite his military failure against Swein; the one clear note of criticism is one that may reflect either Gaimar's own or his patron's local concern, Aethelred's cruel war in Lindsey. Cnut's two sons are simply passed over with the comment that between them they reigned seven years and they weren't the rightful heirs anyway. Gaimar, lines 935–6, 4173–6, 4671–5, 4748–62, where he adds that since the Danes despised the English, the latter were very happy to see them go.
[107] Gaimar, lines 96–8, 169, 187–8, 321–2.
[108] Gaimar, lines 508–26.
[109] Gaimar, lines 2618–95.
[110] Otherwise, for the pre-959 period there is little except a few and very basic expansions of the *Chronicle* in such characterisations of ninth century West Saxon ealdormen in the forefront of resistance to the Danes as *pruz e si vaillant* or *un bon barun*, Gaimar, lines 2395, 2409–12.

an army to restore him to throne. Sigar is a *prodom* so discreet that he is even able to refrain from blurting out his thoughts when in bed with his wife.[111] In the second we have the loyal warrior Buern Butsecarl, *gentilz hom*, *prodom*, *nobles e gentilz*. When his wife is raped, he formally defies Osbrith ('jo te desfi . . . tun humage ci te rendrait, Ja mais de tei rien ne tendrai'), then takes counsel with his kin and together they choose the *chevaler* Ella as an anti-king. To complete his revenge he calls in the Danes, but they then dispose of both Osbrith and Ella, overthow the kingdom of Northumbria, and so pave the way for the great confrontation between Alfred and the Danes which Gaimar sees as the turning-point in Anglo-Saxon history.[112] Another layman who only appears in what is presumably a legendary history is Walgar, *gentilz hom* and *prodom*, the Danish marcher lord who sacrifices his own power base (*Citez aveit e grant cunted*) in order to saves the lives of Edmund Ironside's sons by taking them to Hungary.[113]

On the other hand there are few villains in Gaimar. Apart from the 'false and very cunning' Walter Tirel,[114] who may – or may not – have murdered Rufus, there is the treacherous Ethelwold who tricked King Edgar, and the treacherous Eadric Streona, a felon who murdered his lord (Edmund Ironside) in ingenious fashion and was duly punished for it.[115] The assassin sent by a king of Wessex to kill Edwin of Northumbria in 626 is described as a man of vile birth (*de pute orine*) who committed a great dishonour.[116]

More revealing of Gaimar's outlook is the fact that during the course of his narrative of the Norman period he chose to praise three men who, different though they are, have one thing in common: other extant sources find in them much to criticise. The three are Robert of Bellême, Hereward the Wake, and Earl Hugh of Chester. Gaimar's admiration for them highlights the way in which he judged men by non-ecclesiastical standards.

To Robert of Bellême Gaimar devotes 14 lines, expatiating on his retinue of a thousand knights and his great estates before concluding that 'for war he was the best knight that men could have known'.[117] Not the slightest hint of the stories of Robert's cruelties that came to the ears of Orderic and, nearer to home, of Henry of Huntingdon, canon of Lincoln.[118]

Hereward, to whom Gaimar devotes some 230 lines, first appears as *un gentilz*

---

[111] Gaimar, lines 503–736.

[112] Gaimar, lines 2593–720. For some reason the *Anglo-Saxon Chronicle*'s account of the crisis in Northumbria in 867 misses out these fascinating details. On Alfred's reign as turning-point see above, pp. 121–2.

[113] Gaimar, lines 4497–613.

[114] Gaimar, lines 6300–302, 6318–28.

[115] Gaimar, lines 4393–430, 4449–51.

[116] Gaimar, lines 1171–7. By contrast in the *Chronicle* nothing whatever was said of his birth – though since he was named he was presumably a man of rank, as indeed that fact that he obtained access to Edwin suggests.

[117] Gaimar, lines 5881–2.

[118] Orderic, iv.158–60 etc., HH (ed. Arnold), 234, 238, 310; ed. Greenway, 450–1, 458–9, 602–5.

hom whom the Normans have disinherited. Entirely conventionally Gaimar admires his prowess and bravery. He is as bold as a leopard; in his last stand against the unchivalrous Normans and in the face of overwhelming odds he carried himself *gentement*, and fights fiercely to the bitter end, like a wild boar.[119] What is unusual about Gaimar's version is his insistence that Hereward did no wrong in his assaults on Peterborough and Stamford and that what damage he did there was no more than the monks and townspeople deserved for their misdeeds and trickery.[120] Here Gaimar is presumably rebutting charges made locally against Hereward, some of which can still be detected in the Peterborough Chronicle's account of the attack on the monastery.[121]

Gaimar devoted more space to Earl Hugh of Chester than to any other Norman magnate and he praised him warmly for his lavish hospitality and generosity. Now of all the Norman aristocrats planted in England by the Conqueror, it was precisely Earl Hugh of whom Orderic drew the most vivid and fiercely critical portrait. Hugh was alleged to be 'a slave to gluttony, a mountain of fat given over to carnal lusts . . . He was a great lover of the world and worldly pomp which he thought the greatest blessing of the human lot . . . a lover of games and luxuries, actors, horses, and dogs and other vanities of the same kind. He was always surrounded by a huge household full of the noise of swarms of boys of both high and humble birth.'[122] As his portrayal of the court of Rufus shows, Gaimar took a far more positive view of the pomps and vanities of the world, and it is striking that he gives so much attention to precisely that noble whom Orderic had presented as the embodiment of wordly values and youth culture among the Norman aristocracy. Indeed at times Gaimar's admiring words appear to be putting a positive gloss on some of Orderic's negative comments. Where Orderic wrote that Hugh 'went about surrounded by an army instead of a household', Gaimar's version was that 'the emperor of Lombardy did not keep such a company as he did of his private retinue'. Whereas Orderic wrote that Hugh was 'more prodigal than generous . . . keeping no check on what he gave or received', Gaimar said that 'however much he might give away one day, the next he would remember it and distribute just as much'.[123]

Was Gaimar answering Orderic? In some respects the evidence is against this. There is nothing to suggest that Gaimar knew St Evroul, or indeed that he ever visited Normandy; so far as we know, no copy of Orderic's *Ecclesiastical History* ever came to England. Yet, as Marjorie Chibnall observed of a related problem, it is hard to believe that Orderic and William of Malmesbury were ignorant of each other's existence.[124] Similarly I find it hard to imagine that Gaimar can have

---

[119] Gaimar, lines 5462–694. He also describes Edmund Ironside as 'bold as a leopard', line 4342. On the wild boar motif see Asser on Alfred, fighting *aprino more*, Stevenson, 29.

[120] Gaimar, lines 5550–64.

[121] ASC, E, ad annum 1071.

[122] Orderic, ii.262–3; iii.216–17.

[123] Orderic, ii.260–3; Gaimar, lines 5855–7, 5864–6.

[124] Orderic, ii.xxiv–xxv.

been ignorant of Orderic. We know that Orderic visited Crowland Abbey at some date between 1109 and 1124 – and, given his re-writing of the Life of St Guthlac, his name and his work as an author must surely have remained well-known to the monks there. Gaimar refers to, and appears to have read, a Life of Guthlac – perhaps, but necessarily, Orderic's[125] – and Crowland (in Lincoln-shire) was certainly a place known to him. As Earl Waltheof's shrine it was a place of some importance for those who took a sceptical view of William I. Even though Gaimar may not have known the text of Orderic's *History*, it seems to me likely that he was familiar with the sort of image which monks such as Orderic liked to construct about Earl Hugh, an image profoundly hostile to the 'world's delights, values and activites' which Gaimar celebrated.[126]

For Orderic it was a point of criticism that Hugh of Chester thought more highly of falconers and huntsmen than he did of monks.[127] It would, of course, be strange if kings and nobles had not valued huntsmen highly. They were their companions in their daily pleasures, and the death of William Rufus is only the most famous of reminders of the dangers inherent in this particular pleasure. When men were out hunting they were at risk and hence most in need of companions whom they could trust with their lives.[128] Gaimar's appreciation of the pleasures of aristocratic life suggests that he, like Orderic's Earl Hugh, may have thought more of the values of the falconers and huntsmen than of the monks. According to Gaimar, it was a huntsman who improvised the last rites for Rufus, and huntsmen who made for him a bier out of branches, flowers and fern. According to him it was the huntsmen who spoke the final words of lamentation over the dead king.[129]

IV. *Love and Marriage*

It is clear from the romantic episodes in his history that Gaimar is keenly interested in the subject of love and marriage and that he regards sexual attraction and satisfaction as central ingredients in that relationship, both during marriage and before it. The story of Edgar, Elftroed and Ethelwold is above all a tale of passion. After kissing her Edgar is inflamed (*enlumined*) and thinks that if he does not have her he will die. After his wooing she too is *enluminee*. After Edgar has succeeded in killing her husband Ethelwold, they marry and although Arch-bishop Dunstan appears on the scene to voice his disapproval, their love was such – says Gaimar – that they cared not a jot for his sermonising.[130] A. R. Press

---

[125] Gaimar, lines 1635–7, and lvi for Bell's comment.
[126] Above, p. 235. Cf. Blacker, *Faces of Time*, 93–4.
[127] Orderic, ii.262.
[128] Cf. above, p. 176.
[129] Gaimar, lines 6333, 6372–82, 6405–8.
[130] Gaimar, lines 3810–960. Some of the scenes in this episode are reminiscent of Geoffrey of Monmouth, e.g. the account of Vortigern falling in love and, as Ian Short pointed out, of the love of Utherpendragon for Ygerne. Other scenes, such as the wedding feast and

has plausibly suggested that Gaimar knew William of Malmesbury's version of this story, in which Edgar is criticised, and that he was answering it.[131] Through Oxford or Winchester contacts Gaimar is likely to have known of William.[132] Here too Gaimar appears to be replying to the monks.

Sex is also treated positively in his Haveloc story. The arranged marriage between Haveloc and Argentille, at first a cause of shame and awkwardness between them, works out well as soon as they have made love.[133] In his study of *Erec and Enide*, Luttrell pointed to the similarities in the way these two married couples talked together, especially in bed.[134] In fact Argentille is rather shrewder than Enide and it is consistently her advice – including a cunning battle ruse – which Haveloc follows and which brings him success.[135] In the story of Buern Butsecarl the relationship between husband and raped wife is sympathetically delineated. She tells him what has happened when he returns home from the king's service and finds her pale and drawn. 'Now it is right that I lose my life/ Although that (the rape) was done secretly/ I wish to die openly.' Buern's reply is that because she was taken by force she had no need to feel shamed, and before seeking revenge he makes it clear that he will continue to love her and kiss her.[136] Finally sex has its part to play in Gaimar's account of the exile of Edmund Ironside's sons. The king of Hungary's daughter takes one of them, Edgar, described as *sened* (sensible, well-favoured) as her lover. When she becomes pregnant, her father gets them to marry and, in default of a son, he makes Edgar his heir. Gaimar tells the story of pre-marital sex without a hint of condemnation, indeed he emphasise that one of the offspring of this love marriage was Margaret, 'the jewel', later queen of Scotland.[137]

As usual some of his brief expansions of the *Anglo-Saxon Chronicle* reflect, however palely, Gaimar's attitudes. For example, when translating the *Chronicle* on the marriage of Aethelraed of Northumbria to Aelfflaed in 792, he adds: 'She was deeply devoted to her lord/ and took pains to serve him,/ And therefore he loved her much.'[138] Similarly on the occasion of the West Saxon King Brihtric's

Elftroed's wedding dress are given in the kind of detail which would be characteristic of Chrétien. As in *Erec and Enide*, the question of whom a king can marry is an issue, Gaimar, lines 3619–26.
[131] Press, 'The precocious courtesy', 270–3. Cf. Bell, Gaimer, *Estoire*, lxvii–lxxii.
[132] On the Oxford and, possibly, Winchester contacts see Short, 'Gaimar's Epilogue'.
[133] Gaimar, lines 173–92.
[134] C. Luttrell, *The Creation of the First Arthurian Romance* (Evanston, 1974), 57.
[135] Gaimar, lines 309–12, 771–81. For the wife as wise counsellor see also P. S. Gold, *The Lady and the Virgin* (Chicago, 1985), 8–10, 15. In fact wives had long been presented as giving their husbands crucial advice, e.g. Bede on the two critical decisions made by Redwald of East Anglia, Bede, ii.12, 15.
[136] Gaimar, lines 2643–72. Rape also plays a part in the Haveloc story. On this occasion Haveloc returned in time to prevent it and though outnumbered six to one is able to kill or wound all the assailants, lines 531–43.
[137] Gaimar, lines 4619–48.
[138] Gaimar, lines 2138–40.

marriage to Offa's daughter Eadburh (reported in the Chronicle without comment), Gaimar adds that she was *bele e gentille*.[139]

Is there any sense in which Gaimar's attitude to women and love can be called chivalrous? Did anyone take up arms to help a 'damsel in distress'? Only if the rape or attempted rape of a wife counts as distress. Was anyone inspired to fight more courageously to win the admiration of noble women? There is no scene in Gaimar equivalent to the 'imitation battle' in Geoffrey of Monmouth in which the flirtatious behaviour of the female spectators is said to arouse the knights' fighting ardour.[140] On the other hand Gaimar does envisage women being attracted by a warrior's reputation. A rich lady called Alftrued, having heard of Hereward's prowess, let him know that he could have both her love and her father's honour if he cared to come to her, and eventually Hereward was ready to fall in with her urgings.[141]

V. *Implications and Questions*

Why has Gaimar remained so little known? In part no doubt because his British history does not survive, being rapidly supplanted by Wace's. Hence the Arthurian addicts have passed him by. The few allusions to Arthur in Gaimar's English history present a negative picture of a belligerent tyrant.[142] If his British History had been similarly unenthusiastic about Arthur, it might easily have seemed less cosmopolitan than Wace's version, particularly after the end of the twelfth century by which time the English had adopted Arthur as one of their own.[143] But even specialists in Anglo-Norman literature have thought of Gaimar in terms of his precocious courtliness, not in terms of chivalric values. It may well be significant that some of the military features characteristic of the courtly romances are not to be found in Gaimar. There are, for example, no tournaments and no jousts, no splintering of lance on shield.[144] The single combat between Edmund Ironside and Cnut was to be on foot.[145] That infantry were seen as playing a central military role is clear from Argentille's ruse (advising Haveloc to re-use his dead soldiers by propping up their bodies with

---

[139] Gaimar, lines 2061–2.

[140] HRB c. 157; trans. Thorpe (Harmondsworth, 1966), ix.14.

[141] Gaimar, lines 5586–97. Here too, as in Gaimar's story of the Hungarian princess and Edgar, it was the lady who took the initiative, as so often in the romances. See J. Weiss, 'The wooing woman in Anglo-Norman romance' in Mills, Fellows and Meale, *Romance in Medieval England*, 149–61; J. Gillingham, 'Love, Marriage and Politics in the Twelfth Century', *Forum for Modern Language Studies* 25 (1989), 292–303, reprinted in *Richard Coeur de Lion. Kingship Chivalry and War in the Twelfth Century* (London, 1994), 243–55.

[142] Gaimar, lines 408–15, 512–14.

[143] As he appears in the Haveloc story 'Arthur was still a Celtic hero, not yet fully adopted by the English', Lee C. Ramsey, *Chivalric Romances. Popular Literature in Medieval England* (Bloomington, 1983), 28. For King Arthur in Stephen's reign see above, pp. 33, 37–9.

[144] Gaimar, p. xli.

[145] Gaimar, lines 4251–94.

stakes).[146] There are descriptions of two battles in which cavalry are engaged, one near York in 867 and the Battle of Hastings. In both there appear to be no couched lances; spears are for thrusting or throwing.[147] Since tournaments and jousts developed after 1100, it is not that surprising that they are missing from a history which ended in 1100.[148]

This raises the question of how vital to chivalry are tournaments and knights jousting for love of ladies?[149] The classic virtues of good knighthood are *prouesse, loyaute, largesse, courtoisie* and *franchise*.[150] Obviously prowess is central, even perhaps prowess on horseback, but does this have to mean jousting and couched lance? In the battles of 867 and 1066 Gaimar focuses attention not upon an aspect of technique but upon an aspect of courage. Who will strike the first blow?[151] Those who do, Orin at York and Taillefer at Hastings, die in the battle – but their names live on. Consider Gaimar's King Alfred, the good king, *le gentil rei*.[152] He and his men often rode (*chevalchat*) against the heathen. The Danes feared his prowess (*prueise*); 'for wise he was and a good warrior; he knew well how to make his enemies yield'. Once they had admitted defeat, he treated them with mercy and generosity.[153] Was Gaimar's Alfred a chivalrous king? What is central? The techniques and the setting? Or the virtues and the qualities? If what turns heroic warfare into chivalric warfare is the desire to please women, then Gaimar is not chivalric. On the other hand if, along side the traditional military values, it is the routinely compassionate treatment of high-status enemies which principally characterises chivalry, then Gaimar can very fairly be described as such an author.

And yet the historians of chivalry have ignored Gaimar. Has not the underlying problem been the fact that Gaimar wrote a history of England in England, not of France in France, and everyone knows that 'there were no tournaments and there was no chivalry in England'?[154] That being so, England is not the place to look for early evidence of chivalry. I do not want to dissent from the perception of chivalry as quintessentially French. I think it probably

---

[146] Gaimar, lines 775–94. In the later *Lai of Haveloc*, Argentille's ruse is too good to omit, but the new world of jousting is indicated by the 'wicked' king remarking that he will get his cooks to joust with pots and pans – humour at the expense of the ex-scullion hero, *Le Lai d'Haveloc*, ed. A. Bell (Manchester, 1925), lines 1022–4.

[147] Gaimar, lines 2782–824, 5255–338.

[148] Whether they were also absent from Gaimar's British History is, of course, impossible to say. If they were, this too might have made his work seem old-fashioned by the side of Wace's.

[149] As opposed to warriors winning the admiration of ladies and being encouraged by them, as Beowulf was by Wealhtheow.

[150] Keen, *Chivalry*, 2.

[151] Gaimar, lines 2793–4, 5300.

[152] Gaimar, lines 3155, 3190, 3225–8.

[153] Gaimar, lines 3225–8, 3381–4, 3441–2.

[154] Southern, *Medieval Humanism*, 143 – a judgement based chiefly on the thirteenth century *History of William the Marshal*.

was, but it does not follow from this that all the earliest surviving chivalric literature must have been written in France. Yet chivalric literature, I suggest, is exactly what we have in Gaimar's *Estoire*, and above all in his remarkable portrait of Rufus, the first portrait of a chivalrous king in European history.[155]

Yet very few pieces of historical writing have had as little influence as Gaimar's account of Rufus's reign. For this there are a number of reasons. Gaimar – though clearly a highly educated man – wrote not in learned Latin, but in French verse, a medium believed to be more suited to the fanciful than to the real, hence the protestation in his history's short epilogue: 'This is not a fable nor a dream, but is taken from the true history.'[156] But even if they knew of it, this was not a protestation that impressed learned historians, themselves writing in Latin and most of them churchmen. They preferred to follow the views of their Latin-writing ecclesiastical predecessors. Moreover although c.1300 the author of the immensely popular prose *Brut* adopted Gaimar's overview of Anglo-Saxon history, he chose to set aside Gaimar's account of the Norman Conquest and its aftermath, including William II's reign.[157] Hence although the *Brut* was to be the first English history to be printed, and was then frequently reprinted in the late fifteenth and early sixteenth centuries, Gaimar's portrait of Rufus survived only in manuscript. Until the nineteenth century it remained unprinted and forgotten. This meant that for centuries the 'monastic' portrait had a clear run. It is, for example, noticeable that even when Protestantism and anti-monasticism led to what Callahan called 'the high point of William II's historical image' in the later sixteenth and seventeenth centuries,[158] those authors such as John Bale, John Speed and Sir John Hayward who wished to take a favourable view of Rufus did not have Gaimar to draw upon. Since no alternative contemporary source was known, it is not really surprising that many judicious historians should, in the end, have decided to go along with the monks. As usual the line adopted by David Hume was to be the most influential one. 'The memory of this monarch is transmitted to us with little advantage by the churchmen whom he had offended; and though we may suspect, in general, that their account of his vices is somewhat exaggerated, his conduct affords little reason for contradicting the character which they have assigned him, or for attributing to him any very estimable qualities.'[159]

---

[155] According to Freeman, Rufus 'was certainly the first man in any very prominent place by whom the whole set of words, thoughts, and feelings, which belong to the titles of knight and gentleman were habitually and ostentatiously thrust forward'. Freeman, *Rufus*, i.169.

[156] Gaimar, Appendix, 207. For early suspicions of history in verse, B. Guenée, *Histoire et Culture historique dans l'Occident médiéval* (Paris, 1980), 221–3.

[157] Possibly because Gaimar's criticism of William I and generally ambivalent attitude to the conquest was not to his taste.

[158] T. Callahan, 'The making of a monster: the historical image of William Rufus', *JMH* 7 (1981), 182–3. Yet even Callahan refers to Gaimar as a 'curious exception' who 'gives a fanciful story of Rufus' death' and whose praise for the king is 'rather surprising', 180.

[159] David Hume, *The History of England*, vol. 1 (London, 1871, reprint of 1786 edn), 170.

By the time Gaimar was eventually re-discovered and printed, in part in 1836 and in full in 1850,[160] the hostile image of Rufus was too deeply entrenched to be much disturbed by an author writing in so frivolous a form as French verse and who, in his account of Norman history, showed such a cavalier disregard for chronology. Bishop Stubbs, for example, shows no sign of having used Gaimar when writing his section on the Norman kings, and his judgement on Rufus remained firmly within the venerable ecclesiastical tradition: 'unrestrained by religion, by principle or by policy, with no family interests to limit his greed, extravagance, or hatred of his kind, a foul incarnation of selfishness in its most abhorrent form, the enemy of God and man'.[161] Similarly A. L. Poole's judgement on him as 'from the moral standpoint probably the worst king that has occupied the throne of England', is the view of a historian who neither lists Gaimar among his sources nor ever refers to him.[162] In his essay on the limitations of medieval chroniclers, Galbraith lumped Rufus together with John as the 'objects of a more active misrepresentation by the chroniclers than any or all of the others . . . surviving portraits are unquestionably mere savage caricatures'.[163] To pair the two kings in this way is to write as though Gaimar never existed. Even Emma Mason, taking an avowedly positive view of Rufus, preferred to do so without the benefit of Gaimar whom she described as 'a writer of romance' whose glowing account of William's reign is 'scarcely sober history'.[164]

Gaimar still falls between two stools and two specialisms. Specialists in literature and language see him as, for the most part, a rather dull historian. Historians regard him as all too much influenced by romance and hence as inaccurate and unreliable. In their view Gaimar gets things wrong. The monks, it is acknowledged, exaggerated, but by and large they got things right. Their anecdotes can be trusted. After all, as Hollister has shown, Rufus *did* have 'a system of methodical extortion of the church', more like Henry VIII's than Henry I's.[165] Moreover it was not only churchmen who had reason to complain about Rufus's style of government. That much can be inferred from the terms of Henry I's Coronation Charter. William II wanted his subjects' money whether through taxation or through exploitation of the patronage system. But so far as his treatment of lay society is concerned, it is hard to see that he differed much from his father and younger brother, or indeed from many other

[160] F. Michel, *Chroniques anglo-normandes* (Paris, 1936), printed the history from 1066; T. Wright, *The Anglo-Norman Metrical Chronicle of Geoffrey Gaimar* (London, 1850).

[161] W. Stubbs, *Constitutional History of England*, 4th edn (Oxford, 1883), i.328.

[162] A. L. Poole, *Domesday Book to Magna Carta* (2nd edn, Oxford, 1955), 99. Not even in his chapter on 'Learning, Literature and Art' does Gaimar get a mention.

[163] V. H. Galbraith, 'Good and Bad Kings in English History', *History* 30 (1945), 124–5; reprinted in his *Kings and Chroniclers* (London, 1982). John, of course, did not have a Gaimar.

[164] Mason, 'William Rufus', *JMH* 3 (1977), 16.

[165] C. W. Hollister, 'William II, Henry I and the Church' in ed. M. A. Meyer, *The Culture of Christendom* (London, 1993), 204–5.

kings. It was his treatment of the church which made the critical difference and which shaped virtually all the subsequent historiography.

Yet it seems obvious from William of Malmesbury's account that some at least of William II's contemporaries must have admired or liked him, above all no doubt those who profited from his (in monastic eyes, excessive) generosity. In building his palace at London he, in Malmesbury's words, 'spared no expense to demonstrate the magnificence of his liberality'. This must have employed and pleased many, including no doubt the hordes of knights who flocked to his court from every kingdom north of the Alps and who presumably enjoyed the fashionable life-style which so enraged the monks.[166] What words would those who admired or flattered Rufus have employed if not words like Gaimar's? Indeed Gaimar's portrait may even be derived from their words. Obviously Gaimar's portrait of Rufus is an idealising and distorted one, but it is not obvious that it is any more distorted than, say, Eadmer's. Gaimar, I have suggested, consciously offers an alternative to the ecclesiastical view of Rufus – and, in consequence, this has led to his account being either ignored or dismissed. Yet if we were to follow Barlow's prescription and 'as far as possible judge the king by the standards of the nobility',[167] then Gaimar's portrait ought surely to be the most important source of all. Were such key courtly virtues as 'elegance of bearing' and 'restraint of passion' really absent from William II's court?[168] Yes, if we believe the monks; no, if we believe Gaimar.

In the end though it is not a question of trying to decide whether it was the churchmen or Gaimar who produced the more accurate account of what Rufus or Hugh of Chester were 'really' like. It is simply that, given the long-standing interest in twelfth-century secular culture, it is almost incredible that so little use should have been made of the earliest author to write in French about such subjects as kingship, war and marriage. Whether or not Gaimar consciously rebuts, as I think he does, puritanical monastic views on a number of subjects – on Robert of Bellême, on Hereward the Wake's attack on Peterborough, on King Edgar's love life, and above all on Hugh of Chester and on William Rufus – we should still be prepared to see his opinions on these matters not merely as his alleged mistakes, but also as precious early evidence of an alternative and secular set of values.

APPENDIX. GAIMAR'S IRONY

How should we interpret Gaimar's boast that he could, if he chose, compose verses about Henry I's court describing the fairest deeds, 'about love and gallantry, and woodland sports and jokes, and of feasts and splendour'?[169] 'It is

[166] WM cc. 312–21.
[167] Barlow, *Rufus*, 435.
[168] Hollister, 'Courtly Culture', 11.
[169] Hollister, 'Courtly Culture', 15–16.

hard to see what there was to joke about', was Southern's comment, reflecting his own view of Henry as a 'cold, hard, inscrutable man'.[170] But that, I suspect, was the joke. As a ruler Henry had many great qualities, but being either chivalrous or courtly were not among them.[171] Generous to his friends and loyal supporters he was – a quality nicely illustrated in what may be the only pleasant anecdote ever told about Henry I[172] – but courtesy and chivalry require more than generosity towards those whom you judge to be useful to you. Even in a history dedicated to Henry's son, William of Malmesbury reported the king's death without a word of praise; and in the praise which he had prudently lavished on him while he was still alive there is, very significantly, nothing to match the enthusiasm with which he described the splendour of Queen Edith-Matilda's separate court and the generosity of her patronage. William could praise Henry as 'facetiarum pro tempore plenus', but this contrasts with his descriptions of Rufus: 'multa joco transigebat, facetissimus'.[173] Notorious for his inability to enjoy a witticism at his own expense, Henry's own sense of humour was revealed when he showed Conan the view from the top of the tower of Rouen.[174] Moreover as Hollister noted, 'under Henry I . . . crownwearings gradually became less frequent and less lavish'.[175] Thus although it is possible to find parallels between the politics of Henry I's reign and some of the episodes in Geoffrey of Monmouth's *History*, there is nothing to suggest that King Arthur's court was modelled on Henry's. Hence I suggest that we at least consider the possibility that Gaimar was joking.[176]

---

[170] Southern, *Medieval Humanism*, 230, 233.

[171] On the contemporary charge that Henry lacked chivalry, see above, pp. 52, 223.

[172] He treated kindly a chamberlain who had been helping himself to the king's wine, Map, *De Nugis*, 440.

[173] WM cc. 312, 412, 418.

[174] And then threw him down. WM cc. 392, 394; Orderic, iv.224; Wace, *Rou*, lines 10,505–54.

[175] Hollister, 'Courtly Culture', 3.

[176] Detecting irony in the written word of the distant past is notoriously difficult. But how should we, for example, understand Walter Map's assertion that under Henry I many nobles deliberately committed offences in order to fall into the king's mercy? Map, *De Nugis*, 472.

14

Some Observations on Social Mobility in England between the Norman Conquest and the Early Thirteenth Century*

It may be, as David Herlihy has asserted, that 'the reality and importance of social mobility in the Middle Ages are today unquestioned'. It may also be that no-one any longer believes in the existence of a medieval society based upon 'a system of closed and stable estates in which social mobility was officially discouraged and rarely achieved'.[1] Unfortunately a very great deal depends on just what we mean by 'rarely'. Obviously this is an area in which our approach has to be as quantitative as possible. Particular examples of mobility may illuminate the kinds of process at work, but we are not entitled to use words like 'rarely' unless we know how common they were, both in their own period and compared with equivalent cases in other periods. One difficulty with particular examples is that they are often those which contemporary opinion found remarkable and contemporary opinion is particularly unreliable so in those areas – like social mobility – where misconceptions and prejudices abound. In the twelfth century, as in other centuries, there was a strong current of opinion which disapproved of social mobility. The ideal ruler, like Duke Richard II of Normandy as portrayed in Benoit's *Chronique des ducs de Normandie*, was one who tolerated no 'vilains' at his court and whose officials, one and all, were 'gentil homme'.[2] As a comment which Gerald de Barri passed on King Dermot McMurrough implies, the ruler who was an 'erector humilium' was also easily thought of as a tyrant, a 'nobilium oppressor'.[3] No wonder Becket reacted

---

* Although the conference proceedings did not appear until 1996, this essay was written in response to a request that I tackle the subject of social mobility for a conference of British and German historians on *Germany and England in the High Middle Ages: A Comparative Approach* which took place in 1987. Since 1987 much has been written, especially on the economic history background to this subject, and in the last few paragraphs I have taken some account of this literature.

[1] D. Herlihy, 'Three Patterns of Social Mobility in Medieval Society', *Journal of Interdisciplinary History* 3 (1973), 623–47.

[2] *Chronique des ducs de Normandie par Benoit*, ed. C. Fahlin (3 vols., Uppsala, 1951–67), lines 28, 824–40.

[3] Giraldus Cambrensis, *Expugnatio Hibernica: the conquest of Ireland*, ed. A. B. Scott and F. X. Martin (Dublin, 1978), 40, and cf. 24. This combination had, in Walter Map's opinion, been

heatedly to the charge that the king had raised him 'de exili'.[4] Statements relating to social mobility found in narrative or literary sources and made in a climate of opinion like this cannot safely be regarded as anything other than expressions of the author's own highly subjective stance: a famous example would be Orderic's comment on the men whom Henry I 'raised from the dust'.[5]

On the other hand, among medievalists, the student of English history is singularly fortunate in possessing a wide range of documentary sources capable of yielding quantitative information. Unfortunately not until the period of the manorial surveys and court rolls of the mid-thirteenth century and later do we begin to have the evidence to enable us to tackle the subject of patterns and rates of mobility in the population at large.[6] Before this date we can only skate on very thin ice, using the tentative conclusions of economic historians to draw still more tentative inferences. Undoubtedly the agricultural base of the economy was expanding, but whether there was more – or less – per capita wealth is a much harder question to answer. Even those historians who take an optimistic view of medieval agriculture and its capacity for progress are inclined to believe that greater productivity per unit area was gained at the expense of productivity per capita.[7] Undoubtedly there were more towns, and larger towns, in England in 1250 than in 1050. But it is not easy to know whether or not England at the later date was more urbanised than earlier, or whether a higher proportion of the population was migrating from country into town. In this period therefore the student of social mobility is inevitably very largely, though not entirely, confined to the elite, to the subjects of mobility within it and recruitment to it. Within these limits in Domesday Book and the Pipe Rolls he has sources which, for the period, are remarkably susceptible of a statistical treatment, nowadays computer assisted.[8] Of

Aethelred the Unready's greatest failing – and Edmund Ironside's fatal mistake, Walter Map, *De Nugis Curialium*, ed. M. R. James, C. N. L. Brooke and R. A. B. Mynors (Oxford, 1983), 420–2, 428–30.

4 *Materials for the History of Thomas Becket*, ed. J. C. Robertson (7 vols., Rolls Series, 1875–85), v, 499.

5 Orderic Vitalis, *Ecclesiastical History*, ed. M. Chibnall (6 vols.; Oxford, 1969–80), vi, 16.

6 For a model of what can be done with these court rolls see Z. Razi, *Life, Marriage and Death in a Medieval Parish: Economy, Society and Demography in Halesowen 1270–1400* (Cambridge, 1980), esp. 87–97 for 'a strong downwards social mobility' reinforced by a brisk land market.

7 It occurred therefore where labour was abundant, i.e. cheap where demesne managers were concerned; simply plentiful on the small-holdings of the peasantry, B. M. S. Campbell, 'Agricultural Progress in Medieval England: Some Evidence from Eastern Norfolk', *Economic History Review*, 2nd ser. 36 (1983), 26–46.

8 E.g. J. Palmer, 'Domesday Book and the Computer' in ed. P. H. Sawyer, *Domesday Book: a reassessment* (London, 1985), 164–74; J. McDonald and G. D. Snooks, *Domesday Economy: A New Approach to Anglo-Norman History* (Oxford, 1986); J. McDonald and G. D. Snooks, 'How Artificial were the Tax Assessments of Domesday England? The Case of Essex', *Economic History Review*, 2nd ser. 38 (1985), 352–72; J. D. Hamshere, 'Domesday Book: Estate Structures in the West Midlands' in ed. J. C. Holt, *Domesday Studies* (Woodbridge, 1987); and on the 1130 Pipe Roll, J. Green, *The Government of England under Henry I* (Cambridge, 1986), 220–7.

course there are still problems. The twelfth century, like most centuries, had no clearly articulated system of social classification.[9] More difficult to get around are the familiar problems posed by a period of expansion. In absolute terms, both population and the level of documentation were rising.[10] So we know more about more people, particularly about the elite, those who made their mark. In these circumstances although social mobility undoubtedly appears to increase with the passage of time, it is always possible that appearances are deceptive. Indeed considerations of this sort have allowed a historically minded sociologist to argue that this period actually witnessed a declining rate of social mobility, a reversal of the trend towards accelerating mobility which had, in his view, characterised late Anglo-Saxon society.[11]

Given the limited and problematic nature of the evidence it is thus hardly surprising that historians of the period should, until recently, have paid little attention to the subject of social mobility.[12] They have not ignored it altogether, of course. They have commonly noted its existence, usually in the context of some particularly striking example of individual upward mobility, almost always an individual in crown service.[13] Indeed, in company with the historians of most other periods, they are inclined to think of society in 'their' period as being 'fluid' rather than 'static'.[14] This is doubtless partly because, like most sociologists, they

---

[9] Green, *The Government*, 136–8.

[10] On the proliferation of documentation see above all, M. T. Clanchy, *From Memory to Written Record: England 1066–1307* (2nd edn, London, 1993).

[11] W. G. Runciman, 'Accelerating Social Mobility: The Case of Anglo-Saxon England', *Past and Present* 104 (1984), 3–30.

[12] On the one hand there have been systematic studies of fairly well-defined and numerically small groups like magnates (a main thread in the essays now collected in C. W. Hollister, *Monarchy, Magnates and Institutions in the Anglo-Norman World* (London, 1988)); royal servants (Green, *The Government*, 134–214, 226–81) and judges (R. V. Turner, *The English Judiciary in the Age of Glanvill and Bracton, c.1176–1239* (Cambridge, 1985)). At the other extreme Alexander Murray made the concept of 'social differentiation by movement' the determinative basis of his bold and wide-ranging *Reason and Society in the Middle Ages* (Oxford, 1978).

[13] For example William Marshal, described on the back cover of S. Painter, *William Marshal* (pbk edn, Baltimore, 1967) as achieving 'the extreme degree of social mobility possible in his age'. Or Geoffrey de Clinton and Bernard the Scribe, both made famous in Southern's seminal study of patronage in the early twelfth century, reprinted in R. W. Southern, *Medieval Humanism* (Oxford, 1970), 214–17, 225–8; for further comment on Clinton's career, D. Crouch, 'Geoffrey de Clinton and Roger, Earl of Warwick: New Men and Magnates in the Reign of Henry I', *Bulletin of the Institute of Historical Research* 55 (1982), 113–23. In the thirteenth century there is Walter of Merton who became 'a multi-millionaire' in Henry III's service, M. T. Clanchy, 'England in the Thirteenth Century: Power and Knowledge' in ed. W. M. Ormrod, *England in the Thirteenth Century* (Woodbridge, 1986), 1–14. For Simon of Felsted, an example of a man who rose in the service of a lesser lord, in this case the abbess of Caen, see M. Chibnall, *Anglo-Norman England 1066–1166* (Oxford, 1986), 146–7. For some justified doubts about a method which relies upon 'the perfect example' see C. W. Hollister, 'Elite Prosopography in Saxon and Norman England', *Medieval Prosopography* 1 (1980), 12–14.

[14] E.g. A. L. Poole, *Obligations of Society in the XII and XIII Centuries* (Oxford, 1946), 8.

tend to regard social mobility as a Good Thing – and like to think of their own preferred period as being full of Good Things – but also because they are inclined to compare the social order of their period with one that never existed, i.e. with the ideal-type of a traditional social order within which the families of greater and lesser landlords, dependent tenants and labourers succeed one another in unvarying accordance with inherited custom.[15] Inevitably, by comparison with this ideal-type, all real societies are fluid, are to be likened, in Paul Hyams's phrase, to a handicap race, not to a layer cake.[16] Thus simply to point to the existence of some degree of social mobility in any given society is to state a truism which does not take us very far. In this paper I hope to avoid such unhelpful comparisons. On the other hand I must plead guilty at once to the charge of believing that this period of English history is unusually full of 'Good Things' for the student of social mobility. I begin by picking out five.

1. As a direct result of the Norman Conquest the decades after 1066 witnessed a faster rate of mobility within the ruling elite than any other period in the entire history of England. If ever there was a period that justified Pareto's famous description of history as 'the graveyard of aristocracies' it was this one.

2. The twelfth century witnessed the emergence of primogeniture, a system of inheritance which has hitherto bulked large in discussions of social mobility in England, on the grounds that it compels younger sons to move into other fields if they are to avoid the downward mobility for which their birth seems to destine them.[17]

3. This period saw the disappearance of one type of mobility which had been a feature of most earlier societies: mobility across the great divide between slavery and freedom.

4. As a consequence of the Gregorian and monastic reform movements there was a uniquely serious and sustained attempt to persuade people to become celibate. Since differential fertility and replacement rates are generally considered to be critical factors in determining patterns of mobility, this lends this period a quality all of its own.

5. The emergence of schools and universities, institutions specialising in education, a development of some importance given the central role traditionally accorded education in most studies of elite recruitment.

I take these five points in turn.

[15] I take this summary definition of a traditional social order from Runciman, 'Accelerating Mobility', p. 3. The fact that I do so is an indication of my indebtedness to this article. Although I disagree with many of Runciman's conclusions I found his approach to the problem of how to assess social mobility in the absence of quantitative evidence extremely helpful. As, on the subject in general, I found A. Heath, *Social Mobility* (London, 1981).

[16] P. R. Hyams, *King, Lords, and Peasants in Medieval England* (Oxford, 1980), 268.

[17] Notably in the works of Lawrence Stone.

1. The impact of the Norman Conquest is, of course, writ large in the pages of Domesday Book. For the historian of social mobility Domesday is doubly remarkable. Not only is it a unique record in its almost complete coverage of England at two distinctly dated moments in time, the time of King Edward and 1086; it is also a record which reveals a situation unique, so far as can be seen, in English history: the more or less total overthrow of an established ruling class. By 1086 little more than 5% of Domesday land values was still held by pre-conquest tenants-in-chief.[18] And even those fortunate survivors tended to be, as Eleanor Searle has observed, Englishmen whose heirs were daughters married to Normans.[19] After 1070 Englishmen came to be systematically excluded from high ecclesiastical office.[20] In government few important positions were held by Englishmen after 1071. In the whole of English history no ruling elite ever suffered greater downward mobility than this. This overwhelming downward mobility necessarily created vacancies at an unprecedentedly high rate and, in consequence, a uniquely high rate of exchange mobility within the elite. Into the vacancies moved the newcomers, mostly Normans. Nearly all made enormous gains though on the whole it was not so much the Norman magnates as the younger sons and men of relatively obscure origin who gained most.[21] Most of William's sheriffs were new men whose fortunes had been made by the Conquest.[22] In this turbulent world it is the speed with which a man could rise to the highest rank in secular society which is remarkable. At other times men rose from relative obscurity to the rank of earl – Eadric Streona in Aethelred's reign or Geoffrey fitz Peter and Hubert de Burgh in the late twelfth and early thirteenth centuries.[23] But none surely rose as fast as Robert de

---

[18]   W. J. Corbett, 'The Development of the Duchy of Normandy and the Norman Conquest of England', *Cambridge Medieval History* 5 (Cambridge, 1926), 508; F. M. Stenton, 'English Families and the Norman Conquest', *TRHS*, 4th ser. 26 (1944), 1–12. Against recent doubts Stenton's term 'a tenurial revolution' has been vindicated by R. Fleming, 'Domesday Book and the Tenurial Revolution' in ed. R. A. Brown, *Anglo-Norman Studies* 9 (Woodbridge, 1987), 87–102. Three major studies to appear since 1987 are R. Fleming, *Kings and Lords in Conquest England* (Cambridge, 1991), A. Williams, *The English and the Norman Conquest* (Woodbridge, 1995) and J. A. Green, *The Aristocracy of Norman England* (Cambridge, 1997).

[19]   E. Searle, 'Women and the Legitimization of Succession at the Norman Conquest' in ed. R. A. Brown, *Anglo-Norman Studies* 3 (Woodbridge, 1981), 159–70.

[20]   F. Barlow, *The English Church 1066–1154* (London, 1979), 57–66.

[21]   Orderic, ii, 190. Cf. Green, *The Government*, 143–4, 'The Norman Conquest of England had provided unparalleled opportunities for men of humble origins to win lands for themselves.'

[22]   J. Green, 'The Sheriffs of William the Conqueror' in *Anglo-Norman Studies* 5 (Woodbridge, 1983), 129–45.

[23]   S. Keynes, 'A Tale of Two Kings: Alfred the Great and Aethelred the Unready', *TRHS*, 5th ser. 36 (1986), 213–16. On Geoffrey fitz Peter's origins and early career see Turner, *The English Judiciary*, 93, 99. Geoffrey entered the ranks of the curiales c.1182–3 and was made an earl in 1199; Hubert de Burgh belonged to a Norfolk gentry family, entered royal service in the late 1190s, and was created earl in 1227, for political and military services. On his family see C. Ellis, *Hubert de Burgh: A Study in Constancy* (London, 1952), appendix 1.

Comines, created earl of Northumbria in 1068 – or, come to that, fell so fast, though the effect of the killing of De Comines in January 1069 was, of course, to create another vacancy almost at once.[24] England was a Norman colony, 'a land of enterprise . . . where young men usually of respectable origins but frequently of moderate means, could rise high in the social hierarchy through military, political or administrative service'.[25]

Although it is only the landholders whose fortunes after 1066 can, thanks to Domesday Book, be considered in quantative terms, there can be little doubt that other groups felt the impact of the Norman Conquest. Builders and stone-masons, for example, must surely have been employed on an unprecedented scale in that orgy of demolition and re-building of all the major English churches that followed 1066. There was work for them too in the great surge of castle building – not all of which can have been carried out by forced labour – which was so crucial to the success of the Norman invasion. Another group to find new and greater opportunities were the interpreters – and the mere fact of their existence is itself an indicator of the greater gap, the greater social distance between the French speaking elite and those who only spoke English.[26]

2. Primogeniture. In the first generation after the conquest almost nothing was inherited, virtually everything was acquisition, and acquisition on a scale sufficient to satisfy the ambitions of brothers and younger sons, sufficient to enable them to escape the constraints of Duby's marriage pattern with its inhibition on the marriages of younger sons.[27] But for how long did this last? At what date do we first reach a generation whose chances in life were unaffected by the upheaval of 1066? There is no very clear or obvious answer to this. To some extent the extra-ordinary post-Conquest situation was prolonged by a continuing flow of new acquisitions caused by the succession wars of William II's, Henry I's and Stephen's reigns, i.e. by the ordinary accidents of medieval

---

[24] Simeon of Durham, *Historical Works*, ed. T. Arnold (2 vols., RS, 1882–5), i, 98–9.

[25] J. C. Holt, 'Feudal Society and the Family in Early Medieval England: I. The Revolution of 1066', *TRHS*, 5th ser. 32 (1982), 193–212, esp. 206.

[26] The sheer scale of the building work, and therefore of the economic and social consequences, is emphasised in J. C. Holt, *Colonial England 1066–1215* (London, 1997), 5–12. For an interpreter attached to the abbot of Ramsey's household, J. A. Raftis, *The Estates of Ramsey Abbey* (Toronto, 1957), 51; for the embarrassment of an early twelfth century Somerset parish priest who spoke only English and therefore had to remain silent in the presence of bishop and archdeacon, John of Ford, *Vita Beati Wulfrici anachoretae Haselbergiae*, ed. M. Bell, Somerset Record Soc. 47 (1932), 29; cited by Barlow, *English Church*, 133. Naturally parish priests never became bishops, though this was not a feature unique to this linguistically divided society. The Domesday evidence relating to interpreters has now been helpfully brought together in H. Tsurushima, 'Domesday Interpreters', *ANS* 18 (1995), 201–22.

[27] J. C. Holt, 'Feudal Society and the Family in Early Medieval England: III. Patronage and Politics', *TRHS*, 5th ser. 34 (1984), 15–16.

politics.[28] On the other hand it has been observed that by the time of Henry I land which had earlier been treated as acquisition was increasingly being regarded as patrimony and that those who managed to stay loyal to the king were rewarded by being able to enjoy fairly secure inheritance. Holt moreover has drawn attention to charters which begin, once again, to speak the language of hereditary tenure.[29] At this social level hereditary tenure increasingly meant primogeniture. Why this 'unnatural' law came to predominate still remains something of a mystery. It may be that the circumstances of the Conquest lent greater weight to the interests of lords, enabling lords, and in particular the lord king, to insist on impartible succession, while the interests of the family were at least able to ensure that if only one son were to succeed then the eldest.[30] However this may be, it does at least seem clear that at some stage younger sons, after a generation or two in which they had enjoyed, and perhaps come to expect, increased opportunities, found their prospects diminishing. In these new circumstances what strategies could they, or their parents, adopt? Best of all perhaps would be to find a magic wand which would suddenly increase the number of available heiresses. And indeed they may have found such a wand in the shape of the *statutum decretum*, probably to be dated to the latter years of Henry I's reign, which laid down that, in the absence of a son, the inheritance was to be shared between the daughters instead of going, as hitherto, to a single female heiress.[31]

3.   The ending of mobility across the boundary between freedom and slavery. Whether or not, as Runciman suggests, rates of enslavement and manumission were higher in the tenth and eleventh centuries than they had been earlier, it is clear that by the end of the twelfth century these rates had dropped to zero.[32]

---

[28] Holt, 'The revolution of 1066', 205. See now the chapter entitled 'An open elite? The aristocracy after 1086' in Green, *Aristocracy of Norman England*, 126–40.

[29] R. DeAragon, 'The growth of secure inheritance in Anglo-Norman England', *Journal of Medieval History* 8 (1982), 381–91; J. C. Holt, 'Feudal Society and the Family in Early Medieval England: II. Notions of Patrimony', *TRHS*, 5th ser. 33 (1983), 193–220, esp. 214–17.

[30] Pollock and Maitland, *The History of English Law*, re-issued with introduction by S. F. C. Milsom (2 vols., Cambridge, 1968), ii, 262–74; Chibnall, *Anglo-Norman England*, 174. It is possible that some form of impartible descent had become customary in England outside Kent before 1066; but if so it seems to have been a custom much modified by the capacity of some landholders to bequeathe property widely. This the social conventions of the Normans in England did not permit, Holt, 'The Revolution of 1066', 197–9.

[31] J. C. Holt, 'Feudal Society and the Family in Early Medieval England: IV. The Heiress and the Alien', *TRHS*, 5th ser. 35 (1985), 1–28, esp. 8–10. On heiresses and the *statutum decretum* see J. A. Green, 'Aristocratic Women in early twelfth-century England' in ed. C. W. Hollister, *Anglo-Norman Political Culture and the Twelfth Century Renaissance* (Woodbridge, 1997), 59–82, and J. A. Green, *The Aristocracy*, 361–83.

[32] Runciman, 'Accelerating Social Mobility', 11. In Domesday slaves comprised over 10% of the recorded population; if without households of their own they may have comprised a much smaller proportion of the actual population in 1086. J. S. Moore, 'Domesday

Exactly when and how this happened is something of a puzzle. To judge from the *Leges Henrici Primi*, in the early twelfth century movement into and out of slavery was still something to be reckoned with, a passage requiring the appropriate public rituals.[33] But after the reign of Henry I it is next to impossible to find any references either to penal slavery or to the slave trade within England. The 1102 Council of Westminster was not the first church council in England to prohibit the slave trade, but it was, significantly, the last.[34] According to William of Malmesbury the efforts of Wulfstan of Worcester had persuaded the men of Bristol to give up the slave trade and they had then been an example throughout England. In this passage William's language suggests that he thought of the slave trade as a thing of the past.[35] Once there was no slave trade then the high cost of replacing slaves probably made other forms of labour a more attractive economic proposition. In these circumstances manumissions and the death and escape of slaves may have combined to render slavery extinct.[36]

Although it would obviously be wrong to attribute the end of slavery, a development common to northern Europe as a whole, to the insular experience of the Norman Conquest, it is none the less possible that the aftermath of 1066 may have contributed to the process. Slaves who took advantage of the turmoil of these years to run away may well have found many more people willing to help a fugitive than would have been the case before 1066. English resentment at the plight of the English people, the atmosphere of the *murdrum* fine, could well have come to the rescue of English slaves on the run from their newly installed French masters.[37] Indeed in an economic climate seemingly characterised by labour shortage, some English farmers and landholders may have seen protecting and providing for runaways as an attractive method of acquiring additional labour.

In one sense the runaway slave is no more than a special case of a general phenomenon: the ability of people to rise vertically in society as a direct result of moving horizontally. Even for the non-slave this was rarely an easy matter.

Slavery', *ANS* 11 (1988), 191–220, argues to the contrary, that many may have had families and hence comprised a rather larger proportion of the total population. See now the chapter entitled 'Lies, damned lies and statistics' in D. A. E. Pelteret, *Slavery in Early Medieval England* (Woodbridge, 1995).

[33] *Leges Henrici Primi*, ed. L. J. Downer (Oxford, 1972), cc. 76, 3; 77, 1–3; 78, 1–3.

[34] Eadmer, in *Historia Novorum in Anglia*, ed. M. Rule (RS, 1884), 143.

[35] William of Malmesbury, *Vita Wulfstani*, ed. R. R. Darlington, Camden Soc. 40 (1928), 43–4. On Wales, R. R. Davies, *Conquest, Co-existence and Change: Wales 1063–1415* (Oxford, 1987), 119–20. See *The Letters of John of Salisbury, Volume One*, ed. W. J. Millor and H. E. Butler (London, 1955), 135. This may explain why Gerald gives the impression that slaves were still being imported into Ireland later in the century, *Expugnatio Hibernica*, 70.

[36] J. Hicks, *A Theory of Economic History* (Oxford, 1969), 124–32; Pelteret, *Slavery*, 251–9.

[37] Hyams, 251–3, for a discussion of the way in which English birth 'almost carried a presumption of servility' and cf. *Leges Henrici Primi*, c. 77, 2. On the Norman view of slavery see above, pp. xv, 226.

Competition for labour seems to have meant that in the early period nearly all tenants were tied to their holdings, entitled to leave only with their lord's licence.[38] Those tenants who could give, sell or leave their lands without licence were highly privileged.[39] From Domesday it would appear that approximately three-quarters of the tenant population – *villani*, bordars and cottars – were tied in ways which marked them off from the 14% of tenants who were categorised as *liberi homines* or sokemen. In the case of the Westminster Abbey estates *villani*, bordars and cottars comprised as much as 84% of the enumerated population, with only 3.5% being freemen and sokemen.[40] But by c.1225, the date of the earliest surviving custumal of Westminster Abbey's manors, about 11% of the tenants named were described as being free. Thus Barbara Harvey has suggested that the most striking change in the period after the Domesday survey was 'the rise of a class of free tenants', many of them descendants of men classified as *villani* in 1086. In her view proximity to towns helped some, usually the wealthier, tenants escape from dependence into freedom in the twelfth and thirteenth centuries, but more important still were local opportunities for assarting and colonisation. Yet, she continues, every local breakthrough on this and all other estates might have been in vain had it not been for Henry II's 'vital juridical principle' that royal justice was available to every free tenant.[41] The notion that one of the king's responsibilities was to protect men against seigneurial excess, taken together with the range of remedies offered by the royal courts as a result of the measures taken during Henry II's reign, meant that from then on tenants who wished to loosen the ties that bound them to their lords had a potentially effective ally in the shape of the king's courts. This development could have put the crown in the socially embarrassing position of appearing to help rustics against the *generosi* had it not been for the concomitant emergence of the new common-law doctrines of villeinage and freedom.[42] Thus by the late twelfth century there was a new legal boundary between freedom and unfreedom in place; and once again movement across this boundary could only take place with the lord's approval.[43] It was none the less a significant shift. By

[38] On labour shortage and the flight, enticement and stealing of men see J. Hatcher, 'English Serfdom and Villeinage: Towards a Reassessment', *Past and Present* 90 (1981), 3–39, esp. 26–32. See also Hyams' discussion in his chapter on the origins of common law villeinage, *Kings, Lords and Peasants*, 221–65. For a thorough-going reconsideration of the relationship between lords and peasant tenants in this and earlier periods see R. Faith, *The English Peasantry and the Growth of Lordship* (Leicester, 1997).

[39] Thus in 1142 when 38 *rustici* whose holdings were needed for the foundation of Revesby Abbey were offered the choice of re-settlement elsewhere on apparently identical terms or 'the liberty of going with all their goods wherever they wished' no less than 31 preferred to be landless but lordless; the example cited by Hatcher, 'English Serfdom', 31–2.

[40] B. Harvey, *Westminster Abbey and its Estates in the Middle Ages* (Oxford, 1977), 101–6.

[41] Ibid., 107–15.

[42] Hyams, *Kings, Lords, and Peasants*, 240–50, and note Harvey's observation that many of the free tenants can not really be described as peasants, Harvey, *Westminster Abbey*, 117.

[43] *The Treatise on the Laws and Customs of the Realm of England commonly called Glanvill*, ed. G. D. G. Hall (London, 1965), V.5, including a reference to a former villein being made a knight.

the time of Bracton the unfree could not lawfully be killed or mutilated by their lords, whereas in the mind of the compiler of the *Leges Henrici Primi* a master who killed his slave was guilty of no more than a sin.[44]

4. Under the Normans the English church continued to grow in size much as it had done before 1066. From the mid-twelfth century onwards the picture is in some respects a more static one. There were no new cathedrals after Carlisle (founded in 1133), and it was gradually becoming more difficult to create new parishes. None the less there still seems to have been a growing number of cathedral prebends and vicars, and a continuing proliferation of non-parish churches and altars. Moreover what rigidities there were in the system were very largely the result of the activities of a growing number of canon lawyers.[45] But the old problem remains. In an age of overall population growth and growing, yet always inadequate, documentation, it is hard to know whether or not this meant that the church was becoming proportionally more important as an avenue of social advance. It is at this point that the religious reform movements become so crucial. The most readily quantifiable measure of their success is to be found, as C. N. L. Brooke pointed out, in the rise in the numbers of regular clergy in England in this period.[46] In 1066 there were some 60 religious houses and perhaps 1,000 monks and nuns; by 1216 there were approximately 700 houses and some 13,000 monks, nuns, regular canons and canonesses.[47] No matter what estimate we make of the overall population growth during the same period, what is beyond doubt is that there was a significant increase in the proportion of the population who adopted the monastic way of life. In these circumstances there is clearly a prima facie case for accepting Knowles's contention that very few houses remained 'preserves of the aristocracy', and that during the course of the twelfth century recruits came increasingly from the children of all classes of free men. 'Every indication goes to show that in the reigns of Richard and John the monasteries were recruited almost entirely from what may be called, at the risk of anachronism, the middle class.'[48]

Richard Fitz Nigel, *Dialogus de Scaccario*, ed. C. Johnson, corr. F. Carter and D. Greenway (Oxford, 1983), 53.

[44] *Leges Henrici Primi*, c. 75, 4; 'Bracton', *De Legibus et Consuetudinibus Angliae*, ed. S. E. Thorne (4 vols., London, 1968–77), ii, 37.

[45] On the continuing foundation of new churches, J. Blair, 'Local Churches in Domesday and Before' in ed. Holt, *Domesday Studies*, 265–78, esp. 271–3; the problems of the 'fossilization' of the mid-twelfth century and later are highlighted in Murray, *Reason and Society*, 307–8.

[46] C. N. L. Brooke, 'Gregorian Reform in Action: Clerical Marriage in England, 1050–1200', *Cambridge Historical Journal* 12 (1956), 1–21, esp. 7–8.

[47] D. Knowles and R. N. Hadcock, *Medieval Religious Houses. England and Wales* (2nd edn, Cambridge, 1971), 494.

[48] D. Knowles, *The Monastic Order in England* (Cambridge, 1963), 424–5. And in the thirteenth century the mendicant orders would recruit more widely still.

It is true, of course, that in many contexts the bald figures for numbers of religious houses could be profoundly misleading. Many of the 'new' communities may have been merely transformations of the old secular minsters which were such a prominent feature of the Anglo-Saxon church.[49] None the less in this context there is a significant difference. The old houses were populated by canons who could be, and presumably sometimes were, married. In the new 'regular' communities, however, marriage and children were, to say the least, frowned upon. Thus it is possible that one of the effects of the celibacy campaign was to put a brake on the fertility of the landholding class. Whether or not this could have been on a scale sufficient to form an exception to Herlihy's central principle, that those social strata which commanded the larger part of available resources consistently reared the greater number of children, it is impossible to know.[50] This is to see things in terms of numbers, replacement rates, but in terms of the pattern of recruitment there is one other development which should be borne in mind: the great change in the monastic world of the twelfth century, the ending of the system of child oblates. This major shift in the timing of the moment of entry into the religious life meant that from now on individuals had a much wider and freer choice than ever before. In Southern's words, 'a conscript army was replaced by volunteers'.[51] Here surely was a profoundly important change in the pattern of social mobility, a widening of the opportunities for the exercise of choice.

If reform meant that twelfth-century houses were less and less self-repopulating communities, then it follows, of course, that they would, to an increasing extent, have to recruit from outside. Naturally the Gregorian campaign against clerical marriage tended to affect the secular clergy in a similar way, making the formation of clerical dynasties that much harder.[52] Although among the lower clergy marriage and hereditary succession to benefices remained common until the mid-thirteenth century at least, the higher clergy – the ecclesiastical elite – were distinctly more vulnerable to the pressure of reform. After the mid-twelfth century hereditary succession to prebends was no longer the norm within the cathedral chapter of Hereford, for example, even though as late as the early thirteenth century there were still some individual canons who were married.[53]

---

[49] J. Blair, 'Secular Minster Churches in Domesday Book' in ed. Sawyer, *Domesday Book: A Reassessment*, 104–42.

[50] Herlihy's conclusion was that 'the more rapid expansion of the higher social strata tended to create a top-heavy social pyramid' and therefore 'the dominant direction of social mobility in medieval society had to be downward', 'Three Patterns of Social Mobility', 626–33, esp. 632. For discussion of some of the other problems associated with a high rate of 'upper-class celibacy', Murray, *Reason and Society*, 342ff.

[51] R. W. Southern, *Western Society and the Medieval Church* (Harmondsworth, 1970).

[52] Moreover the monastic expansion may itself have had a direct impact since, as Barlow observed, 'the main way in which the custom of hereditary succession (to churches) was broken was by the impropriation of churches to monasteries and the provision of vicars', Barlow, *English Church*, 131–2.

[53] J. Barrow, 'Hereford Bishops and Married Clergy, c.1130–1240', *Historical Research* 60 (1987).

The effect of this was to increase the rate at which the higher clergy had to be recruited anew in each generation, thus increasing the importance of the church as a channel of vertical circulation.[54] But if clerical sons were no longer to succeed their clerical fathers, then how was the clergy to be recruited? Of course the clergy still had other male relatives, notably nephews, but how was a choice to be made between them? How was their suitability – and that of other candidates – for office to be assessed? In England the question was a particularly acute one for those who did not choose to demonstrate their enthusiasm for the church by entering one of the regular orders; the secular world in which they chose to remain was a fiercely competitive one. In a kingdom where there were very few secular collegiate churches apart from cathedrals (and where half the cathedrals were monastic), prebends were in short supply. Moreover demand was almost certainly rising. As Julia Barrow has pointed out, one consequence of primogeniture was that 'because they could not inherit much property from their families, clerks who were the sons of knights and barons had only the advantage of birth, not the advantage of wealth as well, over clerks who were the sons of burgesses'.[55]

5.   If another aspect of the church reform movement, the campaign against simony, meant that respectable candidates could no longer buy ecclesiastical office, there was at any rate no prohibition against them buying education.[56] Here, it may be, is one of the pressures which brought about the dramatic expansion of education which is such a feature of the twelfth century. It is in this century that we find, for the first time, institutions specialising in education. Hitherto, as Nicholas Orme has emphasised, educational provision, no matter how excellent, had always been ancillary to the main business of the institutions which offered it, whether they were religious houses or royal and aristocratic households.[57] The establishment of numbers of public elementary schools, including some in quite small towns and villages, 'public' in the sense of being open to anyone who could afford to go there, was clearly the educational environment out of which the universities of Oxford and Cambridge developed in the late twelfth and early thirteenth centuries. Southern's view of this period is that 'there were greater opportunities for schools and teachers than ever before. Perhaps these opportunities never again rose so fast until the nineteenth

---

[54]   In Herlihy's opinion, 'this made the church the most visible avenue of social advance in the medieval world', 'Three Patterns of Social Mobility', 624.

[55]   J. Barrow, 'Cathedrals, Provosts and Prebends: A Comparison of Twelfth-Century German and English Practice', *Journal of Ecclesiastical History* 37 (1986), 536–64, esp. 563–4.

[56]   On some of the implications for social mobility of the prohibition of simony see Murray, *Reason and Society*, 214–16.

[57]   N. Orme, *From Childhood to Chivalry. The Education of the English Kings and Aristocracy 1066–1530* (London, 1984), 48–67; N. Orme, *English Schools in the Middle Ages* (London, 1973), 59–60, 167–70.

century.'[58] To judge from a jaundiced comment made by Walter Map, the material advantages which education could bring were widely appreciated. In his *De Nugis Curialium*, a work which vividly reflects the anxieties of a secular clerk seeking patronage in a highly competitive court society, he complains that it was so that their children might get on in the world that the poor and the servile were keen to send them to school.[59]

*

For generations past the traditional way to get on in the world had been through service, and throughout this period it remained so. An ambitious Welshman was advised to enter the service of King Henry I. 'He will honour you and exalt you over your fellows; he will make all your kinsmen envious of you.'[60] The same applied to the service of lesser lords. Jocelin of Brakelond describes how, when Samson was elected abbot of Bury, 'a great crowd of new kinsmen (*novorum parentum*) came to meet him, all desiring to be taken into his service'.[61] But merely to insist upon continuity here is to leave a number of questions unanswered, some of them, no doubt, unanswerable. For example, did the numbers of new opportunities tend to stagnate once new lordships were no longer created at the phenomenally high rate characteristic of the decades after 1066? Or did, as is often asserted, the development of schools reflect a rising demand for educated officials as part and parcel of a general demand, from kings, bishops, monasteries and all great landowners, for administrative servants of all kinds?[62] I shall devote the rest of this sketch to a brief consideration of these two questions.

First, if instead of limiting our view to England we also take the Celtic lands into account, then it is clear that a continuing process of conquest and colonisation enabled new lordships to be created throughout the whole of this period.

'1092. In this year King William went north to Carlisle with a large army and restored the town and built the castle. He drove out the former ruler of that district and garrisoned the castle with his men. Then he returned south, and sent thither very many peasants with their wives and livestock to settle there and till the soil.'[63] This entry from the Anglo-Saxon Chronicle summarises a sequence of events that was to be followed time and time again, notably in Wales and Ireland, though not usually with such direct royal involvement. It seemed to the author of the *Gesta Stephani* that Henry I was turning Wales into a 'second England'; to the Welsh that he was planning to exterminate them completely or

[58] R. W. Southern, 'From Schools to University' in *The History of the University of Oxford*, volume 1, ed. J. I. Catto (Oxford, 1984), 1–36, esp. 1–2.

[59] Map, *De Nugis Curialium*, 12.

[60] *Brut Y Tywysogyon or The Chronicle of the Princes, Red Book of Hergest Version*, ed. T. Jones (Cardiff, 1955), 80–1.

[61] *The Chronicle of Jocelin of Brakelond*, ed. H. E. Butler (London, 1949), 24.

[62] Southern, 'From Schools to University', 1.

[63] *The Peterborough Chronicle*, ed. C. Clark (Oxford, 1970), 19.

drive them into the sea.[64] The pace of advance slowed down after Henry I's death; even so Wales remained a land of opportunity for conquerors and settlers throughout most of this period. Not, it may be, 'a land of easy opportunities or great rewards' – none the less attractive enough for those who were not already well established (e.g. younger sons) in England and Normandy and who were prepared to pay the price of continuing military effort and constant vigilance.[65] Further north, in Scotland, opportunities came in a more peaceful form, particularly in the reign of David I (1124–53) when the eager adventurers found a welcome at the Scottish court and were rewarded with estates covering a vast area in southern Scotland.[66] Then, in the late 1160s, an entirely new field of enterprise was opened up, Ireland, – particularly useful at times when in Wales native political revivals made life awkward for the newcomers. At such times they turned a ready ear to the blandishments, the recruiting offers which came from further west. The early thirteenth-century *Song of Dermot* makes these very explicit.

> Whoever shall wish for land or pence
> Horses, armour or chargers
> Gold and silver, I shall give them
> Very ample livery.
> Whoever shall wish for land and pasture
> Richly shall I enfeoff them.[67]

The second question. Was the apparently growing demand for administrative services real or illusory, and if real, then how important? So far as the central government is concerned, we do have some genuine hope of being able to give relatively concrete answers to some of the relevant questions. For the first time in English history, in the shape of the twelfth-century pipe rolls, there survives the kind of evidence to encourage historians of this subject to adopt a quantitative approach. On the basis of the earliest surviving pipe roll, Judith Green has made a systematic analysis of the origins and careers of the 104 men – at least 96 of them laymen – who were involved in government during the exchequer year 1129–30. Of these 104, 51 came from landholding families; of

---

[64] *Gesta Stephani*, ed. K. R. Potter and R. H. C. Davis (Oxford, 1976), 16; *Brut Y Tywysogyon*, 78–81.

[65] Davies, *Conquest, Co-existence*, 85–6, and, for the settlement of colonists, pp. 93–100. On the south-west of Wales in particular see I. W. Rowlands, 'The making of the March: aspects of the Norman settlement in Dyfed' in *Anglo-Norman Studies* 3 (Woodbridge, 1981), 142–58.

[66] Modern summaries in A. A. M. Duncan, *Scotland. The Making of the Kingdom* (Edinburgh, 1975), 133–42; and G. W. S. Barrow, *Kingship and Unity. Scotland 1000–1306*, 29–36, 44–7.

[67] *The Song of Dermot and the Earl*, ed. G. H. Orpen (Oxford, 1892), 34–5. On the settlement of Ireland see R. Frame, *Colonial Ireland, 1169–1369* (Dublin, 1981), esp. chapters 2 and 4; J. F. Lydon, *The Lordship of Ireland in the Middle Ages* (Dublin, 1972), 84–102; *A New History of Ireland, Volume 2, Medieval Ireland*, ed. A. Cosgrove (Oxford, 1987), 213–24.

these 51, 17 came from greater families (which she defines as those who held more than 5 knights fees in chief from the crown), and 34 from lesser landholding families. The social origins of 53 of the 1130 group are obscure – and it seems reasonable to assume that they were also humble. Out of the total of 104, Green discovered 18 who made very substantial gains from royal patronage; of these fortunate 18, 8 emerged from obscurity – the most famous being Roger of Salisbury. On the other hand no less than 35 of the 53 obscure men seem to have made no gains at all. Morover out of the 17 who already belonged to the greater landholding families no less than 6 made substantial gains.[68] This, doubtless, is not surprising, but it should remind us of Orderic's other comment (i.e. not his one about men raised from the dust): King Henry 'honoured his magnates (*optimates*) generously, he bestowed on them riches and honours, and so by his accommodating policy he won their fidelity'.[69] Unfortunately we still await similarly systematic studies of the personnel of goverment based on later pipe rolls, but here at any rate there may be a way forward, a fruitful field for further research.[70]

Despite the lack of similar work on later records, there can be little doubt that the machinery of government continued to expand. The increasing output of royal documents implies a growing number of clerical staff.[71] William fitzStephen claimed that as chancellor Thomas Becket had no less than 52 clerks in his own and in the king's service.[72] Indeed to all appearances the pace of bureaucratic development accelerated towards the end of the twelfth century, particularly during Hubert Walter's periods of office as justiciar and chancellor (1193–1205).[73] By 1200 indeed the expansion of government had reached a point at which, for the first time in English history, one can detect within it the emergence of a group of specialists: the king's judges, men like Simon of Pattishall and Osbert fitz Harvey, no longer the multi-purpose royal servants of old, but men whose governmental activity was concentrated on the work of justice.[74] In part this development was presumably a consequence of the way in which law was becoming a learned science, and the administration of the law therefore a matter for the appropriately educated expert. But once this was so

---

[68] Green, *The Government*, 283–4. On a closely related subject see S. L. Mooers, 'Patronage in the Pipe Roll of 1130', *Speculum* 59 (1984), 282–307.

[69] Orderic, v, 296.

[70] For a fine example of what can be done with the pipe rolls see T. K. Keefe, 'King Henry II and the Earls: The Pipe Roll Evidence', *Albion* 13 (1981), 191–222.

[71] Clanchy, *From Memory to Written Record*, 44–80.

[72] *Materials for the History of Thomas Becket*, iii, 29.

[73] Clanchy, *From Memory to Written Record*, 68–73. Hubert Walter has been described as 'the son of an obscure East Anglian knight who wielded power over both the English church and secular government in a way not to be seen until Cardinal Wolsey', Turner, *Judiciary*, 292.

[74] This is one of the main conclusions of Turner's study of the careers of 49 justices in this period. Less systematic is R. V. Turner, *Men Raised from the Dust. Administrative Service and Upward Mobility in Angevin England* (Philadelphia, 1988).

then it was not just the judges who needed professional training. In the royal courts of the same period we find, again for the first time in English history, evidence for the existence of a small group of professional lawyers, men who act on behalf of a number of clients and whom a client might employ for just one piece of litigation. From the 1240s we can find men similarly employed in the city courts of London.[75]

As this London example suggests these developments were not restricted to the sphere of royal government. Indeed they could not have been. The greater the output of government documents, the greater the number of individuals who came into contact with them in one form or another. This means, as James Campbell has pointed out, that in the twelfth century 'not only was central government organised in such a way that it could deal directly with more men and institutions, there were also more men and institutions whose status and knowledge were such that they were capable of dealing directly with the central government'.[76] Here we have a two-way relationship which was itself the consequence of social changes: the increasing provision of education, the increasingly large proportion of the population which participated in literacy.[77] Thus during the course of the twelfth and thirteenth centuries we find more men and institutions employing their own clerical staff.[78] The implications of these developmemts are beautifully illustrated by Southern's comment on the silver embossed ivory writing-case with silver inkhorn which Bernard and his brother Nicholas, men of English descent and both of them scribes in Henry I's chancery, presented to the church at Launceston. 'The church converted it into a reliquary. As the instrument by which one English family had climbed back into prosperity, it deserved to be held in honour.'[79]

These changes were then to play an important role in shaping the ways in which lords responded to the crisis of inflation which shook the economy in the years either side of 1200. Until the late twelfth century it appears to have been normal for great landlords to farm out their estates so that they had not only predictable incomes but also only a limited number of individuals to deal with. The stability of the system is indicated by the fact that long-term leases for several lives were common and that these long-term grants had tended to turn into hereditary tenures. Obviously the steep rise in prices around 1200 created severe problems for any lord who continued to live on fixed rents paid

[75] P. A. Brand, 'The Origins of the English Legal Profession', *Law and History Review* 5 (1987), 31–50.

[76] J. Campbell, 'The Significance of the Anglo-Norman State in the Administrative History of Western Europe' in ed. W. Paravicini and K. F. Werner, *Histoire comparée de l'administration* (Munich, 1980), reprinted in *Essays in Anglo-Saxon History* (London, 1987), 181.

[77] Clanchy, *From Memory to Written Record*, 76, has most barons 'using documents' by 1200, knights by 1250, peasants by 1300.

[78] There is some dispute about the chronology of this development, ibid., 54–8.

[79] Southern, *Medieval Humanism*, 227.

by hereditary tenants.[80] The landlords' solution, to take over the direct management of their estates, meant that they now required, and had to deal with, a whole army of professional receivers, treasurers, auditors and bailiffs. 'In place of a single officer with omnicompetent responsibilities, lords employed a variety of officials.'[81] It would have defeated the whole point of the re-organisation if these new officials had been rewarded with newly created hereditary tenures. Thus even the highest ranking of them could normally expect no more than some form of life-grant, and usually in cash rather than in land.[82] Whether or not there had ever before been a price rise as steep as this we cannot know; but what does seem certain is that earlier lords would not have been able to respond in this manner. The switch to direct management, the managerial revolution, was only possible in a society capable of producing numerate and literate men in sufficient numbers. And even Campbell, not a man to underestimate the achievement of centuries before the twelfth, implies that this would not have been possible earlier.[83] From the point of view of social mobility these were major developments. They meant not only that there was now employment for a vastly greater number of officials than ever before, but also that recruitment was more likely to be on the basis of professional competence rather than hereditary succession, though the two, of course, are not mutually exclusive.

Is it possible to draw any broad conclusions? Runciman argued that after the end of Anglo-Saxon England the rate of social mobility was bound to slow down because economically, ideologically and politically there was little prospect of either innovation or disturbance.[84] Clearly this line of argument will not work. The church reform movements, and the Norman Conquest were developments which ideologically and politically, had enormous consequences in the sphere of social mobility, consequences which – amongst other things – tended to increase the rate of mobility. Economic historians are divided on the question of whether, roughly speaking, the whole twelfth century witnessed greater economic activity, or whether it was essentially confined to the latter part of the period.[85] Either

---

[80] P. D. A. Harvey, 'The English Inflation of 1180–1220', *Past and Present* 61 (1973), 3–30, and idem 'The Pipe Rolls and the Adoption of Demesne Farming in England', *Economic History Review* 27 (1974), 345–59. Recent work has somewhat dented the reputation of the 'Great Inflation'. Paul Latimer's analysis of the Pipe Roll figures suggests that inflation was over by c.1204, and the economic, social and political consequences of this for King John's reign have been re-thought by Jim Bolton, see their essays in ed. S. Church, *King John: New Interpretations* (Woodbridge, 1999).

[81] S. L. Waugh, 'Tenure to Contract: lordship and clientage in thirteenth-century England', *EHR* 101 (1986), 811–39, p. 815.

[82] Waugh, 'Tenure to Contract', 813–21. For a discussion of the officials of a twelfth-century aristocratic household see D. Crouch, *The Beaumont Twins* (Cambridge, 1986), 139–55.

[83] Campbell, 'Significance of the Anglo-Norman State', 180.

[84] Runciman, 'Accelerating Social Mobility', 28–30.

[85] R. H. S. Britnell, *The Commercialisation of English Society, 1000–1500* (2nd edn, Cambridge, 1998), xiii, 233–4; and essays in eds. R. H. S. Britnell and B. M. S. Campbell, *A*

way, it seems to me, we cannot ignore the evidence which suggests that for at least some of this period we are dealing with an age not merely of economic expansion, but also of economic intensification. Although the English economy clearly remained under-developed when compared with the economies of Flanders and North Italy, it was, none the less, becoming increasingly market-oriented, with more money and more goods in faster circulation than before. It has indeed been argued that a rise in horse hauling in the twelfth and thirteenth centuries increased the velocity of goods transportation and, hence, the opposite flow of money to pay for them.[86] For these sorts of reasons Barbara Harvey suggested that it was probably in the twelfth century that peasant surpluses became important to the urban market.[87] In terms of social relationships and social mobility this means that we are not dealing with a steady-state, or even a contracting universe which merely appears to be expanding. We are dealing with one which in many critical ways really was expanding. As economic activity intensified, as government became more complicated, so people were presented with more choices, more choices of occupations and – accentuated by the disappearance of both slavery and the system of child oblates – more chance of personal fulfilment.[88]

Commercialising Economy: England 1086–c.1300 (Manchester, 1995) and in eds. R. H. S. Britnell and J. Hatcher, *Progress and Problems in Medieval England: Essays in honour of Edward Miller* (Cambridge, 1996). For a more negative view of the late eleventh and early twelfth centuries see P. Nightingale, *A Medieval Mercantile Community. The Grocers' Company and the Politics and Trade of London 1000–1485* (New Haven, 1995), 16–21, 34. But if the evidence of mints and coins suggests that the drying up of the supply of silver, principally from the Harz, meant an increasing shortage of silver for a century after the Norman Conquest, it also suggests that the process went rapidly into reverse during the last decades of the twelfth century as Freiberg silver came on stream, P. Spufford, *Money and its Use in Medieval Europe* (Cambridge, 1988), 97, 109–12, 196–7. Moreover the effect of inflation at the end of the twelfth century should have been to make the silver penny a still more useful medium of exchange.

[86] J. Langdon, 'Horse Hauling: A Revolution in Vehicle Transport in Twelfth and Thirteenth Century England?', *Past and Present* 103 (1984), 37–66.

[87] Harvey, *Westminster Abbey*, 6.

[88] Cf. S. Reynolds, *Kingdoms and Communities in Western Europe 900–1300* (Oxford, 1984), 337–8. Haverkamp's conclusion, that this period was for by far the greater part of the German population 'ein Zeitalter der Befreiung von persönlichen Abhängigkeiten oder deren Abschwächung', in A. Haverkamp, *Aufbruch und Gestaltung. Deutschland 1056–1273* (Munich, 1984), 308, is a reminder that many of the developments sketched above were the common experience of medieval Europe as a whole. What then were the peculiarly English variations on the theme? I suppose the more systematic application of primogeniture and the high rate of inflation c.1200 (perhaps) and (certainly) the destruction of the old elite as a consequence of the Norman Conquest.

Index

Printed and bound by CPI Group (UK) Ltd, Croydon, CR0 4YY

19/01/2025

14628044-0001